THE DEMOCRATIC EXPERIENCE AND POLITICAL VIOLENCE

Edited by

David C. Rapoport and
Leonard Weinberg

FRANK CASS
LONDON and PORTLAND, OR

First published in 2001 in Great Britain by
FRANK CASS PUBLISHERS
Crown House, 47 Chase Side,
Southgate, London N14 5BP

and in the United States of America by
FRANK CASS PUBLISHERS
c/o ISBS
5824 N.E. Hassalo Street
Portland, Oregon 97213-3644

Website: www.frankcass.com

British Library Cataloguing in Publication Data

The Democratic Experience and Political Violence
1. Terrorism
II. Rapoport, David C., 1929- II. Weinberg, Leonard
303.6'25

ISBN 0 7146 5150 8 (cloth)
ISBN 0 7146 8167 9 (paper)

Library of Congress Cataloguing-in-Publication Data

The democratic experience and political violence /
edited by David C. Rapoport and Leonard Weinberg.
p. cm. – (Cass series on political violence, ISSN 1365-0580; 9)
Includes bibliograpical references and index.
ISBN 0-7146-5150-8 (cloth) – ISBN 0-7146-8167-9 (pbk.)
I. Political violence. 2. Democracy. I. Rapoport, David C.
II. Weinberg, Leonard, 1939– . III Series.
JC328.6. D45 2001
303.6'2 –dc21   00-065973

This group of papers first appeared in a Special Issue of *Terrorism and Political Violence*
12/3–4 (Autumn 2000) 'The Democratic Experience and Political Violence'
ISSN 0954-6553 published by Frank Cass

Printed in Great Britain by
Antòny Rowe Ltd, Chippenham

Contents

Preface

This volume originated in a conference entitled 'Democracy and Violence' held at the Stanford Alpine Meadows Lodge, California in September 1997. The participants came because they were convinced that the connections between the two activities had been ignored, largely because of a widespread reluctance among democrats to consider the possibility that democratic forms often encouraged violence.

The papers led to profitable, interesting exchanges and extensive revisions too. Subsequently, they were sent to others unable to attend the original conference: Adrian Guelke, Andrzej Korbonski, Abraham Miller, Raphael Israeli and Ehud Sprinzak. Those people found they wanted to participate, helping give the project greater focus and breadth. The editors wish to thank all the contributors for their patience and willingness to stay the course, and we are very grateful to UCLA, University of Nevada Reno, Center for International Relations, UCLA Institute of Global Cooperation and Conflict (IGCC) at UCSD for their generous support.

David C. Rapoport
Los Angeles, California
and
Leonard Weinberg
Reno, Nevada

1

Introduction

DAVID C. RAPOPORT and
LEONARD WEINBERG

It is impossible to read the history of the petty republics of
Greece and Italy without feeling sensations of horror and
disgust at the distractions with which they were continually
agitated, and at the rapid successions of revolution by which
they were kept in a state of perpetual vibration between the
extremes of tyranny and anarchy ... If now and then intervals
of felicity open themselves to view, we behold them with a
mixture of regret arising from the reflection that the pleasing
scenes before us are soon to be overwhelmed by the
tempestuous waves of sedition and party rage.

Federalist Paper #9

Opinions regarding the health and future prospects of democracy
sometimes change radically and rapidly. In 1976 during the American
Bicentennial, Daniel Patrick Moynihan wrote: '... liberal democracy on
the American model increasingly tends to the condition of monarchy in
the nineteenth century: a holdover form of government, one which
persists in isolated or peculiar places here and there, and which may
even serve well enough for special circumstances, but which simply has
no relevance to the future.'[1]

Moynihan's prognosis reflected circumstances of the time. Military
juntas and dictators governed much of Latin America, the Middle East
and sub-Saharan Africa, and one-party communist systems ruled most
of the Eurasian land mass. European democracies had difficult
economic problems (i.e. serious inflation and high unemployment).
Britain, West Germany, Italy and Spain experienced spectacular

outbreaks of terrorist violence. The French Fifth Republic was nearly overthrown, and a civil war narrowly averted. The United States was reeling from several painful experiences: a decade of strife associated with the Civil Rights movement, the Vietnam nightmare, assassinations of Robert Kennedy and Martin Luther King, Watergate, and finally several small but shocking terrorist movements.

The pessimism pervading the public scene was reflected in A Trilateral Commission Report, *The Crisis of Democracy*, lamenting the 'excessive demands' citizens placed on their governments and warning that democracies needed insulation from 'extravagant expectations'.[2] Walter Laqueur diagnosed Western Europe as suffering from the condition of *abulia*, a mental state involving a loss of will and direction.[3]

But a decade later, the political scene changed dramatically. The military returned to the barracks in Latin America, the Middle East and sub-Saharan Africa. The Asian 'tigers' (South Korea, Thailand and Taiwan) made significant moves towards democratic rule. By far, the most important events were the collapse of communist regimes in Eastern Europe and then the stunning, wholly unexpected disintegration of the Soviet Union itself. In the wake of these developments, indeed largely because of them, pessimism evaporated. Academics then began to marvel at the irresistibility of liberal democracy, echoing in one way or another Francis Fukuyama's view that history had come to an end.[4]

Today, that euphoria, or what Fidel Castro identified as 'triumphalism' (himself once an embodiment of that sentiment), has evaporated in the wake of another set of current events.[5] Newly established or restored democracies have run into trouble, and the frightening genie of ethno-religious strife has been let loose everywhere, stimulating dormant separatist demands and a variety of new ones as well. Savage civil wars and enormous refugee problems have resulted.[6]

The current situation, *inter alia*, provides new opportunities to rethink the matter and, more specifically, to question the widespread conventional wisdom that democracies are peculiarly predisposed to seeking peace in international and in national affairs. Both contexts are worth examining, but our concern here is with the internal scene.

Why do so many believe that democracies have a special disposition towards peace? The most common reason, and certainly the most compelling one, is that democracies provide dissenters with peaceful ways to achieve their ends. Political violence is less likely because there is no 'need' for it. To put it another way, violence is rare because in democratic states it is difficult to find an appropriate justification.

Yet violence increased dramatically in most contemporary states immediately after democratic forms were introduced. What does this teach us? Most think that this means that democracies require certain preconditions – preconditions which unfortunately do not (and maybe cannot) exist everywhere. Many states, Samuel Huntington notes, unable to become democratic, have 'retrenched', or retreated from efforts to establish democracy, a pattern familiar to anyone acquainted with the history of the form since the French Revolution.[7]

There is an older, but now much less popular, view. Turbulence is an inevitable by-product of democratic principles and processes. Thus, our sombre opening quotation from *The Federalist Papers* emphasizes that history had demonstrated that 'popular governments' have short turbulent lives compared to those of other forms. We must expect, James Madison said in *Federalist Paper* #10, that the liberty necessary for 'popular government' will also stimulate dangerous passions.

Distinguished nineteenth century commentators supported this view. Sir Henry Maine concluded that the right to vote could never fully satisfy democracy's promise to empower the individual, a disappointment which explained why the first great democratic tide in early nineteenth-century Europe produced so much violence. Later, John Stuart Mill wrote that a new democratic tide would destroy the huge multi-ethnic empires, and he wondered whether political forms designed to establish majorities and minorities would prove appropriate for multi-ethnic societies, a moot question still.[8]

Obviously, the two different accounts of the link between democracy and violence (special circumstances and inevitable by-products) are not mutually exclusive. But each emphasizes some features at the expense of others. Our contributors find the second view more congenial, though we accept the proposition that successful democratic systems require preconditions.

The second explanation is supported by the empirical research which the turbulence of the 'mature democracies' in the 1960s inspired. Douglas Hibbs concluded: 'democratic nations experience about as much *mass* violence as non-democratic nations do. [A] democratic world would not necessarily be a non-violent one.'[9] G. Bingham Powell characterized 'democracy as a gamble that discontent can be channeled through legitimate electoral channels'. The term 'gamble' suggests unfavourable odds, but he does not reflect on the implication.[10]

A second theme of those studies is that the characteristics of violence (forms and purposes) vary, depending on the type of state in which they occur. Violence in democratic states normally voices political discontent with policy and/or some aspect of the system. Elsewhere revolutionary aspirations are paramount, a distinction supported by other noteworthy studies.[11] 'Chronic low-level conflict is one of the prices democrats should expect to pay for freedom from regimentation by the state.'[12]

More recent research is suggestive too. Everyone expects 'new democracies' to be peculiarly vulnerable to civil wars and serious rebellions.[13] But most will be startled by a Weinberg–Eubank study showing that terrorist groups appear more frequently in *all* democratic forms (new and old, stable and unstable) than in undemocratic ones. '[T]he likelihood of terrorist groups occurring in democracies is three and a half times greater than ... in non-democracies.' Even more surprising is their claim that with respect to terrorism 'no substantial difference ... between various types of democracy exist'.[14]

This link between democracy and terror, incidentally, is venerable, dating to the time when the first modern democratic tide flooded eighteenth century Europe. The political vocabulary of terrorism derives from the Reign of Terror, which aimed to make the French fit for democracy. The connection between democracy and terror persisted. In late nineteenth century Russia, creators of the modern doctrine and strategy for *rebel* terror announced parliamentary democracy as the aim. After World War II many anti-colonial terrorists claimed to be inspired by democratic ideals.[15]

In this respect, the most recent wave of internal violence, launched after the Cold War ended, is interesting. The 'new' violence reflects ethnic concerns and easily escalates into aspirations for national self-determination, aspirations related to or stimulated by the democratic ethos. Because national self-determination claims cannot be satisfied universally, they are a chronic, albeit intermittent, source of potential violence in democratic states.[16]

Ethnic violence has produced unprecedented carnage, a New York Times editorial laments. 'In no previous age have people shown so great an aptitude and appetite for killing millions of other people for reason of race, religion, or class.'[17] Our age may be unique, but let us remember that the idea of 'total war', one in which distinctions between civilian and military disappears, is a legacy of the French Revolution.[18]

The contributors understand political violence as illegal physical attacks, or threats, on persons, property, institutions and symbols in order to destroy, alter and sustain systems or policies. The attacks may only be alleged (alleged attacks can serve some political purpose) and the persons responsible may be outside or inside governments. We focus on the various forms violence takes in democratic states, but we also discuss *en passant* political problems encountered when those states must use force.

Characteristically, 'democratic violence' is linked to special or unique features of the democratic ethos, which is why elections (an indispensable feature of democratic states) are linked to violence or seem to 'encourage' it. Whatever their initial inclinations and subject, most contributors believe they must discuss elections. Five (more than one-third) of the articles herein have elections as a principal preoccupation: those by David C. Rapoport and Leonard Weinberg, John F. Finn, Martha Crenshaw, Daniel Philpott and Adrian Guelke.

This particular emphasis is unusual, and may say something about predispositions of academics. Rapoport and Weinberg ('Elections and Violence') remind us that while elections may be the most examined subject in political science, few see or wish to see how intimately related ballots and bullets are. Ehud Sprinzak ('Extremism and Violence in Israeli Democracy') complains that Israeli scholars still have not documented the election violence that he witnessed as a youth, and Andrzej Korbonski ('Violence and Democracy in Eastern Europe') discovers to his surprise that the subject has been so neglected in his part of the world that it was difficult for him to gather appropriate materials.

Other subjects discussed are conflicts between domestic and international imperatives, ethnic violence, and three more general concerns: the 'benefits' of violence, why 'democratic violence' never ends, and common explanations of violent eruptions in democracies. The space committed to each varies considerably, and as topics overlap, some editorial decisions to place essays in one category or another are arbitrary. All essays on elections, for example, touch on ethnic violence, while those treating ethnic violence deal with elections too. Guelke's 'Violence and Electoral Polarization ...' could be put in either category. Philpott's 'Should Self-determination be Legalized?' and Crenshaw's

'Democracy, Commitment Problems and Managing Ethnic Violence
...' could be placed in three different places.

Elections

Rapoport and Weinberg offer the most general account. It treats election
as a mode of succession, noting that the succession moment is the most
dangerous recurring one in all political systems. In order to see how the
different character of different succession principles shape violence
patterns, they compare election with heredity, its chief historical rival.
Hereditary systems require, but rarely achieve, clarity in establishing
claim priorities. Election requirements are 'fairness' (competitors
'bend' rules) and 'conciliation' (divisions are created which must be
reconciled). The final section offers a brief taxonomy of typical
justifications for initiating and/or resisting election violence
      Adrian Guelke's essay examines three elections held in May 1996 in
states which suddenly and unexpectedly had an opportunity to engage
in serious efforts to make peace: Israel, Northern Ireland and South
Africa. But the electoral results did not reflect or strengthen the peace
effort; the magnetizing effect of violence, past and present was a critical
ingredient in intensifying division.
      The first two articles treat violence in elections or the impact of
violence on those elections. The last two in this section consider how
one might change the legal order to reduce violence. Finn ('Electoral
Regimes and the Proscription of Anti-democratic Parties') examines a
widespread practice in democratic states of refusing to allow
undemocratic parties to participate in elections. The logic of various
proscriptions is examined to designate respective benefits and costs.
Philpott treats the troubling moral 'right' of national self-determination,
a right he thinks ought to be given a legal basis, and suggests how the
electoral process, the key to that right, might be redesigned to fill this
need. If we are successful in designing that right, both the number of
claims for self-determination and those leading to violence will be
reduced.

Conflicts between international and domestic concerns

Martha Crenshaw's essay is the last in which elections are a crucial
theme; and it is also the first of two treating conflicts between
international and domestic imperatives. She examines an increasingly

significant problem in the post-Cold War period, namely intervention to resolve civil conflicts abroad. When one considers how common intervention has become in our world it is surprising that democratic experiences have not been compared, nor do we know much about differences between democratic and non-democratic state efforts.

Reflecting on a single case, India in Sri Lanka, she sees general lessons for this age of *moralpolitik* where democratic states intervene to end bloodshed, and have to establish groundwork for democratic institutions before they can justify withdrawal. What role do elections play in the process?

A major impediment to quick settlement is the inability of warring parties to make mutually credible commitments, especially on disarmament. An outside enforcer, therefore, must guarantee security for the transition during which democratic institutions are introduced. Distrust invariably prolongs the process, and democracies everywhere experience difficulties in staying the course.

Peacekeeping forces may suffer casualties and usually will kill civilians, difficult-to-bear burdens for intervening democratic governments. As costs increase, interveners are increasingly attracted to have a quick election which will give the intervener a legitimate reason to withdraw. Beyond this, election pressures mount in the intervening state itself; if the government does not get out quickly it may lose its own public. India's decisions both to intervene and withdraw were pushed more by Indian domestic politics than by strategic or international exigencies, and the decisions were disasters for everyone concerned.

Raphael Israeli ('Western Democracies and Islamic Fundamentalist Violence') discusses other ways in which the violence in one state bedevils its relationships with other states. He focuses on Western democracies and friendly states in the Muslim world. The latter are angered by refusal to honour extradition requests, especially when liberal asylum laws enable fugitives to assist attacks on their original homelands. Those friendly Muslim states severely restrict Islamic opposition groups, even when the latter state a willingness to abide by democratic rules and even seem to be doing so. Invariably, democracies abroad will be trapped in moral dilemmas: can they be true both to democratic principles and obligation to respect rights of sovereignty? Beyond this, there are important material and *realpolitik* costs, among which is the possibility that Islamic terrorists may mount attacks in democratic states to influence opinion there.

Ethnic violence

Obviously, ethnic violence is not limited to a particular political system, but national self-determination resonates so favourably in democratic ears, ethnic violence today has a conspicuous and dramatic force. Four essays treat the issue; two deal with the United States. The others examine Israel and Eastern Europe, excluding former Soviet and Yugoslavian territories.

Anna Simons ('Purity is Danger') and Michael Barkun ('Violence in the Name of Democracy ...') illustrate in different ways the unique character of American ethnic conflict. Simons, an anthropologist, confronts the issue explicitly. Barkun does not talk about American exceptionalism. Still, in reading his description of the White right-wing religious racist separatist practices, one is struck by how unusual they are when compared to earlier patterns of American violence and to those in other countries.

Simons distinguishes two kinds of group attachment. One is fixed (usually at birth) and 'pure', supplying individuals with virtually all their needs. The second is 'invented' and 'impure', because the individuals involved also have other group attachments which create conflicting concerns. Members, thus, have 'divisible identities' and individuals are compelled willy-nilly to reassess allegiance relationships periodically. 'Impure' groups thrive best when the state can guarantee rights and create a common identity over and above all other group allegiances.

The 'purer' the contending groups, the more intense conflicts between them will be. Stability depends on having a large number of invented or 'impure' groups, and that in turn is related to the size of the national community (i.e. population and space in particular). The enormous dimensions of the American scene, Simons observes, was an important safety valve for elements hoping to form semi-autonomous purity-seeking communities. But as the state expands its jurisdiction constantly, the ensuing contraction of group space alters ethnic conflict patterns to make them more ominous.

Michael Barkun examines one such pattern, found in three interrelated documents of Christian Identity millenarian churches, critical elements in the radical racist right-wing separatist movement. Millenarian groups, of course, have dotted the American landscape since the colonial period, but the earlier separatists were pacifists with no political agenda or plans to reconstruct the larger social scene (i.e. the Shakers and the Oneida Perfectionists).

Contemporary millenarian separatists are armed and prepared to defend their political agenda, a 'radical localism' which predicates the supremacy of the county and visualizes America as an extraordinary loose confederation of Aryan peoples. The movement sees itself as recreating a democracy which has been lost and bases its claims on eccentric readings of Biblical texts, the Articles of Confederation, the common law and the Constitution.

Sprinzak is concerned with the Israeli scene, particularly with armed attacks by Jews against other Jews. Normally, this conflict would not be considered ethnic, but he explains that 'divisible identities' among Israeli Jews – identities Simons finds so critical for a well-ordered democracy – seem to be collapsing.

Violent conflict between Jews began before independence and has been an intermittent feature of Israeli politics ever since. This experience has been obscured partly because we emphasize Israel's identity as the 'only working democracy in the Middle East', a status maintained under very difficult international circumstances – several wars and numerous Arab terrorist attacks. A second reason is that scholars failed to document early incidents, especially those occurring during elections.

However, the fact is that in the struggle for independence, competing underground fiercely disputed tactics and the future state's boundaries. A threatened civil war was averted when the horror of bloodshed among Jews sank in, a restraint which surfaced again later at critical moments. Pre-state animosities merged with left–right, Sephardi–Ashkenasi and secular–ultra-Orthodox conflicts. The critical point was Israel's astonishing victory in the Six Day War (1967), enabling its troops to occupy ancient Biblical territories and now the Palestinian homeland. Unwise settlement policies made it impossible to avoid momentous polarizing decisions about final territorial dispositions.

Sprinzak draws our attention, too, to the conflict between domestic and international concerns. The invasion of Lebanon, unlike earlier Israeli military undertakings, generated resistance and violence at home – something Americans who lived through both World War II and Vietnam understand well.

Andrzej Korbonski notes that relationships between violence and democracy in Eastern Europe since 1918 have not yet been seriously discussed (Korbonski's Eastern Europe does not include the territories of the former Soviet Union and Yugoslavia). Commentators always describe rebel activity in that part of the world as being inspired by democratic principles, especially when directed against communist governments. It is true that the rebels made democratic claims, but their prime concerns were ethnic interests and specific government failures.

In view of contemporary concerns that international guarantees are necessary to protect ethnic minorities, Korbonski makes the interesting point that in the interval between the two World Wars, ethnic animosities were aggravated by resentments towards the treaties the League of Nations imposed to protect ethnic minorities. Since then ethnic tensions have eased everywhere in the portion of Eastern Europe studied, largely because the size of minority elements have been reduced considerably compared to those numbers prior to World War II. German populations in Poland, the former Czechoslovakia and Hungary were forcibly removed, the Jews were decimated, Polish borders were redrawn to reduce the Ukrainian element, and finally Czechoslovakia dissolved into two states.

The transition from communist rule, the case of former Yugoslavia as always excepted, was accomplished largely through peaceful demonstrations. This striking fact Korbonski relates to the enormous revulsion and anxiety felt for the violence experienced earlier, especially under communist rule – a revulsion, however, which has not prevented those countries from experiencing unparalleled criminal lawlessness.

General issues

Victor Le Vine's 'Violence and the Paradox of Democratic Renewal' initiates the fourth subject by raising a striking question. How sound is Jefferson's contention that rebel violence is not only necessary sometimes to create a democratic state, but also to maintain and renew it afterwards? No other contributor deals directly with this matter, though Sprinzak observes that 'Black Panther' violence in Israel (1972) made Ashkenasi Jews better understand the injustices the Sephardim endured, ultimately helping to heal the latter's wounds. The editors suspect that the other contributors, and most readers as well, could produce additional examples from national histories they know to make the same point. Still, we cannot 'replay' those scenes to see if other means could produce the same result. Equally important, violent actions cannot be understood in their own terms only. Much depends on who emulates or imitates them. The white racist groups Barkun describes claim that their inspiration are those who launched the American Revolution.

Le Vine supplies a list of scholars and activists who support and elaborate Jefferson's paradox. He notes that Jefferson's view is plausible and tries to devise a systematic way to assess it. To that end, he examines three related questions: Are democracies born in violence more prone to periodic violent challenges subsequently? Do periodic challenges make democracies more stable or less? When democracies break down, is it because citizens become accustomed to violence (i.e. develop a 'culture of violence')? None of these questions can now be answered definitively, he explains; but the evidence available confirms our intuition, namely that the pernicious consequences of violence are usually paramount.

The Eubank–Weinberg article, 'The Italian Regions and the Prospect for Democracy', compares northern and southern Italy, a comparison which has intrigued political scientists for a long time. The differences are suggestive; at least they argue that a history of violence need not emasculate a community's potentiality for democratic institutions, and the example runs counter to Le Vine's general picture.

'Civic culture', a precondition of democracy, is much stronger in the north, where the republican tradition goes back to medieval times. Yet strong statistical evidence shows that the north also generated more violence to support Mussolini's drive to seize power: 'The better governed the region in the 70s and 80s, the more likely it is that Fascists and Fascist related violence were most common and widespread ...' And the north, too, had the strongest communist movements which often took to the streets.

The histories of the Italian city republics provided striking histories of violence as well, histories used by *The Federalist Papers* to illustrate links between violence and democracy. Likewise, those histories were utilized by Machiavelli for his comment in *The Discourses* that, once implanted, republican sentiments will survive extensive ordeals of violence.

Eric Gans' article ('Originary Democracy and the Critique of Pure Fairness') argues that even the best and most mature democratic systems have special dispositions to excite envy, an obstacle clearly identified in the opening reflection of the first great encomium to democracy, Pericles' 'Funeral Oration'. No matter how perfect the rules of a democracy, some 'losers' will be unable to reconcile themselves to the outcome and may become violent. A fair democracy will reduce violence considerably, because democratic flaws normally lead dissenters to push for the expansion of the system; and thus whatever their intention they will be more anchored in it as will others. Envy, of course, is an aspect of the human condition, but democracies also exhibit a relentless passion for fairness which, ironically, produces utopian thought or unreal potentially dangerous hopes.

Ancient democracy failed because citizens regarded labour as a contemptuous activity, a feature of ancient life that precluded a market system, an essential feature, Gans contends, of liberal democracy. He argues that ethnic conflict occurs most often in contexts when the market system has not yet integrated disparate elements of the community, especially when the economic power of a group is much greater than its political strength (i.e. the Basques). In the absence of an appropriate formula for secession (such as Philpott urges), violence is likely. However, Gans believes that we have not yet seen how effective integrating mechanisms of the market can be.

The final articles in our fourth section examine how we explain causes or conditions of violence in democratic states. Both articles, one by Christopher Hewitt and the other by Abraham Miller and Emily Schaen, address the American context.

Hewitt's interest is in rebel terrorism. Often in fully democratic states, terrorist violence is seen simply as the work of tiny groups whose concerns are unrelated to the state's larger political dynamics. But this interpretation is difficult to substantiate, and those who reject it link terrorism to the larger political system in one of two ways. One view is that terrorist activity reflects deeply held commitments which the community ignores. An alternative explanation is that the violence is encouraged by important political leaders who indicate sympathy with ends sought but not the means used. Some contend, for example, that President Ronald Reagan's hostility to abortion encouraged anti-abortion violence, even though he denounced that violence.

Which proposition best explains terrorist activity? Using poll data and statements of presidents and presidential contenders since 1954, Hewitt examines KKK activity, black terrorism, the terror of the New Left, and anti-abortion attacks. In *all* cases, many bystanders sympathized with the stated purposes of the violent groups; and in five of the six cases, the violence occurred during hostile, not empathetic, administrations. He also provides data to support the Rapoport–Weinberg argument that elections are linked to violence. More violence occurred during the presidential election years. The only exception was 1968; however, some persons participated in the election for the sole purpose of turning the public around, and when they read the results as meaning the public was impervious to their pleas, the violence began. In a very real sense, ballots provoked the bullets which followed.

The Miller–Schaen article treats mob violence or riots. Riots are more common in democratic than in non-democratic states, partly because democracies provide a right to demonstrate and demonstrations easily get out of control. This fact helps explain why analyses of riots by academics and public figures often betray considerable ambivalence towards the rioters; a proclivity which is enhanced when public support often endorses the legitimacy of a violent outbreak.

Official explanations of two critical recent black riots, the Watts Riot (1967) and the Rodney King 'civil unrest' (1992), exhibit this quality. They focus on background, environmental stresses or perceived injustices, and ignore the internal dynamics of the riots and the need for some comparative perspective. White riots, for example, have been much more common historically, especially in the American South against blacks before segregation ended, and the dynamics of those riots are not related to those by blacks later.

Hope as well as discontent drive riots, and hope is nourished by ambivalent responses, a characteristic democratic governments often display when faced by their own masses. Police reactions are particularly crucial to explain adequately a riot's intensity, duration and scope. This last point brings us back to one made in our first article. Professional police forces initially were established to deal with election riots in nineteenth century Britain and America; and without a proper and effective use of police forces, the legitimacy of the electoral process could not be sustained.

NOTES

1. 'The American Experiment', in Nathan Glazer and Irving Kristol (eds), *The American Commonwealth 1976* (New York: Basic Books, 1976) pp.4–5.
2. Michael Crozier, Samuel Huntington and Joji Watunki, *The Crisis of Democracy* (New York: NYU Press, 1975) pp.1–9.
3. *A Continent Astray* (New York: Oxford University Press, 1979) p.9.
4. 'The End of History?', *National Interest* (Summer, 1989) pp.2–18.

5. Thomas Carother, 'Democracy Without Illusions', *Foreign Affairs* 76/1 (1997) pp.85–9.
6. See Walker Connor, *Ethnonationalism* (Princeton, NJ: Princeton University Press, 1994) especially pp.68–85; and Fred Riggs, 'Ethnonational Rebellions and Viable Constitutionalism', *International Political Science Review* 16/4 (1995) pp.374–404.
7. 'Democracy's Third Wave', *Journal of Democracy* II/2 (Spring 1991) pp.12–34 and also *The Third Wave: Democratization in the Late 20th Century* (Norman: University of Oklahoma Press, 1991).
8. See Sir Henry Maine, *Popular Government* (London: John Murray, 1886, 2nd ed.) especially ch.4; and John Stuart Mill, *Considerations on Representative Government*, ch.38.
9. *Mass Political Violence: A Cross National Causal Analysis* (New York: John Wiley, 1973) p.130 (original emphasis). Hibbs argues against William H. Flanagan and Edwin Fogelman, who see democratic states as experiencing significantly less violence: 'Patterns of Political Violence in Comparative Perspective', *Comparative Politics* III/1 (Oct. 1970) pp.1–20. Hibbs does not indicate that his argument is connected to an earlier tradition.
10. *Contemporary Democracies: Participation, Stability, and Violence* (Cambridge, MA: Harvard University Press, 1982) p.20.
11. Hibbs (note 9); Ekkart Zimmerman, 'Macro-Comparative Research on Political Protest', in Ted Gurr (ed.), *Handbook of Political Conflict* (New York: Free Press, 1980) pp.167–237; and Ekkart Zimmerman, *Political Violence, Crises and Revolution* (Boston, MA: G.K. Hall, 1983) pp.50–52.
12. Harry Eckstein and Ted Gurr, *Patterns of Authority* (New York: Wiley, 1975) p.452.
13. A summary and critique of these findings appear in Harvard Negre *et al.*, 'Towards a Democratic Civil Peace? Democracy Democratization and Civil War, 1884–1992', paper presented at the I.S.A. Annual Conference, Toronto, Canada, 18–22 Mar. 1997.
14. 'Does Democracy Encourage Terrorism?', *Terrorism and Political Violence* (hereafter *TPV*) 6/4 (Winter, 1994) p.426. See comments by Martha Crenshaw, Christopher Hewitt and Abraham Miller in same volume. Todd Sandler's rejoinder 'On the Relationship between Democracy and Terror', which appears in *TPV* 7/4 (Winter 1995) pp.1–10, led to a Eubank-Weinberg response, 'Terrorism and Democracy in One Country: The Case of Italy', *TPV* 9/1 (Spring 1997) pp.98–108.
15. On necessary connections between democracy and terrorism, see David C. Rapoport, 'Terrorism', in Hawkesworth and Kogan (eds), *Encyclopedia of Government and Politics* (London: Routledge, 1992) Vol. 2 pp.1061–83.
16. David C. Rapoport, 'The Importance of Space in Violent Ethno-Religious Strife', *Nationalism and Ethnic Conflict* II/2 (Summer 1996) pp.258–83.
17. *New York Times*, 26 Jan. 1995.
18. This is the theme of Hoffman Nickerson's *The Armed Horde; 1793–1939* (New York: G.P. Putnam's and Sons, 1942, 2nd ed.). When democracies depend upon conscription, they must justify wars as necessary to defend the very life of the community at stake, and the argument when makes 'total war' a compelling possibility, and peace afterwards more difficult. (Nickerson does not address the second problem.)

2

Elections and Violence

DAVID C. RAPOPORT and
LEONARD WEINBERG

No subject attracts political scientists more than elections do. Still, the intimate link with violence has scarcely been noticed. A sparse recent literature exists on how ballots may eliminate bullets in civil war settlements: questions concerning why ballots create occasions for bullets and the relationship between violence-producing and violence-reducing propensities of elections are ignored. This article aims to help fill the gap. It treats election as a mode of succession, noting that the succession moment is normally the most dangerous recurring one in all political systems. We compare election with heredity, its chief historical rival, to see how the different character of each shapes violence patterns. Hereditary systems require, but rarely achieve, clarity in establishing claim priorities. Election requirements are 'fairness' (competitors 'bend' rules) and 'conciliation' (divisions are created which must be reconciled). The final section offers a brief taxonomy of typical justifications for initiating and/or resisting election violence.

> Everywhere else elections are secular events. Ours was more than this, much more. It was a veritable spiritual experience … The black person entered the booth … weighed down by the anguish and burden of oppression … gnawing away at her vitals like some corrosive acid. She re-appeared as someone new, 'I am free, ' as she walked away.with an elastic spring in her step … The white person entered the booth burdened by the load of guilt for having enjoyed the fruits of oppression and emerged as somebody new.
>
> Desmond M. Tutu, *No Future Without Forgiveness*

Zealous Patriots, heading rabbles,
Orators promoting squabbles;
Free Electors always swilling,
Candidates not worth a shilling;

Butchers, Farmers and Car Men,
Half Pay Officers and Chairmen;
Many Zealots, not worth noting,
Many Perjured Persons voting;
Candidates with Tradesman pissing,
Cleavers, Bagpipes, Clapping, Hissing;
Warmest Friends in Opposition,
Hostile Forces in Coalition!
Open Houses, paid to tempt the
Rotten Voters with Bellies empty;
Boxing, Drinking, Rhyming, Swearing,
Some Fools laughin, some despairing;
Fevers, Fractures, Inflammations,
Bonfires, Squibs, Illuminations;
Murd'rers daring all detection,
Pray, gentlemen, how do you like the Election?

'The Election', *Federal Post* (Trenton, NJ) 18 November 1788[1]

Because elections are crucial ingredients of modern democracy, good democrats will be dismayed to learn that elections are often associated with outbursts of violence. At the outset, we show that a paradox exists in this relationship between elections and violence, a paradox inherent in all modes of legitimate succession. We then compare two major historical modes, election and heredity, to see how the issues most specific to each (clarity for heredity, fairness and conciliation for elections) shape succession violence. Finally, we offer a brief typology of election violence, based on those issues.

The important neglected paradox

Newspaper headlines regularly link violence and elections in somewhat contradictory ways. Sometimes elections are used to silence guns, but ballots also seem to provoke bullets. We discuss both links and focus on the second.

The histories of all democratic states provide examples of this double link. Yet political scientists have scarcely noticed,[2] even though *no* subject in that field receives more attention than elections do. Widely admired contributions, such as Duverger's *Political Parties*, Epstein's *Political Parties in Western Democracies* and Rose's *Electoral*

Behavior: A Comparative Handbook, have no entries for violence in their indices,[3] and a voluminous ever-growing literature on violence ignores election settings too.[4] Authoritative studies of democracies and violence (i.e. Hibbs, *Mass Violence* and Powell, *Contemporary Democracies*) note that violence often accompanies elections, but leave the matter unexplored.[5] Kumar's *Post Conflict Elections* (1998) studies the peace-making role of elections in the aftermath of civil war and is a recent valuable exception.[6]

Statistics to detail this double link systematically do not exist, a project we will undertake soon. Here we offer examples from all sorts of states in different historical eras to illustrate various ways, times, forms and outcomes associated with the link. We do not examine the patterns suggested to see how common they are and how they relate to various democratic forms. Our aim here is both more simple and more complex, namely to demonstrate that a link exists in order to justify pondering its significance.

From bullets to ballots

> When electoral results are clear-cut and plain to all, the agitating minorities must become silent in their turn, and the extremists withdraw into the shadows.
>
> Matti Dogan, 'How Civil War was Avoided in France'

When the electoral process works well, we forget the axiom that ballots are substitutes for bullets. But the axiom is crucial to our calculations when serious violence occurs. In negotiations to end civil wars today, for example, elections are regularly proposed as essential ingredients, and literally are opportunities to exchange bullets for ballots. The Nicaraguan election of 1990 was 'the first peaceful transfer of power from a revolutionary government to its opposition' and helped terminate the Contra uprising.[7] Similarly, elections in El Salvador (1991) and Guatemala (1995–96) helped end long civil wars. The 1989 Namibia election terminated a 30-year war, setting the stage for Namibian independence. It is hard to imagine how the long struggle the African National Congress (ANC) waged against various South African governments could have been concluded (and with so little violence in the final phase) without a true election (1994), one in which all citizens could participate.[8]

In France (1968), an election was used to avert a possible civil war. When students and strikers forced President De Gaulle to flee Paris, he rallied the army and then played his trump card: he called an election to show whom France would support. The lesson, Mattei Dogan says, is that when the 'results are clear-cut and plain ... the threat of violence quickly subsides'.[9] (Alas, as the next section shows, a radically different outcome can occur.)

There is another less obvious way to use elections to prevent violence. In cases of civil wars cited, elections are accepted because the parties decide that they cannot win the military struggle or that winning costs too much. But if the war is won, something resembling an election takes place. Those who overthrew Mengistu in Ethiopia held a plebiscite (1992) to justify one-party rule. Every violent seizure of power attempts something similar; violence cannot legitimize itself. Napoleon, the first modern 'democratic' usurper, explained that you can do everything with bayonets, except sit on them! One must have a principle to bestow legitimacy. Fraudulent elections are dangerous, but do usurpers have an alternative? A link to a principle of legitimacy may reduce possibilities for successful violent counterstrokes.

From ballots to bullets

> Prior to most elections, the graph of violence rises. The pot boils over. As Churchill once said, 'democracy may be the casualty of elections.'
>
> Dennis Austin, *Democracy and Violence in India and Sri Lanka*

Ballots may avert bullets; but ballots seem to provoke bullets, too, because violence appears in each phase of the election process. '*Prior to most elections, the graph of violence rises*' in India and Sri Lanka.[10] Jamaica became independent in 1962, and in the lead up to virtually every election since the two principal political parties supply weapons to rival gangs who shoot it out.[11] Israeli Prime Minister Yitzak Rabin was assassinated (1995) because of his role in the Oslo Accords and the hope that without its leader Labor could not make the peace effort a winning issue in the forthcoming election. Pre-election violence may prevent elections from taking place: fears that Papandreou's party would repeat its landslide victory generated a military coup in Athens (1967) to cancel the election,[12] a familiar scene in Latin America.

Street demonstrators cannot mount coups, but they can force governments to abandon election plans (i.e. the Indian state of Assam (1984)). Militia groups, encouraged by the Indonesian army, tried to do the same thing in East Timor (1999), generating a massive turnout instead.[13]

Candidates must be visible *during* a campaign, greatly increasing their risks. Rajiv Gandhi was cut down in the 1991 Indian election campaign, as was the presumptive heir to the Mexican presidency, Ruis Colosio (1995). Senator Robert Kennedy was killed during his run for a presidential nomination (1968). In 1972 former Alabama Governor George Wallace's presidential ambition was destroyed in the primaries when an assassin crippled him. In Japan, during the 1960 national election campaign, a right-wing youth assassinated the leader of the Socialist Party, Asanuma Inejiro, debating a treaty before a national television audience.[14]

Voters and party-workers pay a price too. In 1976, Sandro Saccucci, an Italian neo-fascist parliamentary candidate, killed a young left-wing demonstrator tormenting him.[15] Nineteenth-century English voters found elections so threatening that some 'voluntarily attempted to disenfranchise themselves'.[16] A midwest newspaper wrote in 1884: 'nearly everywhere in America, voting was an arduous task attended by personal danger. Every peaceable man and every household dreads the approach of election day.[17]

In Sri Lanka (1988 and 1989), 14 candidates and nearly 300 party workers were murdered. Successors of the dreaded Haitian *ton-ton macoute* gunned down peaceful voters waiting their turn at a Port au Prince polling station, thus warning everybody not to vote for Aristide. For nearly a century after the American Civil War, violent attacks kept African-Americans from voting in the South.[18]

A month-long Indonesian election campaign (1997) produced 253 deaths, even though the outcome was never in doubt. President Suharto (the incumbent since 1966) regulated 'every aspect of the vote – restricting campaign activities, mobilizing government workers, vetting candidates for all three parties, and reviewing their speeches'.[19] Two years after Suharto fell, street violence by supporters of Ms Magawarti (bypassed in Parliament's vote for president) helped convince Parliament to make her vice-president, a case of bullets giving ballots more power.[20]

The violence often ceases when the voting begins. The militia stopped its harassments on election day in East Timor 1999, but when results were announced it devastated the land, inducing UN intervention. In Zimbabwe on election day (June 2000) the violence which had taken the lives of 29 candidates stopped.

Sometimes a peaceful election generates violence. The American South opted for bullets only *after* Lincoln was elected. When the 1976 Italian national elections returned Christian Democrats to power, extra-parliamentary elements of the left saw it as 'the last straw', organizing the 'Front Line', a revolutionary terror organization. Similarly, after Nixon was elected (1968), anti-Vietnam war demonstrators formed the Weather Underground. Governments may reject unwelcome results. Yugoslavia's Milosevic nullified local elections of 1997, provoking daily, often violent, demonstrations for some three months. The demonstrations could have brought the government down, had it not reversed itself in time.

The Algerian government (1992) moved to create a democratic form, holding 'the first free honest multi-party election in the nation's history'.[21] Unexpectedly, the election revealed the surprising strength of the Islamic Salvation Front (FIS), seemingly poised to take two thirds of the seats in a run-off, making good on its pledge to introduce a new Islamic constitution, which some felt would mean the end of competitive elections. A military coup prevented the run-off, generating an exceptionally brutal and still inconclusive civil war consuming more than 100, 000 lives.[22]

Normally, post-election violence occurs when results are announced, but issues may fester and explode later. In the Congo Republic, claims that the parliamentary elections of 1992 were fraudulent led political parties to arm their supporters in the next election in 1993. When an anticipated vote-counting dispute materialized, some 2,000 were killed. Four years later, the government tried to disarm party militias to have an undisturbed election, but the effort failed when it refused to establish independent mechanisms to guarantee the vote's authenticity.

The succession problem

> Principles of legitimacy are justifications of power, that is of the right to govern ... Every principle of legitimacy establishes a certain number of rules for the acquisition and exercise of that power.
>
> Guglielmo Ferrero, *Principles of Power*

Why do elections have this double, apparently contradictory, meaning? On one level, the answer is obvious. Elections are held to transfer the right to govern. When they fail to perform that function, 'clubs [in Thomas Hobbes' telling phrase] will be trumps'. The ballot–bullet adage, furthermore, goes beyond the election experience and pertains to *all* modes of legitimate succession, which is why Hobbes described *any* efficacious principle an 'artificial eternity of life'.[23]

> Succession moments, we are told, provide unusual opportunities for lawless action which accompany the confusion of an interregnum and comparative weakness of new and inexperienced rulers ... Consequently, passions may be raised to a fever heat at the precise moment when the established order is least capable of effective resistance.[24]

We suspect that the succession moment may be the most violent one in all political systems, but we cannot confirm that proposition now. Still, testimony exists on specific cases. Hoppen says that in the nineteenth century when Irish and English elections were violent, they accounted for most of the political violence in the state. Austin argues similarly for India and Sri Lanka today, and Hewitt has a similar conclusion for recent American presidential elections.[25] Serious election violence occurs more often in 'democratizing states', but they also experience more political violence of all sorts, and one issue is the relationship of election violence to the other expressions in all democratic forms.

How do succession moments in different principles compare? Choosing which to compare is not difficult because the political imagination is much more narrow than we realize. The two major ones have been election and heredity (birth).[26] Lot[27] and appointment[28] were occasionally significant; neither is now, though lot is still used to designate Tibet's Dalai Lama.[29] Most systems use several modes and one normally predominates.

The violence expressed or alternatively averted during elections varies considerably in different states, and similar patterns appear in hereditary arrangements. In the Ottoman Empire, Islam's most successful state which lasted some 650 years, most successions produced violence; half the sultans were deposed and most of them killed. Western figures were once comparable, but when succession rules in the West were clarified everything changed.[30]

After a brief note to explain why one common political form cannot be discussed, we compare the histories of the two major principles from the medieval period. Our purpose is twofold: to establish that succession was agonizing for both[31] and to show that history provides a perspective for seeing the requisites of each principle. The concern is the succession rule itself, and not the broader political context, however crucial that context is.

Government without a principle of succession

Not every political form has a principle of legitimacy. The ancient tyrant and the modern dictator, the modern equivalent, lack one as the etymology of the terms indicates. Tyrants 'seized power and governed without legal right' and dictators rule for 'temporary emergency situations only'. This genetic defect, virtually all political theorists emphasized, made tyranny or dictatorship the most unstable form.[32] '[I]ncalculable hazards of conspiracy and rebellion' regularly influence *all* successions. The dictator has no fixed term, is usually ousted by violence, and may *or* may not be followed by another dictator. Illegitimacy produces intense anxiety in rulers, which they then try to alleviate by making others fearful, a process that distorts all relationships permanently.

Perhaps because succession issues are discussed so rarely, the genetic defect of the tyrant/dictator form, despite its conspicuous presence in the history of political thought, is often overlooked. When, for example, the one-party state emerged in 1917, many thought that the strength of party and ideology had eliminated the flaw. But Soviet experiences simply demonstrated how apt the classical view still was.

> [S]uccession is a fundamental problem [because] there is no established recognized center of decision making ... Supreme authority cannot be said to inhere in either the Government's Council of Ministers or in the Party's Central Committee. At times, the small Secretariat of the Central Committee has been sovereign; at other times, it has been the larger more authoritative Presidium. Most of the time, the power of decision has been in the hands of a dictator, although dictatorial power inheres in no particular office or title; it is unprovided for in the fundamental laws of party and state which establish collective organs of rule without exception.[33]

One-party states normally lack the will and probably capacities to prevent dictators from emerging.[34]

To establish a rule for succession, a dictatorship must transform itself or become another political form.[35] Earlier, when both heredity and election were legitimate principles, one could choose between them. Today, only elections can supply legitimacy.[36] Dictators, therefore, must 'use' elections without really having them: in Ferrero's language, they base their government on 'the people', but refuse to recognize that without an opposition 'the people' are incomplete.[37]

Historical note on two principles

Contemporaries invariably link election with democracy, but the two notions were, and still are, distinct. Elections originated, the Greeks remind us, in aristocracies in order to choose *better* candidates. The lot, which gave everyone an equal chance, was the democrat's principle. Elections signify choice, and choice may be combined with a variety of electoral bodies and forms.

Elections attracted medieval communities enormously. Beyond the republics, the cities of the various kingdoms, guilds and initially even most European monarchies embraced election. Significantly, the Pope and Emperor (the two most august offices of the medieval world) were, Lord Bryce says, 'too holy to be transmitted by descent'.[38]

Despite the appeal of elections, their early history was very troubled, as everyone familiar with the melancholy account of *The Federalist* will remember:

> It is impossible to read the history of the petty republics of ... Italy without feeling sensations of horror and disgust at the distractions with which they were continually agitated, and at the rapid succession of revolutions by which they were kept in a state of perpetual vibrations between the extremes of tyranny and anarchy ... If now and then intervals of felicity, open themselves to view, we behold them with a mixture of regret, arising from the reflection that the pleasing scenes before us are to be overwhelmed with tempestuous waves of sedition and party rage.[39]

A desire to relieve election violence helped transform the Dutch Republic into a monarchy. Most Renaissance city-states, a modern writer notes, abandoned republican forms because 'the threat of civil war hung over *each* annual election'. Some, noting the Greek experience, where lot produced less violence, revived it. Venice, the most important to retain its republican form, chose its chief magistrate by lot, though candidates eligible for the process were screened carefully to eliminate incompetence.[40]

The holiness of the Emperor's office did not immunize it from election chaos:

> The most conspicuous defect of the Holy Roman Empire was the uncertainty of the elections, *followed* as they *usually* were by civil wars ... Its history throws light upon ... elective monarchy in general, a contrivance which has always had attractions for a certain class of political theorists. First, let it be observed how difficult, one might almost say impossible, it was found to maintain in practice the elective principle.[41]

The Polish and Hungarian monarchies were the only other elective ones to survive and paid a high price for the distinction. An observer of the Polish election of 1669 described a scene Poles and Hungarians witnessed often: 'the field was covered with armies, a necessary safeguard to our Golden Freedom.'[42]

But Bryce's second holy office, the Bishop of Rome or Pope, was remarkably durable. The Church made a commitment to elections in its earliest days, the clergy electing the Bishop of Rome – a choice 'the people' ratified. Election disturbances were common; and in the tenth-century, election violence provided opportunities for the Emperors to become 'Pope Makers'. Ultimately, the Church regained its right, but election violence continued. One dispute forced the Papacy from Rome for 70 years in the fourteenth century ('The Babylonian Captivity'). Subsequent disputes created several 'anti-popes', occasioning a century of schisms until the Council of Constance (1414–18) resolved them by producing the most successful electoral process in medieval history, or perhaps ever, for none has lasted longer.

The hereditary principle had an even more difficult early history. Initially, birth and election were combined, a tribal tradition carryover. The choice was between candidates from a single royal family, but the mixture was so pernicious that election gradually gave way, as English history illustrates. The Anglo-Saxons had no unified realm, and the popular assembly (*Witan*) elected the king and deposed him for misgovernment. The Northumbrian experience was a familiar one.

Only two of 15 kings in the eighth century finished their terms naturally. Eleven were murdered and two ousted in a legally prescribed manner.[43] The Norman Conquest unified the realm, provided a more effective royal dynasty, but 'effected no legal change in the nature of succession. Election by the National Council was still necessary to confer an inchoate right to become king'.[44] It took over two centuries to establish an unadulterated hereditary right (1307); in the interval four civil wars occurred, and the laws of succession were changed twice. After 1307 only three monarchs were deposed in three centuries; and in 1547, the rule was perfected by eliminating the ever dangerous interregnum.[45]

Hereditary succession with workable rules became a staple feature of European politics. To ward off chaos produced by unexpected death, the priority of claims had to be established ahead of time. The respective priorities of presumptive heirs were specified in an order extending through 64 possibilities. The object was to transfer power immediately, as the cry 'The king is dead, Long live the king' indicates. The cry also 'betrays in its very assertiveness the sense of anxiety which seizes any political community when its ruler passes away'.[46]

Other systems 'always [retained] the assumption that reigning sovereigns were at liberty to change [succession rules] whenever and wherever they desired to do so'.[47] The Western fiction of a monarch who could not die was unparalleled. It was sustained by three sociological conditions:

(1) the monarch's powers were restrained by nobility, church, cities and parliaments, a restraint which reduced the anxiety of excluded heirs;
(2) monogamy;[48] and
(3) primogeniture, an inheritance rule among the nobility which made it mandatory to pass estates on to the eldest son, giving them a most powerful reason to support the same principle for the monarch.[49]

The Islamic world provides instructive comparisons. Tribal traditions linked birth with election as in Europe; but Islam never separated the principles. Successors came from a royal family, but procedures for selecting and deposing rulers were never clearly specified.[50] The absence of appropriate political requirements (i.e. a functional equivalent of Europe's limited government, monogamy and primogeniture) explains why the rules were never clarified despite the agonies endured.

When the ruler's power is not effectively limited by institutions, succession stakes become too high and eligible candidates cannot resist becoming involved. Polygamy complicates matters by multiplying a man's offspring, and in Islam all potential heirs possessed equal rights to rule.[51]

The Ottoman empire provided gruesome demonstrations of how far one could go to 'solve' the issue. The 'Law of Fratricide' (1442) made mandatory a practice associated with the Empire's birth (1281): 'And to whomever of my sons the Sultanate should pass, it is fitting for the *order* of the world, he shall kill his brothers. Most of the *ulema* allow it. *So act on this.*'[52] Upon his succession, Mehemet III (1595) killed 19 brothers and 15 women pregnant with his father's children. The immediate issue of rivals was 'solved'; then he killed two sons also. Willy-nilly self-preservation led sons and fathers to conspire against each other. Ageing sultans, in addition, might help a favourite by killing all potential rivals, including their brothers and nephews.

In the sixteenth century, another extraordinary arrangement succeeded the Law of Fratricide. Princes were incarcerated in the '*Kafes*' (cages) where they received little education and kept from having children even if infanticide was 'necessary':

> Confinement ... so weakened the virility of those princes who later became sultans, they were completely impotent or fathered such feeble children that the majority ... died in infancy. The 'Kafes' were thus a vicious spiral; a sultan weakened by years of imprisonment gave birth to weak sons, who in turn were confined and later deteriorated.[53]

Nonetheless, the Ottoman dynasty was durable, lasting some 650 years.[54] One reason is that Ottoman succession struggles, unlike the European, rarely produced great outbursts of violence. Interregna normally lasted from 10 to 50 days, and as the demise of a Sultan was concealed until a successor was installed, violence was limited. Only 'The Great Interregnum' (1402–13) produced civil wars and temporarily fragmented the realm.

The empire's highly centralized bureaucratic administration was vulnerable to lightening strokes (i.e. *coups d'état* and demonstrations in the capital). Every post was held at the Sultan's discretion and occupants anxious to end uncertainty sided with a likely 'winner' before he did win, the stampede normally ending a fight before it began.[55] Thus, the third condition, an independent nobility, existed. European nobles could resist lightening strokes, and by the same token they had power to pursue civil wars.

Islamic states still exhibit difficulties in creating a workable hereditary principle. On his death bed (1953) Ibn Saud, the founder of Saudi Arabia, created an election-birth formula to cope with the numerous young aggressive presumptive heirs polygamy generates.[56] A Council of Ministers (*Majlis al Wuzara*) designates simultaneously a new king and his successor, a brother not a son. New monarchs would be older and more restrained. Already overturned once, the arrangement has the unintended consequence of making successors to the throne too old to be effective.[57]

Jordan's parliament removed King Talal in 1952, a year after he succeeded his murdered father, Abdullah. Talal's successor, his son Hussein, was authorized to designate a successor from the ruling dynasty; he chose his brother to be Crown Prince, who served 34 years, and then without warning a few days before Hussein died he removed his brother and appointed his son, Abdullah, successor. Abdullah II upon accession chose his brother Hamzeh to be Crown Prince. Succession expectations which can be changed so quickly are dangerous. Abundant historical evidence indicates that appointed heirs often kill benefactors before they change their minds.[58]

Requisites in different succession principles

The hereditary rule needs certainty or clarity, and in cases where rivals with 'equal' claims exist, as in the Ottoman world, the likelihood that only one candidate will stay alive is strong. European states found that using choice or election as an element in the hereditary process made a monarch's life precarious, which greatly troubled the community's peace. The fiction of a monarch who could not die meant that competence (infants and senile persons held the office[59]) and substantive political issues *seemed* 'extraneous'. But rules cannot exclude serious concerns forever. In the Reformation, for example, religious turmoil made it necessary to introduce religious qualifications. The English Act of Settlement (1700–01) excluded 'Papists' or anyone who married a Papist.

Elections emphasize the importance of efficacious or responsible government more; a candidate's credentials and the issues espoused are crucial matters. Obviously, incomplete rules can be important

ingredients in election quarrels. One dimension of the most notorious
election controversy in American history, the Presidential election of
1876 (Hayes–Tilden), was that the Constitution specified no way to
resolve disputed Electoral College tallies. The ultimate issue was the
fairness of an election deeply flawed by fraud and violence, a question
which appears over and over again in electoral crises. The government
was not overthrown in 1876 and both candidates survived, a common
outcome in electoral violence but much more rare in its hereditary
counterpart.

   The fairness issue develops simultaneously with the emergence of
modern elections in England. Before the Glorious Revolution (1688)
established Parliament's supremacy, legislative seats were seen as a
burden, and as such were often refused and rarely contested.
Afterwards, seats became the object of competition and candidates
often bent the rules. 'By ... 1715 violence and intimidation were
regarded as the most effective means of winning votes', a violence
which political parties initiated and carried on for more than 150 years.[60]
Between 1832 and 1854 Parliament considered 130 petitions to void
elections due to fraud, bribery and violence. Some 90 were annulled; 17
more were found corrupt, though Parliament, unable to trace the agents,
allowed them to stand.[61]

   Parenthetically, the secret of the Church's ultimate success with
elections was that in becoming convinced that electoral mobilization
generated violence, it outlawed campaigning, secluded electors and
made secret ballots mandatory. The principal element in this formula,
no campaigning, is alien to the modern understanding of elections.
While the secret ballot was eventually mandated and the privacy of the
polling booth was protected, this was done because the measures
seemed essential to the integrity of the campaigning process.

   Two institutional factors shape the fairness question. The first is
'permanent' political parties, a distinguishing feature of contemporary
politics created after 1688. Parties organize campaigns, recruit leaders,
nourish ideologies, link local to national concerns, mobilize masses,
and oversee policies when power is won. Most important for our
purposes, they are the agents of first resort for restraining violence or
bringing it about.

   A second institutional factor is the notoriously complex character of
the electoral process. Many administer it (i.e. determine the eligibility
of candidates and voters, count ballots, police numerous polling places,

organize and finance campaigns). All these requirements invariably multiply opportunities for surprises, mistakes[62] and fraud, and, of course, this is a context where allegations of fraud are more likely to be believed.

In the early period and throughout the nineteenth century, so many candidates obviously sought office for material gain, that voters soon demanded their share. In England

> [t]he borough of Sudbury openly advertised for a purchaser. The electors of Grampound boasted that they received three hundred guineas [sic] each for their vote. At Aylesbury the highest bidder was awarded the promise of the election by municipal figures as one awards a contract.[63]

The step from fraud to violence is not a big one.

> When fraud did not seem sufficient ... violence of various kinds was employed. In the earlier days, much of this was due to the natural ebullition of mob spirit enjoying the natural excitement of election time ... By 1776 the uses of violence seem to have become a recognized electoral maneuver and elections in the larger constituencies were characterized by hosts of hired ruffians and bludgeon-men. At Brentford in 1768 both parties ... resorted to terrorism; the object ... was to end polling if the election [went] against [one's] candidate.[64]

> Cases of drugging and abduction were not rare at election time. At Lewes, it was found necessary to put the town in a state of siege to prevent the carrying off and the imprisonment of electors. At Coventry a mob of two thousand roughs were said to have been engaged as bullies to intimidate all who wanted to vote against the Liberal candidates. They received five shillings a day, and had orders to 'beat the electors roundly and leave them alive, but hardly'.[65]

Late nineteenth-century America had its counterparts.

> The United States Marshal for Philadelphia admitted that fraudulent voting and violence were so endemic in that city that 'never an election goes by without a riot' and in 'some wards scarcely an election goes by without somebody being killed. A Cincinnati newspaper reported as a quiet election, one in which

only eight people were killed ... In many cities riots were often orchestrated to keep people away from the polls with protection provided for the 'right party' ticket.[66]

These were familiar local scenes in virtually every election-driven country of the nineteenth century. In America and England they often involved Congressional and Parliamentary seats, but only one serious national crisis precipitated, the Hayes–Tilden election, where results were dubious in four states and violence a factor in three.

Congress appointed a special Electoral Commission. Four months after the election, it decided that Rutherford Hayes, who had fewer popular votes, had won. The incumbent President Ulysses Grant, not a candidate, mobilized the troops stimulating impeachment cries. So uncertain was the nation that the Commission's verdict would be accepted, that Hayes took the oath of office secretly, an act reminiscent of Ottoman sultans!

Many feared a civil war; and one might have occurred if the country had not already just been through one, if Hayes had not jumped on his opponent's platform afterwards, and if the Democratic candidate Tilden had not encouraged supporters to accept the 'Corrupt Bargain of 1876'.[67] Subsequently, the Electoral Count Act (1887) altered the method of verifying electoral counts, to make similar impasses less likely, an impasse which developed in the Gore-Bush struggle.[68]

The Hayes–Tilden election demonstrates that it is crucial for participants to believe an election is credible. Today, states unable to muster their own resources to verify elections can employ international monitors. Monitoring requests began after the League of Nations was established, but the League could not honour them and the last futile tragic plea for help was made in 1931, when German voters in Poland appealed to the League to stop the Polish majority from denying their voting rights.[69] The first successful effort was made in the 1989 Namibia election. Initially designed to stop civil wars, the practice spread to many Third World states thinking that they could not have fair elections otherwise, a list which expands annually (i.e. Nicaragua, El Salvador, Guatemala, Haiti, Surinam, Guyana, Angola, Mozambique, Cambodia, Liberia, South Africa, Chile, Pakistan, Hungary, Georgia, Ethiopia, Peru, Mexico, Zimbabwe, Ivory Coast, etc.).

Are there limits to the value of the process? An Organization of American States (OAS) monitoring team withdrew from a scheduled

Peruvian run-off (May 2000) because fraud and violence 'do not provide a strong basis of legitimacy'. The only challenger (A. Toledo) had withdrawn from what he called a 'butcher house of fraud'. The incumbent (A. Fujimoro) responded, 'globalization does not mean there can be unlimited intervention in a country's internal affairs'. The OAC also criticized Toledo's behaviour and evidence suggests that his support was dissipating; but foreign states are considering sanctions which might backfire.[70]

Election results are rejected for other reasons. No one wondered whether Lincoln's victory was fair in 1860. The count was credible, and the American South made its decision. The American political world had changed dramatically: the old party system collapsed, and the South's minority status and the general hostility to its 'peculiar institution' were permanent. Bullets seemed better than ballots.

Conciliation is important in any succession process. But it has a special prominence for elections as they are mechanisms *par excellence* for pitting elements of the community against each other. The process generates new incentives and opportunities to demonize the opposition; the paradox is that the mutually vilified must live together afterwards. The paradox puzzled Santayana, suggesting that in some important sense people must believe that it makes no difference who wins. Accepting decisions made by 'a majority is like leaving it to chance – a fatal procedure unless one is willing to have it either way. When something important is at stake, as in a criminal charge, we demand unanimity'.[71]

But campaign rhetoric must emphasize party differences to attract voters, and in the process the language exaggerates potential stakes, threatening Santayana's condition for success. The military metaphors employed are particularly striking; the parties wage 'campaigns', employing 'strategy and tactics'. Party faithful are called 'cadre', and areas with many supporters are known as 'strongholds' or 'citadels'.[72]

The campaign divides but partisans must be brought back together again, and a very conspicuous peace-making protocol or conciliation process should appear *immediately* after results are announced. In America, losing candidates 'must' make a concession speech to supporters, telling them in effect that he or she has surrendered, that this 'war' is over, and to 'lay down their arms'. Winners then follow the precedent laid down by Thomas Jefferson, the winner of the first American election driven by parties, declaring that 'we are all Federalists and all Republicans'. Losers are reassured that winners will not press their advantage too far. When the gestures succeed, the winner's popularity normally reaches heights rarely achieved again, that is, until the outcome of the next election is known! The peace achieved becomes a marriage of sorts, as the term 'honeymoon period' used to describe the months after an election suggests.

An Israeli version of this ritual occurred in May 1999 when Ehud Barak calmed celebrating supporters: 'I will be the Prime Minister of all Israel ... We are brothers, and brothers work together'. Uncharacteristically, the loser, Benjamin Netanyahu, gracefully exited from the political scene, an act crucial to an election's success and expected honeymoon.[73]

To play both roles (partisan and peace-maker) well is difficult, especially because it is the party faithful who are most taken with invidious portraits of opponents. And then there is the problem of time. Hereditary succession arrangements can be clear and prompt,[74] but elections take *time*, and often a great deal of time, during which the outcome must have some element of uncertainty. This means that there are temptations to make electoral rhetoric more pugnacious, and the party faithful must exhort themselves, an effort which may make them believe that defeat is unthinkable because the consequences are so serious.

Students of states where elections work note that the election process itself is a socializing agent.[75] Participants gain a firmer grasp of the issues, procedures and nature of their community, and that is one reason why a peaceful election enhances chances that subsequent ones will be too. Indeed, a tradition of peaceful elections, where the credible pluralities and *competent* governments emerge, is a powerful, sometimes essential, ingredient in the ability to do it again.

Yet tensions are an inherent part of the succession process, and may erupt at any subsequent succession. When these anxieties compound with other divisive long-standing political concerns, the consequences may be bitter, prolonged and traumatic, a point which American history demonstrates well. By 1860 the US had completed 15 consecutive presidential successions, including occasions when vice-presidents filled vacant offices. Still the South refused to accept Lincoln's election.

An election experienced as fraudulent shapes subsequent expectations or affects 'socialization' too. Expectations that participants will never learn to contain themselves shape interactions undermining willingness to accept election results. Breakthroughs, or apparent ones, occur. Argentina experienced a century of elections dominated by fraud and violence before its first 'successful' election in 1916, one followed by two more peaceful ones. So complete did the Argentine transformation seem, that one prominent British scholar concluded in 1929 that a military coup was as unthinkable in Argentina as it was in England.[76] Six months later, Argentina had three military coups! Mexican electoral experiences began more dismally. The 1934 election was the first peaceful one; the pattern has been sustained, but it took some 60 years for competition between parties to emerge.

A typology

Liberal democracies are identified by an implicit bargain between representative governments and their citizens, and a specific arrangement which regulates that bargain. The bargain is that the government's legitimacy, its expectation of obedience to its laws, is dependent on its claim to be doing what the citizens want it to do. The organized arrangement that regulates this bargain of legitimacy is the competitive political election.

G. Bingham Powell, 'Liberal Democracies',
Encyclopedia of Government and Politics

The one pervading evil of democracy is the tyranny of the majority, or rather the party, not always the majority, that succeeds by force or fraud to carry elections ... Unequal electorates afford no security to majorities. Equal electorates give none to minorities.

Lord Acton, 'Sir Erskine May's',
Democracy in Europe

The time for election violence varies, and it has many forms, aims and outcomes. It may materialize before, during and after the election, sometimes considerably later. Forms vary widely – riots, demonstrations, civil wars, terrorist campaigns, military coups, and assassinations either by lone individuals or as part of a political conspiracy. Most of the time, violence is designed to influence elections by intimidating voters and striking candidates down. But violence can prevent an election from taking place or a victor from taking charge of the government. Occasionally, the circumstances are bizarre: in Taiwan, Nationalist party members rioted to punish their leaders for losing an election (May, 2000).

Violence is a gamble: it may produce the aim intended, as indicated earlier, or backfire. Anti-Vietnam violence during the 1968 presidential and 1970 Congressional elections unintentionally aided Republicans. The Italian MSI party in the 1970s, perceived to have triggered a series of violent acts, was severely punished at the polls. Violent acts committed for other ends during an election may surprise perpetrators. To avenge a leader the Israelis had assassinated, Hamas organized 'self-martyrdom' bombings during Israel's 1996 election, causing Shimon Peres (the 'peace candidate') to lose important ground to the eventual winner, Benjamin Netanyahu. Hamas did not desire this result again and laid its weapons aside in the next election (1999), its leader, Sheikh Ahmed Yassin, suggesting that it might recognize the state of Israel. Hamas' restraint contributed to the size of Barak's victory over Netanyahu.[77]

A comprehensive typology of election violence is a task too enormous to complete here, but we can briefly suggest some distinctions. Three types are conspicuous: the election principle may be *rejected*; the principle may be valid but the *application* is not, as when citizens belong to different communities; and the most common and complex occurs when participants understand a particular instance to be *unfair*, but they do not explicitly reject the principle or system. Instances of the first two types inspire violence in hereditary arrangements, though the open, lengthy electoral process will induce different dynamics. The third is peculiar to elections, which is why we devote more space to discussing it.

Rejection

Some may never be convinced that competitive elections can provide legitimacy. In outlining a scheme for the violent disruption of Italy's electoral process, the Neo-Fascist leader Giuseppe 'Pino' Rauti declared:

> democracy is a disease of the soul ... I don't believe in elections, I don't believe that Parliament represents the nation. I am convinced, therefore, that in order to count for something in our country we must change tactics and strategy. We must be wolves and make ourselves known as such.[78]

Similar groups appeared during transitions to democracy in Spain, post-Apartheid South Africa, and Latin American states.

In Italy, right- and left-wing elements have traditional antagonisms to competitive elections. When the Communist Party reversed its tradition by adopting 'Eurocommunism' and agreed to consider coalitions with the Christian Democrats, over 100 acts of political violence occurred in the 1976 election in the two-month long campaign. Nearly all attacks came from two extra-parliamentary groups, left-wing elements and neo-Fascist groups who had different reasons to oppose the dramatic Communist decisions.[79]

The mere appearance of candidates believed to be hostile to competitive elections may provoke violence. In Italy's first post-war election, mobs attacked candidates of the Italian Social Movement, even though the victims denied that they wanted to revive the defunct Fascist dictatorship.[80]

Radical political parties often spend more time fighting each other on the streets than organizing for the polling booths. During the interwar period in Europe, Fascist parties in Britain, France, Germany, Austria, Italy and elsewhere developed paramilitary organizations to wage street combat against left-wing opponents.[81]

Application rejected

Parties publicly opposed to free elections seem less significant now, except possibly in the Islamic world. More frequently, some groups feel themselves outside the community and not obliged by elections even when they vote. The election principle *per se*, nonetheless, is accepted.[82] Warring parties in Northern Ireland believe in elections, but see themselves as either Irish or British, not members of the same community. Elections in such contexts express existing antagonisms without resolving them, and may persuade some there is no point in maintaining the system.

The long Sri Lankan agony offers one picture of the process. Riots were first generated by the 1956 elections, when Buddhist monks pushed the Movement for the Protection of the Motherland Party (MEP) to make the state a Buddhist one. Outbursts reoccurred in subsequent elections, intensifying existing gaps between Buddhist and Tamil further. Anti-Tamil riots finally generated a cruel civil war, and the first targets of the Tamil rebels were politicians from their own community who had urged them to continue voting and not give up on the system.[83]

Often, election contests fought out along ethnic or religious lines impose unacceptable conditions on the losers.[84] In the Cameroon,

Nigeria, South Africa and sub-Saharan Africa, the outcome generated secessionist demands, insurgent violence and government repression.

Other results are also common. In sub-Saharan Africa, party differences are wholly ethnic and produce either a series of local adjacent one-party systems within the same state, or a one-party system for the whole country. No matter who wins, elections generally exacerbate and complicate social divisions further.[85] Note the despair of Donald Horowitz:

> What is the point of holding elections if all they do in the end is to substitute a Bemba-dominated regime for a Nyanja regime in Zambia, the two being equally narrow, or a southern regime for a northern one in Benin, neither incorporating the other half of the state?[86]

One is reminded of John Stuart Mill's early prophecy on what a 'premature' breakup of the Western empires would mean for their democratic successors. The most difficult problems would occur when

> nationalities are nearly ... equal [in] power. In such cases, each, confiding in its strength, and feeling itself capable of maintaining an equal struggle with any of the others, is unwilling to be merged in it; each cultivates with party obstinacy its distinctive peculiarities; obsolete customs, and even declining languages are revived to deepen the separation; each deems itself tyrannized over if any authority is exercised within itself by functionaries of a rival race; and whatever is given to one is considered to be taken from all the rest.[87]

Unfairness

Election violence most often occurs to bend the rules, and a useful way to understand the problems is to identify the locations or contexts where they appear. The first two occur in situations where competitive elections are accepted, one is local and the other is national or systemic. A third kind, which is beyond the scope of this article and so is not discussed here, most often occurs in dictatorships offering 'new ' and more 'democratic' types of election under one-party auspices.

Local.   Local election violence is especially interesting. It has been so common: virtually all nineteenth century states displayed significant examples.[88] Good case studies are available and variations are suggestive. It also seems true that local elections compared to their local hereditary counterparts generate violence.

Oddly, repeated local violence can remain isolated in the system, as America's 'Gilded Age' (1868–1906) and the English experience of an earlier period show:[89]

> Most parts of the [American] Union were pure, as pure as Scotland where from 1868 till 1892 there was only one election petition for alleged bribery. Other parts are not better than the small boroughs of Southern England before the Corrupt Practice Act of 1883.[90]

A striking variety of corrupt practices prevailed, bribery, fraudulent election rolls, repeat voting, miscounting, etc.:

> So efficient was the Tweed Ring ... in 1868–71 that the votes cast (for it) were 8% in excess of the voting population. In the New York City elections of 1910, it was conservatively estimated that the number of fraudulent registrations and votes prevented equaled the total number of votes cast.[91]

> The franchise depended very largely upon the registration agents, and they ... controlled the votes. They knew how to create qualifications on flimsy grounds; they knew how to prevent technical objections.[92]

The practices were most flagrant when parties were so evenly matched that slight voting shifts turned elections. In the Presidential election of 1880, Democrat Winfred Hancock carried California by 22 votes; simultaneously, Republican James Garfield carried the nation by 8, 000. Senator George Edmonds (1889) explained the consequences:

> [T]he divisions of parties in several of the States have been so close that the purchase of a comparatively small number of votes could easily turn the scale ... and it can be assumed to be an undisputed fact that such temptation has been yielded to by the active management of both great political parties.[93]

During Reconstruction, practices in the American South confirmed the general argument that closely matched parties could produce serious problems. Election violence was 'so extensive in scope, that it can scarcely be detailed'. But after Democrats regained control via the 'Corrupt Bargain of 1876', violence declined dramatically though still used to prevent blacks from voting.[94]

Adjuncts of local political machines, the police in American cities were extraordinarily busy on election days; a New York state Senate Committee noted:

> Republican ballot clerks, poll watchers, and election inspectors told how the police had threatened Republican voters, ignored Democratic repeaters, tampered with ballot boxes and committed or permitted in the Committee's words 'almost every conceivable crime against the electoral franchise'.[95]

The Chicago police in 1894

> kidnapped 25 prominent Polish Republicans the day before the election and held them incommunicado until the day after.[96]

> If the outcome was in question ward leaders were prepared … to send in hoodlums to keep the opposition away from the polls and to order policemen to help the thugs.[97]

The police were active on election day well into the twentieth century:

> In Chicago where the Democratic organization controlled the police force, ward leaders … in the late 20s forced the officers to distribute partisan handbills on election day though they no longer compelled them to roundup influential Republicans on the eve of the municipal elections.[98]

The British had police problems too. Rural areas were virtually devoid of police. The army dealt with election riots, but just because the military could not act in appropriate time, controversies sometimes became riots.

Indian politics provide a contemporary parallel. Familiar electoral practices in several important states are occasions for bloody Hindu–Muslim riots:

> The injection of large amounts of money, mostly black money, into the election process has become the subject of general complaints and assumed menacing proportions … Along with [this] has come direct tampering with the freedom of the voter.

Widespread rigging and forced booth capturing make a mockery of the election process.[99]

If Muslim votes are unnecessary to win, riots against them occur in tightly contested constituencies (i.e. the winner's margin in the previous election is 10 per cent or less).[100] To win, Stephen Wilkinson explains, Hindu candidates exploit fundamentalist sentiment to bring hitherto indifferent voters to the polls.

> Press accounts of the riots describe how in every case the precipitating event ... was an organized Hindu nationalist attempt to take out an anti-Muslim procession, hold an anti-Muslim public-meeting, or to raise fears that Muslims were just about to turn upon Hindus.[101]

The Indian police problem is critical. Only when states need their votes to maintain majorities will governments give adequate security to local constituencies in riot-prone times.

With one exception, American and British local violence did not threaten the national government's legitimacy, and changes in electoral rules and police arrangements reduced local disorders. A secret ballot prevented buyers from seeing how sellers actually voted. Registration and residence requirements were finally made meaningful. Non-party election officials were chosen, and legislation to maintain polling privacy put in place.

In America the reforms began in 1895 and continued for several decades. Reorganizing the urban police took longer, well into the twentieth century. Severed from local politics, the police became a civil service with narrowly defined law and order functions.

British electoral reforms had a similar dynamic. The decisive turning point was the Redistricting Act of 1883, which extinguished small boroughs and transferred election disputes from Parliament to the courts. The initial British police problem was that there were no police! The army alone was responsible for quelling riots. But the strain on military discipline is always enormous when soldiers are asked to fire on fellow citizens, the Duke of Wellington told Parliament. A professional police force (1832) was then established for London,[102] and step by step expanded to the rest of the country.

Local violence in India poses more difficult problems. The electoral and police reforms so important to America and Britain were already in place before Indian election violence became common. Is there, then,

anything to compare in British and American experiences with Muslim
scapegoating, and can it continue without altering the national scene?[103]
Much depends on whether the army can stay in the barracks. Since 1991
half its forces have been deployed on police duties, and it is called out
three times a day to deal with various kinds of violence.[104] Should
discipline become problematic, the national government cannot escape
the consequences. Each Hindu–Muslim riot also provokes India's
Muslim neighbours, sometimes fomenting violence against Hindus
there and in countries as far away as England – reactions which could
make India's national scene more problematic.

System fraud. We do not know how violence spreads from local to
systemic levels or how special the cases above are. Violence on the
national level does not require local expressions as a precondition.
Difficulties can begin at the national level without an obvious
relationship to the local. Fear of losing power can drive one to alter the
terms of office and/or undermine an election's integrity, a fear which
cannot exist in systems where one receives power for life. The effects
and times of the systemic crisis may be limited. The 'Watergate Break
In' by Richard Nixon supporters was an assault on the integrity of an
election, occasioning the only resignation in American presidential
history.[105] The Allahabad High Court declared in 1975 that Prime
Minister Mrs Gandhi obtained a seat fraudulently and disqualified her
for six years. But in persuading the President that 'internal disorder'
required him to declare a state of emergency, she received extraordinary
powers for two years.[106] Greater effects are common elsewhere. The list
of elected leaders who forfeited their trust by transforming constitutions
is long (e.g. Sukarno (Indonesia, 1959), Rhee (South Korea, 1960),
Menderes (Turkey, 1960), Lee (Singapore, 1967), Marcos (Philippines,
1985)). Some ended their days peacefully; but Menderes was hanged,
Marcos fled, and Rhee ran when Korea's Second Republic crumbled.

Persistent systemic election violence puts the military in a difficult
position between conflicting party and government pressures. Is it an
accident that the favourite time for military coups, the most frequently
employed method to overthrow governments, is during elections?[107]

Once in power, the military may find its own agenda. In Nigeria
(1993), the military annulled a presidential election which it authorized
because the results were unacceptable, breaking its promise for a six-
year transition to civilian government.[108]

When governments change rules to exclude candidates, the disqualified may try to prevent the election from taking place. Alternatively, an opposition may exclude itself because it cannot win or believes that it will not be allowed to do so, and a boycott can prevent elections from bestowing legitimacy. In the National Assembly elections in Nigeria (1998), the turnout was less than 5%, a feat which might have toppled the regime even if the incumbent had not died very soon after.[109]

Conclusions and afterword

Ballots are substitutes for bullets, democrats often say, a slogan reflecting both truth and hope. No principle of succession works every time it is used, and when it fails bullets are trumps, at least for the moment.

History offers two major principles of succession: heredity and election. Each needs clarity and must produce efficacious governments, but heredity gives the first requisite priority, and election adds a third – fairness. Birth works best when it can eliminate choice and reduce uncertainty and interregna (i.e. the king who does not die). The election principle moves in the opposite direction, expanding the realm of choice and the time to make it.

We do not know which principle reduces succession violence more. Earlier distinguished witnesses (the authors of *The Federalist*, Sir Henry Maine and Lord Acton) endorsed elections, fully convinced that they invited more violence. Friedrich articulated the current conventional wisdom: 'Although there have been many uncertainties with ... election[s], the development of mass parties has stabilized constitutional democratic regimes [providing] a certainty of succession which surpasses that of hereditary monarchy.'[110] Still, no systematic examination exists; and when attempted it should compare like with like (i.e poorly and well-designed hereditary states with their two electoral equivalents).

What does seem clear is that each principle generates distinctive tensions and violence patterns. Elections are complicated affairs extended over time, involving many participants widely spread in space to organize and implement the plan. The situation maximizes opportunities for mistakes and is a context where false allegations of fraud are credible and encouraged.

Candidates pit elements of the community against one another, often aggravate existing tensions, complicating contexts in which aroused groups must live together afterwards. Mobilization requires belligerence, but conciliation entails restraint and delicacy.

Conventional wisdom associates election violence almost exclusively with the 'developing democracies', where it is common and has profound consequences. But our examples show that virtually all states have experienced it; the question is why and how the experience relates to the general features of political violence in the same states.

Political parties have the initial responsibility for managing peaceful elections. Sometimes, this is beyond their capacities. Though the Whig party's collapse precipitated the American Civil War, it is difficult to see how party adjustments could have prevented it. Still, even if parties can restrain election clashes, government must help to enforce the rules, and that explains why professional police forces were established when they were.

Political parties, much evidence suggests, largely organize election violence. Winning is always a crucial, perhaps the most important, element on the party agenda. Responsibility at times is indirect. Weak parties provide opportunities for other elements of the community to exploit election tensions and parties may be drawn into the fray willy-nilly.

While discussing particular instances of election violence, we enumerated times, forms and some consequences. We could neither treat crucial questions of frequency and intensity nor show how specific patterns relate to particular political systems. Even though the most important consequence is the repeated rise of dictators, the democratic form is resilient. In India and Sri Lanka, 'democratic institutions persist in most critical respects' even with 'frequent, brutish, and widespread' election violence:

> The killing and the suffering are monstrous [but] … there is no archipelago of prison camps, no suffocating attempts to stifle opposition. Elections are interrupted but not vitiated, parliament is unruly but still central …, politicians rail against each other but accept the legitimacy of opposition.[111]

The Eubank–Weinberg and LeVine articles in this volume provide more evidence of the ability of democratic institutions to endure violence.

We enumerated some domestic consequences of succession and largely ignored international complications. But with respect to the latter, it should be said that although *all* struggles provide opportunities for foreign state intervention, each principle has particular international implications too. European royal families created alliances through marriage, which inevitably meant succession problems in one state often affected others immediately, sometimes generating wars among many powers. With respect to elections in the twentieth century, the international community has assumed important responsibilities for maintaining election credibility.

We distinguished three mobilizing factors for election violence. In the first, the election principle is rejected, a relatively rare occurrence now. A second challenges the basis for community and may lead to secession, but the seceding element normally accepts elections. The third perceives particular elections as unfair, a more frequently made claim, which produces numerous variations. We discussed two examples of this third type, those affecting the local sphere and those threatening national governments.

We looked more closely at cases of persistent local election violence, which did not affect the national sphere decisively. *Inter alia*, the pattern illustrates how tenacious a community's commitment to elections may be. English and American local elections are no longer troublesome, but the future of the Indian counterpart is problematic, as it contains intense ethnic and religious elements, matters which seem particularly difficult for elections to resolve.

The disruption of the integrity of national or systemic elections has no necessary connection to local election scenes, and the intensity of systemic crises vary greatly. Finally, just because they involve so much violence, the most profound interruptions generally make military establishments critical elements on the political scene.

NOTES

1. Leo Snowiss, Leonard Billet, Victor Le Vine, James Tong, Sara Grdan and Paul King read the manuscript at various stages and made helpful suggestions, not all of which, alas, could be taken. My special thanks to Paul King who found the poem.
2. Excellent case studies exist, but we found no general argument. See Dennis Austin, *Democracy and Violence in Sri Lanka* (London: RIIA Chatham House Papers, 1994); Steven Ian Wilkinson, 'The Electoral Incentives for Ethnic Violence; Hindu-Muslim Riots in India' (APSA, unpublished, 1998); Garson and O'Brien, 'Collective Violence in Violence in the Reconstruction South', in Hugh Graham and Ted Gurr, *Violence in America* (Beverly Hills, CA: Sage, 1989) pp.243–76; and Garson and O'Brien, 'New

Perspectives on Election Fraud in the Gilded Age', in Peter Argersinger, *Structure, Process and Party: Essays in American Political History* (Armonk, NY: Sharpe, 1992) pp.103–21. Historians by contrast, as the last two references indicate, are much more aware of the issue. *Cf.* K. Theodore Hoppen, *Elections, Politics, and Society in Ireland 1832–1885* (Oxford: Clarendon Press, 1984).

3. *Cf.* Maurice Duverger, *Political Parties* (New York: John Wiley & Sons, 1959); Leon Epstein, *Political Parties in Western Democracies* (New York: Praeger, 1967); and Richard Rose (ed.), *Electoral Behavior* (New York: Free Press, 1996). Argersinger (note 2) says 'that the propensity by academics to discount observations about the corruption of the electoral process in the Gilded Age is probably due to the vested interest we have in data statistics': p.120. Unreliable statistics make the study of elections less valuable. That may explain our obliviousness to electoral violence too, but there are other causes. See discussion of the two editions of *The Encyclopedia of the Social Sciences* (note 24).

4. See Graham and Gurr (note 2).

5. See Douglas Hibbs, *Mass Political Violence: A Cross-National Causal Analysis* (New York: John Wiley, 1973) ch.7, pp.116–32. Powell discusses specific elections and focuses largely on how parties participate in that violence: *Contemporary Democracies*, pp.168–70.

6. Krishna Kumar (ed.), *Post Conflict Elections: Democratization and International Assistance* (Boulder, CO: Lynne Rienner, 1998).

7. Jennifer McCoy, Larry Gerber and Robert Pastor, 'Pollwatching and Peacemaking', *Journal of Democracy* 2/4 (Fall, 1991) p.101. *Cf.* W. Marvin Will, 'NGO's and IGO's as Promoters of Liberal Democracy in the Caribbean: Cases for Nicaragua and Guyana', in I. Griffith and B. Sedoc Dahlberg, *Democracy and Human Rights in the Caribbean* (Boulder, CO: Westview Press, 1997) pp.51–74.

8. 'The air was electric with excitement, anticipation ... and with fear ... that those in the right wing who had promised to disrupt this day of days might in fact succeed in their nefarious schemes ... Chief Buthelesi's Inkatha Freedom Party [too] had threatened to stay out of the election. We were all bracing ourselves for the most awful bloodletting. We held our breaths and wondered what the body count might be.' Desmond M. Tutu, *No Freedom Without Forgiveness* (New York: Doubleday, 1999) pp.2–4.

9. Mattei Dogan, 'How Civil War was Avoided in France', *International Political Science Review* (1984) vol.3, p.277.

10. Dennis Austin (note 2) p.3.

11. Tony Payne, 'Multi-Party Politics in Jamaica', in Vicky Randal (ed.), *Political Parties in the Third World* (London: Sage, 1988) pp.137–54.

12. Stephen Rousseas, *The Death of Democracy* (New York: Grove Press, 1968) pp.9–12.

13. Seth Mydans, 'Fearful of Militias ...', *New York Times* (hereafter '*NYT*') 29 Aug. 1999, p.3. In fact, a referendum, not an election, was held, but news accounts used the terms interchangeably, and we thought the example worth using.

14. Hiroshi Kawahara, 'L'Intreccio Tradizionalismo-Modernismo nel Terrorismo Giapponese', in Donatella della Porta and Gianfranco Pasquino (ed.), *Terrorismo e violenza political* (Bologna: Il Mulino, 1983) pp.214–15.

15. Franco Ferraresi, *Minacce alla democrazia* (Milan: Feltrinelli, 1995) p.319.

16. Charles Seymour, *Election Reform in England and Wales* (Hamden, CT: Archon Books, 1970, reprint) pp.189–90.

17. Garson and O'Brien, 'New Perspctives' (note 2) p.112.

18. David Chalmers, *Hooded Americanism* (Chicago: Quadrangle Books, 1963) pp.320–21.

19. Seth Mydans, 'Restive Indonesians Find Little Hope in Vote', *NYT*, 29 May 1997.

20. Seth Mydans, 'Indonesians Select Opposition Leader ...', *NYT*, 22 Oct. 1999.

21. Milton Viorst, 'Algeria's Long Night', *Foreign Affairs* (Nov.–Dec. 1997) p.91.

22. httpl//www.arabicneces.com/Daily/Day199062852html

23. *Leviathan*, ch.19.

24. Frederick Watkins, 'Succession; Political', *Encyclopedia of the Social Sciences*

(hereafter 'ESS') (New York: Macmillan, 1937) vol.VII, p.442. Ferrero's forgotten masterpiece, *The Principles of Power* (New York: G.P. Putnam's, 1942) provides the best discussion of the succession problem. Carl J. Friedrich, *Man and His Government* (New York: McGraw Hill, 1963) devotes chapter 28 to the issue. Jack Goody's excellent edited volume, *Succession to High Office* (London: Cambridge University Press, 1966) deals largely with African monarchies. The strength of the earlier discussions of Ferrero, Watkins, Friedrich and Goody is that they focus on legitimacy principles. The most recent study, Burling, *The Passage of Power: Studies in Political Succession* (New York: Academic Press, 1974) treats illegitimate instances and obscures the principles at stake.

The second edition of the ESS eliminates succession and makes other changes which suggest that the new editors were less sensitive to the fragility of institutions, violence and the importance of history. The article on elections discusses violence, fraud and bribery extensively and contains a separate article on 'contested (disputed) elections'. The article on elections in the later edition does not mention violence, fraud or bribery, and eliminates 'contested elections'. The first had articles on riots, assassination, terrorism, violence and praetorianism; all were eliminated in the second edition. Ironically, after the second was published, the last five subjects were 'in subjects', suggesting once again how poor social scientists can be at forecasting events.

25. Hoppen (note 2) ch.5; D. Austin (note 2) p.21; and Hewitt, this volume.
26. Mattei Dogan correctly observed that the principles of legitimacy academics use most frequently (Weber's tradition, reason and charisma) are irrelevant for succession: 'Conceptions of Legitimacy', *Encyclopedia of Government*, pp.116–28.
27. Lot, or random selection, was the mechanism of Greek democracy. Because humans did not influence the choice, it was presumably divinely guided. Biblical priests cast lots to get Yahweh's response to 'yes–no' questions. Lot survives in the jury systems of common law countries. For major offices it seems incomprehensible now: who cannot sympathize with Tilden's rejection of a proposal to choose Electoral Commission members by lot in the disputed American presidential election of 1876? 'I may lose the presidency but I will not raffle for it.' Paul L. Haworth, *The Hayes–Tilden Election* (Indianapolis: Bobbs-Merrill, 1906) p.200.
28. Appointment, Robbins Burling says, is relevant only for administrative and judicial positions: note 24, p.251. The claim is not entirely correct. Roman emperors usually appointed their own successors; but most were assassinated, suggesting that for the major political offices appointment may be the least workable principle. '[T]he chief anxiety of all the emperors is to secure their position; they all dread rivals whose right is equal or superior to their own.' M. Rostovtzeff, *The Social and Economic History of the Roman Empire* (2 vols) Tr. J.D. Duff (New York: Oxford University Press, 1926) vol.I, p.195. *Cf.* discussions of dictatorship and monarchy in Islam below.
29. The Dalai Lama is reincarnated in a male born at the moment of the former's death. The succession form is utilized in other Buddhist orders too. But disputes about the successor can be violent. See Barry Barak, 'Llama Escape Inflames Buddhist Rivalry', *NYT*, 3 Feb. 2000, p.1.
30. A. D. Alderson, *The Structure of the Ottoman Dynasty* (London: Oxford University Press, 1956) pp.59*ff.* Half of the Sultans were deposed, all under the threat of violence. Another instance of violence during a Sultan reign to depose him was violence the Sultan used against persons who might make a claim in the future for his position.
31. Monarchy collapsed in most European states after World War I. After World War II, the Soviets eliminated those remaining in eastern Europe. Others fell one by one: Italy (1946); Egypt (1953); Vietnam (1955); Tunisia (1957); Iraq (1958); Yemen (1962); Libya (1969); Greece (1973); Afghanistan (1973); Iran (1979); and Ethiopia (1979). Monarchies now survive only where they have been long established (e.g. Britain, Japan and the Netherlands). The African monarchies of Lesotho and Swaziland, and that of the Baganda in Uganda, also have traditional roots. New monarchies, like the one Jean-Bedel Bokassa created in the Central African Republic 1976–79, do not last long. Restored ones last longer. The Ethiopian monarchy, restored in 1946, lasted until

1979; and the Spanish monarchy, re-established in 1969, may endure even longer. It survived the disintegration of Franco's system, partly because of its crucial role in sustaining Spain's most recent democratic constitution. The Kubaka (traditional monarch of the Buganda) was the constitutional head of Uganda, until Obote removed him (1986). When Obote himself was ousted (1993), the Buganda got their king back. Afghan, Rumanian and Albanian elements believe it vital that their monarch be restored, a problematic event. But then, monarchy has surprised astute observers before: Aristotle noted that monarchy was out of date, but its greatest successes occurred after he wrote! (*Politics*, 1286 B). We are indebted to Victor Le Vine for some details on monarchial survival.

32. Hobbes is the exception. He thought the term 'tyrant' so misused, he describes it simply as monarchy 'misliked'!

33. Myron Rush, 'Successions in the Soviet Union', *Journal of International Affairs* XVIII/1 (1964) p.69. *Cf.* his *Political Succession in the USSR* (New York: Columbia University Press, 1965). Ferrero (note 24) has the most penetrating discussion of this issue. 'Revolutionary democracies' (his term for totalitarian states) could never produce legitimate successions because their elections were necessarily fraudulent, and even if they lasted a century those states would *suddenly* vanish. He wrote this in *1944*!

34. Mexico may be the only exception.

35. The original notion that dictatorship was a temporary emergency arrangement was stressed in the French Revolution and Marxist theory, but the modern notion, unlike the original, left the time period unspecified.

36. Obviously, as the Ottoman record indicates, life for a Sultan could be frightening too, but a major difference between a dictator and Sultan was that until the dynasty ended, there would always be a Sultan. Dictators usually groom relatives to succeed them, but the latter rarely last long, and no true dynasty emerges. Nicaragua, for example, was often described as having a Somoza dynasty; but it was short-lived. Anastasio Somoza, the founder, governed Nicaragua for 23 years. When he was assassinated, his successor was his elder son, Luis Debayle (1957), who governed until 1963 when he 'appointed' an aged functionary to a term. A younger son, Debayle Somoza, gained power serving only one term. François Duvalier's son, Jean-Claude, ruled Haiti for 15 years (1971–86) before he fled. In Iraq and Syria, the sons of Saddam Hussein and Hafaz Al Assad are now being groomed as successors. Communist dynasties (an oxymoron?) have been attempted with similar results. Mao Tse Tung's wife unsuccessfully tried to succeed him; and Romania's Nicholae Ceausescu's son and wife were slated as successors but he was overthrown (1989) before their 'time' came. See John Sweeney, *The Life and Evil Times of Nicholae Ceausescu* (London: Hutchinson, 1996) p.61. Sweeney displays an official portrait of Nicholae holding a sceptre – a symbol of monarchy: p.116. *Cf.* Mary Ellen Fischer, *Nicholae Ceausescu: A Study in Political Leadership* (Boulder, CO: Lynne Riener, 1989) p.268. North Korea's Kim Il Sung was followed by son Kim Jong Il (1994), but the son was not installed officially as the 'Great Leader' until 1998 when the constitution made the deceased father 'The Eternal President'!

37. Ferrero (note 24) ch.13, 'Revolutionary Government'.

38. James Viscount Bryce, *The Holy Roman Empire* (London: Macmillan, 1961, 4th ed.) p.230.

39. *Federalist Paper* #9.

40. Burling (note 24) p.131, emphasis supplied. Even the most radical Greek democracies maintained elections for some offices where competence was indispensable (i.e. military leaders).

41. Bryce (note 38) pp.230–31 and 242 (our emphasis).

42. Jane Curry, 'Poland: History', *Encyclopedia Americana* (Danbury Conn: Groliers, 1994) vol.22, p.316 and Bernard Kovrig, 'Hungary: History', ibid., vol.14, p.582.

43. T. P. Taswell-Langmead, *English Constitutional History* (Boston: Houghton Mifflin, 1929, 9th ed.; editor: A. L. Poole) pp.25–6.

44. Ibid., p.168.

45. Ibid., p.178.
46. Friedrich (note 24) p.504.
47. Gaetano Mosca, *The Ruling Class* (New York: McGraw Hill, 1939) p.399.
48. Ferrero (note 24) p.148 and Kevin MacDonald, 'The Establishment and Maintenance of Socially Imposed Monogamy in Western Europe', *Politics and the Life Sciences* 14/1 (Feb. 1995) pp.3–40.
49. Primogeniture had different consequences for the elective monarchies because it was established before electoral college rules were resolved, and thus the autonomy of the nobles enabled them to undermine the powers of kings and the coherence of realms.
50. The election elements in the Ottoman system – choice and ratification (some scholars describe them as 'democratic' features) – stem originally as in Europe from tribal traditions. But Islamic jurists were deliberately vague on the workings of those elements: H. A. R. Gibb and H. Bowen, *Islamic Society and the West* (London: Oxford University Press, 1950) p.28.
51. The English kings Henry IV and Henry VIII married several times, and new laws of succession had to be created on each occasion.
52. Gibb and Bowen (note 50) vol.1, p.36, our emphasis. Alderson provides the best discussion of the Law of Fratricide: see note 30, pp.25–32.
53. Alderson (note 30) p.34.
54. The reigns of Ottoman Sultans averaged 17 years, and the closest Islamic competitor were the Abbasid Caliphs who averaged 12. French and English monarchs lasted 21 and 23 years respectively: ibid., p 35.
55. Ibid.
56. The practice of moving through brothers before going to the younger generation is traditional in Islam and elsewhere.
57. David Holden and Richard Jackson *The House of Saud* (London: Sidgwick and Jackson, 1981) pp.172–3; Leslie McLoughlin, *Ibn Saud: The Founder of a Kingdom* (New York: St Martin's, 1993) p.188. With respect to anxieties produced by aging successors, see Douglas Jehl, 'The Wisdom of a Saudi King: Choosing an Heir to the Realm of Abdel Aziz', *NYT*, 24 May 1999.
58. See Goody (note 24) pp.8–16. The difficulties of appointment are indicated in American Vice President's status since the 12th Amendment which allowed presidential candidates to choose a running mate. The Vice President lost autonomy, which severely handicaps ability to develop an identity necessary for a successful presidential run.
59. Presumptive heirs received a political education from childhood, and so the process is really not as random as it appears to one who knows only democratic systems. With respect to regency problems for those unfit, see Goody (note 24) pp.34*ff*.
60. Seymour Charles and Donald Frary, *How the World Votes; The Story of Democratic Development in Elections* (Springfield, MA: C. A. Nichols, 1918) vol.1, p.58.
61. Seymour (note 16).
62. A run-off in a recent (1997) New York primary was cancelled two weeks later because lost ballots were discovered. The judge observed 'irregularities appear to be a *regular* feature of New York City elections' (our emphasis). The losers accepted the decision with equanimity, but at another time or place, a different reaction might have occurred: *NYT*, 20 Sept. 1997, p.11.
63. Seymore (note 16) p.166. Note that the printer probably erred and should have printed three guineas. On the other hand, the electors were boasting!
64. Seymore and Frary (note 16) pp.102–103.
65. Ibid., p.126.
66. Argersinger (note 2) pp.115–16.
67. The election issues were decisively shaped by Civil War Reconstruction. The compromise ('Corrupt Bargain of 1877') was that Southern Democratic electors would support Hayes if Republicans agreed not to contest elections in two states: see Garson and O'Brien (note 2) p.276. The probability of reigniting a recent civil war soon is high, and so the acceptance of the Electoral Commission's decision may be more unusual

than it seems: Hegre *et al.*, 'Towards a Democratic Civil Peace? Democracy, Democratization and Civil War 1934–1992', ISA Paper (March 1997) p.16.

68. Each state must settle election controversies before the Electoral College meets, thus decentralizing the problem. In 2000 that law is a central feature in the controversy surrounding the Bush-Gore election.

69. The League of Nations was pledged to protect minorities in successor states created by the Versailles Treaty. Unfortunately, the pledge could not be kept. See Korbonski's discussion on how the Treaty stimulated ethnic tensions in this volume.

70. Clifford Krauss, 'Angry Election Monitor Leaves Peru 2 days Before Runoff Vote' and 'Fujimori is Victor in Peru's Runoff Despite Protests', and Christopher Marquis, 'U.S. Retreats in Peru Vote', *NYT*, 27, 28 and 31 May 2000 respectively.

71. 'English Liberty in America', *Character and Opinion in the United States* (New York: Charles Scribner's Sons, 1920) pp.206–207. An appropriate civil society in an election-driven system is the functional equivalent for primogeniture in sustaining monarchial succession. Santayana notes: 'It is implicitly agreed in every case that disputed questions shall be put to a vote, and that the minority will loyally acquiesce in the decision of the majority and build henceforth upon it without a thought of ever retrenching it. Such a way of proceeding seems in America a matter of course because it is bred in the bone or imposed by that permeating social contagion which is so irresistible in a natural democracy. But if we consider human nature at large and the practice of most nations we shall see that it is a very rare wonderful and unstable convention. It implies a rather unimaginable, optimistic assumption that at bottom, all men's interests are similar and compatible, and a rather heroic public spirit – such that no special interest, in so far as it has to overrule, shall rebel and try to maintain itself absolutely': p.197.

72. Robert Michels finds the military metaphor indispensable as virtually every page of his classic illustrates. 'The most striking proof of the organic weakness of the mass is furnished by ways in which, when deprived of their leaders in time of action, they abandon the field of battle in disordered flight; they seem to have no power of instinctive reorganization, and are useless until new captains arise.' 'The press constitutes a potent instrument for the conquest, preservation and consolidation of power on the part of the leaders': *Political Parties* (New York: Free Press, 1949) pp.56 and 130.

73. Victory Speech by Prime Minister Elect Ehud Barak (MFA, 18 May 1999 at <http://www.mfa.gov.il.mfa/go.asp?MFHOercO>) 'Netanyahu with a serene look on his face addressed weeping supporters, "the nation decided and we respect that decision." [He stunned] his audience unaccustomed to the sight of their Prime Minister conceding anything': Deborah Sontag, 'In a Sharp Rebuke to Netanyahu, Barak is voted Premier', *NYT*, 18 May 1999. When the Indonesian Parliament (Oct. 1999) by-passed Ms Megawiti, who had a significant plurality, she calmed rioting supporters by asking them to remember 'the unity of Indonesia'. The turbulence apparently influenced Parliament to appoint her vice-president, and she then told the crowd: 'To all my children throughout the nation I beg you sincerely to return to work. Do not be goaded into emotional actions because what you see today is your mother': Mydans (note 20).

74. Automatic succession in election driven systems occurs only when adverse circumstances (i.e. health, political pressures and malfeasance) compel officeholders to leave before completing their terms. But there is a brief interregnum because the successor's term begins when the oath of office is taken. Parliamentary and presidential regimes fill these vacancies in different ways. Presidents normally have successors in place (i.e. Vice President); the people or parliament decide in parliamentary regimes.

75. John Finn, this volume.

76. See David C. Rapoport, 'The Political Dimensions of Military Usurpation', *Political Science Quarterly*, LXXXX, 4 (Dec. 1968) pp.551–72.

77. Rabin's assassination created enormous sympathy for Peres (his successor), who refused to call a snap election (one which most thought he would have won easily),

stating that exploiting Rabin's murder was unseemly: see Adrian Guelke, this volume. In the election won by Barak, Yitzhak Mordechai, a centre candidate who seemed able to force a run-off, withdrew because the extended period would provide new opportunities for violence: 'I cannot shoulder the fear that things could end up in bloodshed': Deborah Sontag, '2 Candidates Quit in Israel before Elections', *NYT*, 17 May 1999.

78. Quoted by Giulio Salierno, *Autobiografia di un picchiatore fascista* (Turin: Einaudi, 1976) p.88.

79. Giacomo Sani, 'Mass Constraints on Political Realignments: Perceptions of Anti-System Parties in Italy', *British Journal of Political Science* 6/1 (1976) pp.16–25; Piero Ignazi, *Il Polo Escluso* (Bologna: Il Mulino, 1989) pp.167–95. The Algerian civil war, as suggested, can be explained similarly.

80. Petra Rosenbaum, *Il nuovo fascismo* (Milan: Feltrinelli, 1975) pp.56–60.

81. Martin Brozat, *The Hitler State* (London: Longman, 1981) pp.19*ff.*

82. See Philpott's discussion in this volume of how elections might be used to resolve this issue.

83. Stanley Tambiah, 'Buddhism, Politics and Violence in Sri Lanka', in M. Marty and S. Appleby (eds), *Fundamentalisms and the State* (Chicago: University of Chicago Press, 1993) pp.589–619.

84. *Federalist Paper* #10 argues that political conflicts involving religious issues pose enormous, perhaps insoluble, difficulties for election driven systems. *Cf.* Anna Simons in this volume.

85. Joel Barkun, 'Early Elections in Transitional Politics', unpublished paper presented at the MIT Democracy Conference 1997, pp.5–6.

86. 'Democracy in Divided Societies', in Larry Diamond and Mark Plattner (eds), *Nationalism, Ethnic Conflict, and Democracy* (Baltimore: Johns Hopkins, 1994) pp.35–53.

87. *Representative Government*, ch.16. *Cf.* Mill's statement with Rabushka and Shepsle's: 'democracy is not viable in an environment of intense ethnic preferences': *Politics in Plural Societies: A Theory of Democratic Instability* (Columbus: Charles Merrill, 1972) pp.69–92. Mill's argument concerning empire is worth repeating. 'When nations [ethnic groups] thus divided are under a despotic government which is a stranger to all of them ... and chooses its instruments differently from all; in course of a few generations, identity of situation often procures harmony of feeling, and the different races come to feel towards each other as fellow countrymen; particularly if they are dispersed over the same tract of country. But if the era of aspiration to free government arrives, before this fusion has been effected, the opportunity has gone by for effecting it.' Ibid, *loc. cit.*

88. Seymour and Frary (note 59) discuss most European and major non-European states.

89. Ibid., vol.1, chs.4–6.

90. James Bryce, *The American Commonwealth* (New York: Macmillan, 1895) vol.2, p.146.

91. Seymour and Frary (note 60) vol.1, p.261.

92. Ibid., vol.1, p.131.

93. Ibid., p.105. The persistent violence in Jamaica's elections mentioned above is related to the equal strength of the two major parties: Larry Rohter, 'Election Violence Fades in Jamaica, *NYT*, International Ed., 14 Dec. 1997, A13.

94. See Garson and O'Brien (note 2) p.243. Elsewhere blacks were bought, not intimidated. Bryce tells us (note 90) vol.2, p.147: 'There is a good deal of bribery among the coloured voters in some cities ...'

95. Robert M. Fogelson, *Big City Police* (Cambridge, MA: Harvard University Press, 1977) p.2.

96. Ibid., p.33.

97. Ibid., p.69.

98. Ibid., p.129.

99. Nikki Chakraverty, quoted by Austin (note 2) p.52.

100. Wilkinson (note 2) p.3.
101. Ibid., p.22.
102. See Rapoport, 'The Political Dimensions ...', (note 76). A professional police force (Royal Irish Constabulary) was established to relieve the army from election duties; 'it was one of 19th century Ireland's most remarkable success stories': Hoppen, *Elections*, p.409. See also Miller and Shaen, this volume, on issues related to police.
103. Immigrants were mainstays of the American urban machines, and election violence was directed against them. But the differences are important. Ethnic votes were *sought*, there were no international ramifications, and the violence appears less severe.
104. Wilkinson (note 2).
105. The 'cover up' was more decisive than the 'break in', but the integrity of the electoral process was the crucial element.
106. After she lost the 1997 election, Mrs Ghandi went to jail for a short time.
107. Rapoport (note 76).
108. Chief Moshood Abiola, the winner, was jailed in 1994, where he died in 1998 on the eve of his anticipated release.
109. *Africa Confidential*, 39/9 (1 May 1998) p.4. The report does not mention apathy, possibly a critical factor. Abacha's death six weeks later was attributed to a heart attack. But there was no autopsy, the burial was hurried, and it did not follow Muslim custom. Rumours persisted that he was poisoned. See ibid., 39/12 (June 12), and *NYT*, 11 July 1997.
110. Note 24, p.506. Friedrich offers no evidence and does not indicate the instances he has in mind. He seems to be comparing countries with successful hereditary and elective systems, most of which are the same countries, an identity which has interesting ramifications.
111. Austin (note 2) p.1.

3

Electorial Regimes and the Proscription of Anti-democratic Parties

JOHN FINN

Elections are central to the theory and practice of constitutional democracy. A decision to exclude particular groups from the political process represents a fundamental choice about the nature and character of legitimate political conflict. Whether in the form of a constitutional ban, as in the case of Article 21 of the Federal Republic of Germany's Basic Law, or in statutory form, as in the US Internal Security Act of 1950, the exclusion of anti-democratic parties constrains the universe of what a people may will and determines who is entitled to participate in the political sphere. Assessing how such proscriptions affect the level and likelihood of political violence requires strict, systematic scrutiny. It leads us to ask a series of questions about which factors motivate exclusion, on what rational grounds such restrictions may be justified, and if and under what conditions the democratic experiment is advanced by such bans. Moreover, the exclusion of anti-democratic parties in transitional states, where democracy is still in its nascent and therefore tenuous stage, may provide for interesting case studies in addressing the issue of how limits on self-governance affect the strategies of political parties as well as regime legitimacy.

Electoral Regimes and Political Violence

At its most general level of abstraction, our shared topic – democratic elections and their relationship to political violence – concerns issues of statecraft: How can we devise durable and stable democracies? More specifically, our common inquiry is whether and how elections in constitutional democracies encourage or inhibit political violence, often the most significant and always the most arresting challenge to the durability of democracies. Implicit in our effort is an assumption I embrace without much critical examination, namely that the choices we make about the design and structure of elections in constitutional democracies can have a significant impact on democratic stability.[1]

At some other time it might be well to explore that assumption, for it informs almost the entire literature on democratic reconstruction. Some students of that process have begun to challenge the claim, arguing that institutional design is significantly less important in democratic reconstruction than the presence of a political culture receptive to constitutionalism.[2] So it may be that elections do little to promote or retard democratic consolidation. Of greater significance might be political leadership, or culture,[3] or even fortune. Similarly, if we are interested in institutional design, we might do well to focus on elements other than elections, such as whether the structure of executive power is presidential or ministerial, or whether centre-periphery relations encourage or inhibit regime legitimacy,[4] or whether there are ways for states to ease the transition to market economies.[5]

Still, there is good reason to focus on elections and the electoral process.[6] In comparison to many of the factors that might influence constitutional maintenance, electoral laws are subject to control and change. Moreover, we have a fairly large stock of experience we can use to inform our analysis. But the most compelling reason for exploring elections is this: elections are central both to the theory and the practice of constitutional democracy. 'Elections, open, free, and fair'[7] are an essential component of democratic legitimacy, and it is the state's legitimacy that sanctions its monopoly on violence. Elections provide much of the political and moral capital behind the state's condemnation of political violence as a means of securing legitimate political change. Consequently, elections are of obvious relevance to questions of regime legitimacy and the authenticity of civic obligation. Even caretaker governments not serious about democratization recognize the importance of elections to regime power (if not always to regime legitimacy), especially in a political universe where non-democratic means of legitimation, such as monarchic rule or appeals to communism, no longer provide a certain or reliable means to legitimacy.

Elections serve four important functions in democratic states:

(1) First, elections may serve an important legitimating function in democratic states by coupling political obligation with consensual participation.[8] To do this, elections must be public, open and free, and citizens must have access to politically relevant information.

(2) Insofar as they bind citizens and parties to the state, elections may perform an integrating function in democratic states.

(3) Elections and the rules that govern them may also play an important socializing role in the teaching and transmission of democratic values to the citizenry.

(4) Elections may provide a certain and conventionalized means for the transfer of political power.

Each of these four functions may help to reduce the incidence of political violence. The integrating function of elections, for example, may decrease violence by privileging other, non-violent forms of political participation. The integrating function may also reduce the likelihood of political violence by incorporating or capturing regime opponents into the larger democratic framework and, equally important, by distinguishing between opposition to specific regimes and opposition to the democratic state as a matter of ideological principle.[9] The socializing function of elections has a symbolic dimension by persuading the public at large that the presence of legitimate, nonviolent avenues of change should foreclose appeals to violence. It thus denies the necessity for, and hence the legitimacy of, political violence as a means of political participation. And as the Weinberg and Rapoport contribution to this volume makes clear, the succession function may (but does not always) suppress violence by providing continuity and certainty at times of great fragility and vulnerability.

Perhaps less obvious is the extent to which elections are not an alternative to political violence, but instead its source. The relationship between electoral regimes and political violence in constitutional democracies is more complicated than we might assume: elections are not simply or always safety valves or a peaceful, non-violent means of political participation. In some cases, elections, if not the source of political violence, are at the least the occasion for violence. Elections sometimes unloose great passion, instead of the 'reason and deliberation' in public affairs so prized by constitutionalists.[10] Indeed, on a fundamental level an election *is* conflict, albeit of a highly stylized sort. Possible sources of conflict in nearly every election include a losing party unwilling to cede power, as well as the tendency of frustrated parties and their supporters, encouraged by inflammatory rhetoric, to 'demonize' opponents.[11]

In addition to fomenting unreason and passion, elections may contribute to violence by employing structures and rules that alienate significant actors and interests, which provide incentives for other, less gentle means of participation in political life. Electoral rules themselves can be the subject of conflict, especially insofar as 'institutions are weapons' in the struggle for political power.[12] And insofar as election violence derives from a failure or inability to solve basic constitutional issues, the rules that govern the electoral process may themselves manifest that larger constitutional conflict, especially when it concerns not only the design, but also the desirability of constitutional forms.

Disputes about the sanctity or priority of democratic and constitutional norms as preferred ways of constructing political community indicate that a critical but largely unexplored question surrounding the relationship between elections and violence is who gets to contest them. Choices about *who* can properly contest for power in the electoral process are no less important to democratic stability than questions of *when* such elections should be held.[13] Decisions about who may properly contest for elections, for example, may have a considerable impact on the integrating and legitimating functions of electoral regimes. Indeed, one purpose of electoral design is to shore up the legitimacy of new and fragile democratic states.[14]

Consequently, issues of electoral design and decisions about who contests for power are a vital part of any inquiry into the relationship between elections and violence. In this article, I consider one aspect of electoral design, largely overlooked by lawyers and political scientists alike, namely constitutional provisions that proscribe anti-democratic political parties and organizations. Such bans are a common feature of twentieth century constitutions. A typical provision looks much like Article 3 of the new Hungarian basic law, which provides that 'In the Republic of Hungary, political parties may be freely founded and may act in freedom provided they show respect for the Constitution and the statutes of constitutional law'. There are similar provisions in the constitutional texts of Austria, the Federal Republic of Germany, France, Italy, Portugal, Rwanda and Venezuela. Among transitional democracies, we find such provisions in the constitutions of Brazil, Chile, Estonia, Ukraine, Romania and many others. If we expand our search to include countries that effect proscription through statutory means, we can include Ireland, Israel, the United Kingdom and the United States.[15]

In every case, the inclusion of such provisions is predicated on the claim that some points of political conflict are no longer open to discussion (e.g., the adoption of democratic and constitutional forms themselves). Continued contest over those forms is a type of political activity that cannot be subsumed, in other words, within the confines of those constitutional forms. Proscription rules, like other rules that regulate the electoral process, thus represent an effort to end or, more often, to change the nature of the conflict.

Given their ubiquity – and the profound jurisprudential and practical problems they raise – it is surprising that there has been so little scholarly attention paid to such bans. The sparse literature that these provisions *have* generated has been concerned almost exclusively with thorny problems of constitutional theory. On what jurisprudential grounds can these restrictions be justified, especially in light of the obvious and not insignificant claim that they offend basic democratic principles of free expression and political association? Both values are necessary parts of free and fair elections; are there limits to these principles that can be squared with the normative commands of constitutional democracy?

Largely neglected is the extent to which jurisprudential concerns must extend also to the practical: What kinds of abuse do such provisions invite? Are there ways to minimize the potential for abuse? Or, more fundamentally, does proscription make a turn to violence by anti-democratic parties more or less likely, perhaps by alienating them or by providing incentives for violent or extremist activity? If so, does proscription subvert the integrating and socializing functions we commonly attribute to democratic elections? Does proscription contribute meaningfully to democratic stability? Recent cases of proscription and fears of electoral violence in Turkey and Austria suggest the continuing importance of these questions.

The answers to these questions are not known. There has been very little systematic investigation into the actual operation of proscription provisions, much less into whether they work.[16] By work, I mean not much is known about whether these bans:

(1) limit or increase the activity of anti-democratic parties; or
(2) channel dissent into peaceful, non-violent forms of political participation or encourage violence; or
(3) contribute to or disrupt the smooth operation of various electoral regimes; or
(4) contribute meaningfully to democratic consolidation and maintenance or undermine it.

I consider below what proscription is (not as obvious as it might seem, and a point of confusion in the literature) and how it works in various democracies. I also examine on what jurisprudential grounds it can be defended. My analysis is brief, in part because I have covered this ground in some detail elsewhere,[17] but more importantly because the end point – democratic consolidation and constitutional maintenance – is no less a matter of what can be justified than of what works.

I consider below how we might try to assess the utility of constitutional bans against anti-democratic political parties. I explore whether it is possible to come to any generalizations about whether and when they advance the project of democratization and constitutional maintenance. One of the premises of this collection is that analysis of the relationship between democracy and violence should be informed by empirical data and by detailed case studies that are lush in political description. There is no such study of proscription, and I lack the resources to undertake one here. Instead, in this more modest effort, I seek simply to identify the kinds of information such studies should elicit.[18] My aim is preliminary: to specify the sorts of considerations that should inform an analysis of whether proscription contributes to electoral stability and democratic maintenance.

The definition and the mechanics of exclusion

In its most elemental form, proscription is a formal ban, effected by the authority of the state, against participation in the electoral process by anti-democratic political parties. Proscription is thus a constitutive part of the electoral regime itself. It represents a fundamental choice about the nature of the state and its relationship to society. Article 21(1) of the German Basic Law, for example, provides that political parties are a central part of the German state. It indicates that political parties 'shall participate in forming the political will of the people'. But it also limits *what* the people can will. Moreover, the internal structure of political parties 'must conform to democratic principles', and subsection (2) states:

> Parties which, by reason of their aims or the behavior of their adherents, seek to impair or abolish the free democratic basic order or to endanger the existence of the Federal Republic of Germany, shall be unconstitutional ...

In short, the Basic Law imposes important substantive constraints upon the democratic process, albeit in the name of protecting that very process. As we shall see, the German case indicates that the constitutional justification for these limits depends upon a particular understanding of time and politics, and of the 'people', that looks both backward and forward. It also rests upon a claim that some kinds of political choices and norms (those that embrace democratic processes) are inherently superior to others.

To understand proscription, we must consider (1) the source of the ban; (2) its application; and (3) its justification.

Source of the Ban

In the Federal Republic, the power to proscribe is explicitly set forth in the constitutional charter. Article 21 has served as the model for several other constitutional states, including Chile and Hungary. Proscription is also an explicit part of the constitutional charters of Italy, France, Portugal, Estonia, Brazil, Portugal and several other states. The constitutionalization of proscription has two important dimensions. First, it underscores the extent to which decisions about electoral rules and regimes are matters of fundamental, constitutional importance – decisions not only about what the rules of the game are, but also about who gets to play the game. Secondly, it structures political debate. Conflict in such cases tends to centre not on *whether* the state has the authority to ban anti-democratic parties, as is often the case in other states (including the United States and Israel), but instead on the *advisability* of proscribing particular parties. By constitutionalizing a settlement concerning a conflict over the very identity and character of the state, it transforms the nature of the debate, reducing it to a matter of policy.

In some other democracies proscription is a function of a complex of statutory rules and administrative regulations. In Ireland, Northern Ireland, Israel and the United States, for example, electoral bans find their source in emergency or antiterrorism legislation. There is no provision in the US Constitution that expressly prohibits anti-democratic political parties. Indeed, there is no provision that speaks expressly to political parties at all. On the other hand, Article IV guarantees the states a republican form of government and protection against domestic violence. Moreover, a decision to ban a particular party might violate other constitutional provisions, such as the Bill of Attainder clause.[19]

In practice, however, attempts to ban political parties (or membership in certain political organizations) are a familiar feature of American constitutional politics. Ostensibly designed to prohibit violent efforts to overthrow the new government, the Alien and Sedition Act of 1798 was used to silence democratic and peaceful (if sometimes ill-tempered) opposition to the Federalists. It was the precursor for more expansive and elaborate efforts to 'reconstruct' the Southern States after the Civil War. The policy of reconstruction included military orders excluding former Confederates from the electoral process and from participating in the state ratifying conventions. The policy received further sanction in the Fifteenth Amendment. Moreover, Section 3 of the Fourteenth Amendment excluded from political office any public official who had participated in the rebellion. In the twentieth century, proscription tended to function against the left, primarily under the Smith Act of 1940 and the Internal Security Act of 1950.

Efforts to ban parties have also occurred in Israel and the United Kingdom. In 1984, the Israeli Elections Committee barred two parties from participating in Knesset elections: the Kach group, led by Rabbi Meir Kahane, and the 'Progressive List for Peace'. The Israeli Supreme Court reversed the decision in *Naiman* v. *Chairman of the Central Elections Committee of the Eleventh Knesset* (1984). In an earlier case, *Yeridor* v. *Chairman of the Central Elections Committee* (1965), the court had upheld a decision by the Committee to bar the participation of candidates who belonged to El Ard, an illegal organization. In the United Kingdom, authorities have proscribed several organizations, including the Irish Republican Army and several loyalist groups (e.g. the Ulster Freedom Fighters and the Ulster Volunteer Force).

In the preceding examples proscription took the cast of a formal act of state power. Exclusion in these cases is sanctioned by law, whether constitutional (as in Germany) or statutory (as in the United States). The exclusion of anti-democratic parties may also result from more informal mechanisms. Non-participation by anti-democratic parties and organizations may be involuntary, but not a consequence of formal state policy. Governing or majority parties may simply choose to 'lock out' anti-democratic parties by refusing to form coalitions with them or to integrate them in any meaningful way in the political process, as has been the case with the Vlaams Blok in Flanders/Belgium and, to a much lesser extent, with the National Front in France. It is not clear whether such practices constitute proscription. First, the exclusion of anti-democratic parties in such instances may or may not reflect fundamental animosity toward the aims or ideology of such groups: it may, for instance, simply reflect a choice about the relative advantages and disadvantages of cooperation. Secondly, proscription is an act of state power: whether informal choices by parties not to interact with anti-democratic parties constitutes state action is at least in part a difficult question about the definition of state power and the relationship of political parties to the constitution and organization of state power.

Alternatively, some anti-democratic parties may choose to boycott elections, whether for reasons of ideology (recognizing that elections sometimes do have integrating or co-opting functions), or for reasons of strategic advantage. They may find it easier to claim that the electoral process is fraudulent or biased than to risk electoral loss. Likewise, they may fear that their participation will endow the electoral process – or the state more generally – with a patina of legitimacy. In such cases, no proscription is involved because the coercive power of the state is not directly implicated in what is essentially a voluntary choice.

Application of the Ban

To understand how proscription actually works, we need to know which parties may be banned, on what grounds, and to which state agency the decision is entrusted.

Proscription is typically applied to political parties – and sometimes to other organizations – that advance anti-democratic programmes. In the normal course, bans apply to entire parties and not simply to particular individuals, although in practice, of course, the division between party and person may be ill-defined.

Similarly, it may be difficult to come to any shared, much less principled, understanding of what constitutes an 'anti-democratic' ideology or programme. Most constitutional provisions speak in grand generalities, insisting, as does the French Constitution, that political parties 'are obliged to respect the principles of national sovereignty and democracy'. Similarly, the German Basic Law prohibits parties that 'seek to impair or abolish the free democratic basic order ...'. Other constitutions are somewhat more specific, such as the Chilean, which prohibits parties that embrace doctrines that 'advocate violence or a concept of society, the State or the juridical order, of a totalitarian order or based on class warfare ...'. In similar fashion, the Ukrainian Constitution provides that:

> The establishment and activity of political parties and public association are prohibited if their programme, goals, or action are aimed at the liquidation of the independence of Ukraine, the change of the constitutional order by violent means, the violation of the sovereignty and territorial indivisibility of the State, the undermining of its security, the unlawful seizure of state power, the propaganda of war and of violence, the incitement of inter-ethnic, racial, or religious enmity, and the encroachments on human rights and freedoms and the health of the population.

The reference to 'inter-ethnic, racial, or religious enmity' reminds us that political parties and organizations are not always or even very often constituted simply on the basis of shared political ideology. Instead, as in Algeria or Northern Ireland, to take two prominent cases, parties may be constituted on the basis of race, ethnicity, religion and regional or tribal identity.

In some constitutions, the problem is overcome not through efforts to give the definition of 'democracy' greater specificity, but instead by simply picking out certain parties by name and making them unconstitutional. Thus the Italian and Austrian constitutions prohibit the reorganization of particular fascist parties.

In every case, including those countries where proscription is statutory, violent activity is clearly a sufficient cause for proscription. In the United States, the primary target has been the left in general and the Communist Party in particular.[20] The Smith Act of 1940[21] represented the federal government's most comprehensive effort to outlaw anti-democratic organizations. The Act made it a crime for any person to knowingly 'advocate, abet, or advise, or to teach the duty, necessity, desirability or propriety of overthrowing or destroying any government in the United States by force or violence, or by the assassination of any officer of such government...'. Interpretation by the Supreme Court eventually restricted the scope of the Smith Act[22] to acts of violence or the imminent threat of violence.

Other federal statutes did not outlaw the Communist Party directly, but the Internal Security Act of 1950 and the Communist Control Act of 1954 effectively criminalized the Communist Party by forbidding any person to conspire to 'perform an act which would substantially contribute to the establishment ... of a totalitarian dictatorship' and to seek elective office without disclosing his or her membership in a Communist organization. These laws also denied passports to

Communists and created elaborate schemes for the registration of communist organizations.[23]

In many other democracies, a ban may be predicated on a lesser showing. A party that simply advocates totalitarianism may be prohibited in Chile, Germany and perhaps in Israel.[24] The German Constitutional Court has declared two parties unconstitutional under Article 21(2). In the first case, the court declared the Socialist Reich Party unconstitutional in 1952.[25] The court reviewed the SRP's policy pronouncements, the statements of its leaders, and considered the party's obvious similarities to the old National Socialists. In the second case, the Communist Party Case,[26] the court reached a similar conclusion, finding that the Party 'rejects principles and institutions whose validity and existence are a prerequisite for the functioning of a liberal democratic order'. It is important to note that the court did not support its decision with any finding about the actual likelihood of harm or threat to the state. Instead, the court specifically noted that '[n]o action in the sense of the criminal code is needed for a party to be unconstitutional'. Among the factors the court identified as relevant to its decisions were the parties' political programs and their internal organization. The court also noted that under Article 21 of the Basic Law, the internal organization of the party must satisfy basic democratic principles.

In Germany, the United States, Estonia and Romania, the decision to ban a political party from the electoral arena is clearly entrusted to the judiciary. This may seem peculiar especially in civil law jurisdictions, as in most of Europe, where the politicization of judicial authority has a long and unhappy history. On the other hand, one of the defining features of twentieth century constitutionalism was the rise of constitutional courts and judicial enforcement of bills of rights.[27] Assigning the proscription decision to judges comports with the underlying sense that the decision implicates political liberties of the first order, as well as with the adjudicatory dimensions of the order. Consequently, even in countries where proscription is an executive function, such as the United Kingdom, there are often calls by critics for at least some kind of judicial review for proscription orders.

In some other countries, such as France, Israel and Rwanda, the constitutional provisions that authorize proscription say little or nothing about who may implement them. It may appear that the drafters assumed such provisions would be self-executing or have no need of execution. It is better to understand such provisions as serving purposes other than the actual exclusion of anti-democratic parties. By making fidelity to democratic and constitutional forms to an explicit constitutional command, such provisions may be said to serve a 'presentational' function because they express 'the condemnation of the community'.[28]

Justifications for proscription

Should political parties that reject the principles of constitutional democracy be permitted to enter the electoral arena? In such cases, should the democratic and constitutional principles of free elections and free association admit challenges that are hostile (because they reject those principles) to constitutional democracy?

The constitutional justification for these policies is not a simple matter. We must first distinguish between overt acts of violence and the political programmes of organizations that challenge democratic principles: banning the former raises no serious issues for constitutional democracies that admit of and have mechanisms for the pursuit of peaceful change. Among those mechanisms must be free and fair elections. Hence, the initial question is: Are elections that exclude opponents of democracy 'free and fair'? Electoral regimes that are not 'free and fair' lack a central component of legitimacy. Without legitimacy, it is doubtful whether elections can advance any of the functions assigned to them.

Secondly, assuming free and fair elections, should states exclude parties, admittedly non-violent, whose political programme is hostile to democratic principles? Should they exclude parties whose putative agenda satisfies democratic values but whose internal organization and political life is itself anti-democratic, as is possible in Germany?

The second question tells us that the difficult issue for constitutional theorists is not the proscription of violence but rather to identify the limits and proper means of regime change. The Basic Law provides that certain constitutive principles, such as the free democratic order, may not be overcome even by constitutional amendment. In contrast, the American statutes typically provided that bans against contributing to the establishment of a totalitarian dictatorship in the United States did not apply to proposals for constitutional amendments. Another difference between the German and American practice concerns the imminence of harm. In the Communist Party Case, the German court did not premise a finding of unconstitutionality upon a showing of actual harm. In the United States, however, such a finding is a likely requirement and a consequence of the court's decisions in *Yates* v. *United States*,[29] *Brandenburg* v. *Ohio*,[30] and *Hess* v. *Indiana*.[31]

Do constitutional or democratic principles require us to countenance appeals to change that would destroy democracy? Efforts to shut down such appeals necessarily involve limits on the kinds of information available to citizens and thus raise important issues about the limits of free expression and, by extension, about our collective capacity for democratic self-government.[32] Secondly, they raise important issues about the nature of constitutional democracy itself, and these issues involve questions about identity: In simple terms, if we understand 'the people', or the democratic 'community', to be a corporate entity that exists in time, then on what authority can the electorate deprive future electorates of the opportunity for democratic self-governance that it itself enjoyed?[33] The constitutional logic of exclusion must thus embrace a theory about the boundary and collective identity of the 'people', as well as of the limits of constitutional change.[34]

Proscription and the jurisprudence of militant democracy

The most sophisticated justifications for proscription were induced by the failure of the Weimar Republic. It is a mistake to think the collapse of Weimar was a singular consequence of well-known defects in its constitutional design. Chief among those defects was Article 48, which embraced an elaborate scheme of emergency powers and entrusted them to the executive. Article 48 was not the cause of Weimar's loss so much as it provided a staging ground for conflict. One of those conflicts was over whether the state should have banned the National Socialist Party from national elections.

It is important to recall that Weimar did possess the constitutional authority to respond to political violence. The triumph of the National Socialists cannot be attributed to a lack of emergency powers in the Weimar state, of which there were many.[35] Weimar fell instead because it 'could not respond to challenges to constitutionalism disguised in the language of democratic legality'.[36] This was made possible, at least in part, because German constitutional thought was dominated by a particular understanding of legal positivism. The most influential of its proponents, Hans Kelsen, advocated a jurisprudence dominated by the study of legal norms 'uncontaminated by politics, ethics, sociology, [and] history'.[37]

I forego a full review of Kelsen's jurisprudence.[38] For present purposes, it is sufficient to note that it provided the basis for a particular conception of electoral politics in Weimar. The 'equal chance' doctrine held that anyone willing to abide by the formal rules of electoral procedure could contest for power. As a consequence, electoral politics in Weimar were not limited to political parties committed to the maintenance of constitutional democracy.

The equal chance jurisprudence of electoral competition is plainly inhospitable to constitutional provisions banning anti-democratic parties. The essence of proscription provisions is their willingness to inquire into the substantive agendas of various political organizations and to measure the validity of those agendas against some set of democratic ideals. In this sense, proscription hopes to save democracy from its own excesses. This is precisely the kind of substantive, normative inquiry Kelsen's jurisprudence considered out of bounds. It was a jurisprudence of procedure and value-neutrality. It was also a jurisprudence wedded to a particular conception of the democratic state's relationship to time, in which the present is under no obligation to the future to preserve for it the same choices it may make for itself.

The Basic Law of the Federal Republic explicitly embraces a radically different understanding of the state and time. The Basic Law entrenches certain core constitutional principles, such as respect for human dignity and the social democratic state, and immunizes them from constitutional change. It rejects the past by rejecting Weimar's equal chance conception of electoral competition. It looks forward in time by guaranteeing to future Germans that the current generation will not abrogate core principles. In making this promise, the German people bind themselves and the future to a particular vision of political life, a vision that limits the kinds of political choices they may make, both for themselves and for their children.

This self-limitation is readily apparent in the concept of 'militant democracy', which appears in several places in the Basic Law.[39] Article 20 provides: 'All Germans shall have the right to resist any person or persons seeking to abolish [the] constitutional order, should no other remedy be possible.' Article 21 provides that political parties 'which, by reason of their aims or the behavior of their adherents, seek to impair or abolish the free democratic basic order or to endanger the existence of the Federal Republic of Germany, shall be unconstitutional.' Article 21 thus rejects the equal chance conception of electoral politics in favor of an electoral process willing to distinguish the friends of constitutional democracy from its foes. It equates elections, as Max Weber and Hans Kelsen did not, with legitimacy.

Assessing the utility of exclusion

Earlier I distinguished between constitutional theory and constitutional politics. Of course, no such sharp distinction exists in the real world. A policy that may be justified as a matter of constitutional theory is not for that reason alone a *good* policy or the best way to promote constitutional maintenance. A ban that sparks violent activity, to take one obvious example, may well do more harm to democratic consolidation than allowing all parties equal access to the electoral arena.

The political factors that lead states to ban anti-democratic political parties are easy to appreciate. Depending upon the strength and number of their adherents, antidemocratic parties may present a significant challenge to fragile state authority. If they succeed in the polls, they may short-circuit the installation of democratic forms by replacing or subverting them with policy agendas and structural-institutional reforms that promote other values. Even well shy of electoral success, the mere presence of antidemocratic parties may confuse the electorate or persuade some portion of it that democratic forces are incapable of governing. The force of persuasion may be in direct proportion to the fragility of the state.

Assessing proscription

The utility of a provision prohibiting antidemocratic parties may appear obvious, especially in transitional democracies. Proscribing antidemocratic political parties may help to contribute to the stability of otherwise fragile democratic regimes in several ways. First, they may contribute to the success of redemocratization 'by channeling dissent into legally accepted means of dispute resolution'.[40] There is some evidence that toleration of political dissent in the Netherlands, for example, has led to the eventual co-optation and integration of dissidents.[41] Secondly, they may contribute to democratic forms by throwing the moral and political weight of the regime behind democratic principles. In this instance the ban might be said to serve 'presentational' rather than practical purposes by reducing the sense of 'affront to the public'.[42] Thirdly, they may limit the number of candidates and parties in the field. In doing so, they may contribute to the policy-making process by streamlining the agenda. In similar fashion, they may help to promote consensus by narrowing and shaping the electorate. Fourthly, and in addition to helping to prevent the splintering of the electorate, these provisions may be useful as a means of focusing political debate and choice, perhaps of especial importance in young democracies. In sum, proscription may in some cases be seen as a means of promoting all four of the functions – legitimating, integrating, socializing and systematizing – we commonly assign to elections.

On the other hand, exclusion can work in ways that undercut the integrating and binding functions attributed to democratic elections. Excluding opponents may contribute to their sense of alienation and isolation, making them more likely to resort to violence. It may change 'electoral losers into antisystem oppositions'.[43] Instead of channelling dissent into non-violent expression, it may encourage it to take more extreme forms. And if the excluded party can claim fairly to represent a significant part of the population, then its exclusion from the electoral process might itself be enough to delegitimate the process in the minds of many citizens by calling into question whether elections are genuinely 'free and fair'. Finally, exclusion may undercut the legitimacy of moderate parties and actors that have chosen to participate, in part by suggesting that electoral inclusion is not proportional to or a prerequisite of political power.[44]

Equally important is the great potential for abuse such provisions present. First, there is the risk that incumbent regimes will use such powers not against anti-democratic parties, but rather against opposition – no matter its ideological character – to the settled regime, as was the case with the Alien and Sedition Acts in the United States and as is common in Latin America. Especially where redemocratization follows upon conservative, bureaucratic-authoritarian regimes, such as Pinochet's Chile, provisions outlawing anti-democratic political parties may be little more than poorly disguised efforts to silence leftist political opposition.

Secondly, the use of such provisions may have a chilling effect on political dialogue more generally. This may take the form of self-censorship by timid parties or a fearful populace, or it may provide the basis for more aggressive state efforts to clamp down on dissidence. Consider the German case. One might argue there has been no such abuse, since only two parties (the Socialist Reich Party and the Communist Party) have been banned under Article 21. But this is an exceptionally crimped way to measure abuse. A more accurate way to assess the possibility of abuse would be to consider how and in what ways the decision to ban these parties may have provided the basis for further state activities designed to censor or harass anti-democratic forces. One estimate, for example, suggests that preliminary inquisitions from state prosecutors increased from 7,975 cases in 1956 to 12,600 just one year later, following the Communist Party decision.[45] If we expand our analysis to consider not simply Article 21, but rather the policy of militant democracy it represents, then the risks such policies present for abuse become profound. In the German case, militant democracy has contributed to an environment that has led to expansive new security laws and loyalty decrees.[46]

In the United States, there are no express constitutional provisions that ban anti-democratic parties. Nevertheless, the logic of proscription has prevailed, as represented so clearly in statutory mechanisms like the Smith Act of 1940, the Internal Security Act of 1950 and the Communist Control Act of 1954. The history of abuse that surrounds these efforts is recalled simply by invoking the name of McCarthy and institutions like the House Un-American Activities Committee.

Conducting case studies

The many possibilities for abuse, coupled with the ease with which banned parties manage to circumvent their bans, either by going underground, by forming party militias, or by simply reincorporating themselves,[47] suggests that proscription provisions are unlikely to contribute meaningfully to democratic consolidation and maintenance. Is there any evidence that proscription contributes to democratic consolidation or maintenance? To get this kind of evidence detailed case studies are needed of countries that have utilized exclusion provisions. The constitutional logic behind proscription suggests that in assessing the utility of these provisions we should concentrate on the following issues:

(1) On what basis can a political party be proscribed? In Germany, Chile, Italy and maybe Israel, no showing of actual harm is necessary. Some provisions, such as Article 21 of the Basic Law and Article 8 of the Chilean Constitution, permit proscription simply on the basis of an agenda or programme that is hostile as a

matter of theory to democratic and constitutional values. Others, such as the United States, permit proscription only upon a showing that some actual, overt harm is a possibility.

(2) If proscription is permitted on the basis of harm, as in the United States, three additional questions must be asked. First, what constitutes 'harm'? Secondly, how imminent must be the harm? Thirdly, how substantial must be the threat?

(3) If proscription is possible simply on the basis of a party programme, what criteria will be employed in the decision? Is a political party committed to the abolition of private property 'anti-democratic'? Is a party committed to the primacy of racial or religious identity over national identity or the ideology of constitutional democracy 'anti-democratic'? Must the anti-democratic aims of the party be reflected also in the party's internal organization, as in the Federal Republic of Germany?

(4) Who assesses the various criteria? To whom is the proscription decision entrusted? Is it subject to independent review? In the Federal Republic of Germany, Estonia, Romania and Chile, the constitution expressly commits the decision to the courts. In practice, the United States follows a similar course, though the interplay between Congress and the Court can be quite complicated. A similar interplay characterizes proscription decisions in Israel.[48] In the United Kingdom, proscription is assigned to the executive. Other constitutions, such as the Austrian and Italian, ban specific parties but do not set forth procedures to implement or enforce those bans.

The foregoing questions speak to the mechanics of the proscription process. There are also several questions we must ask about the consequences of the decision:

(1) Which party was banned and why? Was the party constituted on a political, racial, religious or tribal basis? The answers to these questions may help us to assess whether the ban contributed to – or undermined – the consolidation and legitimization of the state.

(2) What kind of political strength did the banned party claim? A ban that excludes parties certain to face electoral failure, for example, may serve only presentational purposes, or it may reflect fear of the party's increasing popularity.

(3) When was the ban put in place? Bans imposed during the electoral

cycle proper may pose a greater threat to the state's legitimacy than a ban imposed before an election begins. In the former case, citizens may be more likely to see the ban as simple political posturing.

(4) What kind of political activity did the party undertake after the ban was imposed? In Germany and Italy, for example, Fascist parties simply reconstituted themselves under new forms and continued to participate. Banned parties in Latin America followed a similar course, whereas in some Eastern European countries, banned parties ceased to exist.[49] Differences here may have a profound influence on how preexisting party structures influence redemocratization.

(5) In light of (4), above, one should ask: What was the structure and nature of party competition before proscription? There are likely to be important differences here, for example, between Latin America and post-Communist Europe.[50]

Conclusion

Constitutional proscriptions against anti-democratic political parties are a common feature in Western democracies. For reasons of political expediency, they are especially common in transitional democracies. As a matter of abstract democratic or constitutional theory, these provisions present no insurmountable problems, especially if (1) there is included in those theories a recognition that democracies are inherently fragile not only in space but also in time; and (2) a more sophisticated understanding is adopted, also temporal, of the people that constitute the democratic community.

Nevertheless, bans against anti-democratic parties also threaten basic democratic values by limiting the range and kinds of information available to the people, thereby undermining the capacity for self-governance. Moreover, these provisions offer the potential for great abuse. Consequently, a decision to limit the contest for electoral power is a choice about constitutional *politics* in the most elemental sense. The decision takes place in a political arena and in conjunction with a great variety of political considerations, many of which I identify above. All of them will influence the extent to which a ban on anti-democratic parties will contribute to or undermine regime stability. In addition, the installation of democratic forms will be influenced by basic choices about the timing of founding elections, about the structure of executive and legislative power, the literal constitution of the transitional government (caretaker or provisional, military or civilian), and the presence of involvement by various actors in the international community.

APPENDIX

Anti-democratic political parties: Selected constitutional and statutory provisions

Austria

The Austrian Constitution of 1945, fresh on the heels of Austria's independence from Germany following World War II, prohibited the re-establishment of the National Socialist Party and its sister organizations. The provision is similar in purpose to one in the Italian Constitution that prohibits the re-organization and reconstitution of the Fascist party. As in Germany, there is also a wide variety of statutory mechanisms that outlaw secret organizations, as well as parties and activities hostile to the state and the constitutional system (Art. 246).

Chile

Article 8 of the Chilean constitution, modelled in part on the Basic Law, is similarly expansive. It provides:

> Any action by an individual or group intended to propagate doctrines which ... advocate violence or a concept of society, the State or the juridical order, of a totalitarian character or based on class warfare, is illegal and contrary to the institutional code of the Republic.
>
> The organizations and political movements or parties which, due to their purposes or the nature of the activities of their members, tend toward such objectives, are unconstitutional.
>
> The Constitutional Tribunal shall have cognizance of violations of the provisions set forth in the preceding paragraphs.

Estonia

Article 48 (Right to Associate) states the following:

> (1) Everyone shall have the right to form non-profit associations and leagues. Only Estonian citizens may be members of political parties.

(2) The establishment of associations and leagues possessing weapons or organized in a military fashion or conducting military exercises requires a prior permit, the issuing of which shall be in accordance with conditions and procedures determined by law.

(3) Associations, leagues or political parties whose aims or activities are directed towards the violent change of the Estonian constitutional system or otherwise violate a criminal law shall be prohibited.

(4) The termination or suspension of the activities of an association, a league or a political party, and its penalization, may only be invoked by a court, in cases where a law has been violated.

European Convention on Human Rights

Three provisions in the European Convention seem to mitigate against bans against antidemocratic parties: Article 9 guarantees freedom of thought and conscience, Article 10 protects freedom of expression, and Article 11 speaks to freedom of association. Even so, the Commission has upheld efforts by the Austrian government to prevent the reorganization and revival of the old National Socialists.[51]

France

The Constitution of the Fifth Republic of France contains a similar but more expansive provision. Article 4 states simply that 'political parties are obliged to respect the principles of national sovereignty and democracy'. Unlike the German case, however, the text includes no procedure banning such parties.

Federal Republic of Germany

Article 21(1) of the Basic Law provides that political parties are a central part of the German state. It indicates that parties 'shall participate in forming the political will of the people'. But it also limits *what* the people can will. The internal structure of political parties 'must conform to democratic principles', and subsection (2) states

> Parties which, by reason of their aims or the behaviour of their adherents, seek to impair or abolish the free democratic basic order or to endanger the existence of the Federal Republic of Germany, shall be unconstitutional. The Federal Constitutional Court shall decide on the question of unconstitutionality.

Ireland and Northern Ireland

Like the Constitution of the United States, the Constitution of the Republic of Ireland does not contain a provision that directly outlaws anti-democratic political parties. The Republic's statutory law, though, has long included provisions that permit the state to proscribe certain organizations. In other words, some organizations, like the Irish Republic Organization, are banned. In addition to proscription (making membership in such organizations illegal), Ireland's law includes provisions that prohibit support for such organizations and broadcasting bans that prohibit interviews or reports of interviews with a spokesperson for such organizations.

In the United Kingdom, the Prevention of Terrorism Act also permits the proscription of 'terrorist' organizations. A lesser-known statute, the Representation of the People Act 1981, prohibits from serving in the House of Commons any person convicted of an offence and is undergoing imprisonment for more than 12 months. The Act followed the election to Parliament of Bobby Sands, a well-known hunger-striker. Similarly, in Northern Ireland, the Elected Authorities Act 1989 requires that candidates for local elections must take an oath not to support proscribed organizations or acts of terrorism.

Israel

Section 7a (Prevention of Participation of Candidates List) states:
A candidates' list shall not participate in elections to the Knesset if its objects or actions, expressly or by implication, include one of the following:

(1) negation of the existence of the State of Israel as the state of the Jewish people;
(2) negation of the democratic character of the State;
(3) incitement to racism.

Italy

The Italian Constitution includes a clause that expressly prohibits the old Fascist Party from reorganizing. Article XII of the Transitional Section of the text provides: 'The reorganization in any form whatever of the now dissolved Fascist party is prohibited'.

Article 18, section 2 provides more broadly that 'Secret associations and those which pursue political aims even indirectly by means of organization of a military character shall be forbidden'.

Portugal

Article 10 (Universal Suffrage and Political Parties) states:

(1) The people exercise political power through universal, equal, direct, secret, and periodic suffrage and other forms laid down in the Constitution.

(2) The political parties contribute to the organization and expression of the will of the people and respect the principles of national independence and political democracy.

Romania

Article 8 (Political Parties) states:

(1) Pluralism in the Romanian society is a condition and safeguard of Constitutional democracy.

(2) Political parties may be constituted and pursue their activities in accordance with the law. They contribute to the definition and expression of the political will of the citizens, while observing national sovereignty, territorial integrity, the legal order, and the principles of democracy.

Article 37 (Association, Political Parties, Unions) states:

(1) Citizens may freely associate into political parties, trade unions, and other forms of association.

(2) Any political parties or organizations which, by their aims or activity, militate against political pluralism, the principles of a State governed by the rule of law, or against the sovereignty, integrity, or independence of Romania shall be unconstitutional.

(3) Judges of the Constitutional Court, the Advocates of the People, magistrates, active members of the Armed Forces, policemen, and other categories of civil servants, established by an organic law, may not join political parties.

(4) Secret associations are prohibited.

Article 144 (Powers) states:

The Constitutional Court shall have the following powers:

a) to adjudicate on the constitutionality of laws, before promulgation, upon notification by the President of Romania, by the President of either Chamber of Parliament, by the Government, the Supreme Court of Justice, by a number of at least 50 Deputies or at least 25 Senators, as well as, *ex officio*, on initiatives to revise the Constitution;

b)　to adjudicate on the constitutionality of the Standing Orders of Parliament, upon notification by the President of either Chamber, by a parliamentary group or a number of at least 50 Deputies or at least 25 Senators;

c)　to decide on exceptions brought to the Courts of law as to the unconstitutionality of laws and orders;

d)　to guard the observance of the procedure for the election of the President of Romania and to confirm the ballot returns;

e)　to ascertain the circumstances which justify the interim in the exercise of office of President of Romania, and to report its findings to Parliament and the Government;

f)　to give advisory opinion on the proposal to suspend the President of Romania from office;

g)　to guard the observance of the procedure for the organization and holding of a referendum, and to confirm its returns;

h)　to check on compliance with the conditions for the exercise of the legislative initiative by citizens; and

j)　to decide on objections of unconstitutionality of a political party.

Rwanda

Article 7 (Political Parties) states:

Political parties fulfilling the legal conditions shall concur to the expression of suffrage. They shall be formed and shall exercise their activities freely provided that they respect democratic principles and not infringe upon republican form of government, national territorial integrity, and the security of the State.

NOTES

1. Recalling *Federalist Paper* #1, any serious constitutionalist must assure that collective political lives are not governed solely by accident or chance. See Clinton Rossiter (ed.), *The Federalist Papers* (New York: New American Library, 1961) #1, p.33.
2. See e.g. Daniel P. Franklin and Michael J. Baum (eds), *Political Culture and Constitutionalism: A Comparative Approach* (Armonk, NY: M.E. Sharpe, 1995) pp.1–4.
3. For an overview of transition theory, see Marry Ellen Fischer, 'Introduction', in Mary Ellen Fischer (ed.), *Establishing Democracies* (Boulder, CO: Westview Press, 1996)

pp.1–21. For an argument about the importance of a 'cultural legacy' that will inhibit democratic reforms in Eastern Europe, see Kenneth Jowitt, *The New World Disorder: The Leninist Extinction* (Berkeley: University of California Press, 1992) pp.207–24.

4. For a discussion of how different federal arrangements may redirect ethnic conflict, see Donald Horowitz, *Ethnic Groups in Conflict* (Berkeley: The University of California Press).

5. On the possibility that the economic hardship occasioned by such transition may threaten democracy in Eastern Europe, see e.g. Adam Przeworski, *Democracy and the Market: Political and Economic Reforms in Eastern Europe and Latin America* (New York: Cambridge University Press, 1991).

6. As Mark Jones has written: 'Electoral laws alone do not make or break a democratic system. They do however have a significant impact on its functioning.' See Mark P. Jones, *Electoral Laws and the Survival of Presidential Democracies* (Notre Dame: University of Notre Dame Press, 1995) p.3.

7. Samuel Huntington, *The Third Wave: Democratization in the Late Twentieth Century* (Norman: University of Oklahoma Press, 1991) p.9.

8. This point is not obvious. Weber, for example, argued that elections alone did not necessarily confer legitimacy. See 'Legitimate Order and Types of Authority', reprinted in Talcott Parsons *et al.* (eds), *Theories of Society: Foundations of Modern Sociological Theory* (New York: Free Press, 1965) p.233.

9. See e.g. Courtney Young and Ian Shapiro, 'South Africa's Negotiated Transition: Democracy, Opposition, and the New Constitutional Order', *Politics & Society* 23 (1995) p.269.

10. See Rossiter (note 1) pp.33–7.

11. See David C. Rapoport and Leonard Weinberg, 'Elections and Violence', this volume.

12. Barbara Geddes, 'Initiation of New Democratic Institutions in Eastern Europe and Latin America', in Arend Lijphart and Carlos H. Warisman (eds), *Institutional Design in New Democracies: Eastern Europe and Latin America* (Boulder, CO: Westview Press, 1996) pp.18–19.

13. Many folks have written about how different electoral regimes contribute to or subvert efforts at democratic consolidation. Notable works include: Gisueppe Di Palma, *To Craft Democracies* (Berkeley: University of California Press, 1990); Huntington (note 7); and Yossi Shain and Juan Linz, *Between States* (Cambridge: Cambridge University Press, 1995). There is an older literature addressing similar questions, a literature sparked by efforts to redemocratize in Europe after World War II. See e.g. Carl J. Friedrich, *Constitutional Government and Democracy* (Waltham, MA: Blaisdell Publishing Co., 1950, rev. ed.). Questions about the suitability of different kinds of electoral systems, whether single-transferable or proportional, for example, have begun to focus on the question of timing, or about when and where elections should be held to best promote democratic stability. See *Problems of Democratic Transition and Consolidation: Southern Europe, South America, and Post-Communist Europe* (Baltimore: Johns Hopkins University Press, 1996). Unlike most of the literature on elections and redemocratization in transitional democracies, my interest in electoral regimes is not with the admittedly important question about when to schedule founding elections.

14. See Peter Siavelis and Arturo Valenzuela, 'Electoral Engineering and Democratic Stability: The Legacy of Authoritarian Rule in Chile', in Lijphart and Warisman (note 12) p.92.

15. For reasons of economy I do not list them all here or include the legal citations; I have reprinted some provisions in a short Appendix. The number of constitutional documents that contain such provisions is considerable. The block is even more crowded if we expand our scope to include those countries that regulate electoral contests through statutes without violating a superordinate constitutional command. Moreover, exclusion can take a variety of forms, some constitutional, some statutory, and some through the push and pull of daily political posturing by political actors. See pp.xx–xx, *infra*.

16. There are superior but limited case studies of Ireland and the United Kingdom; see Gerald Hogan and Clive Walker, *Political Violence and the Law in Ireland* (Manchester: Manchester University Press, 1989); and for Israel see Dan Gordon, 'Limits on Extremist Political Parties: A Comparison of Israeli Jurisprudence with that of the United States and West Germany', 10 *Hastings Int'l & Comp. L. Rev.* pp.347ff.
17. John Finn, *Constitutions in Crisis: Political Violence and the Rule of Law* (New York: Oxford University Press, 1991).
18. See Gordon (note 16) pp.385–94.
19. See *Communist Party* v. *Subversive Activities Control Board*, 367 US 1 (1961).
20. Other targets include the Klu Klux Klan. The Court upheld one of these efforts in the case of New York *ex rel. Bryant* v. *Zimmerman*, 278 US 63 (1928).
21. For a review of the American statutes *supra* and cases see Walter F. Murphy, 'Excluding Political Parties: Problems for Democratic and Constitutional Theory', in Paul Kirchhof and Donald P. Kommers (eds), *Germany and Its Basic Law* (Balden-Balden: Nomos Verlagsgesellschaft, 1993) pp.182–7.
22. See e.g. *Yates* v. *United States*, 354 US 298 (1957).
23. See *Aptheker* v. *United States*, 378 US 500 (1964); Murphy (note 21), p.187.
24. See Gordon (note 16) p.364.
25. *Socialist Reich Party Case*, 2 BVerfGE 1 (1952).
26. *Communist Party Case*, 5 BVerfGE 85 (1956).
27. See C. Neal Tate and Torbjorn Vallinder, *The Global Expansion of Judicial Power* (New York: New York University Press, 1995).
28. Hogan and Walker (note 16) p.142.
29. *Yates* v. *United States* (note 22).
30. 395 US 444 (1969).
31. 414 US 105 (1973).
32. In addition to my work in *Constitutions in Crisis* (1991), see Murphy (1993); Stephen Holmes, 'Precommitment and the Paradox of Community', in Jon Elster and Rune Slagstad (eds), *Constitutionalism and Democracy: Studies in Rationality and Social Change* (New York: Cambridge University Press, 1988) pp.xx–xx. See also Gordon S. Wood, *The Creation of the American Republic* (New York: W.W. Norton, 1972), p.379.
33. The best work on democratic theory and temporality is James G. March and Johan P. Olsen, *Rediscovering Institutions: The Organizational Basis of Politics* (New York: The Free Press, 1989); see also Michael Walzer, 'Philosophy and Democracy', *Political Theory* (1981) p.379.
34. See Finn (note 17); see also Laurence Tribe, 'Toward a MetaTheory of Free Speech', *Sw. U.L. Rev.* 10/337 (1978) p.239.
35. In addition to Article 48, for example, the Law of the Protection of the Republic of 21 July 1922 and a similar law in 1930 might have provided the basis for a decision to outlaw anti-democratic political parties.
36. Finn (note 17) p.137.
37. George Scwab, *The Challenge of the Exception* (Berlin: Dunker and Humblot, 1970) p.48.
38. See Finn (note 17) pp.170–7.
39. For a discussion of 'militant democracy', see Finn (note 17); Murphy (note 21); and Donald P. Kommers, *The Constitutional Jurisprudence of the Federal Republic of Germany* (Durham: Duke University Press, 1977, 2nd ed.).
40. Shain and Linz (note 13) p.5.
41. See Alex P. Schmid, 'Countering Terrorism in the Netherlands', in Alex P. Schmid and Ronald D. Crelinstein (eds), *Western Responses to Terrorism* (London: Frank Cass, 1993) p.88.
42. Schmid and Crelinstein, ibid., p.180; Clive Walker, *The Prevention of Terrorism in British Law* (Manchester: Manchester University Press, 1992, 2nd ed.) p.56.
43. Sivaelis and Valenzuela (note 14) p.92.
44. See e.g. Giovanni Sartori, 'The Influence of Electoral Systems: Faulty Laws or Faulty

Methods?', in Bernard Grofman and Arend Lijphart (eds), *Electoral Laws and Their Political Consequences* (New York: Agathon Press, 1986) pp.43–68; Arend Lijphart, 'The Political Consequences of Electoral Laws, 1945–1985', *American Political Science Review* 84 (1990) p.482; Siavelis and Valenzuela (note 14) p.92.

45. Donald P. Kommers, 'The Spiegel Affair: A Case Study in Judicial Politics', in Theodore L. Becker (ed.), *Political Trials* (Indianapolis: Bobbs-Merril, 1971) p.15.

46. See generally Finn pp.206–16; Gerald Braunthal, *Political Loyalty and Public Service in West Germany: The 1972 Decree Against Radicals and Its Consequences* (Amherst: University of Massachusetts Press, 1990).

47. See e.g. Gordon (note 16) pp.375–7; see also Justice Jackson's concurring opinion in *Dennis v. United States*, 341 US 494 (1951) p.578.

48. Gordon, pp.348–64 and 399–400.

49. Ibid., pp.30–1.

50. Ibid.

4

Violence and Electoral Polarization in Divided Societies: Three Cases in Comparative Perspective

ADRIAN GUELKE

Three elections, all of which took place at the end of May 1996, are examined in order to analyze the impact of violence on political attitudes in deeply divided societies. They are the Israeli general election of 29 May 1996; the Northern Ireland forum elections of 30 May 1996; and local elections in the Western Cape province in South Africa on 29 May 1996. It is argued that what the outcome of the elections in Israel and Northern Ireland demonstrates is the capacity of the continuing threat of violence (and not just actual episodes of violence) to polarize opinion even in the context of ongoing peace processes. Further, it is argued that fear of change may influence the electoral behaviour of members of the dominant (or previously dominant) community as profoundly as the prospect or even the reality of an end to the conflict, as the case of the local elections in the Western Cape underlines.

The basis of this article is a comparison of three elections: the Israeli general election of 29 May 1996, the Northern Ireland forum elections of 30 May 1996, and local elections in the Western Cape province of South Africa on 29 May 1996.[1] The purpose of the comparison is to explore the relationship between political violence and political polarization through an examination of the campaigns and outcomes of the three elections. These three cases were chosen not simply because of the coincidence in time in their elections, but because of the frequency and influence of the comparison of Northern Ireland, Israel/ Palestine and South Africa as deeply divided societies/territories.

Comparison of pairs of the three societies/territories (particularly the South African–Northern Ireland pair) can be traced back to their origin as political entities. However, academic interest in a comparison of the three cases taken together is more recent and generally can be dated to the 1980s. For example, a workshop on the comparison of South Africa,

Israel, Northern Ireland and Lebanon was held in Freiburg during 1983 under the aegis of the European Consortium on Political Research. That was followed in 1989 by a conference in Bonn sponsored by the Friedrich Naumann Foundation and the Institute for a Democratic Alternative in South Africa (IDASA) that explored South Africa, Israel and Northern Ireland. The principal theme of the conference and the book that came out of it[2] was of the intractability of the three conflicts. It was also an implication of other studies of the three cases.[3] Ironically, just as what might be described as an academic consensus on the implications of the comparison was beginning to emerge, the ground shifted with the break in the political impasse in South Africa signalled by President de Klerk's initiative of February 1990.

The ground also shifted in the Israel/Palestine case with the Declaration of Principles of September 1993 (or Oslo 1). Northern Ireland followed suit with the paramilitary cease-fires of August and October 1994. By this time, the South African transition was virtually complete with the inauguration of Nelson Mandela as President in May 1994 following democratic elections. By the mid-1990s, the focus of academic interest had become the comparison of the peace process in the three cases.[4] The comparison of the three cases also became part of political discourse in the three societies/territories, generally under-pinning optimistic views of the prospects for the resolution of the conflicts. Thus, whereas during the 1980s the comparison had tended to reinforce explanations of the persistence of the conflicts, during the early 1990s it tended to reinforce expectations of the resolution of all three conflicts. By the last week of May 1996, South Africa had moved beyond the politics of transition with the adoption earlier that month of the country's final constitution. In the other two cases, however, progress towards a settlement had been so much slower that in both Israel/Palestine and Northern Ireland, the very survival of the peace process was in question.

In these circumstances, it was hardly surprising that the local elections in the Western Cape attracted very little international attention. The Israeli general election, widely seen as crucial to the Middle East peace process, attracted massive coverage. Northern Ireland's elections also secured considerable attention, with the main focus being on whether they would lead to a renewal of the cease-fire by the Provisional Irish Republican Army (IRA), which had broken down on 9 February 1996. A common feature of the three elections was that each was being held under new complex electoral arrangements, complicating the task of comparing these elections with previous ones. However, as the focus of this article is on what can be learned about the relationship between violence and electoral polarization in deeply divided societies, the new electoral processes are not a major obstacle to the analysis of the implications of these elections. The approach of this article is comparative, but first gives an individual account of each election before examining what comparative points can be derived from the three cases.

Israel

The Israeli case provides the clearest example of the link between political violence and the electoral process. A series of violent events in the run-up to the elections influenced the conduct of the campaign and played an important role in explanations of the outcome, including the assassination of Prime Minister Yitzhak Rabin at a peace rally on 4 November 1995; the assassination of Yehiya Ayash ('the Engineer') by Israeli agents using a booby-trapped mobile phone on 5 January 1996; a wave of suicide bomb attacks by Hamas inside Israel at the end of February and the beginning of March 1996, in which 60 people died; attacks on Israeli soldiers by Hizbollah in Israel's security zone in southern Lebanon in March 1996; Israeli retaliation followed by Katyusha rocket attacks by Hizbollah on northern Israel; and the bombardment of southern Lebanon by Israel in Operation Grapes of Wrath for 17 days from 11 April . These violent events tended to overshadow the most significant development in the peace process in this period: the holding of elections to the Palestinian Authority on 20 January 1996. These were a triumph for Arafat and Fatah. Arafat won 87 per cent of the vote in the Presidential elections, while Fatah and Fatah-aligned independents won an overwhelming majority of the seats on the legislative council.[5]

For the first time Israeli voters had two ballots in the general election: one for the direct election of the Prime Minister, and the other for the party of their choice. Israel used the list system of proportional representation, the effect of which was to multiply the number of parties gaining representation in the 120-member Knesset. A total of 11 parties gained representation in the Knesset elections of May 1996. The direct election of the Prime Minister was introduced partly to counteract the leverage given to the smaller parties in the system. The results of the two sets of ballots are set out in Tables 1 and 2.

TABLE 1
ELECTION FOR PRIME MINISTER OF ISRAEL

Benyamin Netanyahu	1,501,023 votes	50.4%
Shimon Peres	1,471,566 votes	49.5%

Source: Journal of Palestine Studies XXV/4 (Summer 1996) p.151.

TABLE 2
ELECTION TO KNESSET

	Percentage of vote	No. of seats	No. of seats in 1992
Labour Party	26.8%	34	(44)
Likud-Tsomet-Gesher	25.1%	32	(40)
Shas	8.5%	10	(6)
National Religious Party	7.8%	9	(6)
Meretz	7.4%	9	(12)
Yisrael Ba'aliya	5.7%	7	–
Hadash	4.2%	5	(3)
United Torah Judaism	3.2%	4	(4)
The Third Way	3.1%	4	–
United Arab List	2.9%	4	(2)
Moledet	2.3%	2	(3)

Sources: Journal of Palestine Studies XXV/4 (Summer 1996) p.151; and Keesing's Record of World Events (London: Longman, May 1996) p.41117.

In his analysis of the Israeli general election, Benny Morris begins by arguing that the real winner of the Israeli general election was Yigal Amir, the 25-year-old Bar Ilan University student who had murdered Rabin. According to Morris, Amir had calculated accurately that Rabin 'was the only Labor Party leader capable of carrying the nation with him through the peace process'.[6] However, in the immediate aftermath of the assassination, there was a strong backlash against the right-wing opposition and its candidate for the premiership, Benyamin Netanyahu. Morris himself alludes to this in his discussion of why Rabin's successor, Shimon Peres, failed to exploit it by calling swift elections, as many of his followers were urging. He argues that Peres hoped to go to the electorate with a draft peace treaty with Syria achieved, and only decided to call elections in May (ahead of the final date for the elections of November 1996) when he reached the conclusion that no deal was possible with the Syrian leader, President Assad, ahead of Israeli general elections.[7]

The delay reduced the impact of the shock of Rabin's assassination on the election campaign, though from the outset of the campaign the Labor Party signalled that it intended, as David Horovitz of Jerusalem Report put it, 'to make maximum use of one definite election asset: the ghost of the much-mythologized murdered prime minister, Yitzhak Rabin'.[8] A comparison might be drawn between the assassination of Rabin and that of the charismatic South African Communist Party (SACP) leader, Chris Hani, in South Africa in April 1993. Hani's assassination proved entirely counterproductive for its extreme right-wing perpetrators, strengthening the position of the African National Congress (ANC) at an important point in the transition. However, the backlash in Israel against right-wing opponents of the peace process proved temporary.

By contrast, the suicide bombers of Hamas appear to have wrought a more enduring change in Israeli attitudes. Further, there was widespread agreement in commentaries before and after the elections that as a factor in the elections, the bombings helped the candidate of the right, Benyamin Netanyahu. The tactic of the suicide bomb was first used by Hamas in 1994. On 6 April 1994 a Hamas suicide bomber detonated explosives at a bus stop in the northern Israeli town of Afula, killing seven Israelis. There was another such bombing on a bus in the coastal town of Hadera a week later on 13 April, in which five Israelis died. These bombings followed the massacre by Baruch Goldstein of 29 Muslims at a mosque in Hebron on 25 February 1994. There were further suicide bomb attacks by Hamas in the course of 1995. On 24 July a suicide bomb attack on a bus in a Tel Aviv suburb killed six civilians and injured 30. A further attack on a bus in West Jerusalem in August killed five people and injured 107. The bombings in 1994 and 1995 prompted demonstrations against the peace process in Israel. There was a sharp fall in the numbers supporting the peace process according to the opinion polls. However, they did not prevent the progress between the Israeli government and the Palestine Liberation Organization (PLO) in the peace process, culminating in the signing of an interim agreement on Palestinian self-determination in September 1995 (Oslo II).

The resumption of the suicide attacks in February–March 1996 proved far more damaging. On 25 February, there was a suicide bomb attack on a bus in Jerusalem and another such attack at a hitch-hiking post at Ashkelon. There was a further attack on a bus in Jerusalem on 3 March and that was followed by an attack on a shopping mall in Tel Aviv on 4 March. After Netanyahu's election, they tended to be accorded a decisive role in his narrow victory. The account in *Keesing's Record of World Events* is typical:

After the assassination [of Rabin], Peres had refused to call a snap election – which most analysts believed he would easily have won – claiming that it would have been unseemly to exploit Rabin's murder. However, a series of Palestinian Islamist suicide bombings in Israel in February and March 1996 badly damaged his standing and increased support for the more hawkish Netanyahu.[9]

At the time of the attacks, they were reported as a devastating blow to the vision of peace that Peres had once held out of the establishment of open borders between Israel and her Arab neighbours. During the election campaign itself, when the most likely result seemed to be a narrow victory for Peres in the contest for Prime Minister, the thrust of commentary was on the possibility that further attacks by Hamas during the course of the election campaign might undermine Peres's lead. In the event, no such attacks took place. In retrospect, it seems that just their possibility proved of benefit to the challenger. Netanyahu made effective use of the issue in his debate with Peres on 26 May 1996, as Horovitz's account makes clear:

> Five, six, seven times [Netanyahu] charged that the people of Israel were 'living in fear' of further Islamic extremist suicide bombings, ridiculing Mr Peres's vision of a new Middle East peace in the context of such harsh realities.[10]

The impact of Operation Grapes of Wrath on the elections is somewhat harder to judge. Initial assumptions tended to be that it would strengthen Peres's credentials in the area in which Hamas's bombing campaign had made him seem most vulnerable: the safeguarding of the personal security of Israeli civilians. However, after Israeli forces shelled a United Nations base at Qana, killing more than 100 civilians, there was strong criticism of the Israeli government internationally. The right-wing press in Israel was derisive. The *Jerusalem Post* carried a cartoon portraying Syria, Iran and Hizbollah on an Olympic-style victory podium as the winners of Operation Grapes of Wrath.[11] However, a common assumption remained that the Israeli government's actions had strengthened Peres's position among Israeli Jewish voters. But it was also evident that Operation Grapes of Wrath had antagonized Israeli Arab voters so that opinion remained divided on whether it had assisted or damaged Peres's prospects of election overall. Morris argues that the civilian deaths at Qana cast a pall over the whole operation, estranging the Israeli Arab minority at a critical juncture:

In the end, and despite a last-minute effort by Arab politicians and Labor party activists to mobilize the Arab vote, a large number of Arab voters either boycotted the polls or cast a blank vote for the premiership.[12]

Internationally, the contest between Peres and Netanyahu was the main focus of attention in the Israeli elections, with much less space being given to the contest among the parties. The choice between Peres and Netanyahu tended to be seen starkly as a referendum on the peace process itself, with international opinion lined up strongly behind Peres. Although there was recognition of the fears that motivated supporters of Netanyahu, there was generally little sympathy outside Israel for the challenger. The analysis of the elections in the *Financial Times* on the eve of polling underlined external attitudes towards the choice:

> If Israel was any other country the government would be all but certain of victory in tomorrow's elections. Since taking office four years ago the Labour-led government of Shimon Peres has pushed hard to reach for peace with Israel's Arab neighbours in an attempt to end half a century of conflict in the Middle East. The evolving peace process has started to break down Israel's diplomatic and economic isolation, not only within the region but in Asia and Africa as well. This in turn has generated trade and investment flows, which have underpinned an economic performance with which any western government would gladly face its electorate.[13]

It described peace, security and the threat of terrorism from Islamic fundamentalists as the dominant issues of the election, a point graphically illustrated by a cartoon accompanying the article showing Peres holding a piece of paper marked peace process in confrontation with Netanyahu wielding a gun with Arab terrorism written on it. The same piece quoted a columnist of the *Jerusalem Report*, Ze'ev Chafets, as describing the choice as not one between liberals and conservatives but 'an epistemological dispute between rationalists and irrationalists'.[14]

It can be argued that international coverage of the elections overplayed the starkness of the choice facing the Israeli electorate and that factors other than the peace process played a part in the outcome of the election such as the role of the ultra-orthodox parties and of Sharansky's party of Russian emigrants. However, it did not fundamentally distort the picture. The images used in the campaign itself, such as a poster portraying Yasser Arafat as an unexploded hand-grenade, underline the centrality of violence to the elections. Similarly, while after his election as Prime Minister much was made of Netanyahu's commitment to advance the peace, it remained clear that he rejected the precepts that had provided the basis for the peace process under Rabin and Peres, in particular the concept of 'land for peace'. He also indicated his support for the expansion of Jewish settlements in the West Bank and his opposition to Palestinian statehood.

It is therefore hardly surprising that after Netanyahu's election the peace process was beset by a series of crises. The one achievement of negotiations between the parties was the Hebron Agreement of January 1997. This was a significant step because although the previous government had committed Israel to withdraw from Hebron under Oslo II, it signalled Netanyahu's enmeshment in a process that he had denounced in opposition. It upset a number of Netanyahu's allies on the right, which was reflected in the narrowness of the vote to approve the accord in the Israeli cabinet. However, the lack of movement since the Hebron Agreement and Netanayahu's endorsement of the construction of a new Jewish settlement at Har Homa in east Jerusalem have underscored his continuing reluctance to accept the implications of the Oslo peace process for the right's dreams of retaining sovereignty over a greater Israel. An attempt was made by the British and American governments in 1998 to use the achievement of the Good Friday Agreement in Northern Ireland to inject life into the Middle East peace process. However, the conference held in London at the beginning of May 1998 ended in deadlock after the Israeli government rejected minimalist American proposals for an Israeli withdrawal from 13 per cent of the territory of the West Bank.

Northern Ireland

Northern Ireland's forum elections arose out of the Conservative government's difficulties in sustaining majority support within the House of Commons while getting Unionist support for the peace process. It became evident during the course of 1993 both from the government's own contacts with the Provisional IRA and from the negotiations between the leader of the Social Democratic and Labour Party (SDLP), John Hume, and the Sinn Féin President, Gerry Adams, that there was a possibility of an IRA cease-fire. The government tried to steer a course between encouraging such a development, while giving reassurance to Unionists that the IRA had not been offered a secret deal to secure an end to the violence. Sinn Féin was offered a place in all-party negotiations on the future of the province, provided the IRA declared a permanent cease-fire. At the same time, Unionists were told that their position was safeguarded by the fact that any deal would require both the support of Unionist parties and endorsement by the people of Northern Ireland in a referendum.

When the IRA declared a cease-fire on 31 August 1994, with the Loyalist paramilitaries in the Combined Loyalist Military Command following suit on 13 October 1994, the organization did not use the term 'permanent' in its declaration. However, that was eventually glossed over and in February 1995 the British and Irish government published guidelines for negotiations among the parties in 'framework documents'.[15] There was a hostile reaction to these guidelines from the Unionist parties. At this point, the process stalled over the issue of the decommissioning of the weapons arsenals of the paramilitary organizations. In March, the British government made it clear that some decommissioning of weapons would have to take place in advance of all-party negotiations. The Republican movement was equally adamant that it was unwilling to meet this precondition for the inclusion of Sinn Féin in the talks. Sinn Féin's position was that decommissioning should follow a negotiated settlement. The mood among Unionists was reflected in a crisis during the summer of 1995 concerning two issues: the right of the Orange Order to parade through Catholic neighbourhoods, and the election in September of David Trimble, the right-wing outsider, as leader of the Ulster Unionist Party (UUP). The UUP was the largest party in Northern Ireland. Its policies on the conflict were seen generally as considerably more moderate than its chief rival, the Democratic Unionist Party (DUP) of Ian Paisley.

The impasse over decommissioning continued up to the last week of November 1995, when President Clinton was due to visit the province. At this point, the British and Irish governments agreed to the appointment of an international body to seek a resolution of the issue, with the goal that all-party negotiations should begin by the end of February 1996. This step ensured that President Clinton's visit would be a success, injecting new optimism into the peace process. The international body reported its conclusions on 22 January 1996.[16] It argued that decommissioning should take place during the negotiations on a settlement. At the same time it recommended that the parties should be required to sign up to a set of principles (dubbed the Mitchell principles after the international body's chairman, former US Senator George Mitchell). A number of possible confidence-building measures were mentioned in the report, including the holding of elections if they had the support of the parties in Northern Ireland. In his response to the report in the House of Commons, the British Prime Minister, John Major, endorsed the suggestion of elections, to the delight of the UUP, which had proposed this option. Nationalists criticized Major's response as a 'binning' (i.e. rejection) of the international body's report which delayed negotiations by creating the additional precondition of elections.

Even before Major's response to the report of the international body, there had been reports of growing dissatisfaction in Republican ranks over the lack of political progress since the cease-fire, prompting fears of a split among the Provisionals. However, no-one anticipated that the Provisionals would repudiate their cease-fire by bombing Canary Wharf in London on 9 February 1996. Nationalists tended to place much of the blame for the breakdown on the British government, and specifically the proposal for elections in Northern Ireland. Nonetheless, when the British and Irish governments agreed on a package to relaunch the peace process, the holding of elections in Northern Ireland remained one of its elements. A concession to nationalists was the setting of 10 June 1996 as a definitive date for the start of all-party negotiations, on the assumption that there would be a restoration of the Provisional IRA's cease-fire.

Consultations followed between the British government and the Northern Ireland parties on the form that elections should take. The outcome, in part dictated by the government's desperate quest for Unionist votes in the House of Commons, in part by the need to ensure that the two parties linked to the Loyalist paramilitaries would gain representation, was a memorandum endorsed by the leader of the Liberal Democrats, Paddy Ashdown, as the best 'dog's dinner' available. The proposals the government came up with were contrived simultaneously to achieve overrepresentation for the largest parties, while ensuring that small minorities would nevertheless not be excluded.

They provided for the election of a peace forum of 110 members. The all-party negotiations were separate from the deliberations of the forum. Indeed, the nationalist parties made it clear that they intended to boycott meetings of the forum, though not the elections to it. At the same time, election to the forum was to be the qualification to participate in the all-party negotiations (provided in the case of Sinn Féin that the Provisional IRA renewed its cease-fire). Northern Ireland's 18 Westminster constituencies provided the basis for the election of 90 members of the forum. Each constituency was to return five members. The voter had a single vote for a choice of party lists. Seats were allocated using the Droop quota, with partial quotas distributed using the D'Hondt method. A further 20 seats were allocated on the basis of Northern Ireland-wide lists aggregating votes from the individual constituencies for the parties. The 10 most popular parties across the province were each to receive two seats. The results for the successful parties are given in Table 3.

The campaign for the forum elections took place against the background of fear that the Provisional IRA's repudiation of its cease-fire might reignite Northern Ireland's troubles and of hope that electoral process itself might secure a restoration of the cease-fire. As a result of bomb warnings at Dublin airport in early May, there was also some measure of anxiety over the durability of the Loyalist cease-fire. Sinn Féin campaigned for support for its peace strategy under the slogan that a vote for Sinn Féin was a vote for peace. It blamed the British government and the Unionists for the breakdown of the peace process. The campaign was marked by fierce exchanges among the three constitutional Unionist parties, the UUP, the DUP and the United Kingdom Unionist Party (UKUP) of Robert McCartney. A cartoon in *The Irish Times* accurately captured the spirit of these exchanges. Unionists were portrayed as yelling at one another: 'Our flag is bigger than your flag'; 'We'll say no louder than you'll say no'; 'We're more Unionist than you are'; 'We're more intransigent than you'; and 'Our bottom line is lower than your bottom line'.[17]

The most striking feature of the outcome of the forum elections was the success of Sinn Féin. This was the party's best result since the Provisionals' political wing had started to contest elections in 1982 in the aftermath of the mobilization of the Catholic community during the 1981 hunger strike by Republican prisoners. Its previous best result had been in 1983 when Sinn Féin had won 102,701 votes (13.4 per cent of the total vote), compared to 116,377 (15.5 per cent) in the forum elections. The result reversed the decline the party had suffered since the Anglo-Irish Agreement of November 1985 and its further marginalization after the start of negotiations among the constitutional parties in 1991. The hopes attached to those negotiations were reflected

TABLE 3
RESULTS OF NORTHERN IRELAND'S FORUM ELECTIONS:
VOTES, PERCENTAGES AND SEATS

	No. of votes	Percentage of votes	No. of seats
Ulster Unionist Party	181,829	24.2%	30
Social Democratic and Labour Party	160,768	21.4%	21
Democratic Unionist Party	141,413	18.8%	24
Sinn Féin	116,377	15.5%	17
Alliance Party	49,176	6.5%	7
United Kingdom Unionist Party	27,774	3.6%	3
Progressive Unionist Party	26,082	3.5%	2
Ulster Democratic Party	16,715	2.2%	2
Northern Ireland Women's Coalition	7,731	1.0%	2
Labour	6,425	0.9%	2

Source: Sydney Elliott, 'The Northern Ireland Forum/Entry to Negotiations Election 1996', Irish Political Studies 12 (1997) p.119.

in the success of the UUP, SDLP and Alliance Party in the Westminster general election of 1992, when together they had won 66.7 per cent of the vote. In the forum elections, the three parties' share of the vote had shrunk to 52.1 per cent. The turn-out at 64.5 per cent of the electorate was better than had been expected.

The relative success of the DUP was a surprise, especially in the light of the strong showing of the Progressive Unionist Party (PUP) and the Ulster Democratic Party (UDP), parties linked to the Loyalist paramilitaries and appealing to an urban working class constituency from which the DUP also drew much of its support. It confounded expectations that Trimble's leadership of the UUP would extend the appeal of the party among Loyalists. The result was a disappointing one for Trimble, who had done more than anyone else to bring the elections about. As Evans and O'Leary put it:

> The election ... resulted in the lowest share of the vote obtained by the UUP in a comparable election – it has performed worse in European parliamentary elections, but not in the functional equivalent of a local assembly election. The relatively poor performance of the UUP was more surprising because the electoral process and formula was partly designed to address its concerns.[18]

Explanations of the success of Sinn Féin focused on the readiness of previously SDLP voters to back the party so as to increase the influence within the Provisional movement of the leadership of Gerry Adams and

Martin McGuinness, widely seen among nationalists as committed to a peace strategy and best placed to persuade the IRA to restore its cease-fire. (The further increase in the party's share of the vote in the 1997 general election and local elections, despite the absence of an IRA cease-fire, can be seen as a reflection of the fact that much of the nationalist electorate still believed that Adams and McGuinness were working to overcome the obstacles to a new cease-fire, a view eventually vindicated in July 1997 when a second IRA cease-fire was declared.) By contrast, the shifts in the Unionist electorate reflected fear, if not hostility, to the peace process.

An opinion survey of Northern Ireland voters that coincided with polling in the forum elections underlined a much greater disposition on the part of Catholic and nationalist voters to accept compromise than among Protestants and Unionists. A majority of Unionists wanted their leaders to stick to their principles in preference to the option of being willing to compromise. The opposite was the case among nationalists, even among Sinn Féin supporters. Evans and O'Leary summarized the state of opinion in Northern Ireland as reflected in numerous surveys, including their own as follows:

> Protestants and unionists are resistant to multiple forms of constitutional change because it is they who have to do the changing; Catholics and nationalists are more amenable to change because for them most feasible changes would mark a net incremental improvement on the status quo.[19]

The polarization of opinion evident in the forum elections was carried over into a long summer of conflict over Orange Order marches. The absence of an IRA cease-fire led to Sinn Féin's exclusion from the multi-party talks that began on 10 June. The talks themselves soon deadlocked over the issue of decommissioning. No further progress was made in the peace process in 1996 or in the last months of Conservative rule in 1997.

When Labour came to power on 1 May 1997, the Northern Ireland peace process was deadlocked. Immediately on assuming office, the new government authorized contacts with Sinn Féin at an official level. At the same time, the new Prime Minister, Tony Blair, came to Belfast to deliver an important speech reassuring Unionists that he did not envisage a united Ireland in the foreseeable future and making it clear that the establishment of cross-border institutions would not be allowed to develop into a lever for pushing Unionists into a united Ireland against their consent. However, the new government was unable to find a compromise to the demand of the Orange Order that it be allowed to parade down the Garvaghy Road in Portadown. To avoid a long-running stand-off the decision was made to force the march through, against the wishes of its Catholic residents. They chanted 'no cease-fire' as the parade went ahead accompanied by a large contingent of police. Despite these ugly scenes, less than two weeks later on 20 July, the Provisional IRA renewed its cease-fire.

The government gave three assurances to Sinn Féin to secure the cease-fire. First, it agreed that the party would be admitted into the multi-party talks within a matter of weeks of a new cease-fire. The previous formula had been that the party would have to establish its bona fides over a much longer period of time before a decision on its participation was made. Secondly, May 1998 was set as a deadline for the completion of the talks. One of Sinn Féin's fears was that the process of negotiation would be stretched out indefinitely. Thirdly, the government made it clear that the issue of the decommissioning of paramilitary arsenals would not be allowed to delay negotiations on the substantive constitutional questions. Substantive talks then began in October. However, two of the Unionist parties, the DUP of Ian Paisley and the small UKUP of Robert McCartney, walked out in response to Sinn Féin's inclusion in the process.

Initially, the negotiations made very little headway with the parties reluctant to indicate areas where they would be willing to compromise. The minor parties unattached to either the Unionist or the nationalist bloc were the most constructive in actually putting forward position papers on the issues in an attempt to move the process forward. The UUP preferred talking to the British government and to Blair himself rather than engaging with the other parties. Similarly, Sinn Féin did most of its negotiating through the Irish government, headed since the Republic's general election in June 1997 by Bertie Ahern. In December the British and Irish governments tried to get an agreement from the parties on the broad contours of a settlement, so as to provide the basis for more intensive negotiation. However, this attempt failed. In January the two governments put forward their own agreement document to give the process impetus. This proposed a Northern Ireland Assembly operating on a power-sharing basis, a Council of Britain and Ireland, North–South institutions and changes to the Irish constitution and to the 1920 Government of Ireland Act. This proved acceptable to all the parties except Sinn Féin. Its hostile reaction was partly influenced by a leak of the document to a national newspaper ahead of the official publication of the proposals. The leak put a strongly Unionist interpretation on their implications for the future.

By this point the negotiations were in serious difficulty for another reason. Billy Wright, the leading figure in the Loyalist Volunteer Force, an extreme Loyalist paramilitary organization, had been murdered just after Christmas in the Maze prison by inmates from an equally extreme Republican paramilitary organization. As a consequence of this event, imprisoned members of one Loyalist faction taking part in the talks urged their political wing to withdraw from the negotiations. To avert this potentially fatal blow to the negotiations, the Secretary of State for Northern Ireland, Marjorie ('Mo') Mowlam, went in person into the prison to persuade the prisoners to reverse their decision. She was successful in doing so, though some were offended by her readiness to talk to prisoners who had carried out multiple killings. Further, in the event it transpired that members of the paramilitary organization linked to the prisoners, the Ulster Freedom Fighters (UFF), had been responsible for a number of random sectarian assassinations that had taken place in January in revenge for the killing of Billy Wright. As a consequence, the party linked to the UFF, the UDP, was suspended from the talks for a period of four weeks.

A new crisis in the talks occurred at the end of February when the Chief Constable of the Royal Ulster Constabulary concluded that the Provisional IRA had been responsible that month for two murders. These were the killing of a known drug dealer and of a member of a Loyalist paramilitary organization who had been accused of involvement in distributing drugs. Significantly, there was no denial by the IRA of its involvement in these killings, merely a statement that the cease-fire remained intact. The point was that the IRA did not regard action it took in policing its strongholds as a breach of the cease-fire. Sinn Féin for its part argued that it did not in any event represent the IRA. Neither the governments nor the other parties was persuaded by these arguments and Sinn Féin was suspended from the talks, though for an even shorter period than the UDP had been.

The successive exclusions of the UDP and Sinn Féin and the arguments over these absorbed the energies of the parties in the talks, prompting widespread gloom over the prospects for a negotiated settlement. There was a break in the talks in the middle of March to allow the parties to take part in St Patrick's Day celebrations in the United States during which President Clinton strongly urged the parties to make the necessary compromises to achieve a deal. This break was followed by the talks chairman, former US Senator George Mitchell, setting 9 April as a deadline for the conclusion of the negotiations. The reason he set such an early deadline was the realization by the two governments that unless a deal was achieved by Easter, it would prove impossible to hold the elections to the proposed Northern Ireland Assembly ahead of the climax to the Orange Order's marching season in the second week of July, since any deal would first need to be approved in referenda in Northern Ireland and the Republic of Ireland. The fear was that another confrontation on the Garvaghy Road might derail a settlement if the Assembly was not in place by this point.

The achievement of the Good Friday Agreement (on 10 April 1998) came as a surprise to most people in Northern Ireland. In the week of the settlement itself, John Taylor, the UUP Deputy Leader, had put the odds of reaching agreement at four per cent. Even those commentators who were optimistic that an agreement could be achieved had not expected that it would embrace all eight parties. In particular, few expected that Sinn Féin would stay the course. However, it appears that once the leaders of Sinn Féin appreciated that an agreement would be reached with or without their support, fear of the party's marginalization and the concessions that the party was able to secure through the good offices of the Irish government in respect on non-constitutional issues, such as the reform of policing and the release of prisoners, persuaded the party to go along with the Agreement and then to seek to persuade the rank and file of the party of the wisdom of this course of action. The actual contents of the Agreement were much less of a surprise. Their fundamental basis is power-sharing within a devolved government of Northern Ireland, plus an Irish dimension in the form of cross-border bodies to promote cooperation between the two parts of Ireland in a number of largely uncontroversial policy areas. The basic thrust of the Agreement is quite similar to the Sunningdale Agreement of December 1973. Indeed, in a widely quoted witticism, Seamus Mallon, the Deputy Leader of the Social Democratic and Labour Party (SDLP), the party that represents a majority of Northern Ireland's Catholics and nationalists, described the basis of the current agreement as 'Sunningdale for slow learners'.

Factors external to Northern Ireland were evident in the process that led to the Agreement. Thus, a number of accounts of the achievement of the Agreement highlighted as crucial President Bill Clinton's phone-call to the leader of the UUP, David Trimble, in the hours immediately before the announcement of the agreement when the Ulster Unionist party appeared to be wavering over whether to accept the deal. Also widely seen as critical to the success of the talks was the decision of the British Prime Minister, Tony Blair, to leave London and stay in Belfast for the final days of the negotiations. Indeed, all the parties in the talks process praised his role in brokering the deal and that was reflected in the credit he received in polls on the Agreement. His role appears to have been crucial in persuading the UUP to accept a deal, both by offering reassurance to the party on a number of issues, but also making it clear that if Unionist opposition prevented an agreement, the British government would take the actions it considered appropriate. An argument used by the Ulster Unionist leadership to persuade rank and file members of the party to accept the deal was that if there had been no agreement, the British government would have implemented the parts of the Agreement that the Unionists disliked most. Without the Agreement the Unionists would not have secured what they had wanted most, the revision of Articles 2 and 3 of the Irish constitution and the replacement of the Anglo-Irish Agreement.

Referenda in Northern Ireland and the Republic of Ireland on the Good Friday Agreement were held on 22 May, the first time that the people of both parts of Ireland had voted together on the same day, though the actual terms of the two referenda were different since southern voters were being asked to approve a change in their constitution as part of the peace deal. The overwhelming votes in favour of the Good Friday Agreement in both the Republic of Ireland (94.4 per cent 'yes' on a 56.3 per cent turnout) and Northern Ireland (71.1 per cent 'yes' on an 81.1 per cent turnout) gave the appearance of a new consensus on the island. In fact, that was misleading. The vote in the Republic certainly did express a consensus within the south in favour of political accommodation between the two northern communities. In Northern Ireland, the vote in favour of the Agreement disguised the extent of Protestant division: Protestants were split down the middle on the Agreement. The large majority reflected near unanimity on the part of Catholics in voting for the Agreement. Further, what tended to be glossed over in accounts of the outcome was the extent to which the parties who campaigned in favour of the Agreement differed radically in its interpretation, a factor underlined by the distance both the Ulster

Unionist party and Sinn Féin kept from the non-party 'yes' campaign. This is not to underestimate the significance of the Agreement or its endorsement by the Northern Ireland electorate. An historic breakthrough in one of the world's longest running conflicts has been achieved. However, this has not been brought about by a radical change in attitudes within the two communities, as subsequent elections, where voters indicate their party preferences, will no doubt underline.

A substantial obstacle to the implementation of the Agreement remains the requirement that important decisions of the Northern Ireland Assembly will require majorities of both Unionist and nationalist members. The opponents of the Agreement would be in a strong position to wreck the operation of the Agreement in practice if they are ever able to win a majority of Unionist seats in the Assembly. That is by no means an inconceivable outcome, given the division of opinion among Unionists on the Agreement and the scope for disagreement over its interpretation. It took the British Prime Minister's strong engagement to secure the substantial 'yes' vote in the referendum. Before Blair's powerful intervention – dominating all forms of the media in Northern Ireland – opinion polls suggested that a solid majority of Unionists might vote 'no', especially with the trend of the 'don't knows' to the 'no-es'. Another factor in swinging the vote in favour of the Agreement was a pop concert by the band U2 at which the Unionist leader David Trimble and the nationalist leader John Hume appeared together. The image of them shaking hands to the cheers of a teenage audience displaced the pictures from the previous week of prisoner releases that had done so much to upset Unionist voters. Early in the campaign, when the attitude of rank and file members of Sinn Féin was in doubt, an ANC delegation headed by Cyril Ramaphosa played an influential role in helping the Sinn Féin leadership to generate support for the Good Friday Agreement.

However, while Sinn Féin endorsed a 'yes' vote in both referenda, it did not actively campaign for a 'yes' vote. Reaction in Northern Ireland to the result of the referendum was relatively muted. One reason for this was that people recognized that a number of obstacles still have to be overcome if the Agreement was to take root as a final peace settlement. In particular, the Provisional IRA had yet to declare unequivocally that the war was over or to indicate that it was willing to comply with the provisions for decommissioning of weapons under the Good Friday Agreement. Both Blair and Trimble made it clear that Sinn

Féin could not expect to take its place in a power-sharing executive in Northern Ireland unless these issues were addressed satisfactorily. Another problem ahead was the Orange Order's marching season with its potential for generating sectarian conflict, though the Orange Order's support for the 'no' campaign had reduced its influence in the UUP and limited its capacity to generate support for a confrontation with the Parades Commission over its rulings on contentious parades. Notwithstanding such potential difficulties, there was no doubt that the Good Friday Agreement provided Northern Ireland with its best chance for real peace for many years.

South Africa

The holding of local elections in 1995 and 1996 completed the process of South Africa's democratization. Elections to the national assembly and to provincial legislatures had been held in April 1994. The ANC won over 60 per cent of the votes cast in those elections. As a result, Nelson Mandela was inaugurated as the President of South Africa on 10 May 1996. In terms of the interim constitution he headed a Government of National Unity (GNU). The ANC was the majority party in seven of the nine provinces of South Africa. The exceptions were the Western Cape, which was won by the National Party, and KwaZulu-Natal, which was won by the Inkatha Freedom Party (IFP). Local elections were held in the seven ANC-run provinces on 1 November 1995, as well as for 95 transitional councils in the Western Cape. However, as a result of disputes over the demarcation of the boundaries of the local authorities, elections to the Western Cape Transitional Metropolitan Council and its substructures and for the province's rural areas were delayed. So were the local elections throughout KwaZulu-Natal. These were further delayed to 26 June 1996 as a result of ongoing political violence in the province. The remaining local elections in the Western Cape took place on 29 May 1996.

Preparations for the creation of non-racial local government preceded Mandela's election as President. In the end of September 1992 a task group was set up to examine the structures of local government following a breakthrough in relations between the National Party government and the ANC that signalled their intention to cooperate on the country's transition to democracy. The meeting of the task group paved the way to the establishment of the local government negotiating forum in March

1993. The forum's recommendations led to the passage of the Local Government Transition Act of 1993. The first stage in the process of the transformation of local government involved the replacement of all apartheid-based local authorities by nominated transitional local and metropolitan councils. The second stage was to be elections to the newly agreed local authorities. The first stage of the process took somewhat longer than had originally been anticipated so there was slippage in the initial target date for the elections of October 1994.

In the Western Cape, voters outside Cape Town and its environs had two votes: one for a direct election of a ward representative by plurality and another for the party list to elect further members by proportional representation. There were 95 transitional local councils, voting for which occurred on 1 November 1995, and seven rural services councils, elected on 29 May 1996. Cape Town and its environs, encompassing most voters in the province, was covered by the Western Cape Transitional Metropolitan Council, which was broken down into seven substructures. Voters in this case had three votes: one for a ward representative; another for the party list for the substructure; and a third for the party list for the Metropolitan Council as a whole. Wards were distributed between suburb and township according to a formula agreed in the multi-party negotiations in 1993.

Comment on the outcome of the local elections on 1 November focused on the extent of the ANC's successes across the country. Initially, much was made of breakthroughs by the party in dramatically increasing its share of the vote among Coloured voters,[21] but the final totals presented a more muted picture, of relatively little change in party percentages compared to 1994, on a very much lower turnout of voters than in 1994. Nevertheless, the perception of an ANC challenge to the National Party's dominant position in the Western Cape, was very much in voters' minds when polling took place at the end of May. In contrast to the other provinces in South Africa, Africans (or Blacks, the official label from the 1980s that continued to be widely used in post-apartheid South Africa) were a minority in the Western Cape outnumbered even by Whites. The majority of the population in the Western Cape (constituting approximately 60 per cent of the electorate) were Coloureds. The political context gave added importance to the contest.

There had been a political crisis at the beginning of May over the provisions of the country's final constitution. Its adoption required a two-thirds majority, which meant that the ANC needed the support of

other parties to secure its passage. Only a last minute deal with the
National Party averted a deadlock which would have triggered a
referendum if there had been no agreement after a brief period set aside
for conciliation in these circumstances. The final constitution was
adopted with National Party support on 8 May. In contrast to the interim
constitution, this constitution did not institutionalize power-sharing.
The following day (9 May) the National Party resigned from the
Government of National Unity. Its decision to quit the government
prompted a fall in the Rand, which had already fallen sharply on foreign
currency markets since the start of the year.

Withdrawal from the Government of National Unity was welcomed
by those in the National Party who saw it as enabling the party to oppose
ANC policies much more combatively. What attention the May local
elections in the Western Cape received outside South Africa stemmed
from their being seen as a test for the party's new role.[22] During South
Africa's transition, there had been relatively little political violence in the
Western Cape and it was not an issue in the local elections, though in
common with other parts of the country, crime was an issue. Concern
over the issue was reflected later in 1996 in the formation of a vigilante
organization, People against Gangsters and Drugs (PAGAD).

The National Party won the elections to the Western Cape
Transitional Metropolitan Council, with the ANC coming in a strong
second. For the National Party, its victory was a vindication of its
decision to leave the Government of National Unity. The results of the
proportional vote for party lists to the Metropolitan Council are set out
in Table 4. The most striking aspect of the results was the
extraordinarily poor showing of the Democratic Party, the party
identified with English-speaking White opposition to apartheid. In the
context of Cape Town it was closely identified with the city's liberal
traditions. Throughout the apartheid era the city had been a bastion of
opposition to the imposition of social segregation and returned a
number of MPs for the Democratic Party in elections to the country's
White parliament during the 1980s.

The Star reported the outcome of the elections under the headline
'Nats' Cape victories spark fears of racial polarization'.[23] Commentary
on the outcome focused on the polarization of opinion in the city and of
the failure of the Democratic Party in its heartland of the Cape
peninsula. The *Cape Times* editorial on the elections was headed 'The
Cape's flight to the laager':

TABLE 4
PROPORTIONAL VOTE FOR PARTY LISTS FOR WESTERN CAPE
TRANSITIONAL METROPOLITAN COUNCIL

National Party	358,365	48.53%
African National Congress	282,247	38.23%
Democratic Party	29,739	4.03%
African Christian Democratic Party	17,391	2.36%
Pan Africanist Congress	12,552	1.70%
Freedom Front	7,332	0.99%

Source: Local Government Elections Western Cape: 1996 Results at a glance (Cape Town: Project Vote, 1996) p.63.

The National Party may have changed a few of its spots since 1987, the last time it frightened whites en masse into its right-wing fold, but the same sort of tactics again proved successful last week when it campaigned to turn the Cape metropole into a white/coloured laager as a bulwark against black control. Only in one of six substructures, the central city, was it significantly outnumbered by the ANC, a party supported by blacks even more overwhelmingly than the NP was by whites. This polarization suggests that the voters still approach their politics largely on ethnic lines, in spite of the attempt of some leaders, notably Nelson Mandela, to calm white fears and curb black impatience. Trust is clearly still in short supply on both sides. It is also clear that the great majority of voters see South African politics as a two-party fight, and have little confidence in the smaller parties to protect their interests.[24]

In fact, the pattern of party support across the country in post-apartheid South Africa has proved somewhat more complex than implied by this editorial.

Thus, the Democratic Party fared comparatively well in the local elections in June 1996 in KwaZulu-Natal, where Whites had been alienated by the record of the IFP-controlled provincial government. This was explained by R. W. Johnson as follows:

Among whites the DP ... is the cultural expression of this most English-speaking of the provinces, giving the party a new strength and significance. From the 1960s on the Progressives and the other forbears of the DP were always stronger in Gauteng and the Western Cape than in Natal. Now the national conference of DP councillors has to take place in KwaZulu-Natal because the province has more of them than anywhere else: the turnabout is striking.[26]

The turnabout was also ironic considering Natal's association with the origins of segregation in South Africa and its reputation as a bulwark of English-speaking White conservatism.

Johnson argued that the local elections in South Africa in 1995 and 1996 were 'maintaining elections' in contrast to the general and provincial elections of April 1994 which he described as:

> a critical election', that is one in which the universe of political behaviour is given a definite stamp and shape which future elections are likely merely to replicate, with mere short-term fluctuations occurring round that central norm for some time to come.[25]

A comparison of the outcome of the provincial elections in the Western Cape in April 1994 with that of the local elections in the Western Cape in 1995 and 1996 (see Table 5) gives broad support to Johnson's thesis. Apart from the decline in support for the Democratic Party, the most significant change between 1994 and 1995–96 was in the turnout. Only slightly more than half as many people voted in 1995 and 1996 as did in 1994, though there was a higher turnout in the local elections in the Western Cape than those of any other province. Some decline was inevitable as the 1994 elections had taken place without a register and there were fewer registered voters for the Western Cape local elections in 1995 and 1996 than the number who had voted in 1994. Taken as a whole, South Africa's local elections confirmed the ANC's political dominance. They also confirmed the regional basis of support for its main rivals, the National Party and the IFP.

Events since the local elections of 1995 and 1996 have underlined the continuing polarization of South African politics along racial lines. Indeed, the failure of either the country's political stability since 1994 or the new government's adoption in 1996 of a neo-liberal macro-economic strategy to be rewarded by an influx of foreign capital enabling the country to generate higher economic growth rates has exacerbated racial tensions. This was reflected in an extraordinary attack on white political parties by President Nelson Mandela at the 50th National Conference of the ANC in December 1997. He accused them of reneging on national reconciliation by frustrating social

TABLE 5
OUTCOME OF WESTERN CAPE LOCAL ELECTIONS OF 1995 AND 1996,
COMPARED TO 1994 PROVINCIAL ELECTIONS

	1995 and 1996	1994
National Party	48.6%	(53.2%)
African National Congress	37.7%	(33.0%)
Democratic Party	3.4%	(6.6%)
African Christian Democratic Party	1.6%	(1.2%)
Freedom Front	1.4%	(2.1%)
Pan Africanist Congress	1.3%	(1.1%)

Sources: Calculated from figures given in Local Government Elections Western Cape: 1996 Results at a glance (Cape Town: Project Vote, 1996) and from figures provided by the Independent Electoral Commission, Johannesburg, for the 1994 provincial elections.

transformation, citing their opposition to measures to reduce racial disparities in the socioeconomic sphere. He even suggested that crime was being used by a counter-revolutionary conspiracy of elements of the former ruling group deliberately to damage the economy and thereby destabilize the government.[27]

Comparisons

The outcome of the local elections in the Western Cape in May 1996 was not sufficiently significant to attract attention outside South Africa. By contrast, the outcome of the Israeli general elections was greeted with widespread dismay internationally. There was also a degree of concern at the outcome of the Northern Ireland forum elections in Britain and Ireland. Both reactions were encapsulated in a column in the Financial Times by Edward Mortimer. The theme of the piece, entitled 'The awkward squad', was the propensity of electorates to 'show a disturbing tendency not to vote as foreigners think they should';[28] his main examples were Northern Ireland and Israel. While there was a note of irony in his references to the wishes of foreigners, he expressed real exasperation at the likely consequences for the Northern Ireland and Middle East peace processes. Mortimer noted a tendency after the event, however, for the rebuffed international establishment to swing into damage-limitation mode and to find virtues in politicians it previously regarded as beyond the pale. Northern Ireland's summer of conflict following the forum elections provided the inspiration for a cartoon in The Irish Times. It showed two broken tablets marked respectively 'Northern Ireland peace process' and 'Middle East peace process', accompanied by the simple message, 'snap'.[29]

Why do dominant communities seemingly so often embrace the continuation of conflict and reject compromises that offer the prospect of an end to conflict and a measure of peace? This would seem a particularly pertinent question in the case of Israel. It has become less so in Northern Ireland as a result of the Good Friday Agreement. It is no longer relevant to the South African case. But prior to the South African transition, it was common for a similar answer to be advanced to this question in all cases and this was that the explanation was to be found in the siege mentality of the dominant community. In the light of South Africa's transition, such an explanation no longer appears so persuasive. However, closer examination of the South African case suggests that contrary to the common view of the transition as a miraculous change of heart on the part of the dominant community, the country's transformation was the product more of a shift of power than of attitudes. The point is underlined by the racially polarized pattern of voting in the country's first democratic elections in 1994, which was repeated in the Western Cape local elections analyzed in this article. It is noteworthy that F. W. de Klerk, the conservative Afrikaner nationalist who initiated South Africa's transition, remains adamant that the course he adopted was not the product of any Damascene conversion.[30]

Superficially, the subordinate community often appears as unaccommodating in its attitudes as the dominant community because of its readiness to give support to political parties associated with campaigns of violence and the tendency outside of deeply divided societies for support for violence to be equated with extremism. However, it is evident since South Africa, Israel and Northern Ireland embarked on peace processes that the subordinate community, when given the opportunity to express its opinion, has given its support to those committed to engagement in the process and rejectionist elements have been completely marginalized. The most striking example of such marginalization has been the eclipse of the Pan Africanist Congress (PAC), once seen as a serious rival to the ANC. But the proposition even applies to the case of Northern Ireland where increased support for Sinn Féin derived from its promotion of a peace strategy and the credible (and ultimately well-founded) perception among nationalists of the leaders of Sinn Féin as desiring a restoration of the IRA cease-fire. It is also reflected in the very nearly unanimous support that nationalists gave to the Good Friday Agreement in the referenda on 22 May.

How does the issue of violence relate to the different responses of dominant and subordinate communities to peace processes? In examining more specifically the relationship between political violence and elections in the context of peace processes, two broad areas need to be addressed. First, how far are those engaged in political violence motivated in their timing of acts of violence by the possibility of influencing the outcome of polling? Secondly, how do electorates respond to political violence? I do not intend to delve into the first of these areas in any depth, but a common pitfall in the analysis of the motivations of campaigns of violence is worth underlining. This is the danger of inferring motivations from consequences, a weakness of Benny Morris's analysis of the role played by violence in the outcome of the Israeli elections. He too readily assumes that those engaged in violence were able accurately to predict the consequences of their actions as in his contention that Rabin's assassin was the real winner of the Israeli general election of May 1996.

A similar danger exists in the analysis of the impact of political violence on voters. Before the polling in the Israeli elections it was commonly assumed, based on the evidence of the opinion polls, that Peres would win, provided there were no suicide bomb attacks by Hamas during the campaign. It was only after his defeat by Netanyahu that commentators harked back to the bombs in February and March. Yet what really counted was not the electorate's memory of those events, but its continuing perception of the threat of more such violence. The absence of violence in a deeply divided society is not sufficient by itself to stop voters from reacting as in a force field. Thus, in elections in Northern Ireland, perceptions of threat have played at least as an important a role as a factor in the polarization of voting behaviour as actual levels of violence.

Further, somewhat paradoxically, the existence of a peace process may actually enhance a dominant community's perception of threat. This at least is what seems to have happened in Northern Ireland, as Edward Mortimer's account of the summer of conflict in Northern Ireland following the forum elections suggests:

> The Protestant majority in the province, rattled by a 'peace process' which in their eyes means constant British retreat and creeping Irish annexation, has rallied behind an uncouth and menacing reminder of their historic supremacy: the Orange Order marches.[31]

As Mortimer's comments underline, the dominant community's fears are not confined to threats of violence. The threat of change much more broadly may constitute a source of intense concern for the dominant community. Political violence (whether potential or actual) played a very minor role in the polarization of the electorate of the Western Cape along racial lines. The threat of an ANC victory in the metropolitan council elections was enough of an incentive to produce a sharp shift to the right among English-speaking White citizens of Cape Town.

At the same time, the South African case provides one of the most powerful proofs that continuing conflict in deeply divided societies is not inevitable and that change is possible. Quite fairly, analysis of the South African transition has focused on the remarkable role played by Nelson Mandela in allaying White fears and thus making possible the country's negotiated revolution. Yet Mandela could not have succeeded if structural factors had not brought about a shift of power in the society so that the point arrived (in the referendum of 17 March 1992) where Whites came to fear the consequences of what would happen if they rejected negotiations more than they did the prospect of a new dispensation. External pressure was crucial to the achievement of the Good Friday Agreement in Northern Ireland. Recognition by the UUP of the popularity of the Blair government and thus the likelihood, particularly given the scale of Labour's victory on 1 May 1997, that it would be re-elected, for once persuaded a majority of Unionists that defiance of the British government would have worse consequences for their position than the acceptance of a measure of change. The future of the peace process in the Middle East depends on a similar equation.

Since this piece was completed in May 1998 there have been further changes in the three societies examined in it. To consider them in detail would require a whole new article. However, none of the changes that have taken place fundamentally challenge the conclusions reached in 1998. A summary of events since 1998 would shift the focus even further from the elections in 1996.

NOTES

1. The local elections in the Western Cape formed part of nationwide local elections throughout South Africa. In the rest of the country, apart from KwaZulu-Natal, which went to the polls on 26 June 1996, the local elections had taken place on 1 November 1995. However, the main focus here is on the Western Cape elections.
2. Hermann Giliomee and Jannie Gagiano (eds), *The elusive search for peace: South Africa, Israel and Northern Ireland* (Cape Town: Oxford University Press, 1990).

3. Michael McDonald, *Children of Wrath: Political Violence in Northern Ireland* (Cambridge: Polity Press, 1986) contains a sustained comparison of the three cases, as does Donald Harman Akenson, *God's Peoples: Covenant and Land in South Africa, Israel, and Ulster* (Ithaca, NY and London: Cornell University Press, 1992).
4. See e.g. Antoine Bouillon, Sonia Dayan-Herzbrun and Maurice Goldring, *Desirs de paix, relents de guerre: Afrique du Sud, Proche-Orient, Irlande du Nord* (Paris: Desclee de Brouwer, 1996).
5. See Lamis Andoni, 'The Palestinian Elections: Moving Toward Democracy or One-Party Rule?', *Journal of Palestine Studies* XXV/99/3 (1996), p.6.
6. Benny Morris, 'Israel's elections and their implications', *Journal of Palestine Studies* XXVI/101/1 (1996), pp.70-81.
7. Ibid., p.74.
8. David Horovitz, 'Peres leans on Rabin in election bid', *The Irish Times*, 11 May 1996.
9. *Keesing's Record of World Events* (London: Longman, May 1996) p.41117.
10. David Horovitz, 'Netanyahu outperforms Peres in Israel's television debate', *The Irish Times*, 27 May 1996.
11. *Jerusalem Post*, 22 April 1996.
12. Morris (note 6) p.73.
13. Julian Ozanne and David Gardner, 'Peace path's deep divide', *Financial Times*, 28 May 1996.
14. Ibid.
15. They were *A Framework for Accountable Government in Northern Ireland*, which was recommended to the parties by the British government, and *A New Framework for Agreement*, which was recommended to the parties by the British and Irish governments.
16. George J. Mitchell, John de Chastelain and Harri Holkeri, *Report of the International Body* (Dublin and Belfast: 22 January 1996) 20pp.
17. *The Irish Times*, 28 May 1996.
18. Geoffrey Evans and Brendan O'Leary, 'Frameworked futures: intransigence and flexibility in the Northern Ireland elections of May 30 1996', *Irish Political Studies* 12 (1997) p.25.
19. Ibid., p.45.
20. *Financial Times*, 11 April 1998.
21. See e.g. 'No apathy, but plenty of poll errors', *Weekly Mail and Guardian* (Johannesburg), 3 November 1995.
22. See e.g. 'De Klerk faces city vote test', *Financial Times*, 30 May 1996.
23. *The Star* (Johannesburg), 1 June 1996.
24. *Cape Times*, 31 May 1996.
25. R. W. Johnson, 'Understanding the Elections', *KwaZulu-Natal Briefing* (Helen Suzman Foundation) 3 (August 1996) pp.18–19.
26. Ibid., p.18.
27. Mandela's speech (Report by the President of the ANC, Nelson Mandela, to the 50th National Conference of the ANC) is available on the ANC's website, http://www.anc.org.za.
28. *Financial Times*, 5 June 1996.
29. *The Irish Times*, 25 June 1996.
30. See e.g. Patti Waldmeir, *Anatomy of a Miracle: The End of Apartheid and the Birth of the New South Africa* (Harmondsworth: Viking, 1997) p.111.
31. Edward Mortimer, 'As separate as ever', *Financial Times*, 17 July 1996.

5

Should Self-determination be Legalized?*

DANIEL PHILPOTT

Those who recognize that elections and parliaments are not always orderly institutions, civil procedures and triumphs of compromise, but that they often accompany, and even encourage, the power of the gun and the mob, those who recognize, in short, the tension between violence and democracy, will see the problem with self-determination. Philosophers and partisans of self-determination historically have linked the principle with democracy. Mazzini, Mill, Wilson, the American colonists, French-speaking Quebecois, virtually all colonial independence movements have portrayed the independence of nations and colonies as a people's expression of its will, of its desire to govern itself. This democratic impulse is often a violent one, as we have seen again and again since the end of the Cold War. In Europe alone, independence struggles have claimed more lives in the past nine years than have all wars there during the previous 45 years. Self-determination has sprung violently around the globe, too.

But self-determination is not always bloody. If there has been war over Chechnya and Moldova, we must also observe that most of the 15 independent states that emerged from the former Soviet Union departed in peace and have remained at peace. If the Slovak departure from Czechoslovakia and the French-speaking Quebecois' drive for independence have been rife with bitter words, messy procedures, questionably worded ballots and lack of proper plebiscites, we must also notice that these quarrels have thus far been conducted with little malice, and with at least a modicum of democracy.[1] Even warring self-

---

* This article draws from ideas developed in Daniel Philpott, 'Self-Determination in Practice', in Margaret Moore, ed., *National Self-Determination and Secession* (Oxford: Oxford University Press, 1998) pp.79–102.

determination movements may sometimes evoke the democrat's sympathy: the Iraqi Kurd quest for greater federal autonomy under Saddam Hussein, and many colonial independence movements, including, perhaps, the American revolution. Toward other movements, of course, democrats are divided and conflicted: the Scots, the Palestinians, the Croatians, the Bosnians.

The oppression of a group that seeks independence from a tyrannical central power, the harm done by a group that departs from a generally just multicultural democracy, the bloodshed that frequently accompanies self-determination – all pull the democrat's intuitions in different directions. Particularly, the violence of Bosnia, Sri Lanka, Chechnya and elsewhere gives pause to the advocate of self-determination as a form of democracy. Responding to both the intellectual dilemma and the surge of violent self-determination movements in the world, political philosophers recently have again taken up the problem of self-determination. The most thorough work, commendable for its treatment of the many issues that self-determination evokes – maltreatment of minorities, economic grievances, domestic constitutional questions, and many other considerations – is Allen Buchanan's 1991 book, *Secession*. Since then, just as self-determination movements have proliferated, so has the literature on the subject, many of the authors responding to or modifying Buchanan's argument.

Buchanan himself recently has categorized the nascent literature usefully into two broad categories. Broadly speaking, prior to qualifications and strictures, one approach is constrictive of the right to self-determination, while the other is permissive. The constrictive approach, which includes his own theory, he terms 'Remedial Right Only Theories'. It holds that a group is entitled to self-determination (to secession, in Buchanan's version) only when it has suffered certain kinds of threats or grievances. These include prior historical wrongs such as an invasion or an annexation, threats to a group's culture, threats of genocide, and what Buchanan calls 'discriminatory redistribution' – an economic injustice such as that claimed by the American South against the North's high tariffs during the nineteenth century. The Remedial Rights Only approach is like the right to revolution: a people claims it only when it has been wronged.[2] A Remedial Rights Only theory also denies that self-determination is a general right, derived from democracy, obtainable by any group the majority of whose members desire to exercise it. Rather, it burdens a claimant group to show that self-determination would remedy some injustice that it has suffered.[3]

The other broad approach, which Buchanan terms 'Primary Right Theories', argues the intuition of democratic theorists, of Mill, Wilson and colonial independence movements, asserting the very claim that Remedial Rights Only theories deny: that self-determination is a basic right, rooted in democratic theory. Threats and grievances are unnecessary to establish a claim, although they are morally relevant, and may well enhance such a claim.[4] In a 1995 article, 'In Defence of Self-Determination', I argued for this approach – the apparently more permissive one – myself.[5] I also stressed, however, that the right to self-determination is a contingent one, thickly qualified by the same liberal democratic commitments on which it is based. To sustain a claim to self-determination, I require, a group must show that it is at least as liberal and democratic as the state from which it is separating, that its majority prefers self-determination, that it adequately protects minorities within its midst, and that it meets distributive justice standards. I emphasized, too, that secession is only one form – the most extreme, at that – of the right to self-determination, which may also take the form of enhanced autonomy within a federal republic. Self-determination as I defend it, then, is not, simply 'a plebiscitory right to secede'.[6] A separatist group must pass far more tests than a plebiscite; secession is only a last resort. The heart of the difference between the two approaches is that Remedial Right Only Theories deny that self-determination is a general right arising from democracy, but allows it to groups as a remedy for injustices that it has suffered, while Primary Right Theories grant the general right but curtail it for groups that have performed injustices.

Believers in democracy ought to be partisans of self-determination, whose value goes beyond correcting injustices. I said little, however, about the institutions that might (or might not) promote self-determination properly qualified: international law, international enforcement bodies, domestic constitutions and state policies. In this sense, the article was a first step. It is important to get the principles right before deciding what institutions would further them. But heeding self-determination's noisome particularities, in Bosnia, Sri Lanka, Kashmir and Rwanda, acknowledging the killings, the rapes, the refugees, the 'cleansing' of minorities, we may well find ourselves chary towards partisans and philosophers. Even if my theory's qualifications acknowledge these problems and restrict the general right, could these qualifications be secured in practice?[7] Again, it is the violence that gives us pause. Some scholars also argue that a right to self-determination would undermine democracy by allowing a group to use its credible threat of exit as a debilitating form of blackmail. The group would subvert majority decision-making by constantly wielding its veto and by eroding citizens' expectation of a territorially stable political community, on which democratic politics depends.[8]

Such criticisms do not aim directly at the philosophical foundation of self-determination, but rather suggest the ill effects of institutions that promote it. A defence of the principle of self-determination, then, must explain what would be the likely effects of promoting self-determination through international law, domestic constitutions and the foreign policies of states. The most central question is how legalizing self-determination would affect the violence associated with it. Would it increase the violence by encouraging more movements? Or would it help reduce the violence by taming unjust movements? Or would it have little effect at all? Another important question is the one about democracy: would institutionalizing self-determination undermine democratic governance? Today, few institutions to promote self-determination exist, making the question a difficult counterfactual: how would self-determination movements act differently were these institutions to gain legal and political clout?[9] Would the institutions realistically both promote the principle and discourage the perversions? Should self-determination be legalized?

Self-determination and violence: a long tradition

Self-determination movements are as old as nations. In the four centuries before Christ, messianic Jews hoped for the liberation of Israel in the form of an independently governed community. On grounds largely religious, but laced too with economic and political grievances, Protestants in the Netherlands and in the German states fought for decades during the sixteenth and seventeenth centuries to liberate themselves from the alliance of the Holy Roman Empire and the Spanish monarchy and enjoy their autonomy. It was not until the French Revolution that the nation became associated deeply with popular rule, as peoples across Europe came to desire liberation from *anciens régimes*. Popular nationalist movements were behind the wars to unify Germany and Italy, and the wars of several Balkan peoples for liberation from the Austro-Hungarian and Ottoman empires in the late nineteenth and early twentieth centuries, quests which culminated in the settlement of World War I.

During the twentieth century, one of the most common forms of self-determination movements has been the independence struggles of colonies from empires. Of course, such struggles were not new to the twentieth century, for both the American Revolution and numerous revolutions in Latin America were struggles for liberation from European colonial powers. But the rate of decolonization accelerated sharply during the twentieth century, first in Britain's colonies in Ireland, New Zealand, South Africa and Australia in the first half of the century, then sweepingly throughout several European powers' colonies in Africa and Asia after World War II, peaking during the 1960s. Most attainments of independence were without violence, but the exceptions are numerous and notable: Algeria, Indochina, Madagascar, Kenya and Malaya.

But even after colonial independence, violent self-determination has hardly abated. During the Cold War, violent protest and rebellion associated with 'ethnopolitical conflict' – in which a national minority seeks independence or great autonomy – quadrupled.[10] In only two cases outside the colonial context, since the end of World War II, did any of these movements succeed in attaining independence: Eritrea and Bangladesh. Some conflicts were associated with the Cold War division between the superpowers, but this was hardly a central or even concomitant cause. As David Rapoport notes that in only four out of 40 secessionist struggles during the Cold War did Cold War protagonists favour opposite sides in a conflict.[11] In 1993, in the estimation of Ted Robert Gurr and Barbara Harff, 57 conflicts involving ethnopolitical groups were 'serious or emerging' across the globe.[12] In Gurr's view, the republics of the former Soviet Union and the former Yugoslavia were the most likely regions for future violence. In the 1990s, then, violence associated with self-determination is as common and widespread as it has ever been: such is the context in which we now consider an institutionalized right.

The ground of a right to self-determination

An institutionalized right to self-determination is only intelligible if the right has a moral basis. An important preliminary question, then, is: What exactly is the foundation of the moral right to self-determination for which I have argued? I previously defined self-determination as a legal arrangement that gives a group independent statehood or expanded powers within a federal state. Self-determination is itself, then, a form of institution, a new arrangement for governance. Its justification lies in what it promotes – democracy – which is in turn justified by what *it* promotes: the autonomy of individuals who better steer their fate by governing themselves collectively. The details of this argument, which I borrow from theories of democracy, I need not repeat here. It is important to see, though, that self-determination is one of a class of legal mechanisms that institutionalize a democratic impulse. In this broad sense, it is like scores of institutional instruments that give one group or another greater representation or ability to participate – like the right to organize labour unions, or the enfranchisement of women or the working class, for instance. Self-determination is even more similar to mechanisms that give a regional or ethnic group better representation – a subclass of democratic institutions that also includes federalism, minority representation schemes and the like. What uniquely distinguishes self-determination, though, is that the members of the group that claim it are united by an identity, usually a national identity, and by much more than just geographic residency, and want to govern themselves as a distinct group, not just attain representation within a larger whole. Self-determination redraws the political borders of this group in order to circumscribe its residents more locally, enabling them to fashion better their political identity, enhancing their autonomy.[13]

The realized good of democratic autonomy for the members of a group, the enhancement of their self-government, sufficiently grounds self-determination. The members may well seek goods beyond intrinsic self-government, which may enhance their case for self-determination. Keeping alive their culture by strengthening their language, educating their children better, and protecting their religion are examples of such goods. Their case is enhanced, too, if they can cite legitimate grievances or threats to their culture, their economic livelihood or even their lives. But self-government alone adequately grounds their claim to self-determination. In most, if not all, self-determination movements both historical and contemporary, self-government intrinsically desired is at least one element in the movement's alloy of arguments and motivations. Sometimes it is the avowedly central motivation. Consider for example many post-World War II colonial movements for independence from the British empire. Certainly the colonists had suffered harms: slave labour or the near equivalent, shootings of their protesters, quelling of their dissent, all the banal evils of imperialism. Yet in the writings and speeches of these movements' leaders, we read not only about these grievances, but of the intrinsic evil of colonial subordination, the contradictions of a democratic, egalitarian European state holding on to colonies. Consider the following passage from Gandhi's writings:

> [H]as independence suddenly become a goal in answer to something offensive that some Englishman has done? Do men conceive their goals in order to oblige people or to resent their action? I submit that if it is a goal, it must be declared and pursued irrespectively of the acts or threats of others.[14]

This is not to say that colonial self-determination movements were always unproblematic. In India, for instance, the problem of minority treatment – one of the qualifications of self-determination – was quite substantial. It is only to say that Remedial Right Only Theories, focusing only on the grievances, fail to address the central rationale to which colonial movements appealed, the rationale put forth by Mahatma Gandhi, Jawaharlal Nehru and Mohammed Jinnah in India, and by many others throughout the rest of the colonial world.[15]

But if nothing beyond a claim to self-governance is required to establish self-determination, a group's own injustices might limit or invalidate the *prima facie* claim. To show that it avoids these injustices, any movement must pass certain tests, which reflect qualifications to the right to self-determination that also grow out of liberal democratic theory. The rationales and details of these qualifications I explore in the original argument; I summarize them here.[16] To obtain self-determination, a group must uphold basic liberal (including some minority) rights, as well as features of democracy such as elections and representation, upholding these liberal and democratic features at least to the same extent that the larger state upheld them prior to self-determination. The procedure for choosing self-determination itself must also be democratic, meaning a plebiscite in which a majority, perhaps even a supermajority, of the group's members approve of their separation. Liberalism also suggests distributive justice. A group seeking economic independence might pay compensation or maintain a cooperative economic relationship with its former state. A final requirement parallels a criterion of just-war theory: the cost of winning self-determination, and the evil consequences involved in doing so (war, refugees, and the like) must be proportionate to the justice gained. Recognizing that secession is most likely to bring such consequences and least likely to remain a proportionate struggle, I argue that it ought to be a last resort, most justifiable for groups who suffer grievances that are not likely to be remedied short of full independence – the fate that the Bosnian Muslims feared if stranded with the Serbs in a unified Yugoslavia, and the treatment of the Iraqi Kurds at the hands of Saddam Hussein. Appropriately qualified, my own approach attains important commonalties with Remedial Right Only Theories. Both approaches recognize the importance of grievances and the potential dangers of self-determination, especially secession. It might even turn out that in most actual cases, a qualified Primary Right Theory makes quite similar judgements to a Remedial Right Only Theory. The difference lies primarily in the method of justification.

All of this amounts to a qualified moral right to self-determination. But there is a final important point about this right: if I have argued for the justice of self-determination, I do not necessarily think it desirable for self-determination movements to exist, nor that their number be maximized. If people identify their existing nation-state as the group with which they want to govern themselves, then self-determination is not needed to further their democratic autonomy. It is only when the group with which they identify politically does not correspond with existing institutions that the problem of self-determination arises.

Still less have I asserted the undesirability of multicultural democracy. One might worry that by promoting institutions that may create societies with uniform identities, my argument rejects cooperative democratic politics between people of separate identities.[17] But this misconstrues the problem. My justifying reason for self-determination is not its promotion of political homogeneity.[18] As I have argued, it is the group's realization of its political destiny, the furtherance of the democratic autonomy of its members, that justifies self-determination. It is this justification on which a Primary Right Theory rides or falls, not on whether a group becomes more or less homogenous in achieving self-determination. Nor must we confuse the real question at stake in a theory of self-determination, which is not 'Is multicultural democracy desirable?' but rather 'Given that a group already desires separation, should separation be granted?' The question of self-determination arises, after all, when a group (e.g. the Irish, the

Basques, Quebecois, the Nigerians, the Ghanians, the Native Americans) has decided that it no longer belongs to a polity, when the unity of a political order has already been ruptured seriously.[19]

There is nothing incoherent about advocating multicultural democracy while also holding that in cases when it has failed, it may be just for a group to attain self-determination. Such an argument indeed matches many democrats' intuitions about actual cases. Advocates of a multicultural America with political cooperation between races and ethnic groups ought not to be troubled, for very few such groups today seek political separation. The one group which does claim some form of separation is Native Americans, precisely the group whose self-determination most elicits democrats' sympathy.[20] In other cases, self-determination, even in the absence of grievances, will seem justified to democrats even if it increases homogeneity. Consider again the Indians living under the British – or the Nigerians, or the Kenyans. Even acknowledging that the British government advocated their gradual democratization, is it outlandish to hold that the Indians were justified in rejecting participation in the multicultural political entity known as the British Empire?

Need self-determination be institutionalized?

There is no reason that a Primary Right Theory of self-determination, even if defensible as just, must be converted into law or policy.[21] It could be that international law and domestic constitutions in their present condition are too blunt-edged, too lacking in judicial clout and enforcement, to promote just self-determination effectively, upholding all of its qualifications. In this case, self-determination need not be legalized at all. Such a conclusion would not relegate the right to moral irrelevance, for it would still be of concern to all who want to know what justice consists of – statespersons, jurists, advocates, scholars, legislators and citizens. The argument's validity stands or falls on its own terms, apart from whether the right is institutionalized. But I am not yet ready to concede the case for legalizing self-determination. Whether the world's institutions are ripe enough to have self-determination grafted onto them is still an open question.

The question is also speculative. As there is scant precedent for institutionalized self-determination, the case for it lies in our best guesses about its possible effects on the incentives and decisions of nations and states. There are two main forums in which self-determination might be institutionalized, the effects of each of which warrants consideration. First, the right might be promoted through international law. Currently, self-determination resides in United Nations agreements, but remains subordinate to sovereignty, preventing nations outside recognition in their demands for greater autonomy or independence. If international law were to be strengthened, its enforcers would still be states, perhaps acting according to resolutions of the UN Security Council or a regional organization such as NATO. Thus the forum of international law involves both an international organization and individual states. Secondly, the right might be incorporated into states' domestic constitutions. Here, it has rarely previously appeared, with a few exceptions such as the 1993 Ethiopia, 1979 Yugoslavian and the former Soviet Union constitutions, where it was scantly respected.

In turn, I propose three criteria for evaluating how well these forums promote just self-determination. First, what is the forum's capacity to render impartial justice? Can it provide the disinterested officials, the judicial status, the enforcement powers needed to make fair and heeded decisions? Secondly, can the forum minimize self-determination's perverse effects while promoting its component principles? Finally, how utopian is the forum? Might the forum actually become the site of a right to self-determination? Does it build upon precedent? Is there consensus on its behalf? These are the questions that sceptics of self-determination raise, and which proponents of the principle must answer.

The possibilities of international law

Several key UN agreements enunciate self-determination as a major principle of international law, mentioning it right alongside human rights, democratic governance and the rule of law. Such company of principles suggests, with Primary Right Theories, that self-determination is a close cousin of liberalism and democracy.[22] Outside the colonial context, however, self-determination's status has advanced little beyond that of an inspired principle. In international legal consensus and state practice, there is no general legal right to self-determination that trumps the principle of territorial integrity, granting outside recognition or assistance to a people seeking federal autonomy or independence from a state. Self-determination has long lingered in the shadow of state sovereignty.[23]

The impartial enforcement criterion

If self-determination were to become an international legal right, then international law and the bodies which enforce and interpret it would grant recognition to peoples seeking federal autonomy or independence under some circumstances. These circumstances are suggested by the moral theory of self-determination. A claimant people would be required to hold a plebiscite, endorsing the measure though a majority (or supermajority) vote. But it would also have to demonstrate that it meets qualifications of liberalism, democracy, distributive justice, just minority treatment and proportional consequences. In most cases, enhanced federal privileges would be a people's entitlement; secession is reserved as a last resort, accorded to those peoples victimized by the most egregious threats or grievances. This law, with all of these provisions, might be incorporated in a UN covenant or in an agreement of a regional international organization such as the Organization for Security and Cooperation in Europe.

But who would judge and enforce the law? Standards of liberalism, democracy, and distributive justice, threats, grievances and last resort are far from self-interpreting, but are subjective, situational, often needing to be balanced against each other, and matters of degree, rather than of simple fulfilment or non-fulfilment. Their application requires a disinterested and expert third party. We also desire effective enforcement, not only of immediate claims, but of obligations that persist into the future. One can imagine, for instance, the United Nations or a group of states recognizing and assisting a self-determination movement in its initial quest for independence or autonomy, but failing to enforce the movement's continuing economic obligations or its commitment to treat its minorities justly. In our sovereign state system, such guarantees of future compliance are rare, for they require some states or institutions constantly to oversee other states' internal affairs and obligations.

So we look for institutions that could guarantee principles of self-determination impartially, enduringly. Are they possible? A court, perhaps the World Court, would most likely be appropriately disinterested and expert. But its lack of an effective enforcement arm would render it impotent in issues of self-determination, its decisions often deeply politically, even militarily disputed. A UN Security Council might play the role of enforcer, but only in a far more developed UN system.

It is easier to conceive of a Security Council which judges when self-determination is warranted and when to assist it. Because it comprises Great Powers, the Security Council would not easily weigh complex claims. Doubtless, it would be more influenced by its members' economic and strategic interests than the World Court or another judicial body would be, and yet would it be more disinterested than a single state? It is difficult to judge exactly how disinterested the Security Council could be. Some positive evidence exists in several instances in which the Council intervened since the end of the Cold War – in Iraqi Kurdistan, Somalia, Bosnia, Rwanda, Haiti, Cambodia, Namibia, El Salvador and elsewhere – to deliver humanitarian aid, monitor elections, and promote human rights and statebuilding,[24] although the Security Council was not free from Great Power security motives and may have chosen selectively, ignoring cases similar to the ones where it became involved. Each case nevertheless seems warranted on its merits, having involved an injustice or humanitarian disaster that was not simply an excuse for Great Powers to pursue their strategic and economic interests. In many cases the Security Council's proxy armies were at least partially successful in ending conflict, delivering relief, helping to build state institutions, or monitoring elections.[25] The lesson for self-determination is that the Security Council is significantly, if far from perfectly, equipped to determine and encourage a just outcome to an internal conflict, and could promote self-determination according to just criteria.

The activities of a court or fortified Council in promoting the international law of self-determination would include mainly judging claims and enforcing them through its panoply of policy tools: military force, economic sanctions, provision of monitoring teams and others. Another important purveyor of law is diplomatic recognition policy, which resides in the hands of states. Recognition of claims to statehood is a familiar issue in international law. It arises when a larger state dissolves, as did Austria-Hungary at the end of World War I and the Soviet Union in 1991. Here, it mainly applies to secession. The issue at stake is the circumstances under which outside states ought to recognize a nation seeking independence from a larger state. During the Cold War, state practice and international law rarely conferred such recognition except in the case of colonies. Even though self-determination appears in the UN Charter and subsequent declarations, the one case of secession sanctioned was Bangladesh's exit from Pakistan in 1971.

If states promoted principles of just self-determination, they might be more open to recognizing secessionist claims, although there is still insistence that they acknowledge qualifications and the last resort status of secession. But could states be relied upon to recognize and support just cases while discouraging unjust ones? It is difficult to determine how much a state's decision for recognition will affect the respective incentives of a self-determination movement and its opponent. The effects of recognition might include bequeathal of legitimacy, diplomatic or military assistance, and the incentives for recognition will likely involve vagaries of the balance of power, public opinion and legislatures. Here, impartiality is precarious.

For example, in 1991 the European Community (EC) proposed standards for recognizing Croatia and Slovenia, which had just declared independence from Yugoslavia. These standards included democracy, human rights and respect for minorities. Although the EC did not intend here to promote self-determination, insisting that it was only recognizing the new states arising from a dissolved federation, its criteria much resemble those that I want to apply to self-determination claims.[26] Germany then proceeded to grant recognition to Croatia and Slovenia in December 1991, unilaterally, before other EC states were ready to assent. Many criticized Germany's hastiness, arguing that it contributed to the further dissolution of Yugoslavia and to the ensuing war in Bosnia. This claim is controversial, but what is much more clear, and important for our purposes, is that Germany's decision arose from its internal politics, not from its assessment of the merits of the case. The same factors will also likely govern future recognition decisions.

States' ancient political drives and central role in judging and executing the international law of self-determination evoke the general question: were a right of self-determination to become legalized, qualified in the ways suggested, might it come to pass that the claims would attain rampant recognition while the restraints would be ignored? The danger is real, but not inevitable. Legalization alone, the legitimacy that law confers, would not necessarily promote a bias towards enforcing separatism over the qualifications. Human rights, including minority rights, and democracy – constituting a good portion of the restrictions – are currently far more entrenched in international law and state foreign policies than self-determination is, a pedigree that international bodies are not likely to abjure in a single-minded, unqualified pursuit of self-determination.[27]

More worrying is the role of states. The Security Council is comprised of states; states grant recognition; and states pursue primarily their traditional desiderata of security, position and wealth, not legal rectitude. It is not clear that a general secessionist bias will result. Germany and Croatia was only one case; great powers could just as easily discover an interest in opposing the break-up of a state. But even if states' inclinations do not generally add up to one or another sort of decision, we can hardly be confident that states will act rightly in the single case of a Kosovo, a Quebec or a Sri Lanka. As long as we live in a sovereign states system, this is a difficult problem. Hopes for impartial judgement and enforcement depend on confidence in states acting in concert in the Security Council or some regional organization. Again, post-Cold War interventions give some grounds, admittedly tenuous, to expect that the Council can promote the demands of justice. These efforts surely will be imperfect and selective, but not without some prospect for success.

The problem of perverse effects

In designing institutions, we must consider not only how adequately they would provide for judgement and enforcement, both of the principle and its qualifications, but also what kind of perverse effects they might bring. Two sorts of perverse effects are relevant here. First, there are effects relating to the international system. Secondly, there are effects upon the minorities and the overflow populations of particular movements.

The sovereign states system dates roughly to the Peace of Westphalia of 1648, the settlement which ended the Thirty Years War. This war was very much about self-determination, and very violent. Protestant and Catholic armies sought to alter the religious proportions of neighbouring territories, eradicating perhaps a quarter of Germany's population. Westphalia was a *modus vivendi*. Princes and estates agreed not to respect deep common principles of religion or justice, but to refrain from interfering in one another's territory. The norms of state sovereignty and non-intervention that solidified in the century after Westphalia became perhaps the deepest norms in the international system. There is value to the *modus vivendi*. It protects territorial integrity, the right of a state and its citizens not to be attacked or interfered with from the outside. As Buchanan explains, territorial integrity, in turn, provides important goods for a state, including protection of the security, rights and stable expectations of its citizens, and a stable order that gives citizens the incentive to invest themselves in their government over time.[28] The moral intuition that justifies Westphalia is that whatever evils occur within states, it is better to maintain the *modus vivendi* than permit the manifold, self-multiplying claims that can motivate, and serve as a pretext for, widespread intervention.[29]

If self-determination were institutionalized in international law, would the Westphalian norms be enfeebled? The answer depends on the sense in which the question is asked. If it asks whether self-determination challenges sovereignty as the foundational norm of the international system, then the answer must be 'No', for self-determination does not purport to replace the state with an alternative polity. A state, after all, is what a secessionist group seeks to become. Neither does a people seeking federal autonomy, one hoping to remain legally within an existing state, propose an alternative polity. Self-determination may indeed increase the existing number of states, but this only extends, and does not challenge, the Westphalian system.[30] Colonial self-determination, for instance, globalized rather than curtailed sovereign statehood.

But if the question is whether self-determination challenges the absoluteness of sovereignty, then the answer is 'Yes', it does weaken the Westphalian order. If self-determination claims were to gain regular recognition from outside states, then the Westphalian principle of absolute sovereignty, the right of non-intervention which states have enjoyed roughly since the seventeenth century, would be notably compromised. It would not be the first such compromise, for as I argued above, since the end of the Cold War, the UN Security Council has curtailed absolute sovereignty for purposes of humanitarian relief, the promotion of human rights and democracy, state-building, and election monitoring. Legalized self-determination would manifest this same trend.[31] To this date, there is little evidence that these compromises to sovereignty entailed a general curtailment of the Westphalian *modus vivendi* of non-intervention. Occurring under the auspices of the UN Security Council, they have not caused unilateral interventions to swell elsewhere. The Security Council itself has used the term 'intervention' only reluctantly, justifying its interference in states as responses to threats to 'international peace and security', even if it has been directed chiefly against a domestic evil. Self-determination would clearly widen the justifications for intervention, whether they take the form of military, diplomatic or via recognition policies, but similar restraint and consensus in the Security Council ought to guard the Westphalian *modus vivendi*. The value of this *modus vivendi* is genuine, but conditional. Territorial integrity confers benefits, but it is not absolute. Sovereignty, though a force for order, has also sheltered evil, as it did Nazi Germany and other troublesome regimes. If the *modus vivendi* is loosened slowly, if the Security Council approves intervention only where it finds strongest consensus on the injustice involved, then it might preserve sovereignty's contribution to order while scaling back its absoluteness.

There is another potential detriment to legalized, institutionalized self-determination. It might turn out that laws and institutions not only affect the fate of single cases, but also cause further separatist movements to arise, multiply, and radicalize their claims. As nearly every state in the world contains minorities, and as there are far more minorities in the world than can possibly have states, endless secession is a concern. The worry, however, is unfounded in the context of the present argument. The principles alone sharply limit the number of nations entitled to statehood. In fact, there may be quite few cases of self-determination which my theory's principles would endorse but which a Remedial Right Only Theory would strongly restrict. Many of those movements which have avoided significant threats or grievances – towards which Primary Right Theories are more permissive than Remedial Right Only Theories – will be limited in their claims by their own injustices. Consider, for instance, the Quebec case for independence. On one view, admittedly only one side of the controversy, their petition does not rest upon deep threats or grievances *vis-à-vis* Canada, but upon strong French identity claims. Yet even if one takes this view, questions remain about this group's prospective treatment of its own anglophone and aboriginal minorities. Again, the clearest cases which a Primary Right Theory allows but which a Remedial Right Only Theory restricts are those colonies which had experienced relatively mild injustices apart from the sheer fact of colonial subordination, and which then seemed able to govern themselves as justly as they were administered as a colony. But today there are few such colonies left. Most potential secessionist movements harbour qualifying features or questionably demonstrate last resort. An incessant secessionist mitosis does not inevitably follow from a legalized right, at least the qualified sort proposed.

The real problem with such a mitosis is the fate of minorities trapped within self-determination movements, minorities mixed with the populations of the larger state, and whose own members spread across official boundaries. A separatist group will quite often have minorities of its own who fear danger in an independent state (e.g. Croats, Serbs and Muslims in Bosnia). In a new state, these minorities may then come to demand their own independence, secession begetting more secession. Alternatively, they might form irredentist groups which aspire to unite with their own in a neighbouring state (e.g. Catholics in Northern Ireland). They may also inspire secessionists elsewhere, fueling separation through their mere example. These predicaments lead further to the war, the war crimes and refugees which self-determination movements increasingly elicit.[32]

The problem, then, is not with the political end state of self-determination, but with the process of reaching it. Most of these dilemmas are captured by the principles of self-determination, and the qualifications to the principles proposed. When it appears that minority rights are likely to be violated and war likely to break out, then self-determination ought to be curbed. But, one might ask, if violations and war are not just likely, but almost inevitable, if major rifts virtually always splinter into minor clefts which themselves become major rifts, and if any familiar international institution is impotent to stop it, then are such qualifying principles only spurious academic desiderata?

I dispute the inevitability this argument implies. There are many independence movements which, while not without problems, have avoided atrocities – Norway from Sweden, most of the Soviet Republics, Slovakia and Slovenia. The atrocities are not inevitable. But if inevitability were the only issue, we might still accept the argument against self-determination based on fears of minority mistreatment. Widespread minority abuse might still far exceed the unfulfilment of a few just aspirations to self-determination. But this is a skewed analysis of the problem, for it ignores a different source of war, war crimes and the like – the denial of self-determination claims by larger states, a denial that often strengthens, and even creates, separatist movements. Imagine, for instance, a scenario in which the Soviet Union had refused to agree to the independence of its constituent republics, instead choosing to fight for its continued empire. Might not many more wars like that in Chechnya have been fought? If self-determination institutions could promote the ill effects of separatism, so their absence might allow unionist evils. To ignore the unionist evils, however, is to promote a status quo bias. The difficult question is the relative size of the respective effects. So we come back to institutions. Can they be efficacious? Can they discriminate between movements? It is far from clear that institutions capable of sound judgement in matters of self-determination are out of the question.

Possibility of realization

The final criterion for international law as an instrument of self-determination is whether it might develop in the foreseeable future. There are two ways of applying the criterion. First, does institutionalization find precedent in international law, building on foundations which are already present, or is it a novel departure? The second standard is much balder: Is there a political and legal consensus behind change?

Asserting the criterion of precedent, Buchanan argues that a theory of self-determination ought to be 'consistent with well-entrenched, morally progressive principles of international law'. Primary Right Theories suffer by this standard, for they contravene one of the most deeply entrenched principles of international law: territorial integrity. Buchanan waxes Westphalian here, appealing to the benefits of territorial integrity. But he is not an absolutist, for he also proposes standards of legitimacy that a state must meet if it is to warrant outside recognition and full respect for its territorial integrity, including respect for democracy and human rights.[33]

On what basis, however, would we include democracy and human rights as elements of legitimacy, but exclude self-determination? After all, if a claim to self-determination is just, and if a government denies it, then why should we not consider this government's legitimacy thus compromised, and restrict its entitlement to outside recognition? Buchanan here distinguishes between criteria of justice that are 'standard and uncontroversial', including human rights and non-discrimination against minorities, and those which are not widely accepted – like self-determination (or, in his rendering, a right to secede). Basing legitimacy on these standard criteria, Buchanan holds, flies less in the face of precedent – for international law increasingly has treated violations of human rights and democracy as grounds for outside interference – yet leaves territorial integrity generally intact. In a Remedial Right Only Theory, then, a people gains the right to secede only when it has suffered violations of their human rights and their democratic government, but not when it is simply asserting a general right to self-determination.

But to exclude self-determination as an element of legitimacy because it challenges what is standard is to exclude it without an argument. The very purpose of Primary Right Theories is to push out the frontiers of international law, to revise precedent, to make respect for just claims to self-determination a standard criterion for legitimacy. To reject such theories requires a demonstration that they are wrong, not merely an assertion that they contradict well entrenched principles.[34]

It is also mistaken to think that self-determination is a strong departure from international law. Self-determination appears as a principle in the UN Charter and in several subsequent key UN documents and declarations, including the two covenants on human rights. In the case of colonial peoples, it even attained the status of an international 'right'. It is quite true that outside the colonial context, self-determination is not a right and is understood by most international lawyers to be subordinate to territorial integrity.[35] A fortified right to self-determination of the sort proposed would indeed expand this legal status, making the principle a qualified right. But self-determination's continued public enunciation since the days of President Wilson, combined with its articulation in key international legal documents, makes a fortified right far from a novel legal departure. Rather, it would strengthen what is already present.

But I do not expect such a strengthening any time soon. Judging from the current legal and political consensus among major UN members, the will to abridge sovereignty is precisely what the states of the UN are lacking. On this criterion, there is little imminent prospect for a right to self-determination of any kind. As I have mentioned, in approving interventions since the end of the Cold War, the UN Security Council has been loathe to admit that its actions constitute intervention in domestic affairs. Self-determination, far from rivalling any of these values in prestige, is even less likely to take priority over sovereignty in international law. This is just as true of a remedial right as it is of a general right. Indeed, the distance between the present status quo and any fortified right to self-determination is arguably far greater than the distance between my Primary Right Theory and Remedial Right Only Theories, once the qualifications in my principles of self-determination are taken into account.

Is there a scenario in which self-determination would evolve into something like a 'right'? Most likely, it would first occur through the recognition policies of states who support self-determination. To this date, such recognition has not occurred, not even in one suggestive case – Germany's recognition of Croatia and Slovenia in 1991. There has been much debate about whether Germany's decision, joined by the EC, was impulsive. But whatever its effects, there is little evidence that it arose from a conscious endorsement of any general right to self-determination. Far more likely, Germany and the EC were merely recognizing the successor states to a dissolved federation.

Can domestic constitutions effectively institutionalize self-determination?

If self-determination is not about to become a principle of international law, perhaps it will become institutionalized in another form: the domestic constitutions of states. Most often, proponents of a constitutional right to self-determination envision it as right to secede.[36] But a right to secede in a constitution might at first appear an odd hedge against success, somewhat like putting a divorce clause in a marriage covenant: such a reservation might seem to call into question the very association. But the analogy may not be accurate. It is open to question whether a political association requires the absolute commitment to permanence on which a sound marriage depends. Grounds may even be found to allow a substate community within a state the possibility of exit, even at the moment at which the union forms.

The impartial enforcement criterion

Secession clauses are quite rare. When they existed, their efficacy was often doubtful. Witness only the constitution of the former Soviet Union, whose tanks stationed in Lithuania mocked the right of exit. A robust constitutional right to self-determination is a practice the effects of which one can only begin to theorize. Here is what one would expect: it ought to apply the requirements of just self-determination – a plebiscite, and the qualifications for liberalism and democracy, secession as a last resort, and so on. In any effective domestic constitution, a right of self-determination would be prescribed procedures for achieving these requirements. How exacting and onerous these requirements would be depends on how difficult it is believed self-determination ought to be in a particular state. Depending on the status of minorities within potential secessionist regions, the history of conflict in the state, the human rights practices of a regional government likely to become a national government, and other considerations of incentive and cost, the procedures would be made more or less difficult. At the very least a claimant group would be asked to conduct a plebiscite of its members, which is what democracy requires.

These requirements for popular choice, because they can be specified as procedures and identify the proper sequence of activities, are the easiest ones to specify, implement, and verify, even impartially. Other standards for self-determination are much more difficult to determine. Has a group met appropriate standards of liberalism, democracy, and respect for minorities? What are its distributive obligations? Does it merit the last resort of political independence? Such requirements are not met simply by fulfilling a duty, carrying out a procedure which can be verified, but require a judicial body to make the subjective determination of their fulfilment. But where might such a body be found? Within the domestic realm, it is difficult to imagine a court with credible impartiality. A national court would likely represent the larger state; a court within the breakaway region would likely represent the interests of that region. An international judicial body could arbitrate more impartially, but would require even further institutional innovation; its realization is even more distant. There is also a difficult question of ongoing enforcement. Once a region has seceded, its sovereignty makes it difficult for outsiders to enforce its compliance – such is a feature of the Westphalian system. A potential solution, containing possibilities for enforcement, but weaker on the impartiality criterion, is for interested outside states or regional organizations of states to enforce settlements, or at least provide incentives for compliance with them. An example: the US might use trade privileges or NAFTA membership to pressure an independent Quebec to respect the rights of anglophones and aboriginals.

The problem of perverse effects

What is most troubling about a domestic constitutional right to secede is a perverse effect on constitutional orders, especially democracies. It would undermine their stability.[37] The source of the problem would be the blackmail power which separatists would gain. Wielding a right to secede, any group – even one that is only potentially separatist – would become able to blackmail the larger state. In a federal republic, the region could make every question, even vital national questions of defence and providing public goods, a question of secession, threatening to exit should the larger state fail to accede.[38] A variety of ill consequences for civic life might follow. Collective action problems in providing public goods would become ever more intractable. A group constantly threatening separation might also undermine civic unity, destroy the cultural identity that eases cooperation in all common projects.[39] It is at the birth of a state federation that the problem of unity would be most acute, for then a right to secede might prevent cohesiveness from forming. With this reasoning, Cass Sunstein opposed including secessionist clauses in newly formed Eastern European constitutions.[40] Over the course of a state's growth, a right to secede might encourage a nascent separatist group to radicalize its unique identity. In reaction, a central state government, anticipating this dynamic, might repress this identity by forbidding freedom of speech and worse.

Is the problem of blackmail, then, so formidable that it makes a domestic constitutional right to secede unworkable? In fact, the presumption of inevitability is too simple and hasty. Even to refer to all separatist groups' potential leverage as blackmail is already tendentious, and prejudges the appropriateness of this power. It is true that some separatists might well exercise something quite like blackmail. These are groups whose intention to depart is weak or ephemeral, but whose leaders capitalize upon latent separtist urges in order to extract concessions. Wayne Norman aptly calls their demands 'vanity secessions'.[41] But we can imagine other groups with sincere demands, the majority of whose members prefer separation, groups who satisfy the criteria of liberalism, democracy and minority treatment. Such groups may suffer mistreatment at the hands of their central government as well. These are indeed the groups for whom is desired a moral right of self-determination and a strong negotiating position against their central governments. One ought to conceive their leverage as 'empowerment', rather than 'blackmail'. Their claim ought to be balanced against territorial integrity, not subordinated to it. Of course, most groups fall between the vanity secessionists and the ideal group described. But as long as there are groups which do not merit the description of blackmailer, it should not be assumed that all groups are subverters.

It is not necessarily the case that a right to secede would undermine democracy, either. If the appropriate qualifications to a right to secede are judged and enforced, then the leaders of vanity secessions will find their distributive claims rejected, the votes they need to sustain their claim lacking, and their exit threats thus robbed of their credibility, no longer effective. In other cases, one could imagine a right to secede helping a federal state to form; perhaps it would induce a wary group to join in the first place.[42] If a region's members did develop a separatist cause over time a constitutionally prescribed procedure might even help to avoid bloodshed, temper radicalism and perhaps defuse popular support for secession. Rather than give a group blackmail power to veto the state's decisions on a constant basis, the right might give them the leverage they need to negotiate a lasting settlement based on a new, decentralized system. Failing to grant leverage to a group, by contrast, may prove to be the very measure that leads to a hostile and violent break-up.

Again, one of the problems with predicting the effects of a right to secede is that there is so little empirical evidence. But a couple of cases serve well as thought experiments: Quebec and Slovakia. Quebec is a region the inhabitants of which voted against secession by a thin margin; Slovakia is a region which in fact seceded; and both cases are ones in which some blood was shed over the question. Now in neither case did the larger state's constitution (Canada, Czechoslovakia) contain a right to secede. But in both cases, the larger state's government as well as the separatist region were willing to abide by common political procedures, and, in the case of Quebec, a referendum. It is this mutual consent that makes these regions experimental proxies for constitutional secession. Now, both cases admittedly provide reasons to be sceptical. From a democratic standpoint, the procedures were contested and deeply imperfect. The Canadian referenda worded the question of independence confusingly; Slovakia never held a bona fide referendum; in both cases, minority rights guarantees were questionable. But the crucial question is: rather than imperfect procedures for separation, what if there had been no (approximation of a) right to secede at all? What if the Czechoslovakian and the Canadian governments had failed to allow even the possibility of secession?

It seems difficult to doubt that the separatist drive would have been considerably fueled, that the procedures would have been far more hotly contested, and that blood would far more likely have been shed, had the central government refused to consent to any procedure for considering secession. Nor is there evidence in either case that it was an implicit right to secede that helped to establish or deepen separatist identities. We must not make the mistake of thinking that messy separatist procedures are necessarily the fault of institutions; rather, they could be, and usually are, the result of deep conflicts the roots of which lay in remembrances of historical injustices, and linguistic and cultural identities. This, I believe, was true in both Quebec and Slovakia. There is also little evidence, in either these or in other hypothetical cases, that an actual right to secede would have brought central government to quell separatism pre-emptively. Historically, perceived centralized resisitance has in fact contributed to the formation and radicalizing of national identities, only augmenting separatist drives. The nations of the Austro-Hungarian empire and the American colonies are two examples. Democratic procedure, by contrast, may well dampen separatist vigour.

It is still possible that blackmail and destabilized democracy could result from a right to secede. But salutary and unifying effects may result, too. How are we to know which effect will prevail? Much will ride on how a constitutional right to secede is designed. Constitutions can make secession easier or more difficult through the procedural hurdles which they raise. High procedural hurdles can best deter blackmail and assist secession or the attainment of federal autonomy where it is justified. Victimized groups will most likely be united in favour of secession, the most likely to sustain claims to grievances and threats, and, fittingly, the most likely to clear high procedural hurdles. The same hurdles would hinder what I have called elsewhere an 'arbitrageur of separatism', the leader who relies upon shaky popular support for self-determination to extract concessions from the larger state, to conduct blackmail. After all, in order to exert this leverage, such a leader must be able to make a credible threat of secession, likely only if he or she already enjoys strong popular support. Otherwise, the claim will fade into the background of the affairs of the federation's politics –where it ideally belongs. It is difficult to say what such high procedural hurdles consist of, for constitutional design is highly contextual. They might include supermajorities, clearly worded referenda, and perhaps a requirement for multiple referenda over a specified time.[43]

The most difficult dilemma of the moral right to self-determination is finding the terms of a just settlement (e.g. the economic obligations involved). Is there a form of arbitration that could realistically attain the assent of the disputants and prove capable of delivering a just settlement? The question is difficult to answer; solutions are likely to vary. Several possibilities have potential. The highest court of the larger state might serve well, if it is independent enough. An international board of arbitration, a consensual third party arbiter, or some other forum might also work. In constitutional design, moral theory has limits. Its purpose is to propose what constitutions ought to discourage, and what they ought to allow.

Possibility of realization?

The world does not seem any closer to constitutional rights to secede than it does to an international legal right. With limited exceptions such as the Ethiopian Constitution of 1993, few states are proposing to adopt one. Yet in some locales like Quebec and Slovakia, as I have suggested, something like an implicit right to secede emerged, and was agreed upon. Both parties respected the outcome of a procedure, even if they disputed some of its terms or its execution. It is in such cases that the right of self-determination has come closest to being realized in the domestic context.

Conclusion

Legalizing self-determination in international law or a domestic constitution seems far from realization, and judging its effects is a speculative enterprise. But insofar as philosophers' conclusions are heeded, perhaps it is for the best that they take up the question well in advance. At least the problem will be well considered. The first step has been to determine the appropriate moral principles involved. I have proposed such principles in my previous argument that self-determination is a basic right, but a qualified one. Its value lies in its promotion of democracy for a people. Here I have asked: What would be the effects of legalizing such a right? Should just self-determination be promoted through international law and in domestic constitutions, or should it be confined to moral advocacy? The questions are important, for the perverse effects of poorly designed institutions of self-determination may well take the form of increased violence, which accompanies proliferation of claims where minorities are endangered and may fracture democratic institutions. Would institutionalizing self-determination reduce this violence, increase it, or have little effect on it?

My concluding answer is most unsatisfying: it depends. It depends on all the factors that are most difficult to predict. We do not know how effective a strengthened international legal right or a domestic constitution would be in bracing just self-determination claims while enforcing the qualifications, discouraging unjust claims, and limiting violence. If it were the case that these institutions are certain fiascos, that virtually all self-determination claims are likely to bring evils far disproportionate to any injustices which separatist peoples suffer within their larger state, and if virtually all self-determination movements are blackmailers, fomenters of vanity secessions, then we should not make self-determination any easier.

I have tried to make the case that this description is not necessarily accurate and that competent institutions are conceivable. Given the limited evidence, I make no stronger claim. In an anarchic world of sovereign states, the Westphalian world, institutions to promote self-determination will be incapable of perfect enforcement. But the world in which self-determination movements occur is also imperfect. Apart from whether self-determination is legalized, movements will arise, many of them violent, many of them yielding new states which do violence to new minorities, bringing forth familiar evils. The vital question is whether, in a world in which self-determination exists, institutions would, on balance, channel them justly? Would institutions improve the situation or make it worse? That, again, depends. It depends on the effectiveness of the institutions, and on how likely self-determination movements are to be affected by them.

NOTES

1. Note that the Quebecois case did produce some acts of terror in the 1960s.
2. A. Buchanan, 'Theories of Secession', *Philosophy and Public Affairs* 26/1 (1997) p.35.
3. See Allen Buchanan, *Secession: The Morality of Political Divorce from Fort Sumter to Lithuania to Quebec* (Boulder, CO: Westview Press, 1991); Buchanan (note 2); and Allen Buchanan, 'Democracy and Secession', in Margaret Moore (ed.), *National Self-Determination and Secession* (Oxford: Oxford University Press, 1998) pp.14–33. Lea Brilmayer's perspective also requires grievances; she focuses mainly on historical grievances. See L. Brilmayer, 'Secession and Self-Determination: A Territorial Interpretation', *Yale Journal of International Law* 19 (1991) pp.177–202.
4. As Buchanan points out, they are thus Primary Right Theories, not necessarily Primary Rights *Only* Theories: Buchanan (note 2) p.41.
5. See D. Philpott, 'In Defence of Self-Determination', *Ethics* 105/2 (1995) pp.352–85. Other perspectives falling into this category include Thomas Pogge, 'Cosmopolitanism and Sovereignty', *Ethics* 103 (1992) pp.48–75; M. Walzer, 'The New Tribalism', *Dissent* 39 (1992) pp.164–71; H. Beran, 'A Liberal Theory of Secession', *Political Studies* 32 (1984) pp.21–31; Yael Tamir, *Liberal Nationalism* (Princeton, NJ: Princeton University Press, 1993) pp.73–4; D. Donnelly, 'State and Substates in a Free World: A Theory of National Self-Determination', *Nationalism & Ethnic Politics* 2/2 (Summer 1996) pp.286–311; C. Wellman, 'A Defence of Secession and Political Self-Determination', *Philosophy and Public Affairs* (1995) pp.142–71; D. Gauthier, 'Breaking Up: An Essay on Secession', *Canadian Journal of Philosophy* 24 (1994) pp.357–72; and K. Nielsen, 'Secession: The Case of Quebec', *Journal of Applied Philosophy* 10 (1993) pp.29–43.
6. See Buchanan (note 3, 1998).
7. See especially Donald Horowitz, 'Self-Determination: Politics, Philosophy, and Law', in Moore (note 3) pp.181–214.
8. See A. Buchanan (note 2) pp.46–9; and Buchanan (note 3, 1998) pp.15–18. See also Wayne Norman, 'The Ethics of Secession and the Regulation of Secessionist politics', in Moore (note 3) pp.34–61.
9. On the current status of self-determination in international law, see Hurst Hannum, *Autonomy, Sovereignty, and Self-Determination: The Accommodation of Conflicting Rights* (Philadelphia, PA: University of Pennsylvania Press, 1990). Although it is sometimes thought that the treatment of eastern European peoples in the minority treaties that ended the First World War was an example of self-determination, in this case, as part of the vision of Woodrow Wilson, self-determination was only realized to a limited extent. Plebiscites were held and borders drawn to accommodate the aspirations of minority peoples, but the treaties largely recognized states that had already come into *de facto* existence, not peoples within already established states. More importantly, no lasting institutions to promote self-determination beyond the settlement itself were created.
10. Ted Robert Gurr, *Minorities at Risk: A Global View of Ethnopolitical Conflicts* (Washington, DC: United States Institute of Peace, 1993) p.316.
11. David C. Rapoport, 'The Importance of Space in Violent Ethno-religious Strife', *Nationalism & Ethnic Politics* II/2 (Summer 1996) p.265.
12. Ted Robert Gurr and Barbara Harff, *Ethnic Conflict in World Politics* (Boulder, CO: Westview Press, 1994) p.160.
13. Philpott (note 5) pp.355–62.
14. In V.V. Ramana Murti, *Gandhi: Essential Writings* (New Delhi: Gandhi Peace Foundation, 1970) p.226.
15. Philpott (note 5) pp.360–62.
16. Ibid., pp.371–85.
17. Buchanan (note 3, 1998) p.23.
18. In interpreting my argument, Buchanan cites a passage from 'In Defence of Self-Determination' in which I explain that the institution of self-determination redraws a

group's political boundaries (I use a hypothetical group, 'the Utopians') so that they circumscribe the group as tightly as possible: Buchanan (note 3, 1998) p.23. In arguing that I am advocating homogenous politics, though, Buchanan takes the passage out of context. First, the purpose of the passage is typological, explaining how self-determination is distinct from other sorts of democratic institutions such as local government and minority representation schemes. Secondly, I explain elsewhere that the central justifying reason for self-determination is its promotion of democratic autonomy, not homogeneity. Elsewhere in his piece, Buchanan takes issue with the autonomy justification, but here he argues as if homogeneity is the central motivation. Thirdly, it should be kept in mind that 'the Utopians' – a people united in their desire for separation and without minorities – are an heuristic, a bracketing device, that I adopt provisionally in order to demonstrate the rationale for self-determination. I spend the second portion of the article dealing with the many complications that exist in our non-Utopian world.

19. Buchanan recognizes that in some cases a 'condition of radical pluralism' of religious and cultural identities will erode the 'background condition' of commonality required for democratic decision. Here, it is best to 'redraw political boundaries to reflect the fact that there are two political communities, not one'. This is an odd exception for Buchanan to make, as he now seems to be endorsing separation even in the absence of a grievance. Nor does he offer a standard for how much pluralism there must be before we 'redraw boundaries', making it difficult to know how wide this exception is supposed to be. But most importantly, Buchanan ignores that in all self-determination claims, a group has already identified itself as one with a separate identity – usually it calls itself a nation, sometimes it is defined ethnically or racially – and in almost all cases it (or a majority of its members) asserts that its separate identity can only be realized through some form of political separation. Its very claim, then, is that the background condition of commonality required for cooperation in a common polity does not exist. We may lament that a people has chosen thus, and desire that they choose to remain and cooperate, but the fact is that they have not – and this is the predicament that a theory of self-determination must address. Of course, some self-determination movements will be nothing more than elite attempts to extract economic concessions, will lack a majority, will be illiberal or undemocratic, and/or will mistreat their own minorities. But in these cases, the theory's very qualifications provide that such claims will not pass. The achievement of homogeneity, though, is not a disqualification, nor does it particularly enhance the moral quality of a self-determination claim.

It might be objected that the real threat of self-determination to multi-cultural democracy is not that it allows a separatist group to leave, but that it encourages separatist movements to arise in the first place, or that it allows a potentially separatist group to use a threat of exit as a constant veto over the state's decisions, thus undermining democratic decision-making. Both objections I deal with below. Here I only argue that self-determination is not inherently a rejection of the ideal of multicultural democracy.

20. I mean this only in the general sense that most Americans do not object to apportioning tracts of land for Native Americans to live and govern themselves. I do not deny the many contentious issues surrounding the terms of this separation.

21. Buchanan makes a similar point: note 2, pp.56–9.

22. On self-determination's legal status, see Hannum (note 9).

23. Ibid., p.49.

24. See T. Franck, 'The Emerging Right to Democratic Governance', *American Journal of International Law* 86 (1992) pp.46–91; and David Scheffer, 'Toward A Modern Doctrine of Humanitarian Intervention', *University of Toledo Law Review* 23 (1992) pp.253–94.

25. On humanitarian intervention, see Anthony Clark Arend and Robert Beck, *International Law and the Use of Force: Beyond the U.N. Charter* (New York: Routledge, 1993).

26. On the legal significance of the EC's criteria, see M. Weller, 'The International Response to the Dissolution of the Socialist Federal Republic of Yugoslavia', *American Journal of International Law* 86 (1992) pp.569–607.
27. On international legal instruments for human rights, see Hannum (note 9) pp.3–118.
28. Buchanan (note 2) pp.46–7.
29. A classic article on Westphalia and its significance for the international system is L. Gross, 'The Peace of Westphalia', *American Journal of International Law* 42 (1948) pp.20–41.
30. Self-determination does not always increase the number of states. It could take the form of fusion: witness the unification of Germany and Italy in the nineteenth century. Of course, this form of self-determination is hardly a challenge to the Westphalia system either.
31. See Franck (note 24); and Scheffer (note 24).
32. Donald Horowitz emphasizes these problems in his 'Self-determination: Politics, Philosophy, and Law' (note 7).
33. Buchanan (note 2) pp.42, 51.
34. Buchanan does attempt such a demonstration in 'Democracy and Secession' (note 3). His argument concerning international law, however, is independent of this demonstration, and may be criticized independently.
35. See Hannum (note 9) pp.27–49.
36. A right to general self-determination, one that might include revisions to the terms of a federation but less than independence, is almost unheard of (although not wholly implausible, in my view).
37. Several critics raise the issue. See C. Sunstein, 'Constitutionalism and Secession', *The University of Chicago Law Review* 58/2 (1991) pp.633–70; Buchanan (note 3) pp.47–9.
38. For the logic of exit and voice, see Albert Hirschman, *Exit, Voice, and Loyalty* (Cambridge: Cambridge University Press, 1970).
39. On the importance of civic unity and shared identity for the functioning of democracy, see David Miller, *On Nationality* (Oxford: Clarendon Press, 1995) pp.66–73, 81–8.
40. Sunstein (note 37).
41. See Norman (note 8) pp.52–5.
42. Buchanan mentions this possibility in his helpful discussion of a constitutional right to secede in Buchanan (note 3, 1991) pp.127–46.
43. For a more extensive discussion of these procedures, see Norman (note 8) pp.53–5.

6

Democracy, Commitment Problems and Managing Ethnic Violence: The Case of India and Sri Lanka

MARTHA CRENSHAW

Based on a case study of the Indian intervention in Sri Lanka's ethnic war from 1987 to 1990, this article explores the conditions under which democracies can act as effective third parties to resolve civil violence. India's experience as guarantor of a peace settlement in Sri Lanka suggests that not only the intractability of civil conflicts but the power of domestic pressures shape intervention policies and outcomes. Decision-makers depend on the support of important domestic political elites – political parties, interest groups, press, and governmental bureaucracies – as well as the approval of the public who can reject them in periodic elections. In order to enforce peace settlements, third-party guarantors must have a firm sense of the belligerents' intentions and resources, sensitivity to the dynamics of the conflict, and freedom of action. At the same time, democratic leaders must consider the role of timing, the influence of internal bargaining, the importance of credible 'staying power', and personal reputation.

This article considers the relationship between democracy and effective third party intervention to resolve civil violence. What impact does a democratic form of government have on a state's capacity to act as an external mediator, peace-enforcer, or peace-builder in ethnic conflicts?

Recent research on civil war settlement stresses the problem of credible commitments.[1] Even if a negotiated compromise is reached that is acceptable in principle to both government and opposition, the combatants themselves are unable to guarantee that they will abide by its terms in the long run. Nor can they promise credibly not to try to exploit the other side during the transition period of demobilization, disarmament, and disengagement. Distrust between the former belligerents is too great and the incentives for defection from cooperation are too high. Thus an outside mediator or enforcer is necessary to guarantee both security and the implementation of new power-sharing arrangements.

Successful mediation and peace enforcement require, first, that third party commitments be appropriately timed. As Zartman explains, the 'ripe moment' of a 'hurting stalemate', the window of opportunity when a settlement is possible, is both objective and subjective. It depends on both the military balance of power and the perceptions of all parties, who must feel that they have no option except reconciliation, even if it is considered second best.[2] The mediator must know when to expend political resources on negotiations, and a guarantor must know when the dynamics of the conflict permit the construction of a settlement that is worth supporting with military force.

A second requirement is 'staying power'. No commitment is credible unless the third party can see it through. Intervention will be ineffective if it ends prematurely.[3] Outside guarantors must stay until a new government is consolidated, with a security force trained and equipped to maintain order. The guarantor thus needs adequate resources and motivation to stay the course, as well as the ability to estimate how long it will take to accomplish the task of reconstruction. This is a distinctly future-oriented requirement.

How well can a democracy be expected to perform this role? As Vertzberger argues, political capabilities are as important as military and economic resources.[4] Accountability is the hallmark of democratic leadership, and the internal and external legitimacy of policy must always be at the forefront of decision-makers' attention. At the societal level, as the costs of intervention mount, the 'theatre of war' is extended to include the home front.[5] Waterman also emphasizes that democratic leadership is based on an ability to form coalitions.[6] Decision-makers depend on the support of important political elites in domestic politics – political parties, interest groups, press, or government bureaucracies – as well as the approval of the public who can reject them in periodic elections. Vertzberger adds that a democratic leader's freedom of decision is constrained by both the size of his or her parliamentary majority and the formal and informal rules and laws that set the limits of authority.[7] In addition, interest group demands are channelled through bureaucracies, and the degree of openness and complexity of the political system will thus affect the regime's susceptibility to outside influence.

The formulation of policy involves internal political bargaining as well as assessment of external conditions and conceptions of foreign policy goals. Third parties care about the terms of the settlement not just because they seek an end to the fighting, but also because they are concerned about their own reputations. A failed intervention is costly in terms of prestige as well as material resources. Furthermore, since external mediation is often required for negotiations to succeed, it is likely that the mediators will become the guarantors of the settlement they have helped arrange. This prior involvement increases their stakes.

These conditions impose constraints on the types of warfare democracies can practice and the type of outcome they can support.[8] Vertzberger refers to 'moral, value-based, self-imposed limitations' combined with the problems of conducting war in a civilian environment.[9] The peace keeper cannot take full advantage of military superiority. A recent collection of case studies focuses on the stages of 'getting in, staying in, and getting out'.[10] The study concludes that the initial decision to intervene is more oriented toward strategic interests, while staying in and getting out are more sensitive to domestic pressures. The proposition that democracies seek to avoid casualties, both among their own troops and among the population of the targeted state, is also supported.[11] Furthermore, Downs suggests that democratic leaders are attracted to a strategy of 'gambling for resurrection': the withdrawal of military forces is unlikely to be accomplished by an administration in power at the time of deployment.[12] Once the military is committed, a leader's political future depends on success; it is better to stay on and gamble to win than to withdraw with a loss that will certainly end a public career. Vertzberger concurs: 'intervention decisions are often difficult to make, but once taken are equally or even more difficult to reverse.'[13] In democracies, intervention decisions require heavy investments of time, internal bargaining and involvement of personal reputation. A democratic leader will be reluctant to reverse the decision even if the results are negative. Adjustment of policy comes at a high domestic cost.

Whether the prescription for a durable peace settlement is a new institutional structure based on negotiation and mutual acceptance of future power-sharing, or an imposed settlement based on the domination of one side by the other, remains an open question.[14] If a compromise is necessary for long-term political stability, then the outside guarantor must encourage moderation over extremism on both sides of the conflict and engage elites and publics in the process of accommodation to a new order that will be perceived as legitimate.

However, Licklider, analyzing data from 91 post-1945 civil wars, found that in wars over identity issues, settlements based on military victories were more enduring than those based on negotiated compromises.[15] Moreover, Betts claims that an intervening power will have to choose between peace and justice; if peace is what is wanted, the outside power should support the stronger side regardless of legitimacy.[16]

Nevertheless, democracies will not usually support a settlement that is undemocratic, although it might be more stable. This constraint involves normative conceptions by both elites and the public. Simply ending the conflict, perhaps by supporting one side's decisive victory over the other, will not suffice even if this solution saves the most lives and is the most stable over the long term. There may indeed be a tension between peace and justice, as Betts argues, but democracies may not be able to enforce a solution that is not perceived as morally right. For example, Peceny has suggested that American military interventions follow a pro-liberalization tendency in order to forge a domestic political consensus, not for security reasons.[17] The public and Congress, especially liberal internationalists in the Democratic Party, will not support military action that is not intended to promote democracy. Claims based on establishing international security do not have the same appeal.

This does not mean intermediaries must be strictly neutral in the conflict. Recent work suggests that they need not be impartial; in fact, security may be enhanced if the third party favours the minority group in the conflict.[18] Betts refers to impartiality as an 'Olympian presumption'.[19] In fact, he argues that if the purpose of intervention is to make peace, not just preside over it, impartiality is likely to prolong the conflict.[20] Self-interest is to be expected, and patronage can be an important source of leverage over the combatants. Altruism is not required.

The case used to explore these issues is the Indian intervention in Sri Lanka's ethnic war, from 1987 to 1990. This analysis illustrates some of the difficulties that democracies may face as mediators and guarantors. Ironically, at this time India and Sri Lanka were the only two democracies in South Asia, and they became jointly embroiled in a protracted conflict over Tamil nationalism. India was also beset by separatist insurgencies at home, principally in Kashmir and the Punjab, and Sri Lanka faced a radical Sinhalese opposition movement. This analysis thus does not focus on the unique qualities of the Indian political system or the individual leadership styles of Prime Ministers

Indira and Rajiv Gandhi. It simplifies a series of complex events and omits discussion of competing explanations for Indian behaviour, such as strategic conceptions. Fortunately there are numerous accounts both of India's involvement and of the Sinhala-Tamil conflict.[21]

The timing of intervention

Consider first the timing of India's initiatives. Indian involvement began with covert assistance to Tamil rebels against the Sinhala-dominated government in Colombo.[22] Discrimination against Tamils in Sri Lanka (a minority of about 18 per cent of a population of 18 million) had increased steadily since the 1950s, and as moderate demands for equality of access to political and economic resources were rebuffed, extremist groups gained the ascendancy. In 1983, deadly anti-Tamil riots in Sri Lanka, which the government of J. R. Jayewardene failed to control, provoked Indira Gandhi to furnish sanctuary, weapons and training to the various Tamil militant groups, including the Liberation Tigers of Tamil Eelam (LTTE). But the critical determinant of the Indian initiative was the effect of communal violence in Sri Lanka on political elites in the southern Indian state of Tamil Nadu, whose support Mrs Gandhi needed. The Tamils in Sri Lanka are a minority within Sri Lanka, but if borders were reconfigured and the 60 million Tamil citizens of India were added to their number, Tamils would form a regional majority. Refugees from Sri Lanka were pouring into India. Cross-border sympathy and connections were running high, and Mrs Gandhi felt intense pressure from Tamil Nadu politicians who were already competing to help the 'boys'. Openly supporting a Tamil independence movement was out of the question for a multi-ethnic state already struggling with secessionist minorities, although Mrs Gandhi did send a special emissary to facilitate discussions between the Sri Lankan government and Tamil groups. Covert support for the Tamil opposition seemed the best way of controlling the extremists, gaining leverage over the Sri Lankan government, maintaining the loyalty of political allies who could keep the Congress (I) party in power, and forestalling eruptions of Tamil nationalism that might threaten the integrity of India.

J. N. Dixit, former Indian High Commissioner to Sri Lanka, refers to 'a perception that if India did not support the Tamil cause in Sri Lanka and if the Government of India tried to question the political and emotional feelings of Tamil Nadu there would be a resurgence of Tamil separatism in India'.[23] His view is that if Mrs Gandhi had remained 'detached' or 'just formally correct' about events in Sri Lanka, she risked 'disenchantment' in Tamil Nadu. The 1983 riots precipitated her decision. So, for both domestic political ('Emotions were high in Tamil Nadu') and national security reasons, Mrs Gandhi had to respond.

In 1984, Mrs Gandhi was assassinated by her Sikh bodyguards, and her son Rajiv replaced her as party leader. A large sympathy vote gave the Congress Party an overwhelming majority in parliamentary elections. In his first year as Prime Minister Rajiv Gandhi was enormously popular, and he did not have to face new elections until 1989. He initially took a much more conciliatory approach to India's ethnic conflicts than his mother had done and, extending this attitude to Sri Lanka, in 1985 began a series of mediation efforts, bringing together the Sri Lankan government and the Tamil opposition, including the armed militant groups. Possibly the security of his political position allowed him to take some risks to try to resolve the Sri Lankan conflict. The general euphoria that accompanied his first year may also have made him over-confident: mediation proved to be extremely frustrating. Neither side would make concessions. Talks went on from the summer of 1985 through the summer and winter of 1986, with one proposal succeeding another. India replaced negotiators, offered new ideas, cajoled both sides, all to no avail. Rajiv Gandhi had little to show for his close personal involvement in the negotiations. Clearly the conflict was not 'ripe for resolution', whatever that might mean. By February of 1987 he suspended his efforts.

Elsewhere in Indian politics the honeymoon period was definitely over. The Congress Party lost a series of state elections. Gandhi's promises to reform the authoritarian structure of the party and to liberalize the economy remained empty. An accord he had brokered in the Punjab broke down. A major corruption scandal involved arms purchases from the Swedish company Bofors. A cabinet minister resigned to join the opposition. Gandhi was criticized for inexperience and inconsistency. Furthermore, elections were now less than two years away.

In Sri Lanka negotiations broke down, and the conflict escalated abruptly. Both sides appeared bent on a military solution. The LTTE, which had relocated from Madras to Jaffna, declared the independence of the northern Tamil province. Jayewardene responded with a combined military offensive and economic blockade designed to crush

Tamil aspirations for once and for all. As the Sri Lankan army advanced on Jaffna, leaving numerous civilian casualties through indiscriminate bombings and artillery fire, dismay and anguish grew in Tamil Nadu. More refugees fled the fighting in Sri Lanka and sought asylum in India (reportedly 150,000 by the end of 1987). Gandhi then initiated a sequence of military actions. In June the Indian air force launched an airlift of humanitarian supplies to the besieged residents of Jaffna, a largely symbolic gesture that nevertheless violated Sri Lankan sovereignty, demonstrated India's vast military superiority, and compelled the government to announce a cease-fire. In July, India signed a bilateral accord with the Sri Lankan government that provided for substantial devolution of power to Tamil interests, in return for which Sri Lanka was to refrain from becoming too friendly with powers perceived as hostile to Indian interests. Jayewardene promptly invited India to guarantee the mutual accord, and India agreed. On 30 July 1987, the Indian Peace-Keeping Force (IPKF) was deployed to Sri Lanka. In Tamil Nadu, elsewhere in India and internationally, the action was praised. Gandhi was even proposed for the Nobel Peace Prize.

India's national interests may have dictated that India respond to this crisis on her southern border. However, as Manor suggests, the crisis did provide a convenient opportunity in terms of domestic politics.[24] Dixit emphatically disagrees:

> The allegation that Rajiv Gandhi desired a diplomatic success to divert attention from domestic criticism which he was facing over Bofors and other issues is not valid from what I recall ... I never discerned any subconscious motivation or undercurrent of thought processes on the part of Rajiv Gandhi linking his involvement in the Sri Lankan situation with his domestic political predicament.[25]

Dixit recognizes that Gandhi might not have been frank about his intentions, but he insists that Gandhi's advisers would have talked about domestic concerns had they been critical. Nevertheless K. M. de Silva argues that Gandhi signed the Accord for four reasons: he needed a political 'triumph' to offset recent electoral failures; he wanted to settle the conflict while the Tamil Nadu Chief Minister, M. G. Ramachandran, was still alive to keep order in Tamil Nadu politics; he was tired of acting as a mediator and wanted to end the problem; and he wanted a settlement while President Jayewardene was still in power.[26]

This account suggests that democracies are not free to choose the timing of their interventions. It is the effect of external crises on internal politics that drives decisions, not the international environment *per se*. Decision-makers must react to demands from constituents, which become particularly acute when cross-border ethnic identities are involved. Furthermore, it was not necessarily the central government's perception of crisis in Sri Lanka or a reaction to a general groundswell of public opinion across the country that dictated action. Dixit admits: 'The details of the Agreement were not publicised and discussed in detail by the media or Parliaments, either of Sri Lanka or of India. Had such discussions preceded the finalisation of the Agreement, it would never have come about ...'[27] Rather, it was pressure from influential local political elites. In Tamil Nadu concern was generated not only by ethnic identification but by political rivalry between two Tamil parties and the exigencies of India's federal and parliamentary system. Democratic states are thus prone to the 'process bias' that Sisk warns against: 'any yes will do'.[28] Furthermore, if third parties are motivated primarily by domestic political considerations, the difficulty judging the intentions of the adversaries in a conflict will be exacerbated, although it is essential to the timing of effective intervention.[29] At the least, even if democratic leaders are motivated more by national security interests than by domestic pressures, they are vulnerable to charges that they are creating a diversion.

Guaranteeing security during the transition

In principle, a key obligation of the third party in conflict resolution is to provide security during the transition period, so that the warring parties need not fear each other during a period of high mutual vulnerability and uncertainty about the future. This role involves enforcing the terms of a cease-fire so that the fighting stops, and it often involves facilitating the demobilization and disarmament of the combatants. Walter argues that credible security guarantees by third parties must fulfil three basic conditions: the outside enforcer must have an interest in doing it, be willing to use force, and be able to signal resolve.[30] However, she found that disarmament had a negative effect on security, because 'adversaries had no illusions about their former enemy's ability to hide or procure weapons if they so chose'.[31] Letting the combatants keep some weapons made them more likely to implement the peace agreement. Although disarmament has conventionally been a central part of peace enforcement operations, it is recognized as one of the most vexing elements because it is rarely consensual.[32]

In official terms, the Indo-Sri Lankan Accord was simple, direct and optimistic. There was to be an immediate cease-fire. Shortly after, the Sri Lankan army stationed in the northern and eastern provinces was to withdraw to barracks. The Tamil militants (i.e. the LTTE, now clearly the dominant faction) were to surrender their arms in return for an amnesty. Indian troops, deployed at the request of President Jayewardene as soon as the Accord was signed, would supervise the cease-fire and receive the surrendered weapons. All this was expected to be accomplished within the week.

How well did the IPKF provide security? Although the Accord was not popular, the Sri Lankan army was not a problem. Paramilitary forces were disarmed. More than half the troops in the Jaffna peninsula were quickly shifted to fighting a Sinhalese insurgency in the south of the island; in fact, Indian aircraft helped ferry them down from the north to Colombo as they transferred in the IPKF. But the LTTE, after a few token surrenders of weapons, did not disarm. Within two months they had renounced the Accord entirely. The conflict was transformed into a war between the IPKF and the LTTE.

The first obstacle to effective enforcement was that the IPKF entered the fray with no clearly stated mission, inadequate intelligence (particularly about the LTTE's intentions and capabilities) and only a small number of military forces. Why? One reason was the haste with which the mission was organized, owing to lack of anticipation of the need to send troops. According to Dixit: 'There was hardly any time to give detailed briefings to Indian Commanders and army personnel, because New Delhi did not envisage any large-scale induction of its armed forces into Sri Lanka. They were rushed into Jaffna at a few hours' notice.'[33] The commander of the IPKF saw his responsibility as limited to maintaining law and order in the areas from which the Sri Lankan army had temporarily withdrawn, not enforcing the agreement.

There was also a mistaken expectation that although the LTTE was not a party to the peace Accord, and continued to insist on full Tamil independence, they would acquiesce. De Silva claims that the exclusion of the LTTE was at the insistence of the Sri Lankan government, with whom India agreed in order to ensure that her foreign policy concerns about Sri Lanka's pro-Western orientation were addressed.[34] Dixit argues that LTTE leader Vellupillai Prabhakaran did not initially wish to sign the Accord, but then changed his mind. In any case, Indian policy-makers believed that the institutional arrangements proposed in the Accord offered Tamils the best deal yet, better than they ever could have achieved without Indian help. Up until that point the Sri Lankan government had refused to join the northern and eastern provinces because of the mixed population of the latter, but they now agreed to the concession. It was thought that India's superior military power as well as her affinity for the Tamil cause would give her leverage with the LTTE. However, if the LTTE did resist, victory was expected to be easy. India explicitly assured Sri Lanka that the LTTE would be disarmed by force if necessary. Dixit now concedes that Rajiv Gandhi was given bad advice by the military and intelligence agencies, as well as by Dixit himself.[35]

The IPKF had been in the field for only two months when relations with the LTTE soured. The LTTE not only refused to disarm but proceeded to attack rival militant groups in an effort to dominate the Tamil population, a pattern of internecine rivalry established earlier when they were all headquartered in Madras. The LTTE also used terrorism to drive Sinhalese and Muslim civilians out of areas with mixed populations. They began to criticize the IPKF in public and to organize popular protests, including a hunger strike by a prominent LTTE leader. A group of LTTE militants taken prisoner by Sri Lankan authorities committed suicide. Then in early October the LTTE directly attacked Indian soldiers.

Apparently the commanding general of the army's Southern Command opposed a direct confrontation with the LTTE; his preference, he later said, was to cut off their supply routes. A strategy of attrition would take longer, but the alternative he predicted was a full-fledged insurgency with India taking the role of the government.[36] His advice, however, was overruled at the top, in his view. The decision was made at the cabinet level to launch a military offensive against the LTTE, despite the fact that the IPKF units in Sri Lanka were not up to strength and probably were not yet adequate to the task, in terms of training and specialization.[37] Indian policy-makers were unwilling to wait for full mobilization and acquisition of the necessary intelligence.

Muni, quoting the Indian press, states that the Defence Minister and the Chief of Army Staff worked out the offensive strategy during a visit to Colombo on 9 October because the LTTE had broken an agreement it had made with Dixit.[38] He adds that Jayewardene pressured Indian leaders to take a firm stance, which was also what the LTTE wanted. Dixit agrees that it was the LTTE's reneging on an agreement about power-sharing arrangements and their assault on Indian forces that prompted India to use force.[39] Top-level military and intelligence officials supported Rajiv Gandhi in deciding to 'neutralize' the LTTE, whatever the scale of the operation.

India then proceeded to do what it had warned the Sri Lankan government against: seize Jaffna, which took longer than anticipated because of faulty intelligence. The LTTE was larger, better-disciplined, better-informed and better-armed than anyone had suspected. As the LTTE melted away into the jungles to conduct a classic guerrilla and terrorist campaign, over the next two years India deployed more and more troops to contain the insurgency. Dixit estimates that by the end of 1987, India had four divisions and two independent brigades in Sri Lanka.[40] Military operations were constrained by the need to avoid civilian casualties and to gain the support of the Tamil population. This meant that the military not only had to defeat the LTTE, but engage in winning 'hearts and minds', a task for which they were ill equipped. There were unforeseen terrain and logistics problems. The Indian press began calling the conflict 'India's Vietnam'. Moreover, the government in New Delhi was unwilling or unable to close off the sanctuary of Tamil Nadu. Small boats found the shallow waters of the Palk Straits no impediment to transporting arms and ammunition. Tamil Nadu Chief Minister M. G. Ramachandran, an avid supporter of the LTTE, died in December 1987, and the power struggle that followed exacerbated intra-elite competition for the Tamil nationalist constituency.

Nevertheless, as the IPKF acquired both experience and reinforcements, security was restored in some areas. In July, the government even cracked down on the LTTE in Tamil Nadu. This is not to say that the LTTE was destroyed, however. Muni describes confusion over whether the IPKF was ordered to destroy the LTTE as an organization and kill Prabakharan or whether military action was meant to coerce the LTTE into accepting the Accord.[41] Furthermore, while the military was taking casualties in order to defeat the LTTE, India's civilian intelligence agency (the Research and Analysis Wing, or RAW) continued to negotiate with them. Dixit concludes:

> Rajiv Gandhi could be partially blamed for the contradiction which characterised Indian policies. Though he had to instruct the armed forces to confront the LTTE, once they reverted to

terrorism, there was perhaps an emotional and psychological inhibition on his part to take drastic action against the LTTE. He had an innate sympathy for the legitimate rights and aspirations of Tamils. It is perhaps because of this mind-set that he permitted representatives of our intelligence agencies to continue negotiations with the LTTE even as the Indian forces were engaged in military operations against them.[42]

What led to these mistakes – the lack of preparation of the initial deployment, the misjudgment of the LTTE's intentions and capabilities, and the premature attempt to disarm and then 'neutralize' them? Was India's ambivalence about the military mission of the IPKF, in pursuit of what Dixit calls a 'two-track policy', a sensible carrot-and-stick approach, or simply confusion?

Possibly some of these disjunctures were owing to India's emphasis on civilian control of the military. Military leaders are often cautious about the use of force, especially in the absence of clear objectives, missions and rules of engagement. Most observers agree that the Indian military has a singular lack of influence over the policy-making process, a result of the distancing of the military from society generally.[43] Access to the political arena is through a civilian defence ministry. There is no equivalent to the American position of Chairman of the Joint Chiefs of Staff. The services have no unifying institution; they operate under separate command with little coordination.

Decisions on Sri Lankan policy were made by a small group of close advisers to the Prime Minister, including the Army Chief of Staff. It does not appear, however, that the level of consultation went very deep into civilian or military bureaucracies. Lack of communication, coordination and intelligence led to a serious gap between policy ambitions and military capabilities. Military intelligence was weak. In fact, army intelligence officers were taken by surprise when the IPKF was deployed. Information about the LTTE came from the RAW, and the failures of that intelligence and well as RAW's relationship with the LTTE caused resentment. Lines of authority were not clear, and information and advice did not move up from operational levels of command. Dixit is particularly critical of the lack of coordination between RAW and the IPKF, which he sees as placing 'operational limitations' on the IPKF.[44] He sees bureaucratic politics dictating RAW's role in the conflict. Dixit reports that all his advisers, except RAW and Tamil Nadu political interests, supported Rajiv Gandhi's firmness toward the LTTE.[45] He points out that Gandhi had to deal with 'recalcitrant Tamil political groups' who were prominent supporters of the LTTE and whose assistance to the LTTE could not be curtailed: 'It was of course physically impossible to control these activities in Tamil Nadu if local authorities, sections of its police force, and segments of their political leadership were not willing to conform to the overall policies of the Government of India.'[46] According to Dixit, Gandhi wanted to be firm with the LTTE, but he also had an 'equally greater' (*sic*) concern to avoid a hostile government in power in Tamil Nadu. Thus he allowed RAW to pursue back channel communications with both the LTTE and Jayewardene.

Why then the initial decision to disarm and then 'neutralize' the LTTE? Why not choose a strategy of attrition? Clearly Gandhi's aim was not to destroy the LTTE but to coerce them into compliance with the agreement. Certainly it was in Gandhi's interest to end the conflict quickly, since he was facing national elections at the end of 1989. The need to make it a quick rather than protracted intervention may have motivated him to ignore some of the military's warnings that the consequence of an offensive strategy would be the opposite (assuming that these warnings were communicated to him). He also had other advice that supported his inclination to order the IPKF to strike hard, and continued to offer the carrot of negotiations via RAW.

The conduct of the military operation was strongly affected by democratic norms and requirements as well as contradictions in policy that stemmed from domestic politics. The switch from seeing the LTTE as a potential ally to regarding the group as an enemy was disorienting. The IPKF tried to avoid civilian casualties, which meant no indiscriminate methods such as aerial bombing or heavy artillery. Scrutiny of military operations by the media heightened sensitivity to charges of atrocities and brutalities. Apparently the hasty induction of the IPKF had resulted in human rights abuses and indiscipline that were corrected as the scope of the engagement became clear to military commanders. But criticisms in the Indian and Sri Lankan press and among international human rights agencies made the Indian military defensive.[47] Dixit says that by the spring of 1988 Sri Lankan policy had lost public support, and military leaders were well aware of their isolation.[48]

Enforcing power sharing arrangements

The Accord provided for a merger of Sri Lanka's northern and eastern provinces in a single administrative unit, which would have a Tamil majority with Muslim and Sinhalese minorities. An interim administrative council would be appointed, later to be replaced by an elected provincial council. The timetable shows how quickly India expected to restore order. Elections were planned for December 1987, less than a year after the Accord. After a year had passed, a popular referendum would determine the extent of support for the united province. The Accord, however, was weak on detail, and its implementation depended on the cooperation of the Sri Lankan government, which promised to amend the constitution to permit a devolution of power to the provinces. The LTTE was not a party to the Accord and rejected it within a few months. From the outset Jayewardene's official acceptance of the idea of a merger of the northern and eastern provinces with significant devolution of power was not supported even within his own government, much less by the Sinhalese public. His prime minister, Premadasa, and half of the cabinet did not support him.

Why then did Indian policy-makers think the Accord would work? They might reasonably have assumed that the presence of the IPKF would compel short-term acquiescence and that realization of the benefits of peace might dawn on both parties. India expected to exert leverage over the LTTE, and Jayewardene appeared to want the IPKF. Furthermore, the LTTE was not the only representative of Tamil opinion. Perhaps a moderate coalition would form in support of the settlement. But the fact that Indian decision-makers were worried about support for the new arrangements is demonstrated by the secrecy with which the final Accord was negotiated. Furthermore, moderates will not participate unless they are protected from the retaliation of the extremists. From the beginning moderate Tamils were at risk from the LTTE, and moderate Sinhalese were at risk from the radical Sinhalese terrorist organization that the Sri Lankan government had not managed to defeat, even when freed of its obligations in the north.

India started by proposing a bargain. The LTTE would be permitted to dominate the appointed interim council, and in return they promised to participate in elections for a permanent governing body. However, after a dispute over appointments to the council, the LTTE pulled out of the deal, which was one of the reasons the IPKF took the offensive against them.[49] The LTTE then opposed holding elections, which created an unpleasant impasse.

Now the question was whether to hold the elections without the LTTE. Apparently, in June 1988, Gandhi convened several meetings to discuss the issue.[50] Jayewardene supported holding the elections. However, other Sri Lankan parties, ranging from Buddhist pro-Sinhalese factions to moderate Tamils, were opposed. Tamil leaders wanted to see a significant devolution of power to an interim administration first. They also questioned the voting lists supplied by the government and voiced apprehension about prospective terrorism from the LTTE. Within the Indian bureaucracy, RAW wanted to wait until the LTTE could be persuaded to come aboard. The head of the Intelligence Bureau (M. K. Narayanan) warned that the IPKF would have to conduct the elections and that the new provincial government would have to be supported by India. Other civilian officials also felt that devolution of power should precede elections, which should be administered by Sri Lankan civil authorities. Dixit, however, felt that since the LTTE was obdurate, India 'had no choice'. Gandhi apparently agreed.

Consequently the elections were held under IPKF administration in November 1988. (None of the 20,000 Sri Lankan officials asked to staff the polling booths would agree to do so, according to Dixit.[51]) As expected, the LTTE boycotted the elections, and Tamil parties friendly to India gained a majority. The turn-out in Jaffna, still loyal to the LTTE, was low, but voting was high in the eastern province, which was where the council was eventually located. However, even Dixit, who favoured holding the elections, admits that this aspect of the implementation of the Accord was 'tenuous' and that the 'prospects of this new Provincial Council settling to normal work were dim'.[52] Any Tamil party that India supported or even that might win in Indian-sponsored elections was perceived as a tool of India, not a legitimate representative of the Tamils. Moderates were bound to be labelled as collaborators. And as is frequently the case, the new provincial council members had faults of their own such as inexperience and corruption. The result was a weak institution trying to operate under conditions of extreme insecurity and uncertainty about the future. Furthermore, Sri Lankan politicians were now preoccupied with the upcoming national parliamentary and presidential elections and did not act immediately to devolve power.

Perhaps the dilemma of the Tamil moderates could have been overcome through sustained peace-building efforts. However, General

Sardeshpande (head of the army in Jaffna, then at IPKF headquarters in Madras) claims that 'political and economic steps had not been commensurate with the military effort and had lagged far behind'.[53] He continues:

> The NEPC's demands [the provincial council], difficulties and complexities rose by the day. No group of advisers came to guide or help them in their new experiment in the prevailing hostile environment. Nothing seemed to be moving anywhere–except the IPKF and LTTE detachments gunning for each other. [The council had] no powers, no resources, no politico-economic-organisational-secretarial support. It did not even enjoy popular support in vital areas ...[54]

On the other hand, Dixit contends that one of India's main tasks was to provide security and credibility for the new Tamil government.[55] To this end, India continued to press Jayewardene to implement power-sharing arrangements and also asked him to create a Sri Lankan Tamil police force for the new province – which India would fund and train. In Dixit's view, the main obstacle to these plans was the assistance the LTTE continued to receive from 'different political circles in Tamil Nadu and even from a segment of the Tamil Nadu provincial police and security forces', a trend that New Delhi could only marginally control.[56] He claims that the LTTE now received intelligence, arms and even sanctuary from the Sri Lankan security forces, encouraged by Prime Minister Premadasa and other anti-India officials.

From this account it is clear that the new governing arrangements in Sri Lanka did not provide for genuine power-sharing, nor were they enforceable. India faced a complicated set of trade-offs. To gain Sri Lankan support for devolution, India had to disarm the LTTE. To justify the military offensive, India had to produce some concrete gains for the Tamils. 'Neutralizing' the LTTE without first securing an equitable power-sharing arrangement would alienate Tamils, but the Sinhalese were unlikely to make concessions until the LTTE was defeated, if then. Presumably the military offensive strengthened India's bargaining position on devolution in India's eyes.[57] There might be Tamil opposition to destroying the LTTE even if it resulted in a stable peace settlement with substantial devolution. Handing power in the new provincial council over to the LTTE without holding elections would be equally unjustifiable at home, even if the LTTE's rivals lacked credibility in Sri Lanka. (However, initially India had been willing to guarantee LTTE control over the appointed interim council.) So India needed to pursue both peace and justice at the same time. Holding the provincial elections thus took on a symbolic significance for India that was out of proportion to the political gain in Sri Lanka.

One problematic and often neglected element in the peace-keeping and peace-building dilemma is post-transition security. Who is responsible for maintaining order after new power-sharing institutions are in place? Immediately after the provincial elections India began to train and equip a 'Tamil Volunteer Force', which subsequently became the 'Tamil National Army'. The Sri Lankan government was consulted, but the initiative seemed to have been primarily General Kalkat's.[58] The LTTE was deeply opposed, as was to be expected. But the Tamil population was also apprehensive about the 'volunteer force', and even about the provincial administration itself. The Sri Lankan government complained of Sinhalese discontent and acted as though India's moves were unilateral. The bottom line was that these forces were hastily recruited and trained, their conscription angered the Tamil population, and the Sri Lankan government undermined them.

Staying power

Outside guarantors of settlements must commit to staying long enough to see the transition through. If the election of a new administration is expected to herald a change of policy, then the dissatisfied combatants need only wait for elections, while making the intervention experience as unpleasant as possible.

The constraints that theories of foreign military intervention designate operated in Sri Lanka. One obstacle to staying is mounting casualties among the security forces. As the IPKF became embroiled in the fighting after October 1987, casualties mounted, eventually reaching around 1,500 deaths. Another source of domestic discontent was reports of atrocities by the Indian troops. From the autumn of 1988 on there was little support among the general Indian public or the media for Sri Lankan policy.

Ironically, the last straw came as a result of democratic elections in Sri Lanka. In December 1988, Premadasa replaced Jayewardene as President. His antagonism toward the IPKF had been obvious from the start, and he wasted no time in calling Dixit in to demand the ouster of the IPKF and declare his intention of negotiating directly with the LTTE.[59] The February 1989, parliamentary elections then returned a majority for his party, which strengthened his sense of having an electoral mandate. Furthermore, the government was still involved in combating the Sinhalese insurgency in the south, one of whose demands was the ouster of the IPKF. On 2 June, Premadasa publicly demanded that India withdraw by the deadline of the second anniversary of the Accord, thus in two months. In a subsequent exchange of correspondence with Rajiv Gandhi in early July, which barely met the standards of diplomatic courtesy, he revealed that he had reached an agreement with the LTTE and that a cease-fire was eminent.

Gandhi promptly rejected the ultimatum. He argued that institutional arrangements for power-sharing had not yet been implemented (although elections to the provincial council had been held, the referendum on its future had not), that the LTTE was not disarmed, and that the Accord was a bilateral agreement that could not be unilaterally abrogated. He had already, however, agreed in principle to withdraw some units; the issue was whether to agree to a complete withdrawal by July. Gandhi was clearly angry at Premadasa's offensive tone and especially at his deliberate leaking of their correspondence to the press. In January, Gandhi had already warned Premadasa that 'India will not accept a situation where in public perception an impression may be created that the Indian army was abruptly expelled or withdrawn', and now Premadasa was doing exactly that.[60] Premadasa's original demand, for example, threatened to confine the IPKF to barracks; later Premadasa threatened to declare war on the IPKF (all of which provoked a stern warning from the IPKF commander, General Kalkat). Premadasa's response to Gandhi was that the IPKF was in Sri Lanka only at the invitation of the government, that it had failed in its mission of disarming the LTTE, and that the two objectives of the peace settlement – security guarantees and new power-sharing arrangements – were not linked. India, he said, had been asked only to provide the first, not the second. Devolution was Sri Lanka's business, and the LTTE's willingness to negotiate had now resolved the security problem. In fact, he continued, the presence of the IPKF only complicated the process of peace-making.

Regardless of the effect of withdrawal on the conflict or on Indo–Sri Lankan relations, the timing of Premadasa's announcement could not have been worse in the context of domestic politics. Even Dixit points out that at this time, facing elections at the end of the year, Gandhi was 'enmeshed in domestic political controversies'.[61] Lloyd Rudolph summarizes Gandhi's domestic difficulties. In January 1989, the Congress Party finished third in the Tamil Nadu state elections, although Gandhi had made 11 campaign trips to the state. This outcome was disastrous:

> the party's and the prime minister's reputations were badly damaged by the gap between their aspirations and their performance ... After its defeat in Tamil Nadu, the Gandhi government was eager to find a way to stem the downward trend in its political fortunes.[62]

In April he imposed President's Rule in the state of Karnataka, which critics saw as an unconstitutional move that presaged a return to the authoritarianism of his mother. The Congress party was demoralized and there were defections in other important states. He had already lost badly in a crucial election in Uttar Pradesh, India's largest state, with 16 per cent of the seats in the Lok Sabha. To make it worse, that election was a direct challenge from his national rival, V. P. Singh. There was also disarray at the top, with 13 cabinet reshuffles by the end of 1988. In desperation, in March Gandhi recalled to his cabinet one of his mother's aides, a move that was unpopular with his supporters as well as his opponents. The situation in the Punjab was depressing; over 1,500 people were killed in 1988, including more than 1,000 civilians. Just as he was exchanging acerbic letters with Premadasa, the old corruption scandals were revived. In July, most opposition members resigned from the Indian parliament to protest the government's handling of an official report on the matter, an action regarded as an attempt to make corruption a major issue in the upcoming parliamentary elections. The contest between the Congress party and the opposition occupied the centre of attention in national politics; if the opposition parties could unite it was expected that they could defeat Congress. Adding insult to injury, the newly elected leader in Tamil Nadu was a key player in the opposition.

Under these circumstances, as Rudolph puts it, domestic political imperatives made it difficult for either Premadasa or Gandhi to back down, yet if they persisted in confrontation it would be costly. 'For Rajiv, only five months away from a national election, a fiasco in Sri Lanka, where he had taken direct command of foreign policy, could prove particularly costly.'[63] Best, perhaps, to gamble on resurrection or at least hedge. At a minimum, he could not appear to bow meekly to an ultimatum.

India had been considering its options well before Premadasa's move. Dixit (who by this time had become Ambassador to Pakistan) thought that Gandhi had already decided on a gradual withdrawal, culminating in 1990, with the expectation that the IPKF would have finished its military operations and that Premadasa would have become disillusioned with the LTTE.[64] General Sardeshpande recounts that by May 1989, the IPKF's early sense of mission had given way to complacency and a 'tactical stand-off', a passivity he attributes to the awareness that the LTTE was still receiving support in Tamil Nadu.[65] In his view, the Indian government was pursuing a military offensive for its own sake, without any effort to support it with political and economic planning. In an assessment report filed in the spring of 1989, he predicted that it would take 10 years to bring some semblance of normality to Sri Lanka. He also noted that at the time he felt that the constraints of the military effort were not understood at the political level, perhaps because the army leadership was not making itself heard at the top. Apparently India's political leadership wanted to reduce troop levels and let the new provincial council and its 'Citizens Volunteer Force' maintain law and order. He reports that the view held at the top in New Delhi was that some elements of the IPKF should be kept in certain vital areas as 'points of pressure' while the rest of the force would withdraw.[66] Another body of opinion advocated staying in for the long haul, until there was stability, and a third favoured a complete and immediate withdrawal, letting the Tamils and the Sri Lankan government sort it out. The latter two views were more commonly held in the military.

Now India's hand was forced. Gandhi refused to comply with the 30 July deadline, but withdrawal would have to proceed, and it would have to be complete: there could be no 'pressure point' strategy. Thus Premadasa was informed that the IPKF would begin a phased withdrawal, with the aim of completion by the end of 1989 or early 1990. The consequences for the Tamil provincial government were disastrous. As soon as the IPKF began to withdraw, members of the 'Tamil National Army' either fled to India or fell victim to the LTTE. The chief minister of the provincial council eventually left for exile in India.

The Congress Party did not gain a sufficient majority in the December 1989 elections to be able to form a government. The new National Front government immediately agreed to the prompt withdrawal of the IPKF, promising a pull-out by March 1990. Election commentaries, interestingly enough, do not list the Sri Lankan quagmire as a cause of Gandhi's difficulties. Atul Kohli stated that: 'One should not look for dramatic failures of Rajiv Gandhi to explain Congress's defeat in the 1989 elections.'[67] He concludes that generally poor performance kept Gandhi from implementing any of the major goals that he had defined initially as his priorities. Short-term electoral pressures often led to policy failures in all areas. Sri Lanka was only one of India's many problems.

Conclusions

The requirements for successful intervention to secure peace settlements in ethnic conflicts are rigorous and complex. Commitment problems often impede effectiveness. To calculate the timing of their actions, third parties must possess excellent knowledge of the belligerents' intentions and resources, sensitivity to the dynamics of the conflict, and freedom of action. To provide security during a transition period, a third-party guarantor must be able to accept military casualties, avoid civilian casualties in the host country, prevent atrocities or human rights violations by the military, and use force against groups with whom their own populations or even armed forces may sympathize.

At the same time, the intervening power must limit the use of military force to secure compliance with the peace agreement. Victory is not the goal. If the use of force is to be legitimate, the enforcer also has to see that democratic institutions are established. The settlement has to involve genuine power-sharing. Justice cannot be sacrificed for peace. To justify disarming an opposition movement (especially a former client and especially if the fight is bloody), the third party guarantor has to produce a positive outcome. Thus the peace-maker must promote the formation of moderate coalitions on both sides of the conflict. Holding elections is typically the most visible symbol of new arrangements. Finally, an obvious requirement for both security and reform is that the guarantor has to stay the course despite frustrations and setbacks.

The obstacles to effective performance of this role are numerous. Militaries are rarely equipped to perform political and administrative functions, nor are they trained to fight without winning. 'Moderates' favoured by the outside power in a civil conflict will probably be perceived as collaborators. An outside presence in a conflict will provoke nationalist reactions. Cross-border ethnic affinities will complicate any peace-keeping effort. India's decisions in Sri Lanka were also affected by a series of particular factors: the determination and ruthless efficiency of the LTTE, India's acute vulnerability as a multi-ethnic state to secessionist demands, Rajiv Gandhi's inexperience and impetuousness, the isolation of the Indian military from civilian authority, the centralization of decision-making in a small circle of personal advisers to the Prime Minister, and India's desire for regional dominance and the exclusion of foreign powers.

Although this analysis has not compared vulnerability to domestic pressure in democratic regimes to that in authoritarian regimes, India's experience suggests that the sensitivity of democracies to domestic politics matters considerably to intervention policy. Even the decision to 'get in' was not purely strategic. India reacted not only to the trajectory of the conflict between the Sri Lankan government and Tamil militants, but to the impact of these developments on political alignments in Tamil Nadu. Rajiv Gandhi's need for success on the home front often coincided with his initiatives in Sri Lanka. Because of a particularistic sort of accountability to constituents in Tamil Nadu, the central government in New Delhi was unable to cut off material assistance to the LTTE or to pursue a consistent military strategy. While India felt compelled to try to coerce the LTTE into compromise, progress in establishing power-sharing institutions was essential in order to justify the policy. Gandhi adopted a 'two-track' policy that included negotiating with the LTTE via civilian intelligence agencies while conducting a military offensive. Because of a need for policy legitimacy, holding elections for a new Tamil provincial council became a crucial objective that in the end served no useful purpose. Staying on became increasingly costly, not only because of the obstinacy of the parties to the conflict in Sri Lanka but because of lack of public support at home. Gandhi resisted demands for immediate withdrawal, perhaps because he was 'gambling for resurrection'. It is impossible to conclude that the involvement in Sri Lanka was responsible for the electoral defeat of the Congress Party, given the multiple problems he faced. However, Gandhi's successor campaigned against staying on and withdrew the IPKF immediately.

India's experience may not be unusual. Regional powers with ambitious aspirations are often the most likely third-party mediators and guarantors of peace settlements in ethnic conflicts in Africa and Asia. Many democracies have centralized and personalized decision-making processes. They are also likely to be multi-ethnic states faced with disintegrative forces. Leadership at the centre often depends on the support of local political elites, and decisions are the result of internal as well as external bargaining. Transnational ethnic affinities are increasingly common. Under these conditions, effective military intervention to resolve civil conflict is difficult to achieve.

NOTES

1. Barbara F. Walter, 'The Critical Barrier to Civil War Settlement', *International Organization* 51/3 (Summer 1997) pp.335–65; James D. Fearon, 'Commitment Problems and the Spread of Ethnic Conflict' (unpublished paper, University of Chicago, 1996); and William I. Zartman (ed.), *Elusive Peace* (Washington: Brookings, 1995). See also Barbara F. Walter and Jack Snyder (eds), *Civil Wars, Insecurity, and Intervention* (New York: Columbia University Press, 1999), especially Walter's 'Designing Transitions from Civil War', pp.38–69.
2. Zartman, ibid., pp.343–4.
3. Walter (note 1) p.361. See also Sisk (note 14).
4. Yaacov Y. I. Vertzberger, 'National Capabilitites and Foreign Military Intervention: A Policy-Relevant Theoretical Analysis', *International Interactions* 17/4 (1992) pp.361–6.
5. Vertzberger, ibid., p.352.
6. Harvey Waterman, 'Political Order and the 'Settlement' of Civil Wars', in Roy Licklider (ed.), *Stopping the Killing: How Civil Wars End* (New York: New York University Press, 1993) pp.292–302.
7. Vertzberger (note 4) p.361.
8. They also impose constraints on the ability to mediate: see Thomas Princen, *Intermediaries in International Conflict* (Princeton: Princeton University Press, 1992) pp.222–4.
9. Vertzberger (note 4) p.356.
10. Ariel E. Levite, Bruce W. Jentleson and Larry Berman (eds), *Foreign military intervention: the dynamics of protracted conflict* (New York: Columbia University Press, 1992).
11. See particularly Charles A. Kupchan, 'Getting In: The Initial Stages of Military Intervention', and Eliot A. Cohen, 'Dynamics of Military Intervention', in Levite, Jentleson and Berman (eds) (note 10) pp.241–60 and 261–84, respectively.
12. George W. Downs, 'The Lessons of Disengagement', in Levite, Jentleson and Berman (eds), ibid., pp.285–300.
13. Vertzberger (note 4) p.362.
14. Timothy D. Sisk, in *Power Sharing and International Mediation in Ethnic Conflicts* (Washington, DC: United States Institute of Peace and Carnegie Commission on Preventing Deadly Conflict, 1996) pp.77–86, argues for power-sharing. An outside guarantee might not be needed if the settlement were imposed on the defeated party by

a clearly superior victor, but one can imagine tenuous balances of power where the winner cannot maintain a peace that has been imposed.

15. Roy Licklider, 'The Consequences of Negotiated Settlements in Civil Wars, 1945–1993', *American Political Science Review* 89/3 (September 1995) pp.681–90.
16. Richard K. Betts, 'The Delusion of Impartial Intervention', *Foreign Affairs* 73/6 (November/December 1994) pp.31–2.
17. Mark Peceny, 'Two Paths to the Promotion of Democracy during U.S. Military Interventions', *International Studies Quarterly* 39/3 (September 1995) pp.371–401.
18. Walter (note 1) pp.361–2, and Zartman (note 1) pp.344–5. See also Princen (note 8).
19. Betts (note 16) p.20.
20. Ibid., p.28.
21. See e.g. Alan J. Bullion, *India, Sri Lanka and the Tamil Crisis 1976–1994: An International Perspective* (London: Pinter, 1995) and Mahnaz Ispahani, 'India's Role in Sri Lanka's Ethnic Conflict', in Levite, Jentleson and Berman (eds) (note 10) pp.209–40. See also Maya Chadda, *Ethnicity, Security, and Separatism in India* (New York: Columbia University Press, 1997) and Dennis Austin, *Democracy and Violence in India and Sri Lanka* (Chatham House Paper, Royal Institute of International Affairs. London: Pinter Publishers, 1994).
22. India also issued public statements of concern about the treatment of Tamils in Sri Lanka, but this involvement was minor compared to active intervention.
23. J. N. Dixit, *Assignment Colombo* (Delhi: Konark Publishers, 1998) p.328.
24. James Manor, 'Politics: Ambiguity, Disillusionment, and Ferment', in Marshall M. Bouton and Philip Oldenburg (eds), *India Briefing, 1988* (Boulder: Westview, 1988) pp.19–21.
25. Dixit (note 23) pp.336-37.
26. K. M. De Silva and S. W. R. de A. Samarasinghe (eds), *Peace Accords and Ethnic Conflict* (London: Pinter, 1993) p.127.
27. Dixit (note 23) pp.188–9.
28. Donald Horowitz, a personal communication, quoted in Sisk (note 14) p.94.
29. See Sisk (note 14) pp.113–14; also Zartman (note 1)
30. Walter (1997) pp.340-41.
31. Ibid., p.362.
32. United Nations Institute for Disarmament Research, 'Managing Arms in Peace Process: The Issues', *Disarmament and Conflict Resolution Project* (New York and Geneva, 1996). The controversy over implementation of the Good Friday accords in Northern Ireland owing to the IRA's reluctance to 'decommission' is a further example of the significance of disarmament.
33. Dixit (note 23) p.194. He also adds: 'There is a theory bandied about that India had planned the sending of its armed forces to Sri Lanka months in advance of the negotiations and signing of the Agreement. This is not true.' See p.186.
34. K. M. De Silva, *Regional Powers and Small State Security: India and Sri Lanka, 1977–90* (Washington, DC: The Woodrow Wilson Center Press and Baltimore/The John Hopkins University Press, 1995) p.125.
35. Dixit (note 23) pp.337–8.
36. See Depinder Singh (Lt. Gen.), *The IPKF in Sri Lanka* (Noida (i.e. New Okhla Industrial Development Authority, UP, India): Trishul Publications, 1991). Of course, in these later observations he had the benefit of hindsight.
37. Stephen Peter Rosen, in *Societies and Military Power: India and Its Armies* (Ithaca: Cornell University Press, 1996) p.253, claims that the Indian military was not good at quick responses and that cooperation among units was difficult, which he attributes to social fragmentation rather than the democratic process.
38. S. D. Muni, *Pangs of proximity: India and Sri Lanka's ethnic crisis* (New Delhi: Sage Publications, 1993) pp.134–5.
39. Dixit (note 23) p.212.
40. Ibid., p.218.
41. Muni (note 38) p.142.

42. Dixit (note 23) p.339.
43. Stephen P. Cohen, 'The Military and Indian Democracy', in Atul Kohli (ed.), *India's Democracy: An Analysis of Changing State-Society Relations* (Princeton: Princeton University Press, 1990); Ragu G. C. Thomas, *Democracy, Security, and Development in India* (New York: St Martin's Press, 1996). See also Rosen (note 37).
44. Dixit (note 23) pp.233–4.
45. Ibid., pp.227–8.
46. Ibid., p.228.
47. For a discussion of this problem, see Muni (note 38) pp.144–5, and Dixit (note 23) p.252.
48. Dixit (note 23) pp.237 and 248.
49. It is interesting that one of the LTTE's complaints was Indian media criticism; Dixit promised to restrain the official media. Ibid., pp.203 and 205.
50. Ibid., pp.224*ff*.
51. Ibid., p.253
52. Ibid., p.254.
53. S. C. Sardeshpande (Lt. Gen.), *Assignment Jaffna* (New Delhi: Lancer Publishers, 1992) p.89.
54. Ibid.
55. Dixit (note 23) pp.268–9.
56. Ibid., p.269.
57. Ibid., pp.221–2.
58. Ibid., pp.282–5.
59. Ibid., pp.277–8.
60. Ibid., p.281.
61. Ibid., p.290.
62. Lloyd I. Rudolph, 'The Faltering Novitiate: Rajiv at Home and Abroad in 1988', in Marshall M. Bouton and Philip Oldenburg (eds), *India Briefing, 1989* (Boulder: Westview, 1989) p.14.
63. Ibid., p.25.
64. Dixit (note 23) p.290.
65. Sardeshpande (note 53) pp.88–91.
66. Muni (note 38, p.152) says that Gandhi and Jayewardene had already agreed on a phased withdrawal in December 1988, immediately after the elections to the provincial councils. However, he says, the Sri Lankan army asked for a slowdown. India's intention would scarcely have been encouraging to the new provincial government.
67. Atul Kohli, 'Epilogue: India's Democracy under Rajiv Gandhi, 1985–1989', in Atul Kohli (ed.), *India's Democracy: An Analysis of Changing State–Society Relations* (Princeton: Princeton University Press, 1990) p.331.

7

Western Democracies and Islamic Fundamentalist Violence

RAPHAEL ISRAELI

On 18 November 1997, Islamic radicals killed 58 foreign tourists in Luxor, Egypt. President Mubarak then accused Britain and other countries of protecting terrorists: 'terrorists are present and living on English territory and other countries where they collect funds and plan attacks.'[1] The British retorted: 'We are not protecting terrorists. We unreservedly condemn all forms of terrorism. We are committed to taking action against anyone who uses the United Kingdom as a base for terrorist activity elsewhere.'[2] Home Secretary Jack Straw added: 'Tackling international terrorism is a top priority for this government. We already have tough anti-terrorism laws. And we intend to strengthen them further.' He denied that Britain granted asylum to convicted terrorists, saying that asylum was only granted on the grounds established under the United Nations' 1951 Convention on Refugees,[3] which provided the possibility for politically persecuted individuals to seek shelter in countries (usually democracies) willing to safeguard their human rights.

The news media noted, nevertheless, that Yasser al-Serri, facing a death sentence in Egypt for the 1993 attempted murder of Egyptian Prime Minister Atef Sidki, has lived in Britain since 1994:[4]

> A gaping hole in Britain's anti-terrorist laws lends some credence to Egyptian President Hosni Mubarak's accusations that it harbours international terrorists, experts say ... Currently, it is not an offense in Britain to plot an attack abroad – and countries like Israel, Saudi Arabia and Algeria have long complained that this has made London a safe haven for their extremist opponents; Six Britons ... were among the 58 foreign tourists killed in Luxor ...

Mubarak effectively said: I told you so. If you do not want your sons to be killed, why do you protect killers? There are people who carried out crimes and who were sentenced in Egypt who live on British land and in other states ...

Aside from the legal loophole, London has for many years been a magnet for dissidents from around the world who are attracted by comparatively liberal asylum laws and Britain's ancient tradition of free speech. Opposition groups have taken advantage of good communications to set up dissident newspapers that are distributed in their home countries ... France and Algeria have repeatedly accused Britain of harbouring members of Algeria's most militant guerrilla group, the Armed Islamic Group, while Israelis believe that the Islamic fundamentalist group Hamas has been operating from the British capital. Saudi Arabia charged Britain with playing host to a range of groups committed to ending the rule of King Fahd. Last year there were angry protests from Tunisia and Bahrain over a huge rally in London planned by the Islamic fundamentalist Muhajirun group, which calls for a Jihad, or holy war against governments in the Middle East. The organizers ... were forced to cancel when the venue demanded huge costs for security. Instead, the Muhajirun held a legal rally in Hyde Park ... 'These British, and many Western countries are strange. They raise their voices on the necessity of combating terrorism around the world, but they are some of the best supporters of this terrorism ... by opening their doors for the shelter of leaders, planners and financiers', al-Akhbar said: 'Such protection is an open invitation to carry out more terrorist crimes not only against Egyptians, but against British citizens too, as in the Luxor massacre'.

Earlier this year, Egyptian officials expressed dismay when an Egyptian lawyer who defended Islamic militants, set up the International Office for the Defense of the Egyptian People in London to expose alleged human rights violations in Egypt ...[5]

This odd debate illustrates some interesting issues and problems which bedevil the relationships of the West to governments and Islamic fundamentalist oppositions in the Muslim world. Many difficulties derive from misunderstanding the different meanings of democracy employed by the parties, and the attending notions of legitimacy of power connected to them. The purpose of this article is to point out those differences as well as to expose the difference between democracy and democratization which are sometimes blurred and generate the seemingly inconsistent attitudes of the West towards some of those countries. The West, furthermore, fails to see that others use democratic rhetoric but seek legitimacy elsewhere. Understanding that might help reduce the level of violence in and from Islamic societies.

Muslim fundamentalists and democracy

On the functional level, the term 'democratic' in the West has three criteria: the ultimate locus of power is an elected body, the legitimacy of the opposition to government, and a smooth transition of power. In most of the Islamic countries today, including those who claim to be 'democratic' or 'democratizing', the head of state occupies the ultimate locus of power by retaining the supreme authority of government, using parliament as a mere rubber-stamp. If the opposition is too critical or too shrill, it finds itself not in parliament but in jail. And power is usually for life, as long as the ruler controls the military, though provision is usually made for the ruler to succeed himself or bequeath his rule either through the perpetuation of the ruling house (Jordan, Saudi Arabia, Morocco, Kuwait), or through the designation of an heir (Saddam, Assad, Qaddafi). No one opposes the ruler for re-election, and his return to power is assured by 99 per cent of the vote or more. In monarchies, 'elections' are held to legitimize parliament, though the autocratic ruler calls the tune.

We speak of the 'people' as the sovereign or the source of legitimacy; Islamists (or Muslim radicals or fundamentalists in other appellations), in contrast, hail Allah as the only sovereign of the universe and brand any attempt to impute sovereignty to humans as *shirk*, namely imparting divine qualities to anyone other than the Almighty. As this is seen as blasphemy deserving capital punishment, fundamentalists do not recognize most governments in the Islamic world, and are particularly incensed by monarchs who dub themselves 'sovereign'. The only form of government acceptable is the ancient Caliphate where the Caliph was the Vicar of the Prophet, not a sovereign.

In the fundamentalist Muslim belief system, Allah has given the most perfect of legal codes, the *shari'ah* law, and any attempt to supplement or supplant it is blasphemous. When a Muslim fundamentalist refers to democracy, he means the rule by *shura*, an appointed or elected body distinguished by its knowledge of and submission to the Islamic legal system. The first successors of the Prophet, the *Rashidun*, had been elected by the *shura*, a council of elders, made up of the closest associates of the defunct Prophet. Today, the Saudi King allows an appointed *shura* in his kingdom; and Egypt, in an attempt to placate Muslim constituencies, has a *shura* – an upper house to supplement the 'elected' parliament.

In the West, consensus is the fruit of political bargaining based upon a give-and-take process between ethnic, political, religious, cultural and linguistic groups, or lobbies of particular interests, which recognize the relativity of the truth and need to balance various interests. Muslim fundamentalists, however, have enormous difficulties in compromising, because the Truth is one and eternal, an either–or affair, anchored in a demand for everything now. Since most existing governments are viewed as anti-Islamic, violence should be used against them. Existing regimes, normally resting on the military, are identified as an enemy of Islam and associated with the West which aims to undermine Islam by promoting permissiveness through education and the media.

The justification to launch war against such evil enemies is distilled in the quintessential doctrine of *jihad*. Etymologically, this word designates intellectual 'striving', and by extension also a physical striving, for a cause. In Islamic *shari'a*, however, *jihad* principally has one meaning: military action designed to expand the outer borders of the realm of Islam or to protect the borders of *Dar-al-Islam* (Pax Islamica) from encroaching unbelievers. Muslim fundamentalist luminaries, such as Sayyid Qut'b (executed by Nasser in Egypt in 1966), have consecrated *jihad* as a tool to battle un-Islamic regimes domestically as well as on international levels.

Four totally Islamized countries exist to date, in which those principles are applied to a great extent: Saudi Arabia, Iran, Sudan and Afghanistan. In the rest of the Islamic world (some 50 countries), where various degrees of democratization are under way, the entire gamut exists from absolute autocracy (Iraq, Syria, Libya, Oman, Qatar and Brunei), through milder forms of authoritarian rule (Jordan, Morocco, Tunisia, Algeria, Kuwait and Egypt), to close replicas of Western democracies (Turkey, Malaysia, Indonesia and Senegal). All contain lofty constitutions, but rulers often put them aside to rule by *diktat*. Parliaments are elected, but are subservient to the ruler. The frequency of 'new' constitutions goes apace with the coups mounted by new rulers against their predecessors and demonstrates the will of the ruler to have his own writ of legitimacy to cover his uncertain grip on power, rather than fulfilling the country's need for a basic iron-clad set of principles to restrict government. In the West, constitutions provide stability and predictability by their very continuity in the face of constant changes in government; in Islamic countries, constitutions are the expression of instability and unpredictability. The ultimate locus of power is the ruler. Even Turkey, until recently the only border case of a functioning democracy, has known in our lifetime three military takeovers, and the ouster of a democratically elected Islamist Prime Minister (Erbakan), under military pressure in the late 1990s. In non-Islamized Muslim countries, Islamic legitimacy is deemed threatening to the regimes in place, and therefore shunned, discarded and feared because of its potency and popular appeal.

Opposition may exist, if it is 'loyal' and does not cause 'division'. When the opposition takes its duty seriously, it is often branded an 'enemy of the people' undermining the state and the regime, and treated accordingly. In Algeria, free elections were permitted for the first time (1992), but when the victory of the Islamists became apparent, the results were reversed and a military junta took over power. A democratizing regime such as Mubarak's in Egypt, for example, does not allow fundamentalists – even the more placid among them, the popular Muslim Brothers – to run for elections for fear that an Algerian scenario might occur. In Jordan, fundamentalists have run for the Parliament and succeeded; but the King dubbed them dangerous to state stability and imprisoned some.

Thus, the regimes in most of these countries have a hard time claiming a credible legitimacy. No-one has elected them in truth, and they have either inherited monarchical absolute power or have it by force. To acquire some legitimacy, some take Islamic titles: the Curator of the Holy Places of Islam for the Saudi King, the Heir of the Prophet and the Guardian of al-Aqsa Mosque for the Jordanian monarch, for example. Even the atheist Saddam Hussein, during the Second Gulf War (1991), added the Islamic war-cry 'Allah Akbar!' ('Allah is Greater!') to his national flag, to make his war against the Americans (the 'New Crusaders'), a new version of the war of the Believers against invading non-Muslims. Other forms of legitimacy, such as championing pan-Arabism (Egypt's Nasser) or Arab unity (the Ba'ath in both Syria and Iraq) or the Palestinian cause (practically all of them) have failed, hence the return to Islam.

When they confront autocratic rulers, one hears Islamic opposition groups speaking for democracy and clamouring for human rights. They are, therefore, often perceived as moderate, reasonable and operating within the system, so long as they do not use violence to attack or overthrow the regimes in place (the Muslim Brothers in Egypt, Jordan and Israel, Islamic movements in the West). But when they do, they are ruthlessly oppressed, usually with the silent support of the West (Turkey, Egypt, Algeria, Jordan, Morocco, Saudi Arabia, the Palestinian Authority, etc.). A double contradiction builds up in these countries as a result: the governments are furious against the West when it supports non-violent Islamist opposition groups which seek to remove their rulers by questioning their legitimacy and demanding democratization; at the same time these opposition groups themselves feel betrayed by the west for its failure to pursue its logic of democracy and to support their democratization drive by means of Islamic legitimacy (the Algerian scenario).

Where East and West differ

In 1940, Ferrero perceived that legitimacy in the modern world stems from the democratic principle, a principle which can be manipulated fraudulently, and create new domestic and foreign policy problems.[6] Ferrero had in mind totalitarian governments which sought legitimacy through a form called 'revolutionary democracy', but since their regimes (whether Nazi or Marxist) were inherent distortions of the democratic principle, they could never acquire legitimacy. This is precisely the plight of the autocratic, non-Islamized regimes in most Muslim countries, except for those who have Islamized, as explained above, thus obtaining another (this time Islamic) base of legitimacy. The problem with these Islamic regimes is that they cannot subscribe to the democratic principle, which was posited by Ferrero as a prerequisite for legitimacy.

In classical Islam the acceptance of the ruler was performed through the *Bai'a* (the oath of allegiance) in the public square, which was then ruthlessly translated into popular legitimacy, and any insurgence challenging it was deemed rebellion against the legitimacy of the ruler. But it was evident that the true legitimacy of the ruler (Caliph or Sultan) remained based on the capacity of the ruler to enforce the *shari'a* law and protect it. Today, rulers use the terms 'democracy', 'human rights', 'elections' and such, but they profoundly misunderstand them. It is not that they understand and manipulate, or behave 'fraudulently', but they seem to manipulate because one cannot imagine that others fail to comprehend what is the obvious to us.

There is a link between legitimacy and succession. Mubarak or Qaddafi have 'succeeded' themselves again and again and genuinely regard themselves as legitimate. They cannot be opposed during an 'election', genuinely believing that opposition and competition, the trademarks of Western democracy, are signs of division and controversy which are inimical to the rule of unity. They sense that since they were overwhelmingly chosen by the masses, they are entitled to cite those results as proof of legitimacy, often with the approving nod of Western powers. In other words, the fake act of unopposed 'elections' seems sufficient to these regimes to claim legitimacy. In the case of moderate President Khatami in Iran, he could play the game of democracy by running against an opponent (Nateq Nuri), though both candidates in the election had to come from among the ranks of the mullahs. That meant that the base of their legitimacy was the Shari'a Holy Law, as embodied in their Islamic creed. Others representing civil society have been either executed or removed, have fled or live as an opposition in exile. Yet the terms 'democracy', 'elections' and 'candidates' were profusely used by both Iranians and others, as if the campaign took place in the mid-West, not the Middle East. In other words, when Islamic legitimacy is established, paradoxically it can allow a certain democratic leeway as long as all candidates swear their allegiance to it.

The frequent changes of constitutions in the Islamic world, and the enthusiasm with which these changes are usually welcomed, are in themselves an indication of this mammoth misunderstanding in concepts and terminology. When a new ruler overthrows his predecessor, he also finds it necessary to wipe out the record of the latter's accomplishments (de-Stalinization, de-Nasserization, etc.) together with the basic documents which had provided the ideological underpinnings of his rule. Sadat's 'October Paper' (1973) replaced Nasser's similar personally drafted documents (The March 30 Announcement). The masses never regard an existing constitution as a basic document protected by a court of law independent of the ruler, but as a legitimate declaratory programme moulded by the ruler and likely to be modified as the ruler lingers in power, emasculated when the ruler finds it necessary to disregard it, or totally discarded when he believes time has come to revitalize his rule, or by the succeeding dictator when he takes over. An exception to this rule is the Charter of the PLO, which has shown a tremendous resistance to change because the PLO has been a revolutionary movement seeking power. The Charter is a blueprint for annihilating the enemy (Zionism), not a platform for domestic conduct. But in Islamized countries such as Iran, the *shari'a* law being the supreme, eternal and immutable rule of Allah, a new legitimacy is not sought by changing constitutions.

In the past decade the international media have penetrated local restrictions and made the idea of a global village applicable to authoritarian Islamic countries, eroding the nature of governments there. The sight of tyrannical regimes collapsing in Eastern Europe, shown in real time over the silver screens everywhere, has provoked a dramatic rise in the belief in people's power, and the ability of a determined and well organized mass, to force down the tyrant. It was seen in 1978–79 in Iran, when the Shah fell. In Afghanistan, the popular movement led by the Taliban took over power, and in Indonesia massive upheaval brought Suharto down. In all three cases, violence was necessary to overthrow the tyrant, who had no legitimacy, but in his stead Islamic legitimacy was provided by the new government (albeit in a milder form in Indonesia). Aspirants of power have yet to be seen demoting that Islamic legitimacy and reinstalling in its place tyrannical rule. The international media have also produced a sense of community among Muslims everywhere, and so far only fundamentalist Islam had the ideological stamina and the organizational skill to embody it. Another lesson too is that the Islamist ascendance to power through democracy, based on Islamic legitimacy as experienced in Turkey and Algeria, proved more fragile than the violent takeovers in Iran or Afghanistan.

To achieve their goal, the Islamist movements are striving to participate in the 'democratic' game, more specifically that part of it which would allow them to seize power, by popular vote. Banned often, in autocratic regimes, from participating in elections as political organizations, they focus on widespread welfare, educational, medical and social activities to increase their appeal and at the same time expose the failure of governments to provide the same services. They also provide exemplary leadership by immensely charismatic sheikhs who come from the people, live modestly with the masses and feel their daily concerns, in contrast to the corrupt illegitimate leaders who retrench themselves into their palaces and rely on brutal military force.

These movements cry for elections as their only hope to take over power, hopes backed by their recurrent successes when allowed to participate but dashed when they were ousted from power by the enemies of Islamic legitimacy.

These movements often win domestic and international support for their 'readiness to accept the rules of the game'. But what would they do once in power? If the West listens to their insistence on the *shari'a* state and rule by *shura*, then perhaps they would abolish free elections. Meantime, their democratic language gains political asylum for their persecuted leaders in the West, and enables them to collect funds under the cover of charitable front organizations, publish pamphlets and magazines banned in their countries of origin, and expose those regimes. In turn, rulers of those countries recognized by the West as legitimate accuse the West of sheltering the dissidents who seek their downfall.

In contrast with Islamists who have accepted the rules of the game and seek power through elections knowing they are no match for the military forces which support the autocratic regimes, the militant Islamic movements (Gama'at in Egypt, Hamas and Islamic Jihad in Jordan and Palestine, GIA in Algeria), press for a solution here and now, through elections if possible, by violent means if necessary. In that struggle, all means are viable: killings of policemen and military; shooting and scaring off foreigners; massacring helpless civilian populations suspected of collaborating with the regime/enemy; and undermining their states in order to show fellow citizens and the West the weakness, illegitimacy and fragility of the state structures.

In spite of the abuses of human rights, these militants seek, and often obtain, refuge in Western governments that are reluctant to move against individuals or organizations of this sort unless caught with blood on their hands within their territories. Muslim militants like Sheikh Abdel-Rahman could find political refuge in America, while fleeing a regime he sought to undermine in Cairo. Similarly, Ghanouchi of Tunisia and Muslim radicals from Egypt seek shelter in Western Europe in spite of the latter's support for the countries those fugitives had fled from. It was not until the implication of the Sheikh in the Twin Tower explosion in New York that the US government moved to freeze the assets of these groups and put them under surveillance. France did likewise after the recurring explosions in its metro system, but Britain, Germany and other Western countries still have a long way to go before such similar measures are put in place.

These violent groups abhor the West as the more quietist ones do too, only more virulently so. In Lebanon, Palestine, Iran and elsewhere they perform the ritual of burning American and Israeli flags, often dubbed the 'Great Satan' and 'Little Satan'. Very often, the more moderate among the Islamic movements, and even the countries within which they operate illicitly, tacitly align themselves with the crowds in order to maintain their popular appeal. Arafat has often been seen watching tremendously popular re-enacted scenes of martyrdom staged in public to hail Hamas and Islamic Jihad heroes, his fierce political rivals, who committed 'suicide bombings'. Islamic leaders participated in the Teheran Islamic Summit (December 1997) despite the role Iran plays in supporting and financing such groups across the globe, including within many of the countries represented in the Summit.

The militant groups are cultivated by Islamic fundamentalist countries. The latter provide living proof that an Islamic regime is feasible and workable in the modern world. Those regimes in turn support militants elsewhere to achieve the same. (Iran sustains the Hamas, the Hizbullah, the Bosnian Muslims and others; Sudan provides training grounds and launching pads for activities against the Egyptian regime and other African Islamic groups; and Afghanistan turns its attention to the former Soviet Central Asia, notably to Islamists in Tajikistan and China.) These militant Islamic regimes provide an umbrella and a hinterland for rainy days. Iran, by far the most powerful and most devoted to the cause of Islamic militants, foots the bill in many cases and assists the militants militarily and diplomatically (recently, the Argentine government publicized the support of the Iranian Embassy to the Hizbullah group which blew up Israeli and Jewish targets in Buenos Aires). It also organizes meetings of the Terrorist International in Teheran to oppose reconciliation of the Islamic world with Israel in accordance with these militants' agenda.

Among Islamic countries, Saudi Arabia stands out as a special case: it has one of the most oppressive regimes in the Islamic world, yet because of its vulnerability and total dependence on Western markets, it treads the road of 'moderation' and adopts pro-American ways. The West does not reproach the Saudi record on human rights and democracy, but does disparage the Chinese and Sudanese. Moreover, trade continues: oil to the West, and a vast arsenal of weapons to Saudi Arabia (and other Gulf states for that matter). Even when Saudi Arabia, or wealthy Saudi individuals, support international terrorists like the Hamas, the West looks the other way. If you have oil, your lack of ballots does not matter, and you can even discretely support those who wield bullets.

The dilemmas of the West

Violence in Islamic societies invariably has emanated either from the hopelessness of removing rulers who lack legitimacy and are pro-Western or from the frustration of winning elections through the ballots and being prevented from following up on their gains, usually with Western connivance. Their disenchantment with the West feeds on disbelief and disarray. The West has cultivated and propagated the idea of substituting ballots for bullets, but aligns itself with those who deprive the Islamists from showing their mettle in the ballot. Paradoxically, the Islamists clamour for the democratic process, and are ready to use violence to attain it, while the seemingly 'democratizing' regimes accused of suppressing it are challenged as being the cause of violence. Conversely, when the West gives asylum to those same Islamists who are persecuted by the regimes they seek to overrun in their own countries, it is attacked by 'loyal adepts', like Mubarak, for professing one thing and doing another. The West ends up as the villain in the eyes of both government and opposition.

Western leaders have declared repeatedly that they will not deal with governments which hold no respect for democratic principles. But everyone can see the close relationships, the alliances and commercial deals made by Western democracies with the worse autocracies. They can see that insistence on human rights and democratic values hinge on:

(1) whether economic interests are likely to be harmed/served;
(2) whether the relative strength/weakness of their target makes it permeable/ impermeable to their bashing or sanctions;
(3) whether criticism of human rights in Islamic countries could hurt the Western critics domestically; and
(4) the fact that often Western leaders' hands are not clean as far as the historical records of their country are concerned.

These concerns affect the decision-making process in the West. But they embarrass Western governments caught in the inextricable contradiction between their statements and deeds. Islamists observe Western democracies behaving as generous, peace-loving promoters of human rights and champions of democracy only at the expense of others, while disregarding their own deficiencies in such matters, and forgetting that these notions are culture-bound and rarely respond to universal criteria.

It took the United States 50 years to apologize for incarcerating the Japanese during World War II who did not menace the national security. It took over 100 years for America to apologize officially for slavery and for mistreating the Black population, but Americans are quick to indict Muslim states for far lesser offences against parts of their populations. In two centuries Americans systematically eliminated tens of thousands of Native Americans without any apology or redress, but they stood most vigorously against Apartheid horrors in South Africa or human right violations in China, the Communist world and elsewhere. Seen in perspective, even the Afrikaners were gentler to the native Black population: despite ruthless discrimination, they never systematically eliminated them as subhumans.

Islamists cite their legendary tolerance of other minorities, compared to that of the Christian West, as a justification for their brand of 'democracy' and human rights. But their concept of tolerance is quite different from that in the West today, which sees tolerance as equality. When one tolerates the other, differences between them (in skin colour, religion, sex, nationality and political outlook) are overlooked, set aside and not value-judged (i.e. I accept you, in spite of the differences). When an Islamist addresses a non-Muslim, the message is: I accept you in spite of your inferiority. Islamic society had been historically compartmentalized, unlike traditional Christian society which was, at least theoretically, uniform and homogenous. This meant that although the Scriptural minorities were second-rate citizens in the Islamic polity (the status of *dhimmi*), their life and property was protected by the Islamic ruler, unlike medieval and even modern Christianity which expelled, forced conversion upon and massacred multitudes of Jews and Muslims. Therefore, in their anti-Western discourse, the Muslim radicals (and Muslims in general for that matter) cite their own 'tolerance' of others who submit to Islamic rule as against the narrow-mindedness, the opportunism and the expediency of the West.

What can be learned?

From the radical Muslims, point of view, the West does nothing when its 'friends' (i.e. Jordan, Algeria and Egypt, or close allies in the Gulf) act violently against their own citizens in attempts to fight Islamic fundamentalism. It actively supports regimes without legitimacy and overlooks the issue of eliminating fundamentalists in elections they may win. This perceived hypocrisy generates violence against the West.

Political bargaining in contemporary Islamic societies, owing to the totality of the Islamic claim, is difficult. The rulers in place can choose, in theory, between total democratization, to which they pay lip-service but by which they may be swept away from power, or total oppression, banning, exile, execution and exclusion of the Islamists. A small degree of liberty is not possible here, because once given, more will be demanded, often backed with violence. The murder of Sadat by Muslim radicals whom he had helped emerge from clandestinity, and the removal of the political reformers in the Soviet Bloc who had attempted part-time liberty (the Gurbachev's, the Kranz's etc.) are evidence of the futility of the half-way syndrome which in the end consumes its initiators.

Islamic groups cannot be shut off by oppression. They are accumulating popularity and power, paradoxically under the protective wings of the Western democracies which shelter them. But, at the end, both the Islamic groups and the regimes in place will turn against the West, the former because of their ideological commitment, the latter, by their current manifestations of international Islamic solidarity, because of perceptions best articulated by President Mubarak after the Luxor massacre that Western democracies indeed shelter terrorists.

Western societies have a hard time comprehending the 'democratizing' process in Islamic countries. The elections in Jordan and Algeria of late were reported by the Western media and were nonchalantly commented upon by Western politicians as if they were describing elections in the American mid-West or in Yorkshire. Terms like 'democracy', 'pluralism', 'multi-party elections', 'percentage points' etc. have quite a different meaning when votes are rigged, parties banned from running and candidates imprisoned.

The West has been conversing with the Islamic world in a language that Islam does not understand, or show any propensity to learn. There are 55 Islamic countries, and none is democratic in the Western sense. Turkey and Pakistan respond partly to the criteria of democracy, but in view of the violence in the democratic process and especially the transition of power, it is doubtful whether either has truly internalized and accepted the democratic principle. Unfortunately, many believe that they are practising democracy (Mubarak is convinced that his country is democratic and Jordanian kings proclaim their autocracy as a 'constitutional monarchy'). What hope is there for a democratic change when those directly involved do not perceive the problem?

Instead of taking sides between fundamentalists and their oppressors, the West should encourage the democratic process and accept its consequences. If the current autocrats should win, though this is difficult to envisage, they will achieve legitimacy and perhaps become less autocratic; if the fundamentalists should win, then, as in Iran, the constraints of government might moderate them in the long run despite a commitment to Islamic legitimacy of their rule. Legitimate governments, sure of themselves, might in turn reduce violence and promote democratization, within the boundaries of their regimes and the authoritarian limitations of their traditions. Those who continue to oppose them would then do so as part of the internal political process, and will no longer need to seek refuge in Western lands or resort to violence to make their point. In this idyllic but unlikely setting in the foreseeable future, ballots will make bullets no longer necessary.

NOTES

1. Al-Akhbar, Cairo, 24 Nov. 1997.
2. Clarinews, Internet, 25 Nov. 1997.
3. Reuters, London, 24 Nov. 1997.
4. Ibid.
5. Ibid.
6. See Rapoport and Weinberg in this volume.

8

Purity is Danger: An Argument for Divisible Identities

ANNA SIMONS

This article explores two very different, yet related, sets of reasons to help explain the absence of widespread identity-based communal violence in the United States. First, Americans can afford to treat identity situationally, and only recently have they begun to bump up against the outer limits of who it can be agreed the state should protect. Secondly, the government has proved increasingly vigilant in its response to separatist groups that pledge their primary allegiance to themselves rather than to the state, and who by doing so invite the use of force.

One of democracy's great strengths has to be its wide appeal to people of all backgrounds. Yet background can also subvert democracy within states and lead to violence under certain sets of conditions. For instance, in many of the places where democratization has been pushed, but extended families and other communal solidarities persist, there has been extensive bloodshed: in Kenya, Nigeria, Rwanda, Sri Lanka, Bosnia – the list is long, while the rationale for how ethnic fissures can lead to ethnic violence seems clear.

Put most simply, people want to be represented by individuals who they know will look out for their interests, over whom they have some sort of leverage, and with whom they feel solidarity. Where such ties also carry moral weight – as they do among members of extended families, clans, tribes and churches, for instance – communal trust is already implied. In fact, it may be *immoral* to vote for anyone outside of the community so long as someone from within the community is running for office. This means that there may be far less choice for people in many societies about who and why they vote than we presume. Choicelessness, in certain instances, may even be said to *define* societies within states, so much so that sub-national groups then win individuals' allegiance, loyalty and compliance away from the state.

A variety of conditions will produce choicelessness.[1] Either the state cannot be trusted to meet citizens' basic needs, or there has never been enough wealth to go around. Regardless, when citizens are haunted by a future they consider to be uncertain and insecure, they invariably fall back on institutions and individuals they know they can trust. In solvent states, government-sponsored social welfare safety nets tend to be wide, deep and inclusive enough to offer sufficient assistance. By contrast, where chronic insecurity emanates *from* the state, people have nowhere else to turn *but* to members of their family, clan, tribe or church. Meanwhile, the more people rely on others easily identifiable as kin (or kindred), the more definition, visibility and substance this lends groups and the more group membership appears to matter. The slide is short and slippery between group identities mattering and members of 'other' groups not mattering at all. Actually, neglecting non-members may represent a best-case scenario. Far worse is when people consider those outside their group to be competitors and rivals. Then, their very existence demands removal.

In 1991–92, members of powerful Somali clan-families neglected drought-stricken members of other clan-families. In 1994 Hutus related to Rwandan President Habyarimana's wife's family incited tens of thousands of other Hutus to pre-emptively murder Tutsi 'power-seekers' in a gambit to retain power themselves. Between 1992 and 1995, Serbs, Croats and Bosnian Muslims committed atrocities in an effort to establish (or re-establish) strongholds where they would prevail socially, economically and politically. And these are but three recent cases of large-scale ethnic conflict. In each case dissolution has followed hard on the heels of government promises to be more inclusive.[2] Elsewhere, in places as far removed as the Congo, India and Indonesia[3] elections have also triggered communal violence.

So far, the United States has escaped this brand of deadly identity politics. How? And why does democracy work so effectively here, but cause so much strife elsewhere?

In this article I suggest two very different, yet related, sets of reasons to help explain the absence of widespread identity-based communal violence in the United States. First, Americans can afford to treat identity situationally, and only recently have they begun to bump up against the outer limits of who it can be agreed the state *should* protect.

Secondly, the government has proved increasingly vigilant in its response to separatist groups that pledge their primary allegiance to themselves rather than to the state, and by doing so invite the use of force.

A confluence of conditions

In the final years of the previous century, American democracy was said to be on trial,[4] full of discontent,[5] and in need of reinvention,[6] vigorous leadership[7] and even a new enemy.[8] The tone was clear: democracy is hurting. But is this democracy's fault? And what is American democracy anyway: a social system that creates people as Americans, or their creation subject to incremental but (in the end) substantive change?

More than 200 years after the establishment of the state, it may no longer be possible to say whether democracy emerges from or grants Americans the freedoms they consider Creedal. As Samuel Huntington notes, if Americans do not worship they at least privilege liberty, equality, constitutionalism, liberalism, limited government and private enterprise. And this, more than anything else, distinguishes them.

> In some societies, some people subscribe to many of these ideas and in other societies many people subscribe to some of these ideas. In no other society, however, are all of these ideas so widely adhered to by so many people as they are in the United States.[9]

However, there is more to American exceptionalism than her political ideas and institutions.[10] As Bellah makes clear, her civil religion is critical to national solidarity.[11] But not even this would be possible without her resource base, and the freedoms that come with room in which to manoeuvre and escape.[12] America could never have seemed such a promising 'promised land' without bounty and (apparent) emptiness. It certainly would not have attracted the numbers of indentured servants and impoverished early immigrants as it did. And likewise, it would not have supported them earning their way as eventual equals under the law. As Jack Greene describes the Thirteen Colonies, they were rankless, not classless: 'all free people occupied the same social status in respect to the law and enjoyed an equality of opportunity to strive for and earn respect'.[13]

Although national myths suggest that US independence was a direct result of the struggle for equality, fairer representation and more republican (and local) governance, one cannot ignore the extent to which environmental givens also favoured liberty and certain 'rights'. In fact, some of the constitution's most basic guarantees may well amount to little more than ethnographic truths. For example, Americans already bore arms and assembled to protect and govern themselves long before the revolution. Other freedoms were likewise entrenched, with far too many religious sects and presses for a weak central government to be able to control. Or, to turn this around, there may have been no way for any eighteenth century government to rein back these liberties, as ingrained as they already were. Just spatially, the Thirteen Colonies were far too inchoate. But also, one generally finds that people will strive to remain independent yet equal according to their own laws wherever they are able to disperse, live off the land and escape one another's surveillance.

Significantly, up through (arguably) the 1930s individuals, families and even entire communities could find large stretches of unmonitored space into which to disappear. Attendant gaps in communications and transportation systems would have helped people remain socially and even economically disengaged. Citizens who chose to could not only subsist comfortably without government assistance, but they could likewise avoid government interference – a luxury which may be in the throes of finally vanishing.

Individuals and factions

In one sense, individuals continue to remain highly divisible. Throughout American history, rights have been fought for on the basis of our inalienable status as separable people, not *peoples*. Traditionally, whenever the Supreme Court (or a constitutional amendment) has reversed customary discrimination of a category of people (e.g. Blacks, women) the point has been to break individuals out of denigrated groups in order to reintegrate them into a broadened society.[14]

Thanks, too, to the intense fusion of democracy with capitalism, Americans have come to compete with one another in virtually all spheres: for jobs, for labour, for votes, for representation. Essentially, individuals serve as *the* political and economic unit of account. However, democratic and capitalist principles do not always mesh in practice.

While Americans may be enjoined legally not to discriminate against others for being members of this or that group, rampant economic competition ensures that judgements about who to hire, fire, befriend, support and associate with are made constantly. The easiest way to make such choices is to pre-judge others based on (1) personal past experiences, and/or (2) the experiences of trusted friends, family members, mentors and others.

There may be no way around it: people constantly compare and categorize; nor does it seem difficult to map people's comfort zones. For everyone, there are people who they are (reflexively) alike, and there are people who they are not like, while clearly the more circumscribed their experiences, the closer-to-home are their choices about who to throw in with. Meanwhile, too, because the United States is a democracy, people *have* to group. Otherwise, their voices are drowned out as soon as those with whom they are in disagreement (or competition) begin to cluster. Thus, it is not just that there is a human penchant to categorize others; there is a political responsibility to group.

This, in turn, means that certain latent tensions persist and are likely always to be present. The challenge comes in preventing these from leading to permanent and/or divisive group-based fissures. One solution is never to allow groups themselves to become permanent. And notably, the founders designed a system which would ensure that this would not have to happen.

Realizing the extent to which voters would align themselves according to self-interest rather than disinterest, the founding fathers devised a system full of cross-cutting checks and balances. To address the issue of factions they built enough flexibility, redundancy, overlap and competition not only into government, but into its interstices, that new interest groups could always be accommodated, and individuals would always be tempted to join new groups. As Madison argues in *The Federalist Paper* #10, the more expansive the system, the more long-lived the union would likely be.[15] The more factions, too, the less likely it would be that any one interest could capture and hold government hostage, as occurred among the ancient Greeks.

Essentially, too, by placing no limits on *who* the Constititution and Bill of Rights applied to, the founding fathers left open a whole series of social frontiers. Given systems of governance and market relations designed to accommodate growth, along with bountiful conditions in this 'new' promised land, government could well afford to be increasingly expansive. Even neater, the faster the country expanded – demographically as well as spatially – the less likely it became that any one faction could ever lock in everyone else.

The proof of the founders' genius endures. Who, at the end of the eighteenth century, could have forseen the shape of states, parties, movements, labour unions or special interests yet to come? Even the multicultural identity politics that alarm so many Americans today should reassure them of the founders' foresight.

Identity politics

Consequently, too, identity politics in the US differ from identity politics abroad. In the US there are no official subnational identities. Although there is a plethora of possible affiliations from which to choose, none carries an official imprimatur: none is a trump. In fact, not only is there tremendous choice in how identities can be fashioned, but identities can be changed much as if they were fashions. Consider some of our most public figures. Michael Jackson, Dennis Rodman, Madonna, Prince, even Bob Dylan, routinely transform themselves. These entertainers have switched colour, sexual orientation, religion – precisely those things which many might say are bred into us – and yet none can be said to have suffered as a result.

Significantly, there is no single factor that the US government or even a majority of Americans uses to categorize all other members of the population. At different times and in different regions, religion, place of birth, class and race may have seemed all-important. But none has been paramount across the country over time. This is in sharp contrast to identity elsewhere, where people carry national identity cards which list their ethnicity (as in Rwanda) or, at a more local level, are acutely aware of one another's heritage.

For many Americans heritage is a hobby and a curiosity. Some do pay keen attention to their past(s), but because the United States is a country founded by waves of different immigrants there is no single, let alone common, past everyone can plug into. Likewise, there is no divisive issue around which Americans can all take sides in a fight. For example, most Bosnians agree on what divides them: differences grounded in locally shared history and mutual slights and depradations. Ditto Rwandans, Sri Lankans and residents of Northern Ireland. By contrast, what are the faultlines that Americans could *all* agree on?

The only civil war fought in the US cannot easily be refought. Even now, historians can hardly agree on whether its causes were economic, political or moral. Resuscitating slavery is on no one's agenda. Not only have grievances shifted radically, so have populations.

The availability of government assistance in the United States also puts the lie to the need for subnational regroupment. No matter where Americans move to or with whom they choose to align themselves, government is generally just a disaster away. This is not the case in many other places where, when catastrophe strikes, central authority fails to protect people, and offers nothing in the way of individual social welfare. Then citizens find themselves turning to the same networks and institutions their parents and grandparents would have trusted: family, church, anything which promises (and has proven) long-lasting, overarching security.[16]

In contrast (and at least so far), conditions in the US offer too many counter-incentives to large-scale, multi-generational, subnational groupings persisting or claiming the exclusive allegiance of members.[17] Or, to come at this from a slightly different angle, few American ethnic interest groups have much moral cohesiveness. Identity politics, in this sense, have broad but shallow roots.

Individuals who self-identify as Blacks, Chicanos, gays or Americans with disabilities, for example, may well feel affinity for others who seem tied to them by virtue of a shared colour, language or stigma. Socially such markers might seem as though they link such individuals together from birth. But morally they do not. It takes more than a shared mode of production, a set of traits or lifestyle to bind people morally. Either webs of mutual obligation are thick, involuntary and inescapable, or members unquestioningly support one another because they believe themselves impelled to by some higher authority. Far too much mobility (and affluence) has precluded the former from developing or persisting in the United States. But the latter?

The issue of allegiance

On the one hand, incorporating all citizens into the state can be viewed as a triumph of social equity. On the other, it can reflect an unhealthy, overly controlling interest. Who reads the situation and how is likely to be morally contingent, while the catch for any central government is to impel (not compel) all citizens to accede to *it* as the overarching moral authority. In a democracy, nothing is more important.

To attain this, government essentially makes citizens a deal. A citizen can be gay and American, or white, gay and American, or straight, black and American; he or she can choose to whom he or she belongs. No one else is supposed to pick individuals' labels for them. The ethos of the United States promises this pluralism, and more: provided Americans grant the state their primary allegiance, the state will protect them no matter what their affinities may be.

Of course, there are two potential hitches to this contract. First, not all Americans believe everyone is equal or that all individuals, given their affinities, are worth protecting. Secondly, problems arise if the government cannot live up to its promise, oversteps its bounds, or is thought to be captured by one particular interest or group.

Failures on all these counts have led to dissolution elsewhere. For instance, once the Somali government could no longer perform even its most basic function –protecting citizens' safety – the 31-year-old Somali state formally fell apart.[18] Most Somalis never regarded the central government as a source of moral authority. Therefore, government actions easily inspired opposition, which triggered fighting and fed further insecurity. Similar patterns can be traced in, for example, Afghanistan, Sudan, Lebanon, Sri Lanka and Northern Ireland.

In the Somali case, as in so many others, government inequity and the presence of separable societies turn out to have been glaringly concomitant. Not only did Somali clans predate the establishment of 'Somalia the state', but the national government proved unwilling or unable to break individuals out of their kinship groups. Subnationally, Somalis openly conducted business and categorized one another according to long-lived genealogical affiliations, and thus the only thing that wound up effectively linking all Somalis was the understanding that clans were where individuals' primary loyalty lay (including, most blatantly, members of government).

Clearly, other countries which have recently dissolved – Afghanistan, Liberia, the former Yugoslavia – do not share Somalia's precise clan structure. However, there do seem to be commonalities. Hindsight suggests that in each of these places the state proved incapable of encouraging and supporting the proliferation of cross-cutting ties which could have kept individuals separable and their affiliations mixed. The morality promised by a civil religion did not sufficiently override or dissolve pre-existing attachments. People instead were able (or were forced) to fall back on, and reinvigorate, networks which obligated them to treat people who did not belong to their particular 'us' as members of alien 'thems'. This, in turn, facilitated ethnic targeting. Without the intercession of credible central authority, members of some groups could all too easily cleanse others simply for belonging to groups they had a moral, often historic, and invariably economic, imperative to dislike.

Still, insecurity and group fears cannot be the sole explanation for how and why ethnic or group violence topples states. There has to be something more – or less. The fact that the government (and not just the faction controlling government) also becomes a target suggests that capturing the state has value, precisely the thing the founding fathers were so keen to prevent any one group from being able to realize.

In virtually all countries, the government controls resources worth having, and/or there is little of worth that those who seize the levers of government cannot (and will not) control. Therefore, we should expect a scramble, though this in and of itself cannot explain why competition has to lead to conflict, or why disaffected, disenfranchised and disgruntled individuals do not simply withdraw, escape and set themselves up elsewhere, as so many immigrants did in coming *to* the US or, once in the US, as others did by moving west.

Separable societies

The short rejoinder to the exit option is that it is decreasingly an option: often there is nowhere else for people to go. The longer answer depends on local conditions.

Again Somalia, as exemplar of a fractured state, may be instructive. Two subclans continue to inhabit and fight over control of the former national capital, Mogadishu. One clan has erected its own government in the former British Somaliland, and considers the region independent (though the international community still does not). In north-eastern Somalia, meanwhile (where members of a third clan predominate), there seems to be peace and a second self-declared state (Puntland). Finally, there is everyone else, scattered throughout the countryside, resident in refugee camps, chased from place to place, with no space to call their own, no one to guarantee them safety and no way to start over. Many of these dispossessed people were nomads to begin with. Yet even they have a bleak future, at least in part because they are too hemmed in by what others have carved up and control.

Somalia, to be sure, is somewhat unusual. Few countries today support nomads at all, let alone the percentage of the population (60 per cent) nomads were said to comprise prior to Somalia's formal collapse.

But if it is impossible for groups of former nomads to move around in Somalia, imagine countries with settled populations, where land has long been a commodity to control. Or, consider the United States.

Historically, there have been communities which have succeeded in separating themselves from broader American society or, having been chased out of one region, have been able to establish themselves elsewhere. Certainly, numerous religious sects have successfully removed themselves. So have communes. Nor can we ignore the hollows and pockets full of people who simply allowed (or could not help) being passed by because there was nothing worth developing where they lived. Most often, though, people in places like Appalachia already owned their land – or no one did.

Significantly, in few (if any) of these cases did residents deny, let alone contest, the central authority of the US government. Individuals may have actively avoided the long arm of the law, but they did not take up weapons *en masse* to protect their separateness; they did not engage in separatist confrontation – with one notable exception.

American Indian tribes are the one set of separable societies the US government *has* officially recognized. Yet the entire relationship between the federal government and American Indians has been (and continues to be) fraught, largely because the US government has always been ambivalent about what Indians are.[19] Are they Americans first, in which case individuals should be pried out of tribes, something the government has, at times, worked hard to do? Or, are Indians members of sovereign nations, in which case the tribe (and community), not the federal government, is the only authority to whom individual Indians owe any allegiance?

The 1973 seige at Wounded Knee, vicious battles over fishing rights and the ongoing tussle to control gaming all indicate just how difficult it has been for the federal government to countenance societies that the law insists must be treated as separate but equal to itself. There are several bitter realities which serve to buttress Indian tribal rights. For one, Indians have already been beaten; they are under control. Secondly, their numbers cannot suddenly swell (since membership depends on blood). Also, these societies make no claim to self-sufficiency; instead, the government is heavily involved and invested.

In other words, and legally speaking, tribes may present certain challenges to federal authority. But Indians cannot pose a threat to democracy *as* Indians, since tribes (and Indians) have been treated as something separate and apart since the founding of the United States. This is not a privilege that marks off any category of individuals. Blacks, women, Chinese and Japanese, for instance, may have been singled out for differential treatment in the past, but only Indians have been awarded supra-constitutional rights granting them *group* sovereignty.

The issue of authority and the association/dissociation challenge

This is noteworthy because the government projects (and may well have to project) a very different attitude toward self-segregating, *non*-Indian societies. While increasingly many are labelled 'anti-government' (and then lumped together), not all are separatist in the same ways.[20] Some, for example, have simply been millenarian and seek neither a confrontation with nor the overthrow of government. They are not particularly antagonistic toward authority; members simply want to be able to answer to a higher authority of their own choosing, on their own terms. Or at least this is one way to interpret the activities of groups such as the Heaven's Gate 'cult', which (apparently) went unmonitored, even by the government.[21]

Problems inevitably arise, though, when the ever-expanding range of choices some Americans make rub up against what other Americans refuse to countenance. As Lindholm and Hall put it, 'civility in society ... depends upon a particular social agreement to live together with difference'.[22] But, again, nothing in society guarantees that all individuals will assent to this. This means that when people treat identity as though it *is* a value, and grant it moral weight, they can (and likely will) use identity to cleave those they regard as morally inferior from members of the population at large.

This – assigning others' identities a value and, worse, choosing identities for them – may well represent the ultimate challenge to the moral authority of a democratic state, which depends on individuals being free to choose and change their own associations. No democracy can afford to be tweaked like this for long, and certainly not by those who would attempt to create an alternative power structure rather than work within the political system.[23]

Actually, the issue of authority, perhaps even the existence of the state, presents democracy with a tricky problem. All governments must flex their muscles from time to time in order to demonstrate that they (still) have them. Usually, control is easy to display. If the country is not at war, there is still crime for state authorities to counter, or taxes for them to collect. To maintain control, though, means also engaging in surveillance.

Surveillance is troublesome in a democracy, yet necessary in a state.[24] From the perspective of individuals already sceptical and critical of federal power, any oversight can suggest that their freedoms are under seige. Driver's licences, licence plates, checking accounts, phone records, social security numbers – all of these permit government (and other large institutions) to track people without their permission, or even their being aware. It is no coincidence, then, that these are precisely the documents that self-proclaimed sovereigns rip up.

As Michael Barkun explains in this volume, there are many reasons beyond suspicion and paranoia for individuals to dissociate themselves from broader society. Put most broadly, people disengage because on some level they consider their principles and society's to be out of synch. Either society is too permissive or not permissive enough. So long as these individuals stay solitary, they present government with little reason to interfere. In fact, if they are very good about keeping to themselves the government may not know *to* interfere. Ted Kaczynski, the Unabomber, is the perfect example of just such an individual. But so was Chris McCandless, the subject of Krakauer's bestselling biography about an intense young vagabond who starved to death alone, while on a journey of self-discovery in Alaska.[25]

Group a Kaczynski or McCandless with others just like them, though, and the dynamic shifts. Then society and government are faced with a social, and not just anti-social, problem. A democratic government may be able to accommodate dissociative individuals – in fact, it may have little choice – but not separable societies. For one, democracy depends too heavily on the social contract being made directly between individuals *and* the state. Individuals who break this contract put themselves at risk, but this is their choice, just as the state's responsibility is to then punish them should they harm others. Because Ted Kaczynski did inflict damage, he will now spend the rest of his life in prison.

However, when a group denies the government's right to punish any of its members – the position taken by adults in Randy Weaver's cabin, and in compounds occupied by the Branch Davidians, the Montana Freemen and the Republic of Texas – people move from dissociation to opposition, from being a collectivity of defiant individuals to being a group defiant in its differences, and the government then has little choice but to react *with* (and as) authority.

The problem is that whenever this occurs the hierarchical – not democratic – organization of authority is revealed. Citizens already wary of government may read this as betrayal. Worse, by surrounding a compound and ordering the surrender of all its occupants, government agents expose the extent to which they regard the occupants as group members, not as individuals. This too highlights the government's hypocrisy when it comes to the democratic presumption that the state will always protect citizens *as* individuals first.

The problem compounded

Unfortunately, though government officials may have little or no choice about how they respond to collective defiance, by responding as they do they also offer their critics little choice in how monolithically they then view 'government officials'. Both sides thus wind up trapped in a vicious cycle from which there is no easy exit. This, at any rate, is what the literature on militias and the anti-government movement suggests.

However, the literature may understate both the history of dissociation in the United States and the significance of exit options. Though it is now *pro forma* to trace the jumbled pedigrees of militias back to the Ku Klux Klan and 1866,[26] separable societies have always formed. So why suddenly do they cause so much alarm? The answer is presumably because they engage in anti-government activities, their members are heavily armed, and they proselytize. Probe a little further, though, and it is also likely that they have taken this turn because their options are increasingly constrained. Both literally and figuratively, the disaffected have run out of room.[27]

Not only have millenial fears boxed in those who believe in Tribulation, but free land no longer exists. New arrivals to an area will rarely go unnoticed, while even if people are able to hide, they cannot do so for long if they seek to recruit new members. Organizations like the Anti-Defamation League of B'nai B'rith and the Southern Poverty Law Center track and condemn any group they suspect is separatist or supremacist, augmenting whatever surveillance government agencies may already be conducting. Just in terms of daily life, escape for any group seeking autonomy proves difficult, if not impossible.

But also, on an altogether different plane, there are very few individual rights left to be won in the US. Thanks to identity politics, individuals in virtually every imaginable category are now protected by law. In this more existential sense Americans may be fast approaching a truly destabilizing set of limits, as they increasingly bump up against certain impossible determinations: Do the unborn have rights? When does life begin? Do the terminally ill and dying have rights? When should life end?

Who are we, meanwhile, to make such determinations? This is the most haunting question these others raise, while the fact that they have become issues at all is a reminder that, regardless of status as fellow citizens, joined together beneath the tent of a common (culturally American) civil religion, US citizens may not in fact share even the most fundamental of values, let alone a common world view. Small wonder, then, that some dissociate.

Solutions: Huntington's temptation

No wonder, too, that those who have studied nationalism and American history voice their alarm. Eight years ago Schlesinger Jr. critiqued the disuniting of America,[28] while two years later Huntington forecast the disuniting of the world.[29] One can sense the same passion underlying both arguments: something has to be done in order to restore Americans' indivisibility, or else. Schlesinger advocates a rethinking of the education system. Huntington, on the other hand, casts about for the US's most likely external enemy.

Since the end of the Cold War it has become all too standard to claim the US needs an enemy.[30] Determining who the next foe of the United States might be is tactically prudent. It is also clever strategy, since leaders have long recognized that having a suitable villain without unites people within.

What is interesting about Huntington's approach is that he does not seem to be promoting a hot war. Instead, his clash of civilizations argument stokes the fires for a cold war between democracies versus anyone/everyone else. At first glance this appears quite clever. The Cold War was everything a nationalist could have hoped for: Americans faced an enemy that perpetually attacked but never directly fought them, and to boot, Communists were easy to demonize.

But was it really the Cold War which kept Americans united? *Were* they united? How one answers clearly depends on how much attention one wants to pay to movements that were just beginning to fight for civil, women's and other rights in the 1960s, which themselves suggest that not all Americans felt equally included, accepted or united.[31] Perhaps, then, it was the homogenizing effects of the Second World War which had still not worn off, holding everything together. Not only did World War II intensify large scale internal migrations in the US, thus mixing populations, but conscription did the same for individual Americans.

In many regards, conscription may be the ultimate democratizer, not only because individuals are its unit of account, but because the military is effective in fusing individuals into a whole greater than the sum of their equally interchangeable parts. In this sense, the draft during World War II may have comprised a far more effective crucible for promoting nationalism than did combat. From all accounts, combat *per se* contributes little to civility. Instead, soldiers routinely find themselves *forced* to get along whenever they are not engaged in firefights. In most wars (if not in the military generally) individuals spend an inordinate amount of their time learning how to be peaceably bored together. Thus, to borrow from Ortega y Gasset, war*time* and not war may be more significant for teaching men how to 'nationally live together'.[32]

At first glance this would seem a further reason to embrace Huntington's cold war temptation. But if we reanalyze the nature of solidarity and cohesion from the level of the individual on up, the national need for a next enemy is not what should preoccupy Americans. Instead, they should be more worried about what vehicle they might have (apart from conscription) for forcing civility – particularly as they run out of elbow room.

The problem already solved: a counterintuitive solution

One thing *The Federalist Papers* make clear is that *civil* order depends on the kaleidoscopic ability of individuals to move in and out of social groups of their own free will, shifting affiliations as their interests shift. Only this can guarantee the persistence and proliferation of groups which, so long as there are enough of them, means none is likely to persist 'as is' for very long. In other words, if democracy is to be kept humming there must be room for flux and reflux.

From the outset, the federalists had scale on their side. But they also had space, and time. Who had declared a revolution before? It took the British months to wheel themselves into place and prepare to do battle, only to then find themselves having to locate and pin down colonial forces that had more to gain by remaining disengaged. Quick victory was impossible. In the meantime, this first 'national' war never galvanized all or even most Americans.

Having said that, though, the aftermath of the Revolutionary War did afford the founding fathers innumerable opportunities to experiment with fresh Enlightenment ideals, and a relatively unspecialized division of labour. In contrast, how much creative socio-political engineering can leaders afford to engage in today? Not only is the country more crowded and compressed in practically every sense but, even more to the point, the landscape in which the founding fathers and successive governments operated was still relatively empty. Whatever did not fit the codified scheme of things could be removed, segregated or ignored. Thanks to so much land, so small a population and so little surveillance, democracy – and those who disagreed with one another – had breathing space. Inclusiveness included the possibility of exclusion – whereas now? Today, purity is danger.

For the United States to function as well as it has requires individuals to remain separable, and to be held accountable as individuals first and members of groups second. Separable societies which fix (and fixate on) singular identities pose a series of dangers. No matter how counterintuitive it may seem, this is also why allowing individuals to claim as many identities as they want as often as they wish only makes sense. The government should want identities to morph. The reason? The more mixed up people are in terms of how they identify themselves, the more difficult it becomes for them to be divided.

Presently, neither class nor race seems nuanced enough to serve as *the* salient divide in the United States, while the more hairs people split the more unruly all of their labelling becomes. For example, something so seemingly straightforward as 'male' or 'female' hardly captures gender which, as a concept, is being stretched increasingly to refer to sexual preferences, sexual orientations and past sexual history. Similarly, there are whole batteries of ethnic categories from which to choose, so that on some government forms Hispanics are granted a completely separate category from Whites (who are of European descent) or African-Americans (who are of African descent), though Hispanics can be of Spanish origin, implying presumably that Spaniards are non-European *and* non-White.[33]

Although the current welter of choices is full of contradictions and is nothing if not confusing, all this divisibility actually represents a politics of intense engagement, not disengagement. Even better, by going along with (if not fostering) such a refractive selection process, the government proves itself ever-expansive and inclusive at every level. By soliciting and being so solicitous of how citizens *self*-identify, and by nurturing a contentious, non-coherent, but also non-exclusive nation, government puts the state up for grabs but also keeps it out of any one group's permanent grasp. Even better, the more the state affords people the opportunity to switch allegiances from group to group, and protects their rights to act as free agents on their own, the less fixed or separable any of their factions can become, the more equitable government seems, the more secure citizens feel, and the less anything approaching a primordial identity *has* to matter.

In the end, the fact that Americans seem unable to stay *socially* (never mind geographically) put may prove the greatest antidote to communal violence.

NOTES

1. See Anna Simons, 'Democratisation and Ethnic Conflict: The Kin Connection', *Nations & Nationalism* 3 (1997) pp.273–89.
2. As Marina Ottaway wrote in 1995, 'Sometimes political openings themselves can set in motion reactions that become obstacles to democracy ... Ethnic conflict has intensified in Burundi, Ethiopia, Kenya, and Nigeria, all countries that held elections recently': 'African Democratization: An Update', *CSIS Africa Notes* 171 (1995) p.5. For example, Melchior Ndadaye was kidnapped and killed by Tutsi extremists in October 1993, less than six months after he was elected president of Burundi. His death led to ethnic violence which claimed the lives of as many as 50,000 Burundians and helped trigger the consequent 1994 genocide in Rwanda. More recently, the 1997 civil war in the Congo grew directly out of campaign violence preceding elections in that country.
3. See Rapoport, this issue.
4. Jean Bethke Elshtain, *Democracy on Trial* (New York: Basic Books, 1995).
5. Michael Sandel, *Democracy's Discontent* (Cambridge, MA: Harvard University Press, 1996).
6. Amitai Etzioni, *The Spirit of Community* (New York: Simon & Schuster, 1993).
7. Arthur Schlesinger Jr., 'Has Democracy a Future', *Foreign Affairs* 76/5 (1997) pp.2–12.
8. Samuel Huntington, 'The Erosion of American National Interests', *Foreign Affairs* 76/5 (1997) pp.28-49.
9. Samuel Huntington, *American Politics: The Promise of Disharmony* (Cambridge, MA: Harvard University Press, 1981) p.15.
10. I draw from James MacGregor Burns, *The Vineyard of Liberty* (New York: Vintage Books, 1982); Jack Greene, *The Intellectual Construction of America* (Chapel Hill: University of North Carolina Press, 1993); Walter MacDougall, *Promised Land, Crusader State* (Boston: Houghton Mifflin, 1997); Walter Millis, *Arms and Men* (New Brunswick, NJ: Rutgers University Press, 1981/86); and Gordon Wood, *The Radicalism of the American Revolution* (New York: Vintage Books, 1991) among other works.
11. Robert Bellah, 'Civil Religion in America', *Daedalus* 96/1 (1967) pp.1–21.

12. As Albert Hirschman has put it, 'Even after the closing of the frontier, the very vastness of the country combined with easy transportation make it far more possible for Americans than for most other people to think about solving their problems through 'physical flight' than either through resignation or through ameliorating and fighting *in situ* the particular conditions into which one has been "thrown"': *Exit, Voice, and Loyalty* (Cambridge, MA: Harvard University Press, 1970) p.107.

13. Greene (note 10) p.206.

14. It seems critical to note that these are most often 'groups' only when looked at from without. They have little sustained coherence when considered from within – and thus, are probably better referred to as categories.

15. See James Madison, Alexander Hamilton and John Jay, *The Federalist Papers* (New York: Penguin Books USA, 1788/1987).

16. Charles Lindholm and John A. Hall discuss trust in the public sphere – one of the attributes of culture-based American exceptionalism – in 'Is the United States Falling Apart?', *Daedalus* 126/2 (Spring 1997) pp.183–209.

17. 'Ethnic' mafias, whose members aim to contravene the law and evade federal authority, are one glaring exception.

18. This is a process I explain in Anna Simons, *Networks of Dissolution: Somalia Undone* (Boulder, CO: Westview Press, 1995).

19. See e.g. Fergus Bordewich, *Killing the White Man's Indian* (New York: Doubleday, 1996).

20. In this section I draw from works by James Aho, *This Thing of Darkness: A Sociology of the Enemy* (Seattle: University of Washington Press, 1994); Alan Bock, *Ambush at Ruby Ridge* (Irvine, CA: Dickens Press, 1995); Joel Dyer, *Harvest of Rage: Why Oklahoma City is Only the Beginning* (Boulder, CO: Westview Press, 1997); Philip Lamy, *Millennium Rage: Survivalists, White Supremacists, and the Doomsday Prophecy* (New York: Plenum Press, 1996); and Kenneth Stern, *A Force Upon the Plain: The American Militia Movement and the Politics of Hate* (Norman: University of Oklahoma Press, 1996).

21. Arguably, Heaven's Gate members escaped government surveillance for four reasons: first, they were not heavily armed; secondly, they did not engage publicly in inflammatory rhetoric; thirdly, they did not actively or aggressively dissociate themselves from broader society (if anything they hid by operating just as any other citizens would); and fourthly, children were not involved.

   In no sense, then, did Heaven's Gate constitute a truly separable society. The group was not striving to be self-sufficient, and it certainly was not capable of self-reproduction. Only if one considers members' ultimate separation (from their containers, as they put it, or life, as we know it) can one construe the group as having had unusual control over individuals. But in no other way did members pose a threat to democracy, or by extension the government. If anything, their very association reaffirmed the potential limitlessness of what a democracy will foster and accept: adults choosing their own company, constructing their own identities, and charting their own futures.

22. Lindholm and Hall (note 16) p.201.

23. However, subversion from within frightens some people far more than does rebellion from without. As Jennifer Taw reminded me, government can be co-opted by those who gain positions of authority, with dire conseqences. If people who assign a moral weight to identity gain election to political office, who can those they condemn turn to for assistance? Genocides have resulted from just such transfers of power. Yet one of the unforseen benefits to plural, fluid identities in the US is that it is difficult to imagine a consensus forming around who to target. In this sense, Americans are acephalous, and threats from a self-defined monolithic group will likely cause others to group in response, and large-scale warfare (rather than genocide) would result.

24. See Anthony Giddens, *The Nation-State and Violence* (Berkeley: University of California Press, 1987).

25. For McCandless' vivid 'biography' see Jon Krakauer, *Into the Wild* (New York: Anchor Books, 1996).

26. See e.g. Stern (note 20) p.43.
27. This is a point that Nancy Rosenblum makes in a different context in 'The Right of Association and Paramilitary Groups: Conspiracism and Clear and Present Danger' (unpublished manuscript, 1996).
28. Arthur Schlesinger Jr., *The Disuniting of America* (New York: W. W. Norton & Co., 1992).
29. Samuel Huntington, 'The Clash of Civilizations?' *Foreign Affairs* 72/3 (1993) pp.22–50.
30. See e.g. Tom Engelhardt, *The End of Victory Culture: Cold War America and the Disillusioning of a Generation* (New York: Basic Books, 1995); and Aho (note 20).
31. See Engelhardt, ibid., and also David Halberstam, *The Fifties* (New York: Ballantine Books, 1993).
32. Jose Ortega y Gasset, *Invertebrate Spain* (New York: Norton & Co., 1937) p.43.
33. See e.g. the University of New Mexico's Voluntary Equal Opportunity Information Survey.

9

Violence in the Name of Democracy: Justifications for Separatism on the Radical Right

MICHAEL BARKUN

Over the last 30 years, figures on the American radical right have sought to justify the use of violence against the national government. This can be seen in three key texts: the charter of the United States Christian Posse Association (1972), the Nehemiah Township Charter and Common Law Contract (1982), and Louis Beam's essay, 'Revolutionary Majorities' (1984). All three are characterized by antipathy toward the state, a desire to demonstrate the legitimacy of violence, a sense of membership in an elite, and a fusion of religious and legal fundamentalism.

There is nothing novel about users of violence claiming legitimacy by linking their actions to interpretations of law, the Constitution or democratic theory. Indeed, late nineteenth-century vigilantes were particularly fond of demonstrating, at least to their own satisfaction, that not only had they done nothing wrong in executing alleged malefactors, but that they had acted wholly within the framework prescribed by the American constitutional system.[1] Nonetheless, such highly elaborated rationalizations for violence are normally few in number and rarely visible to the larger population.

The present time, however, enjoys the dubious distinction of having given birth to a large body of such material. Most of it is associated with what I refer to here as the 'radical right', a term of art which should be taken as encompassing paramilitary organizations; neo-Nazis and other racialist groups; self-identified Klans; Christian Identity groups; and other anti-government 'patriot' coteries.[2] By way of bringing some semblance of coherence to this amorphous and fragmented universe, I concentrate here on three interrelated documents composed during the last 25 years.

The first, 'United States Christian Posse Association', provides a rationale for that organization, one of two broad groupings within the posse comitatus movement. Although undated, it was almost certainly published during or about 1972. It appeared in a publication issued by the late William Potter Gale, founder of the Association and an important Christian Identity minister and tax protestor. Gale was almost certainly the author.[3]

The second document, 'Nehemiah Township Charter and Common Law Contract', was prepared in Kootenai County, Idaho, in 1982 and was meant to provide the basis for a new political unit of 'Aryan Freemen'. The Charter was signed by 28 individuals, many of them then or later prominent on the radical right, including Richard Girnt Butler, the founder of Aryan Nations, as well as several subsequent members of the insurgent group known as 'The Order' (e.g. Randolph Duey and David Lane).[4]

The third document, 'Revolutionary Majorities', is a 1997 web posting of an essay first published in 1984. Its author, Louis Beam, is a former Texas Klan leader now closely associated with Aryan Nations. He is perhaps the most influential strategic thinker on the racialist right, linked to the concept of 'leaderless resistance' (i.e. the doctrine that violence should be committed by unconnected individuals or small cells who decide independently when and how force should be employed).[5]

Behind each of the documents lies a vision of an ideal America, a millenarian conception of a perfect polity. The linkage of political programmes with millennial visions is, of course, scarcely a novelty. From the image of the 'city on a hill' in the seventeenth century, through Manifest Destiny, to post-Cold War conceptions of America as the world's bearer of political democracy and free market economics, millennial visions of America and its global role have been commonplace. What differentiates the documents considered here is not their fixation upon an ideal America, therefore, but the *kind* of ideal they seek. For it is an America with little or no central government, made up of small, autonomous local communities from which Jews and non-Whites have been systematically excluded or reduced to a servile status and in which women have been returned to traditional roles.

The issues that consume democratic theorists – conflicting interests, intensity of preferences, and the like – seem totally absent here. William Potter Gale's 'Christian citizens', the Nehemiah Township Charter's 'Aryans' and Louis Beam's 'patriots' are assumed to manifest natural harmonies of interest, such that none require elaborate mechanisms for decision-making and conflict resolution. Indeed, none even raise the possibility of serious disagreements within the community of those entitled to the rights of citizenship. The only real conflicts, as far as they are concerned, are those that set citizens against outsiders – the 'other' in the form of racial and religious adversaries and their white, nominally Christian allies. In this polarized political universe, the forces of light and darkness are destined to collide in a final, apocalyptic battle. But within the domain of the children of light, only harmony reigns.

The United States Christian Posse Association

Like other posse comitatus groups, the United States Christian Posse Association adopted an inverted view of the American political system, in which small units trump large ones. In particular, the county represents the pinnacle of legitimate governmental authority, 'the highest authority of government in our Republic as it is the closest to the body political (the people), who are, in fact, the GOVERNMENT'. Accordingly, the sheriff is 'the only legal law enforcement officer in the United States of America'.[6]

Not surprisingly, this elevation of the county, its sheriff and, by extension, the posse contains ample potential for violent confrontations with other jurisdictions. For example, Gale asserts that the sheriff is responsible for protecting his county's citizens from 'unlawful acts, even though such are committed by other officials of government'. A sheriff who fails to act against law-violating officialdom must be removed from office.[7] Lest there be any doubt as to what might constitute governmental law violation, the document reminds posses that they should be particularly vigilant toward state and federal tax collection agencies 'who unlawfully assume judicial powers when they are in the performance of their duties'.[8] Indeed, in 1987, the year before Gale died, he and five associates were convicted of threatening the lives of IRS employees and a Nevada justice of the peace.

Any group of seven or more 'Christian citizens' could apply to the Posse Association for a charter, after which a Christian posse could be organized in their county. It was clearly conceived as a paramilitary force since, in addition to a Posse Commander, it was to be governed by Assistant Commanders in charge of personnel, intelligence and investigations, operations and communications, and logistics and supply.[9]

Gale took a dim view of democracy, which he equated with 'mob rule', preferring republican government, which he termed 'a government of LAW'.[10] He was particularly anxious that his activities be perceived as entirely legitimate. The legitimacy of the posse movement, in his view, rested on two tightly interrelated factors: revealed Christian religion, and a complex of legal sources, foremost among them the Articles of Confederation, the Constitution and the Common Law.

Gale linked the US indissolubly with Christianity. Not only is 'The United States of America a Christian Nation! [*sic*]', its law and foundational documents spring directly from divine sources. The nation is itself a product of Christianity's advance, 'holding aloft a triumphant banner – the Name of Yahweh our Yahshua, He whom we call Jesus the Christ'.[11] America's divine nature is manifested and reinforced by the agreements that brought it into being.

Unlike most others, Gale believed that the Articles of Confederation had not been superseded by the Constitution. They remain in effect, buttressing the sovereign authority of states and protecting them from federal encroachments.[12] Lest the point be lost, Gale made clear his conviction that the Articles derived their authority from more than merely legal or historical considerations: 'Its source is the Holy Bible.'[13] The same divine authority extends to the Constitution itself, since it was, allegedly, 'lifted from the Articles of Confederation'.[14] Under these circumstances, it is little wonder that posse members were exhorted to see themselves not simply as serving the nation but as serving God.[15]

Beyond the religious factors lie a host of legalities that further support posse organization. Gale conceived the American constitutional and political structure in terms of a radical devolution of power, in which authority is related inversely to the size of the unit: the smaller the unit, the greater its authority. Hence the county is the most constitutionally potent unit, while the federal government is both the most legally problematic and the most likely to overreach. The description of the Posse Association is studded with citations from the US Code, *The Federalist Papers*, Supreme Court opinions and other legal documents – all of them read in ways that simultaneously limit federal power while empowering localities.

In short, the United States Christian Posse Association sought to establish in as many counties as possible groups of armed adult Christian men constituting themselves as the sheriff's posse. Where the sheriff is willing to lead them in ways they find appropriate, they will submit to his authority. Where he fails to do so, he risks removal by force. In similar fashion, posses claim the right to nullify laws they find unconstitutional and to use armed force against officials seeking to enforce such laws.

The Nehemiah Township Charter

In many respects, the Nehemiah Township Charter was a direct descendant of the posse movement. While Gale himself was not a signatory,[16] the Charter envisioned posses as an important part of a restructured American polity. In one respect, however, the Charter was a significantly more radical document. While the description of the Posse Association assumed that the existing county structure would provide the framework within which posses operated, the Charter envisioned an entirely new governmental unit, 'Nehemiah Township'. It is unclear whether the signatories ever intended to actually create such a jurisdiction beyond its paper formulation. If they did, I have been unable to find any evidence of it. It appears to have been one of several exercises in separatist politics typical of racialists during the 1980s. The Charter was not intended for publication. Instead, it was conceived as a legal document, duly notarized, and filed with the Clerk of Kootenai County. While filing with the county clerk reflects the radical right's customary elevation of the county unit, the filing itself reflects what, in Jerome Frank's phrase, might be called 'legal magic' (i.e. recourse to legal ritual as an intrinsically powerful act).

Many of the themes present in the posse material reappear here, albeit in exaggerated form. The prominent religious motifs are here linked far more explicitly with a conception of racial hierarchy. The drafters seek to establish a government that is both 'Theocratic and Republican'. Indeed, so committed are they to biblical law that they dispense with a formal legislature, 'since GOD Himself has already legislated the only laws necessary to our preservation and prosperity'.[17] Divine law, however, is intended not for humanity in general, but only for 'our own Racial Nation' (i.e. Aryans). God's commandments are 'the organic Life-Law of our Race'.[18]

The political unit that they seek to construct is one in which rights accrue only to 'Aryan Freemen'. All others will live at their sufferance. Non-Aryans, for example, cannot speak in any governmental or legal proceeding except as witnesses.[19]

Supreme governmental authority will be vested in a 'National Court' comprised of 70 judges who in theory would not legislate but would 'execute decisions according to God's Law for the ordering and well-being of our people'. It and lesser tribunals could override the laws of any external political units, including the federal government. The court's veto power would be shared with that of the Township's citizens, since just as 'Judges shall have veto power over ... outside statutes', so 'No member of this association or Guilds shall be bound by State, Municipal, local, or Federal statute, ordinance, usage, or taxation except as he himself may will'.[20]

The Charter's drafters clearly anticipated confrontations with outside authorities and, as a consequence, made provision for both a posse comitatus and a militia, although the distinction between them was not always clear. Both are authorized to 'defend and execute' God's law, as determined by the Township's members and institutions. The incumbent sheriff of the county where the Township is located would be given the opportunity of leading the posse, but should he decline, the posse would choose its own commander, much in the manner of Gale's Posse Association. In theory, the relationship of posse and militia would mirror that between police and military forces. That is, 'The Posse Comitatus shall confine its activities to the Shire wherein it is chartered', while the militia may operate without geographical constraints. However, the posse's geographical limitations may be waived in cases of 'fresh pursuit, rebellion, invasion, governmental lawlessness, war and siege by insular enemies and treason'.[21]

If Gale's description of the posse comitatus was saturated with citations from American constitutional law, the Nehemiah Township Charter reached even further back in legal history. The document is filled with references to early English law, from 'wergild' to 'socage', giving it a curiously archaic flavour. The signers clearly anticipated future violence, for they declared just before affixing their signatures 'that any attack or challenge to any signator or subscriber hereto shall be deemed to be an attack against the entire Township'.[22] Although the institutions described in the Charter were apparently never set up (at least not in a systematic manner), the signers' apprehensions were well grounded, since within a few years, several had committed acts of violence for which they were sentenced to lengthy terms of imprisonment.

Beam's 'Revolutionary Majorities'

Louis Beam's essay, 'Revolutionary Majorities', appeared on the Internet in 1997, prefaced by the cautionary note that it is 'distributed for educational/informational purposes only'. Beam's stated aim is to reflect on the contemporary meaning of the American Revolution. While at one level his essay presents a revisionist view of the Revolution, at another it is clearly intended to suggest parallels to current anti-government protest groups. The nub of Beam's argument is simple enough: the American Revolution, he claims, was never a mass uprising. Instead, 'it was a very unpopular rebellion of a politically radical minority'.[23] Most of the population was supportive of the British administration, politically uninvolved, or too unsophisticated to grasp the salient issues. Confronted with this imbalance between a small number of revolutionaries and a much larger number of the uninvolved or opposed, the revolutionaries adopted terror and intimidation as their major weapons. While Beam is willing to concede that Washington's generalship 'made victory possible', he insists that 'the American Revolution was won more by mob action than by armed conflict'.[24] Such a scenario suggests that a 'revolutionary majority' is a virtual oxymoron, since Beam defines it as 'any number of citizens sufficient to initiate general hostilities against a destructive government'.[25] Hence a 'revolutionary majority' will often be a numerical minority.

Beam's excursion into eighteenth century history is intended as more than mere academic revisionism. As far as Beam is concerned, America now suffers under a tyranny at least as harsh as that imposed by the British Crown: 'the manacles of slavery and destruction once forged in London by the King are now forged in Washington'.[26] His bill of particulars runs heavily towards misdeeds of the FBI and IRS, the entry of illegal (and presumably non-White) aliens, and 'enforced equality'. His implied remedy is, not surprisingly, a second American Revolution, produced by 'a new revolutionary majority coupled with the resurrection of the spirit of '76'.[27] However, Beam also sees differences between contemporary America and the 1770s.

First, he insists that the present federal government is not legally constituted, its violations of the Constitution having rendered it 'an unlawful body'. Rather, it is the 'Constitutional Revolutionist' of the 'patriot' movement who operates within the law by seeking to reclaim the true meaning of the Constitution.[28]

If the users of violence are the real law-abiding population, what then of the compliant majority? Here Beam finds the second difference between the American Revolution and what he hopes will be its successor: a population even more supine than its eighteenth century predecessors. In part, that is the result of government-controlled media that produce 'methodical thought control [begun] during ... childhood ... and continued at a subliminal level' thereafter.[29] This zombie-like population has been further demoralized by the corrupting influence of a consumer society whose members 'gladly exchange their freedom for the right to accumulate material possessions'.[30]

These corrosive forces, Beam contends, have produced an American population not only unable to free itself but unworthy of freedom. His new revolutionary majority must consequently adjust to these facts. First, they require a 'period of grace' when acts of violence are suspended, or at least limited, while the numerical majority is given time to achieve a higher level of political awareness. Beam is not precise about how long the grace period should last, but he implies it ought not to be prolonged, and he certainly does not expect it to yield much in the way of conversions. Rather, it will serve as a justification for subsequent violence against collaborators, since by then 'all excuse for collaboration with the enemy will have been removed'.[31] The second, and related, adjustment is a direct result of the invincible ignorance of the numerical majority. Since they are unworthy, the revolution will provide 'its blessings for the stronger, more noble elements of the race' in the expectation that more enlightened future generations will replace the benighted contemporary population.[32]

Reviewing the documents

While each of the documents described above has its idiosyncratic characteristics, they also share some notable common attributes: a profound anti-statism, a desperate desire to demonstrate their legitimacy, an elitism separating adherents from the population at large, and (finally) a fusion of two forms of fundamentalism.

The anti-statist nature of the documents appears not only in their hostility towards the federal government, but in their apparent distaste for any large governmental unit, no matter what its ideological foundation. It must be said that not all on the radical right share this view. William Pierce's novel, The Turner Diaries, looks forward to an age when not simply America but the world will be governed by a single racialist regime. Nonetheless, the anti-statism manifested here is representative of an influential tendency in extremist politics.

That tendency, which I have elsewhere called 'radical localism', is most clearly evident in William Potter Gale's design for the United States Christian Posse Association, predicated as it is on the supremacy of the county over all other governmental units. Gale's attachment to the Articles of Confederation implies a vision of America as no more than the loosest of federations in which, for all practical purposes, county-based localities would be free to conduct public business as they wish. Prior to the transformation of the entire system into such an arrangement, he foresees the creation of posse groups in as many counties as possible, each capable of challenging putatively unlawful conduct with armed force. The spread of the posse movement, especially in the upper Midwest and Great Plains during the 1970s and early 1980s, suggested that Gale's design could readily be implemented, often with violent results.[33]

The same radical localism lay behind the Nehemiah Township Charter, although the posse is here placed within the context of an elaborate local governmental structure. It is, if anything, even more anti-statist and insular than the posse idea, for Nehemiah Township aspires to cut itself off utterly and completely from all but consensual interactions with the larger society. Its architects seem perfectly prepared to endure a life of chronic warfare with the outside world, carried on through the twin instrumentalities of posse and militia. Indeed, the first on the list of signers, Richard Girnt Butler, had himself been a posse comitatus member.[34]

The anti-statist theme is more muted in Louis Beam's 'Revolutionary Majorities' essay. However, it may still be discerned in the prominence he gives to such local insurrectionist groups as the Sons of Liberty and the Committees of Correspondence. His subsequent essay, 'Leaderless Resistance',[35] recommends violence by groups and individuals operating in isolation from one another. Each would somehow 'read' the meaning of events in similar ways and thus would know simultaneously when and where to strike, but their lack of connection with one another would protect the movement from destruction by government infiltration. Beam, then, presents a model of small, autonomous groups less as an ideal than as a tactical necessity for a violent movement that seeks to survive in a hostile environment.

While in varying degrees all the documents reflect a distaste for large political units, they are at the same time preoccupied with demonstrating that their positions are entirely consistent with the core values of America. Like the late nineteenth-century vigilantes,[36] these latter-day users of violence insist upon their own legitimacy. In part, their claim to legitimacy rests on the assertion that the federal government has forfeited its own claim through various misdeeds; hence those who oppose it have broken no fundamental law. But beyond this lie more elaborate conceptions.

These conceptions rest on two foundations: links to sacred documents and to mythic pasts. The documentary foundation is clearest in the material on the United States Christian Posse Association, whole pages of which are patchworks of lengthy quotations from legal texts. The Nehemiah Township Charter invokes repeatedly the Common Law as the basis for its provisions, and Louis Beam links contemporary revolutionaries with both the Magna Carta and the Constitution. The message in all three cases is the same: radical, even violent, dissent from governmental authority is entirely consistent with American legal and constitutional traditions. Yet the treatment of American history is as fragmentary as it is romanticized, for this is the work of autodidacts who know only fragments which they then selectively retrieve. Thus, while they appear to owe something to theories of constitutional 'original intent', their piecemeal and unsystematic approach is quite different.

At the same time, they hark back to mythic pasts when these traditions were allegedly most vibrant. For William Potter Gale, it is the early Republic, when America was White, Christian and devoted to local autonomy. For the drafters of the Nehemiah Township Charter, it is an even more remote idealized past when 'ARYAN FREEMEN under the ancient English King's GRANTS [enjoyed] FREE AND COMMON SOCAGE'.[37] Louis Beam, for his part, invokes an era of sacred revolutionary violence in which the Continental Congress and its army fade into the background, while revolutionary mobs and terror squads created American independence. Thus they employ two foundational myths: one derived from a romantic reconstruction of the Anglo-American past, the other drawn from the Aryan myth of racial superiority.

The quest for legitimacy has two consequences. First, it sanitizes violence, providing users with a mandate while delegitimizing the use of violence by opponents. The government's use of sanctions becomes illegitimate, while acts of anti-government violence are regarded as defences of constitutional and legal values. The quest for legitimacy also gives to political extremists a sense of their own self-worth: they are the only true Americans, the only ones who genuinely understand the core beliefs of the Republic, and the only ones uncorrupted by materialism.

This self-image leads readily to a conception of constituting an elite, those whom Louis Beam refers to as 'Constitutional Revolutionists', the 'mental as well as physical descendants of the Founding Fathers'.[38] As has been the case with other self-identified 'revolutionary vanguards', this one finds in its sense of eliteness a necessary consolation. It implies access to special knowledge and insight not possessed by their fellow citizens; only they understand the true meaning and direction of history. At the same time, the belief in elite status compensates for the failure to secure a mass following.

They must at some level confront the fact that the public finds their message not only unappealing but repugnant. In part, as we have seen, they do so by describing the public as lazy, conformist and easily bought off. 'Patriots', in contrast, have penetrated the government's and media's window dressing to see behind appearances. They claim to understand why their numbers are so pathetically small: others have been co-opted or lack the strength of will to take on powerful adversaries. Thus, the very smallness of their followings validates their beliefs. Only the knowing and resolute few, they say, can handle such ideas. Radical localism and anti-statism are thus attractive not only because they may be tactically rational or because ideology favours small group independence: they also attract because they are compatible with a movement unable to secure a mass membership. This is reflected in the audiences to whom the texts were directed. Gale was clearly preaching to the converted, in a small-circulation periodical likely to reach only those already attuned to his message. The drafters and signers of the Nehemiah Township Charter wrote only for themselves, preferring the act of filing with the County Clerk to dissemination to a wider audience. While Louis Beam reaches a large potential audience of the curious through the Internet, his essay first appeared in a sectarian publication as distant from the mainstream as Gale's.

Finally, the documents present two varieties of fundamentalism, understanding fundamentalism as the drive to recapture a pristine tradition from its corrupters. One manifestation is religious fundamentalism. The drafters of these documents are wholly or largely

Christian Identity believers.[39] William Potter Gale was one of the three major figures in the first generation of Identity leadership (the other two were Wesley Swift and Bertrand Comparet). Several Identity leaders signed the Nehemiah Township Charter, notably Swift's self-appointed successor, Richard Girnt Butler. Louis Beam has become a major figure in Butler's political organization, Aryan Nations, and has been mentioned as a possible successor to the aging Butler.[40]

The United States Christian Posse Association was formed under 'the auspices of the Ministry of Christ Church', which Gale founded and led. That church, like all Christian Identity churches, claimed that other denominations had wilfully distorted, hidden, or ignored the true meaning of Scripture, which believers must retrieve. In much the same vein, the Nehemiah Township Charter seeks 'our return to the law of our EVERLASTING GOD, YAHWEH, YAHSHUA, JESUS THE CHRIST'. Those who sign the document commit themselves to 'learning the law of God as set forth in both the Old and New Testaments'.[41]

At the same time, the documents reflect another kind of fundamentalism, 'legal fundamentalism'. Here, too, there is the presumption that the true meaning of the law must be recaptured from the corruptions of its allegedly authoritative expositors. As with religious fundamentalism, believers in legal fundamentalism assume that a text's plain, literal sense can be extracted by any committed, intelligent student. This is the case whether the text is the Constitution (as it is for Gale), the Common Law (as it is for the Charter's drafters) or the narrative of the American Revolution (as it is for Beam). In some sense, too, all of the writers are autodidacts. They either have rudimentary formal educations or were trained in fields having little to do with their present political and religious commitments. Gale was a career Army officer before he became an Identity minister, a role for which he had no formal theological training. Richard Butler was an engineer. Beam has apparently had no education beyond high school. None, to my knowledge, has had any formal training in law, philosophy, history or related areas. Yet each assumes that the essence of the legal system and constitutional history can be grasped by any well-intentioned student. The results, not surprisingly, are idiosyncratic and decontextualized. It could scarcely be otherwise for individuals attempting to penetrate such arcane subjects as English legal history. Yet, paradoxically, the very quirkiness of their conclusions becomes proof to the authors of their profundity. For the conclusions inevitably veer away from received ideas, identified with the educational and governmental institutions that these outsiders so thoroughly reject. The very peculiarity of the conclusions, therefore, seems to testify to their correctness, for if committed students reach conclusions so at variance with what is taught in places where Satan's influence is rife, these divergent conclusions must constitute the truth.

Religious and legal fundamentalisms are mutually reinforcing. By extending their beliefs to the legal realm, religious fundamentalists secure ready access to the means for translating their faith commitments into action. If the law mirrors the certainties of religion, that opens a path to the implementation of religion in both public policy and everyday life. Those in 'patriot' circles who emphasize the sacred and immutable character of the Common Law or the 'organic Constitution' find in religious fundamentalism a worldview congenial to their legal ideas. Millenarian religion in particular places legal fundamentalism in the larger context of a divine plan for the culmination of history. From this perspective, unchanging legal concepts must be honoured not simply in the interests of consistency, but because God's scheme requires it.

Yet a tension persists between this millenarian thrust and the separatist goals of radical localism, with its goal of political self-determination, albeit in miniature. Stable community life will always be at odds with apocalyptic expectations. Such tension, however, is neither unprecedented nor unresolvable. Indeed, it may be found in many of the classic communal societies of the nineteenth century, including the Shakers, the Oneida Community, and the Fourierists, all of which linked community formation with millenarian yearnings; and although all dissolved, their dissolutions stemmed from causes other than the tension between institution-building and chiliasm. Clearly, the egalitarian pre-Civil War communities could scarcely have been more different ideologically from the groups considered here. However, there is no reason to suppose that contemporary racial separatists would be less successful in pursuing simultaneously what to the outsider may seem irreconcilable goals. If such an interweaving founders, it is most likely to do so because of external factors.

This interweaving of the legal with the religious can best be seen in action in the case of the Montana Freemen, whose 1996 standoff with the FBI has been the most dramatic incident involving the radical right since Oklahoma City. The Freemen were predominantly Christian Identity believers who before the standoff had as their primary mission the teaching of 'patriot' doctrines about law and the Constitution, mostly to farmers and ranchers from the Plains states eager to learn how to keep impatient lenders at bay. The Freemen's fusion of religion and law was prefigured in a 1994 document by Rodney Skurdal, who in the following year joined the group and ultimately became its chief of security. Skurdal's so-called 'Edict', filed in a local Montana court case, fused the Biblical exegesis of Christian Identity with the statutory exegesis of legal fundamentalism.[42]

Although the Freemen standoff ended peacefully, the potential for violence was clear from the beginning. The precise origins of the Freemen's ideas have yet to be determined, but they exemplify clearly the radical localism already seen in the United States Christian Posse Association and the Nehemiah Township Charter. At the same time, the Freemen had no qualms about direct challenges to the federal government, in line with Louis Beam's exhortations to form 'revolutionary majorities'. The combination of radical localism with armed confrontations suggests the inner instability of groups committed to withdrawal from the larger society.[43] Groups that live, as it were, 'off the grid', in self-sufficient enclaves claim only the desire to be left alone. But their armed formation, whether posses or militias, implicitly challenge the state's monopoly over the legitimate use of force. To withdraw on such terms is, therefore, not so much to secede from the larger society as to declare war upon it.

The millenarian dualism inherent in these documents thus sits in uneasy coexistence with radical localism. At one level, Gale, the Charter drafters and Beam all anticipate a perfect America that will emerge after a climactic struggle with what they see as the forces of evil and corruption. At another level, however, they, like many millennialists before them, disagree about the timing of apocalyptic conflict and the best tactic to adopt before it occurs. The radical localists – pre-eminently Gale and the Nehemiah Charter drafters – are prepared to bide their time, to defer an open struggle with their putative adversaries, although clearly they are prepared to adopt immediate paramilitary measures in preparation. Only Beam exhorts 'patriots' to imminent revolutionary agitation. The others hope their survivalist retreatism will allow them to pursue unhindered local utopian experiments in opposition to the larger culture.

As I have already pointed out, such experiments have flourished in the American past, notably in the decades before the Civil War, when groups like the Shakers and Oneida Perfectionists created millenniumsin-miniature, extending the limits of available social alternatives. Yet that occurred in what was in many respects a different America, with a far weaker central government and a far less elaborate fabric of laws and administrative regulations. The groups themselves were also groups that either had no manifest political agenda or whose political agenda was widely shared by others (e.g. anti-slavery). Hence past tolerance for communal withdrawal provides little basis for assuming that radical localism can pursue its logic of separation. Instead, both Louis Beam's 'revolutionary majorities' and the posse's and Charter's local paramilitary forces stand in a volatile posture of confrontation with the instrumentalities of the state.

NOTES

1. Richard Maxwell Brown, 'The American Vigilante Tradition', in Hugh Davis Graham and Ted Robert Gurr (eds), *The History of Violence in America* (New York: Bantam, 1969) pp.154–217.
2. In fact, there are significant overlaps among neo-Nazis, Klan members, Christian Identity believers and other right-radical styles. Hence, such terms do not refer to mutually exclusive categories.
3. 'United States Christian Posse Association', *Identity* 5/4, pp.1–16. The issue is undated, but the publication sequence indicates that it almost certainly appeared in 1972.
4. 'Nehemiah Township Charter and Common Law Contract', filed with the Kootenai County, Idaho, Clerk, 12 July 1982.
5. Louis Beam, 'Revolutionary Majorities', http://www.ftcnet.com/~freedom/text/revolutionary_majority.html. The essay first appeared as 'On Revolutionary Majorities', in *Inter-Klan Newsletter and Survival Alert* 4 (1984).
6. 'United States Christian Posse Association', p.3 (emphasis in original).
7. Ibid., p.6.
8. Ibid., p.9.
9. Ibid., p.13.
10. Ibid., p.3 (emphasis in original).
11. Ibid., p.10.
12. Ibid., p.1.
13. Ibid.
14. Ibid., p.2.
15. Ibid., p.13.
16. This may have been because of a breach between Gale and followers of Gale's fellow Christian Identity pastor, Wesley Swift. For the convoluted story of these rivalries, see the discussion in Barkun, *Religion and the Racist Right: The Origins of the Christian Identity Movement* (rev. ed., Chapel Hill, NC: The University of North Carolina Press, 1997) pp.66–9.
17. 'Nehemiah Township Charter' (note 4) p.1 (emphasis in original).
18. Ibid., p.1.
19. Ibid., p.2, para. 5.
20. Ibid., p.3, paras 12 and 13.
21. Ibid., p.4, para. 22.
22. Ibid., p.5, para. 31.
23. Beam (note 5) p.1.
24. Ibid., p.2.

25. Ibid., p.1.
26. Ibid., p.4.
27. Ibid., p.4.
28. Ibid., p.6.
29. Ibid., p.6.
30. Ibid., p.5.
31. Ibid., p.6.
32. Ibid., p.5.
33. See e.g. the shootout between posse member Gordon Kahl and federal marshals in North Dakota in 1983: James Corcoran, *Bitter Harvest: Gordon Kahl and the Posse Comitatus. Murder in the Heartland* (New York: Viking, 1990). On 'radical localism', see Barkun (note 16) pp.217–23.
34. Kevin Flynn and Gary Gerhardt, *The Silent Brotherhood: Inside America's Racist Underground* (New York: The Free Press, 1989) p.54.
35. Louis Beam, 'Leaderless Resistance', in 'Special Report on the Meeting of Christian Men Held in Estes Park, Colorado, October 23, 24, 25, 1992, Concerning the Killing of Vickie and Samuel Weaver by the United States Government', pp.20–23. The conference was organized by Christian Identity pastor Pete Peters.
36. Brown (note 1).
37. 'Nehemiah Township Charter' (note 4) p.2 (emphasis in original).
38. Beam (note 5) p.6.
39. On the relationship among the posse, the Nehemiah Township Charter and Christian Identity, see Barkun (note 16) pp.218–22.
40. 'Beam Moves Near Aryan Nations Compound', *Klanwatch Intelligence Report* 70 (December 1993) p.8.
41. 'Nehemiah Township Charter' (note 4) pp.1 and 5, para. 27 (emphasis in original).
42. Barkun (note 16) pp.286–7. One of the fullest descriptions of the Freemen episode is Jean E. Rosenfeld, 'The Importance of the Analysis of Religion in Avoiding Violent Outcomes: The Justus Freemen Case', *Nova Religio 1* (October 1997) pp.72–95.
43. Michael Barkun, 'Millenarians and Violence: The Case of the Christian Identity Movement, in Thomas Robbins and Susan J. Palmer (eds), *Millennium, Messiahs, and Mayhem: Contemporary Apocalyptic Movements* (New York: Routledge, 1997) pp.247–60.

10

Extremism and Violence in Israeli Democracy

EHUD SPRINZAK

This article was written under the impact of the two most violent acts in Israeli recent memory, the February 1994 massacre of 29 praying Palestinians by Dr Baruch Goldstein in Hebron's Cave of the Patriarchs, and the November 1995 assassination of Prime Minister Yitzhak Rabin. The article explores the role of extremism and violence in Israeli politics since the 1948 foundation of the Jewish state, and tries to resolve the seeming contradiction between Israeli's success to establish the only viable democracy in the Middle East, and the unexpected rise of Jewish violence. Like other writers in this volume, I conclude that democracy does sometimes produce violence, and oddly that violence may on some occasion strengthen the foundations of civic politics and democracy.

The Middle East recently has been associated with a dramatic rise in religious radicalism and extremist fundamentalism. Ayatollah Khomeini's revolution in Iran; the assassination of President Sadat in Egypt and the ferocious fundamentalist effort to bring down the Mubarak regime by terrorism; the violent eruption of Shiite terrorism in Lebanon; the rise to power of Sunni fundamentalists in Sudan; the bloody struggle of Islamic radicals in Algeria; and, most recently, the dramatic rise of Hamas and Islamic Jihad terrorism among the Palestinians, have all contributed to the identification of the region with religious violence and fanatical terrorism.

For years, however, there was one exception to this turbulent image: the state of Israel. The Jewish state was perceived as an island of democracy, secularism, pragmatism and non-violence. But events of the late 1980s and early 1990s raised the question of whether, within its borders, Israel was in fact isolated from the atmosphere of political violence that prevailed in most of its neighbouring countries. Thousands of young yeshiva (Jewish orthodox seminary) students took to the streets during this period to fight the establishment of a Mormon university in Jerusalem, to stop archaeological digs all over the country, to burn bus stations where 'obscene' commercial advertisements had been posted, and to stop the screening of movies on Friday nights in Jerusalem. Such incidents were somewhat reminiscent of fanatical street demonstrations in Tehran or Beirut. The vigilante violence of the young messianic settlers of Gush Emunim (the Bloc of the Faithful) in the West Bank, culminating in the 1980 assassination attempts on three West Bank Arab mayors and the 1983 terror attack on the Muslim college in Hebron, approximated the type of religious terrorism that has been highly visible in the Middle East. The 1984 election to Israel's Knesset of Rabbi Meir Kahane, a preacher and teacher of Jewish holy violence, was another indication of the changing character and direction of Israel's political culture.

During 1994 and 1995 the violence of Israel's religious right reached unprecedented heights. On 28 February 1994, a Jewish physician in the military reserve, Baruch Goldstein, broke into Hebron's Cave of the Patriarchs, a shrine sacred for both Jews and Muslims, and sprayed the people praying there with live bullets. In less than three minutes, the doctor unloaded four magazines containing 111 bullets. Twenty-nine Muslims were killed instantly, and over 100 were wounded. A series of confrontations between protesting Palestinians and Israeli soldiers all over the West Bank and Gaza, which followed the massacre, ended up with an additional nine dead Palestinians and nearly 200 wounded.

All hopes for Israel's ability to insulate itself from the external violence practised between Jews and Arabs in the occupied territories were brutally shattered on 4 November 1995, in Tel Aviv's Kings of Israel Square. A huge peace rally in support of the government of Israel was concluded by the fatal shooting of Yitzhak Rabin, the ninth prime minister of the state of Israel. Rabin, who had just concluded the rally with a big hug of Foreign Minister Shimon Peres and with a small chat with the organizers of the rally, was shot at the door of his armoured car. At 11:10 pm, he was officially pronounced dead.

The purpose of this article is to place the recent rise in Israeli extremism and violence in a broader political and cultural perspective. The question the article addresses is not just why and how a Jewish physician could become a political mass murderer and a Jewish law student the prime minister's killer, but what the political and cultural conditions are within which a significant number of Israeli Jews, for years proud of their success to establish 'the only democracy in the Middle-East', have increasingly come to consider violence and assassination legitimate political means.

This article shares the conclusion of most contributors that the democratic process may, under certain circumstances, enhance violence. The article shows, however, that the major reason for the great intensification of extremism and violence in Israeli politics has not been an endemic flaw in the nation's democracy, but the unexpected and unplanned conquest of vast Arab territories in 1967. The Jewish 'return' to ancient Greater Land of Israel, with all its mystical, religious and messianic connotations, has forced upon the newly created democracy an enormous burden, a heavy load of primordial and undemocratic drives it could not properly handle. It led to the rise since 1967 of militant messianic religiosity which, given the intensification of the Israeli–Palestinian conflict, was bound to produce extremism and violence regardless of Israel's restraining democratic mechanisms.

The article also shows, however, that in other areas of Israeli domestic conflict, potential violent consequences were anticipated by Israeli leaders, acted upon early on and contained. The article suggests, consequently, that democratic cultures, which reject violence in principle, are open to anti-violence learning processes which can reduce significantly the likelihood of bloodshed.

The background: past Israeli extremism and violence

Though largely peaceful and formally democratic, Israeli politics have never been devoid of extremism and violence. The intensity of the Zionist revolution – always focused more on Jewish national revival than on liberal-constitutional principles –, the non-democratic Eastern European origins of the early pioneers, and the critical issues involved in nation building before the establishment of the state produced over-heated ideological debates even among mainstream political parties. Three areas of conflict with intense potential of militancy and violence have either preceded the institutionalization of Israel's democracy or evolved in conjunction with this process:

- the conflict between ultra-Orthodox and secular Jews;
- the conflict between Sephardi and Ashkenazi Jews; and

- the conflict between the Israeli left and right over the borders of the state of Israel and its relations with the Arabs.

The oldest area of Israeli militancy involves the haredim, ultra-Orthodox Jews who live in Israel but reject the idea of the Zionist state on religious grounds. The most extreme Haredi factions have always been involved in occasional confrontations with the secular authorities over issues such as traffic on the Sabbath, sex shops, pathology doctors facilitating human organ transplants, archaeological digs in ancient Jewish cemeteries, and the commercial exhibition in public of so-called 'obscene' posters. Their intense denunciation of the Jewish state and its secular mores, however, has never led the haredim to practice extreme violence or take up arms against it. Never reaching the level of a national crisis, Haredi violence has mostly been expressed in street demonstrations, rock throwing and occasional physical clashes with the police.[1]

An area of significant tension in Israeli society since the 1950s has involved the relationships between Sephardim (Jews born in the Middle East and North Africa) and Ashkenazim (Jews of European origins). The Zionist venture in Palestine, started in 1882, was, until the establishment of the state, a project of ideologically motivated and highly educated Ashkenazim. But the vast majority of the immigrants who came to Israel after its 1948 independence neither originated in Europe nor were inspired by Zionism: they were penniless immigrants forced out of the Muslim world by the after-shocks of the 1948 war.

Poor, unskilled, devoid of Western education and Zionist background, and incapable of expressing themselves in Hebrew, the Sephardi immigrants had a rough absorption. In spite of their instant naturalization and formal admission to Israeli society, they experienced enormous difficulties in settling down, integrating into Israel's pioneering ethos and competing in the job market. The social tension born out of the Sephardi–Ashkenazi rift has been expressed since the 1950s in various militant ways. But it reached crisis proportion in two particular series of events: the 1959 Wadi Salib demonstrations and the 1971–72 Black Panthers' riots. Both series involved a high level of street violence, confrontation with the police and a large number of wounded people. However, the constructive response of Israel's establishment, which from 1971 recognized the existence of the problem, allocated significant resources to Sephardi communities and started to recruit young Sephardim to political leadership positions, had greatly reduced the acuteness of the problem. Since the mid-1970s, Sephardi disenchantment has hardly been expressed in violence.[2]

The political conflict with the heaviest volume of militancy and violence in Israeli history was the ideological rift between the nation's secular right and left and the historical debate over the borders of the Jewish state. Starting in the mid-1920s, that conflict produced years of animosity, misunderstanding, intolerance and communication failures. From its inception, the Revisionist Movement of Vladimir Jabotinsky represented a challenge to the Labor Movement, the dominant force in Palestine's Zionist politics. At stake were deep policy disagreements over the relations with the British, the Mandatory power in control of Palestine, and strategies of Israeli nation building. Since both ideological camps had their roots originated in the non-democratic Eastern Europe of the early twentieth century and their leaders were deeply influenced by the extreme left and right of their countries of origins, the confrontation was hardly held in an atmosphere of civility and mutual recognition. Both movements believed themselves to own a monopoly on the truth and all but ignored the convictions of the other side.[3] The intensification of the conflict in Palestine between the Jews and the Arabs greatly radicalized the internal Zionist debate.

While focused on substantial issues of national borders, the formation of a new society and the desired structure of its government, the debate also involved the question of violence. Against the better judgement of the Zionist left (who believed in incremental social and political nation building), the right had increasingly been enchanted by violence, terrorism and a military liberation struggle. Indiscriminate Palestinian terrorism in the 1930s and an increasing pro-Palestinian British position led to the formation of the Irgun and Lehi, right-wing organizations that resorted to terrorism and guerrilla warfare against the Arabs and the British. Fighting leaders such as David Raziel, Abraham Stern, Menachem Begin and Yitzhak Shamir became right-wing heroes. Fighting a 'war of national liberation', they were responsible for the formation of a culture of violence which remained in the background of Israeli society long after the establishment of the state.[4] They also became the reason why the powerful Labor Party, under the aggressive leadership of David Ben Gurion, was increasingly eager to demonstrate, by force if needed, its uncontested hegemony over national politics.

The left–right confrontation in the critical years of the establishment of the state produced the bloody events surrounding the Altalena, an

arms ship brought over in 1948 by Menachem Begin's Irgun
underground and sunk under the orders of Prime Minister David Ben-
Gurion. The armed struggle between the army of the newly created state
and the Irgun was the closest the nation ever came to civil war.[5] Another
dramatic event of that era was the assassination of Count Folke
Bernadotte, the UN mediator in the 1948 war, by members of Lehi
under the command of Yitzhak Shamir.[6]

The right–left conflict produced in the early 1950s two small anti-
government undergrounds, which conspired to topple the Labor
government and were responsible for a few sabotage acts.[7] It was also
expressed in the 1952 aggressive assault on the Knesset, following a
fierce debate over the Holocaust reparations from Germany.[8] Election
campaigns were also marked by aggressive confrontations between the
left and right, and by occasional violent exchanges.[9] The 1957 political
assassination of Dr Israel Kastner, a leader of Hungarian Jews charged
by the extreme right as a former collaborator with the Nazies, was also
a product of the old rift.[10]

Right-wing violence in the 1950s was, however, a declining
phenomenon. On the eve of 1967, Israeli politics were marked by a
significant operative consensus, strong democratic and parliamentary
politics and almost no violence.[11] It is highly likely that a natural
continuation of the pre-1967 political process would have led the
Jewish state into greater democratization, political stability and less
political violence.

The Six-Day War and the birth of messianic politics

The Six-Day War transformed the map of Israeli political
consciousness. The unexpectedly short war, which ended with the
complete defeat of three Arab armies and the occupation of territories
three times larger than the state of Israel, dramatically changed the
nation's political landscape. Only a small fraction of this change
involved an immediate extremist challenge to the government, but it
was bound to have significant effects on the entire political system. The
most meaningful feature of Israel's new agenda was the division of the
nation into two nearly equal political and ideological camps, the
maximalists and the minimalists. The maximalist camp organized itself
around the ideas of the greater Land of Israel, the conviction that the
Arabs were mentally incapable of making peace with Israel, and the

belief that security is solely a function of territory. The minimalist camp supported territorial compromise with the Arabs, strongly believed that the war created realistic chances for peace, and was convinced that peaceful settlement, not territories, would guarantee Israel's security.[12]

The major difference between the old and the new maximalists (i.e. members of the right), which challenged the pragmatism and minimalism of the ruling Labor government, was the prominent role of religious and messianic ideas in shaping the new-politics. While the traditional followers of the right were excited about the new Land of Israel maximalism, the radical leadership of the new camp was assumed by young orthodox Jews. Two Israeli religious elements had become particularly relevant to the emerging maximalist extremism: *Gush Emunim* (the Bloc of the Faithful) and Kach (Thus! followers of Rabbi Meir Kahane).

Gush Emunim, officially established in 1974, is an energetic and modern religious messianic movement. Unlike the haredim, Gush Emunim views Zionism positively and considers the state of Israel and its secular institutions as an essential, though nascent, stage in the process of Jewish redemption and the expected establishment of the Kingdom of Israel. The movement, which follows the ideo-theology of the Rabbis Kook, the father and the son, had slowly emerged as a unique orthodox school since the beginning of the 1950s, involving strict observance of *Halakha* (Orthodox Jewish law), open-mindedness toward modernity, and a desire to fully participate in the building of modern Israel. The school was boosted enormously by the 1967 Six-Day War. Convinced that the miraculous victory meant that God had finally decided to redeem the people of Israel, the founding fathers of Gush Emunim started the settlement movement in the West Bank and have become the political spearhead of the entire 130,000 large settler community. Though never organized as a political party, Gush Emunim has come to wield considerable political influence. The powerful Israeli right, which constitutes about 35–40 per cent of the nation's voters, considers Gush Emunim settlers great pioneers and Israeli patriots.[13] During the 1977–92 right-wing control of Israel's government, Gush Emunim settlements enjoyed full political support and received very generous state allocations.

Kach was established in 1971 by Rabbi Meir Kahane (later assassinated in New York in 1990), following the rabbi's immigration to Israel. It was the Israeli branch of Kahane's Jewish Defense League, born in 1968 in the US as a Jewish self-defence organization. Theologically, Rabbi Kahane can be located between the haredim and Gush Emunim. While in his life he displayed a Haredi-like hostility to the secular leadership of Israel, because of their Gentile-like sinful behaviour, he, like Gush Emunim, recognized the hand of God in the creation of the state of Israel. Kahane was also thrilled by the Six-Day War and, like Gush Emunim, believed that the great victory signified the beginning of the messianic era. Since its establishment, however, Kach has been a negative organization mostly engaged in protest, conflict, and street hooliganism. Unlike the haredim, who created in Israel a large ultra-Orthodox subculture involving secluded communal life for hundreds of thousands of Jews, or Gush Emunim, which established in the occupied territories over 100 settlements, Kach was never engaged in any constructive project. The movement failed to establish even a single settlement and never recruited more than several hundred activists.[14]

Jewish messianism, democracy and the idea of violence

The original Gush Emunim theology did not call for violence. The movement's founding fathers truly believed in the aftermath of the 1967 victory that the Arab enemies of the state of Israel no longer posed a real threat. Gush leaders were consequently ready to allow a Palestinian presence in the occupied territories, and some of them even considered the Palestinian villages an essential part of this Biblical landscape, similar, perhaps, to Israeli Arabs who did not leave the country in 1948, and became full citizens. The Palestinians were expected, of course, to fully accept Jewish sovereignty and dominance over the entire biblical Land of Israel, but following the devastating Arab defeat, this did not seem a major problem.

Although committed to the theocratic vision of the Kingdom of Israel, Gush Emunim did also not challenge Israeli democracy. Full of optimism about the imminent coming of the Messiah, who would open everybody's eyes for the great light, the Gush concentrated on its educational mission of explaining the great meaning of redemption. Israeli democracy, which among other things produced the great victory, was not perceived as a menace. Fully certain of their exclusive understanding of the true meaning of the great days, Gush youngsters approached everybody within the political system with love and compassion. It was, after all, just a short time before the great transformation and the democratic game was disturbing nobody.

Anti-Arab violence gradually crept into the Gush milieu following the growing friction between Jewish settlers and Palestinian villagers in the West Bank and the unexpected refusal of the Palestinians to recognize and respect the great Jewish redemption process. Hebron's Cave of the Patriarchs, which in 1994 became the site of Goldstein's massacre, has always been the most explosive place because both Jews and Muslims struggled over prayer rights in the same shrine. Gush Emunim's anti-Arab violence has, thus, developed out of settler *vigilantism* and a feeling that the Israeli army was unable to provide them with full protection against Palestinian aggression. It has been legitimized by biblical concepts used to justify the Jewish conquest of Canaan.[15]

Gush Emunim's growing disappointment with the slow realization of the messianic process, as well as its intensifying militancy, had also brought it to a growing conflict with Israeli democracy. The young members of the movement were increasingly bitter about the government's refusal to allow free settlement in the occupied territories. The fact that the duly elected government of Israel had a full authority to decide settlement policy, including prohibiting settlement in densely populated Palestinian areas, was not acceptable to them. The issue, according to the movement's ideologues, was not legality but legitimacy. Admitting that government policies were legal and democratic, the movement launched a massive campaign of illicit settlement based on the argument that they were bound by a higher law, the law of Zionism and Judaism, which made settlement of Jewish areas superior to everything else.

The most extreme form of Gush Emunim violence erupted in the early 1980s. It involved an organized conspiracy to blow up Islam's Dome of the Rock on Jerusalem's Temple Mount and several terrorist attacks on Palestinian targets. The discovery of the Gush Emunim underground and the arrest and trial of its members dealt a major blow to the movement. Several of its revered rabbis were very critical of the terrorism of the group and warned their followers to never again consider it.[16] However, the 1987 outbreak of the Intifada, the Palestinian uprising in the occupied territories, and the inability of the Israeli army to provide the settlers with full protection against Arab attacks forced Gush adherents to resume their intense self-defence. Gush Emunim vigilante violence with a limited rabbinical approval became routine.

The Jewish rule of 'He who comes to kill you, you kill him first' was used as a justification.

Kach, though much smaller than Gush Emunim, has been, by far, the most violent of all Israeli religious schools and the most anti-democratic. The desirability of a physical struggle against the Gentiles had been a major Kahane *motif* since the 1968 establishment of the Jewish Defense League. Over the years, however, he developed this revenge instinct into a fully fledged philosophy of violence. According to Kahane, the essence of 2,000 years of Jewish exile is their persecution, vilification, humiliation and killing. Gentiles did this because they wanted to desecrate the name of the God of the Jews and to prove that He did not exist. The essence of Jewish revival and the establishment of the state of Israel is, according to this logic, to prove the might of God by reversing this history of humiliation, by fighting back, and by showing to the world that Jews can humiliate the Gentiles by the use of physical force. Rabbi Kahane never considered the use of violence as a necessary evil, a practice Jews must resort to for self-defence or because of the lack of a better alternative. Rather, Jewish violence was sanctified and glorified for its own sake. The new Kahane Jew was encouraged to resort to violence against the enemies of the people and to feel good about it. This glorification of violence, which was developed by Kahane before his immigration to Israel, reached its peak in his treatment of the Arabs. The Arabs, who had been determined, according to the rabbi, to wipe out the Jewish state, had been collectively depicted as a legitimate and desirable target for Jewish violence'.[17]

While he never instructed his followers to actually kill innocent Palestinians, Rabbi Kahane welcomed and praised every individual who committed such crimes. Several cases of non-Kach Israelis who conducted murderous anti-Arab revenge attacks are noteworthy. Once Kahane heard of such cases he immediately glorified the perpetrators as modern-day *Maccabees* (the Maccabees were ancient Jewish heroes). They were made honorary members of Kach and were offered financial support for their legal defence.[18] Baruch Goldstein may have gone through a personal crisis, that led him to cross the river between word and action, but he was educated and socialized into the idea of legitimate killing by years of intense Kahane teaching. A close disciple of Rabbi Kahane, he immigrated to Israel from the US in order to carry out Zionist pioneering in a Kahane spirit.[19] All indications suggest that until his last moment, Goldstein believed he was glorifying the name of God in the way recommended by the late rabbi.

Early 1980s ultra-nationalism and violence and Kahane's election to the Knesset

Had Meir Kahane been a more balanced and moderate politician, he might well have been elected to the Knesset (Israel's parliament) in 1981, along with other radical right leaders. His analysis of the Arab situation was, from the angle of the radical right, realistic. His forecasts were correct. His solution of evicting the Arabs was far more consistent than the suggestions of many of his competitors. But the Kahane of the streets was an altogether different person from the analytic Kahane of the books – a bundle of unrestrained emotions, violent eruptions and an insatiable thirst for publicity. Apparently, those who might have voted for him needed, in addition to good analysis, a credible and legitimate communicator. The leader of Kach did not project this image in 1981, and most of his potential supporters voted for Menachem Begin. By 1984 the situation had changed a great deal. Begin was gone. Kahane was still an outsider, but the rhetoric of the Likud and the growing radicalism of the radical Tehiya party and Gush Emunim made many of his opinions and beliefs acceptable. Two events in particular, not of his creation, helped the spread of 'Kahanism' and played to the hands of its creator: the Likud electoral campaign of 1981, and the intense conflict between the government and Peace Now during the Lebanon War.

The Likud, Begin's party, entered the 1981 election campaign with a serious drawback. The ailing Menachem Begin had for months been hardly functional and his inner cabinet projected intense personal rivalries. Inflation skyrocketed and the polls indicated a large, almost unbridgeable gap between Labor and Likud. Likud leaders, who just four years earlier took over the government after 30 years of opposition, experienced enormous anxiety. The spectre of a premature return to the Knesset's backbenches loomed large in their minds.[20] Nervous and bitter, they were ready to do anything to stay in power. Against this background it was decided to replace Yigal Horowitz, the unpopular finance minister, with Yoram Aridor, soon to become popular by cutting sale taxes on imported goods and appliances. The fear of electoral collapse must have also been the reason for the miraculous recovery of Menachem Begin who not only returned to his 1978 vigorous self, but appeared able to relive his bellicose 1950s. Begin radicalized his rhetoric against the Syrians and the PLO in Lebanon, would soon order the air attack on the Iraqi nuclear reactor, and was uncharacteristically ready to confront the American administration.

The most significant dimension of Begin's comeback, which filled his old Herut comrades with great jubilation, was his vitriolic attack on the Labor party. Going almost 30 years back, Begin lashed out at Labor and its subsidiary Kibbutzim. But unlike his unrestrained campaign against the German reparations and David Ben-Gurion, conducted from a total political isolation, Begin was now the Prime Minister of Israel, a leader of stature and prestige. Stressing Labor corruption and paternalistic attitudes to the Sephardim (Jews of Middle Eastern or North African origins), mostly exemplified by the Kibbutzim's reluctance to share their wealth with the Sephardim of the development towns, Begin helped get the ethnic genie 'out of the bottle'. Likud's large Sephardi constituency was reminded repeatedly that the people responsible for the rough and paternalistic immigration absorption it experienced in the 1950s – the Ashkenazi (Jews born in Europe) Labor party – were trying to return to power in order to reinstate the same discriminatory policies.[21]

It is not clear whether the scrupulous Likud leader really wished the campaign to become violent, but this is exactly what happened. Incited Likud strongmen started to ravage Labor offices and physically attack its activists. They were particularly rude to Labor leader Shimon Peres, who in 1981 was the subject of an unprecedented character assassination. There were Likud hecklers everywhere Peres went, and he could only move in the countryside with dozens of bodyguards. The violence reached its peak when Likud operatives ransacked the Petah Tikva offices of the Labor party and pushed burning trash barrels to a Peres election meeting.[22]

The brutality of the 1981 campaign was exacerbated by two exceptional events that gained massive media coverage: the uncalculated attack on Likud activists by former chief of staff, Lieutenant General (res.) Mota Gur, and the slip of tongue by comedian Dudu Topaz. Trying to silence Likud hecklers at a Labor election rally, Mota Gur screamed, 'We f--ked the Arabs and will f--k you the same way'. Dudu Topaz told, on the contrary, a captive audience in a Labor stronghold that he was glad he was surrounded by real Israelis and not by Likud *chach-chahim* (vulgar, lower-class oriental Jews). Betraying a supremacist and paternalistic attitude of the Ashkenazi elite toward the oriental 'newcomers', long suspected by the Sephardim of having remained under the Israeli rhetorical egalitarian veneer, the two incidents turned the elections into an ugly and physical Sephardi–Ashkenazi conflict. Labor charges of negative campaigning and election violence, mistakenly believed to be an advantage that would alienate the Israeli middle class, produced additional tension and violence. It may have been appealing to a number of Ashkenazi Jews, but simultaneously drove almost the entire Sephardi public to the bosom of the Likud. Menachem Begin, the indefatigable street fighter, never heard before the expression chach-chahim, but knew how to use it. In a huge Likud rally in Tel Aviv, on the eve of the elections, he asked the cheering crowd, 'have you heard what he called you?' and then, in his unmatched theatrical manner which nobody else has ever succeeded in duplicating, Begin reached into his pocket and slowly took out a slip of paper, '*Cha..ch.. cha.him*. Are you *chach-chahim*?' Begin asked the excited crowed. 'No!' was the loud and angry answer. Fully aware of the explosive effect of the moment, Begin ordered his enthusiastic supporters to instantly go home to their telephones, call all their relatives and friends, and tell them what the Labor party was thinking of them and what should they consequently do in the voting booths.[23]

Likud's marginal victory over Labor, 48 Knesset seats against 47, which made it possible for Menachem Begin to form a narrow coalition government, helped to add legitimacy to the use of electoral violence. None of their brutal activists were ever brought to trial and life went on with business as usual. Shortly after the formation of the government, the Israeli public was mesmerized by a television series which documented the elections. The award-winning series, produced by Chaim Yavin, the nation's Mr Television, showed the violence with great accuracy. Most viewers did not seem to care a great deal about the unsavoury scenes. They concluded, instead, that in the 1981 elections violence and rhetorical violence were the winning cards.

The post-1981 era was marked by a growing ideological rift between the Israeli right and left. Begin's new government greatly differed from the previous administration. The relatively pragmatic policy team of Menachem Begin, Yigal Yadin, Moshe Dayan and Ezer Weizmann, responsible for the spirit of Camp David, was replaced by a very hawkish axis: Menachem Begin, Ariel Sharon and Yitzhak Shamir. Begin was still committed to the full implementation of peace with

Egypt, including the painful evacuation of Yamit and the neighbouring moshavim, but he was equally determined to kill the Autonomy Talks, aimed at producing a compromise in Judea and Samaria. His Camp David strategy had come now to full light, a return of the entire Sinai to the Egyptians in exchange for peace on the southern front and the facilitation of massive Jewish settlement in Judea and Samaria. The November 1981 assassination of Egypt's President Sadat, the Iran–Iraq war and the invasion of Afghanistan by the Soviet Union diverted regional and international attention from the occupied territories and created positive conditions for a massive Jewish drive into the West Bank.[24] No one was better suited for overseeing this venture than Ariel Sharon, Israel's new minister of defence.

The new government's policy resulted in a dramatic escalation of violence in the occupied territories. It also shook up Peace Now, hardly heard from since the signing of the Camp David Accords. Radical Palestinians recruited high school students for demonstrations and rock throwing. Lacking experience in dealing with rioting civilians, let alone high school students, the army used excessive force, leading to the killing of 16 young Palestinians in three months. In the end of November 1981, the IDF responded to rock and molotov cocktail throwing by blowing up three houses in Beit Sahur, a village adjacent to Bethlehem. Alarmed by the new situation, a group of Peace Now activists went out to Beit Sahur to protest the brutal measures. Unknowingly, they started a new chapter in the history of the movement. Since there was little doubt about the architect of the new policy, Peace Now started to talk about 'Arik's Spring'. It did not take long before the situation evolved into a bitter conflict between Peace Now and Ariel (Arik) Sharon.[25]

The confrontation between Israel's aggressive defence minister and the peace movement reached new heights during the Lebanon War. Sharon's desire to find a proper excuse for invading Lebanon, in order to deal the PLO mini-state there a crushing blow, was no secret. The only pending questions involved the conditions and justifications for the invasion. Already a year before the war, a rally of 3,000 Peace Now activists protested against staging military activity. The immediate fear in 1981 was that the excuse to go to war would be the Syrian anti-aircraft missile batteries stationed in Lebanon's Beka. The final countdown for the war started in April 1982 and only Begin's strong denials that war was imminent averted Peace Now demonstrations.[26]

The first anti-war protest took place a few weeks after the outbreak of the war, when Peace Now reservists on active duty received a few days' break. The 120,000 demonstrators in Tel Aviv made history: never before had any Israeli movement dared to protest a war involving most of the Israeli army. The Likud felt betrayed. Labor governments engaged in wars never faced such opposition and could always count on the automatic support of the opposing camp. But now, upon starting what he considered an unavoidable war against PLO terrorism, Menachem Begin, the biggest peace-maker in the history of the nation, could not count on the opposition's loyalty. Most activists of the right did not consider Peace Now anti-war activities either acceptable or legitimate. Praises to Peace Now by the besieged Yassir Arafat in Beirut further exacerbated the situation. In the eyes of the right, the peace activists were simply traitors, Israeli Quislings. Developing the theme of treason, supporters of the government maintained that Peace Now was engaged in 'stabbing the nation in the back'. While losing his battle with the IDF in Lebanon, Arafat was going to win the war in the streets of Tel Aviv, courtesy of Peace Now.[27]

While the Lebanon situation triggered the rise of extremist and ideological anti-war movements such as Yesh Gvul (There is a Limit), and Chayalim Neged Shtika (Soldiers Against Silence) – with almost no relation to the large but relatively moderate peace movement, Peace Now was increasingly singled out as the real 'enemy from within'. Leading activists of the movement started receiving telephone threats and hate letters. Accusations flew regarding the involvement of foreign interests, including secret Saudi financial support. Protesting the war had become a risky endeavour since aggressive supporters of Menachem Begin, Ariel Sharon and Meir Kahane began to resort to violence. The huge rally sponsored by Peace Now in September 1982, against the massacre of Sabra and Shatila, brought the conflict between the left and the right to unprecedented intensity: Nearly 400,000 Israelis protested the killing in Lebanon of several hundred Palestinian refugees and demanded that a state investigation committee study the Israeli involvement in the atrocity. The demand to investigate a massacre, clearly executed by the Christian militias, stunned the Israeli right. Most of their activists could not understand why a massacre of Muslim Arabs by Christian Arabs was of any concern to Jews. Why had so many Israelis attended the rally? Something was wrong with these 'self-hating' Jews.

A tragic day in the history of Israel was 10 February 1983. Emile Greentzweig, a Hebrew University graduate student, was killed in Jerusalem during a Peace Now demonstration demanding the resignation of Defense Minister Ariel Sharon. Found by the Kahan Commission partially responsible for the Sabra and Shatila massacre, by not taking pre-emptive measures against the predictable event, Ariel Sharon was expected to resign. His reluctance to do so and Prime Minister Begin's hesitation to fire him led Peace Now, already deeply involved in the anti-war struggle, to launch a large anti-Sharon rally. Just as they reached the prime minister's office in Jerusalem, the rally's leading column was broken up by a single hand grenade. The explosion that occurred four seconds later killed Greentzweig instantly and wounded a score of others. Greentzweig became Israel's first martyr for peace. Author Shulamit Har-even, a member of Peace Now, gave a graphic description of the march and the last moments before Greentzweig's murder.

> Already at the start, marching from Zion Square up Ben Yehuda Street, the demonstrators noticed that this was neither the ordinary clash of opinions nor the usual level of marginal violence. A group of violent people and strongmen had been waiting for the demonstrators even before they gathered; they repeatedly broke into the marchers' lines with a powerful and strong wedge. Screaming, yelling, beating, plenty of beating, crushing in. The police are not prepared for this kind of violence. Here and there you see a policeman struggling against a group of thugs. To my right I see a lovely policeman, looking more like a father of a large family on his way to pick up the kids from the matinee and bring them home. He is trying to stop the deluge with his body, but fails. – The march goes on. Non-stop beating. Spitting. Rocks. A burning cigarette is thrown at Amiram's face. Anat is hard hit. A thug later tries to extinguish a cigarette on Taliah Ziv's face, an artist from the Israel Museum. These are not the ordinary marginal hecklers; somebody must have organized them. – The marching people are holding themselves in check, they do not strike back. There is a strong feeling that the street is on the verge of civil war which must be stopped by all means. I see Yarom, and Zohar, and Alon, Emile, Amos and Shaul, all (reserve) paratroopers, holding tight each other's hands and staying put, a

thin row facing the violent intruders so that the demonstration may go on ...[28]

The unruly eruption of Sephardi–Ashkenazi animosities in the 1981 elections and its great intensification during the Lebanon War played to the hands of Rabbi Meir Kahane. The evolution of ultra-nationalist and ethnic violence was, in fact, more than what 'he bargained for'. While most of the people involved in the attacks – on Ashkenazi Laborites in 1981 or on Ashkenazi Peace Now activists in 1983 – were bitter Menachem Begin and Ariel Sharon devotees, not Kahane's, they looked increasingly like classical Kahanists. Hating the PLO, pro-PLO Israeli Arabs and Israeli 'Ashafistim' (PLO-ers) and their 'treason' during the Lebanon War, and still suffering from deep-seated ethnic anxieties, they came to consider street violence as legitimate behaviour. When two additional conditions were created in the Israeli public arena, the 1983 collapse of Menachem Begin and the apparent failure of the Lebanon War, a large number of these individuals were ready mentally for the aggressive rabbi. Thus in 1984, frustrated settlers, angry residents of developing towns, young soldiers and insecure people all over the country – 25,906 of them in all – joined forces to lift a 10-year-old ban from the head of Kach and install Meir Kahane safely in the Knesset.

'When prophecy fails': the crisis of militant messianism

A most intriguing aspect concerning religious messianism is its response to major theological crises, that is to setbacks in the evolution of the faithful that either contradict the imminent coming of the Messiah or are clearly opposed to God's will. The realities of the peace process have since 1992 created for Gush Emunim and Kach a devastating predicament. Both movements had believed since their establishment that redemption, which is currently imminent, could only take place within the biblical boundaries of the Land of Israel, which include the occupied territories. They also have come to believe that redemption is irreversible.

Trouble in the post-1967 messianic reading of modern Israeli history started as early as the 1973 Yom Kippur War. The expectation of linear progress toward redemption has been challenged occasionally by unforeseen political moves by the government and potential disconfirmations. The most dramatic of these came in 1918 when Israel's prime minister, Menachem Begin, returned the Sinai to the

Egyptians in exchange for full peace. Begin also made a commitment regarding future Palestinian autonomy in the West Bank and Gaza. There were plenty of explanatory excuses, however. Begin maintained, for example, that he returned the Sinai (a relatively unimportant southern region) in order to make peace with Israel's most dangerous enemy, thereby saving Judea and Samaria (which compose the West Bank), the heartland of the Land of Israel. The disconfirmation of the redemption process, implied in the Camp David accords, was further moderated by the intense efforts of all Likud governments to settle Jews in Judea and Samaria. The relative success of the settlement process was seen by many true believers as a reconfirmation of the 1967 messianic promise.

Conditions for the recent and most unequivocal disconfirmation of the hope for redemption were first created in 1992. Israel's Labor Party, committed to a large territorial compromise in the West Bank, won the national elections. This was followed by a government freeze on settlement in the occupied territories and completed by the 'shocking' Oslo agreement between Israel and the Palestinian Liberation Organization (PLO). The determination of an Israeli government to recognize the PLO, implement Palestinian autonomy in the West Bank and Gaza, evacuate eventually most of the territories and facilitate the creation of a Palestinian entity constituted unquestionably the worst thing that could ever happen to Zionist messianism in Israel. Not only was it a complete falsification of the messianic predictions, but it also contradicted everything their movements had been telling their followers and the rest of the world for over two decades.

Students of religious extremism have long been interested in the response of messianic movements to undeniable disconfirmation of their predicted salvation. In his classic study, 'When Prophecy Fails', Leon Festinger argued that disconfirmation does not produce movement collapse but instead leads to reinvigorated activity, intensified proselytization and reinterpretation of salvation. Festinger showed that while isolated and weak messianic individuals become desperate and abandon their beliefs, messianic collectivities survive. Hyperactive religiosity and group support help members overcome the painful cognitive dissonance of discrimination.[29] Studying the relationships between messianism and terrorism, David C. Rapoport argued that a conviction regarding an imminent salvation and a danger of its disconfirmation may push true believers to undertake a catastrophic terrorist endeavour. Out of their extraordinary messianic frenzy, they may either try, by suicide, to blackmail God into keeping His original salvation plan or prove to Him through such an act that His most dedicated servants do not deserve to be deserted.[30]

Following Festinger and Rapoport, it appears that three courses of potential action are theoretically available for messianic believers who face unequivocal disconfirmation: rejecting the belief and individually dropping out of the movement; finding a biblical excuse for the setback, accepting the inevitable, and slowly turning away from activism to passivism; or turning to hyper-religious activity, including terror and suicide. All three options have been observed recently in Israeli messianism, and all three are bound to have considerable consequences for the future of the nation and the peace process.

The February 1994 massacre in Hebron and the November 1995 assassination of Yitzhak Rabin were, in my judgement, clear expressions of messianism in an acute crisis. They also signalled the potential movement of a number of messianic types to the violent option.

From the information held today about Baruch Goldstein, it is clear that, like other Kach's members, he suffered a severe crisis in the months before the Hebron massacre. Not only was the future of Judea and Samaria put in great doubt, but the neighbouring Palestinians became increasingly aggressive and violent. As the community's emergency physician, and the doctor responsible for first aid to Jewish victims of terrorism, Goldstein was exposed to the consequences of these circumstances more, perhaps, than anybody else. Several victims of the intensifying religious Palestinian terrorism died in his hands. There are a number of indications that Goldstein slowly came to the conclusion that unless stopped by a most dramatic act, an act that would shake the foundations of Earth and please God, the peace process could disconfirm the dream of redemption.[31]

Goldstein, it should also be remembered, was a personal student of Kahane and a very methodical individual. Like his rabbi, he believed that redemption was inevitable but that it could come in two ways, an easy and smooth one or a difficult and catastrophic one. In several of his essays, Rabbi Kahane wrote that the gates of heaven were opened wide in 1967 and that God was ready to redeem the people of Israel instantly. If only they followed the right path, returned to the faith and kicked the Arabs out of the Land of Israel, the Jews could walk straight into the Kingdom of Israel. If they did not, however, Kahane warned, redemption would come the hard way, through trials and tribulations, bloodshed and enormous suffering.[32] There are numerous indications that following the 1990 assassination of the rabbi, whom Goldstein loved dearly, and the consecutive disasters after the 1992 elections, especially the Oslo accords, Goldstein started slowly to move into a desperate messianic defiance: he felt that only a catastrophic act of supreme Kiddush Hashem (sanctification of the name of God) could change, perhaps, the course of history and put it back on the messianic track. A responsible person who never was trigger happy, he had to carry out this exemplary mission.[33]

Unlike Baruch Goldstein, Yigal Amir, Rabin's assassin, was not a member of an organized messianic movement. But Amir was a product of the same cultural and theological milieu of Gush Emunim and Kach. He studied in the Gush Emunim-oriented Yeshivat Kerem De-Yavneh' and, as a student in Bar Ilan University, devoted much of his time to religious studies in the Kollel Institute of High Halakhic Learning. The Oslo accords, signed on 13 September 1993, galvanized Amir. Associating the agreement with a government treason of the first order, Amir became active within the settler milieu, with a special attachment to the Kach people. Goldstein's massacre in Hebron was perceived by Amir as an act of Kiddush Hashem and a model to follow.[34] Amir increasingly was struck by the fact that, in spite of his good intentions, Goldstein failed to create the catastrophe necessary to move God to stop the peace process. He had slowly reached the conclusion that the prime minister of Israel, not a score of innocent Palestinians, had to be killed for the peace process to stop.

It is doubtful that the disconfirmation of the messianic expectation alone would have been sufficient to drive true believers like Goldstein and Amir to commit their atrocious acts. Neither of the two had been identified as a pathological murderer and both were products of a long Jewish tradition of non-violence. The conditions for both atrocities were created by an additional element: the devastating impact of Palestinian terrorism.

Responding to the Oslo accords but especially to the unprecedented series of Hamas and Islamic Jihad suicide bombings inside Israel, which took the lives of 87 Israeli civilians, wounded 202, and traumatized the entire nation, several prominent rabbis from Judea and Samaria began in the winter of 1995 to explore the possibility of putting Rabin and Peres on trial according to *Din Rode* (the Halakhic ruling about a pursuer) and *Din Moser* (the ruling about a Jew who surrenders Jews to Gentile authorities).[35]

A *Moser* and a *Rodef*, according to the Halakha (Orthodox Jewish Law), are among the worst kind of Jews. They betray the community through acts that may result in the loss of innocent Jewish life. A *Moser* is a Jew suspected of providing the Gentiles with information about Jews or of illegally giving them Jewish property. Since the Halakha refers to the Land of Israel as a sacred property of the Jewish people, Jews are obliged to kill the *Moser*. A *Rodef* is a person about to commit, or facilitate the commitment of, murder. The purpose of his immediate execution is to save innocent Jewish life. This rule does not apply to a killer caught after the murder, who has to go on trial. *Din Rodef* is the only case in which the *Halakha* allows a Jew to be killed without trial. While there is no indication that any rabbi or rabbinical court ever ruled that Yitzhak Rabin was *Rodef* or *Moser*, studying the two rulings had become increasingly popular in radical yeshivas and closed extremist circles. The rhetorical demonization of the government in right-wing demonstrations and the depersonalization of its leaders had gradually created the mental readiness among hot-headed yeshiva students to commit murder if and when a clear order was given.

Yigal Amir almost certainly had no specific rabbinical sanction to kill Rabin. The assassin told his investigators that he had discussed the issue of *Din Rodef* and *Din Moser* with several rabbis, with the intention of executing the prime minister, yet none of the rabbis was ready to give him a green light.[36] But this young and self-driven radical – who felt increasingly humiliated and betrayed by the government and by Rabin personally – found his way, nevertheless, through the ancient Jewish doctrine of zealotry. This doctrine maintains that under the most extreme circumstances and if disaster for the nation is evident, a God-loving Jew can kill the person responsible for the trouble without asking permission. The tradition goes back to Pinchas, son of Elazar, who killed, during the Exodus, another Jew. That person, Zimri, the son of Salue, was among many Israelites who made love in the desert to Midianite women publicly within the boundaries of the community, thereby violating a sacred space. In killing Zimri, Pinchas committed an unauthorized murder of a fellow Jew. Nevertheless, not only was his act forgiven by God, 'for he was zealous for my sake among them' (Numbers 25), but a plague that had already killed 20,000 Jews was instantly terminated by God. Pinchas' entire line of descendants were made priests of Israel.

Yigal Amir convinced himself that, in killing Rabin, he was acting in the best tradition of Jewish zealotry. In order to save the land and the nation, Rabin had to be assassinated. He was certain that this was God's will, which other believers recognized but were hesitant to carry out. Amir told his investigators that on at least two previous occasions, he was armed and ready to kill Rabin, but that on both occasions he had a 'sign from Heaven' not to act. On one such occasion, Rabin did not show up; on another, Rabin was heavily protected by security. On the night of 4 November 1995, Amir received the signal to go ahead. He easily negotiated the Kings of Israel VIP parking lot and waited patiently for 40 minutes. According to Amir's testimony, God made it clear that He wanted Rabin dead.[37]

Democracy and violence: some conclusions from the Israeli case

The complex relationships between democracy and violence cannot be exhausted by a single and unrepresentative case study such as Israeli society. The essays in this volume provide a rich sample of this complexity. This study seems to support several of the observations made by other writers in this volume, and to also highlight a few additional dimensions.

Democracy, competition and violence

It goes almost without saying that Israel's case lends support to Rapoport and Weinberg's general proposition that democracy and violence are neither contradictory nor mutually exclusive.[38] It shows, in fact, that Israel's free electoral process has not led to the containment of violence, as might have been expected from classical democratic theory, and that in the 1950s as well as in the 1980s it elicited several waves of violence. This is especially true of Israel's post-1992 politics. In spite of the democratic fair play which brought Labor back to power, the Israeli right had resorted increasingly to militancy and violence in order to stop the Oslo accords, the election results notwithstanding. And the interplay between Israeli politics and violence was not, as shown by Adrian Guelke, a one-sided process. Following the intensification of Palestinian terrorism, the Israeli voters, though stunned by the Rabin assassination, switched loyalties and moved to the right. It is almost certain that without the cycle of Palestinian–Jewish terrorism in 1995 and 1996, the Likud and Mr Netanyahu would have never been elected.[39]

This article is, however, more specific in identifying the sources of strain and violence in Israel's democratic society, and provides additional examples to Anna Simons' discussion of divisible identities.[40] Examined through the prism of violence, Israel's case suggests that most democratic societies contain within their boundaries small or large sociocultural enclaves whose commitment to democratic values and procedures is partial at best. These identity enclaves, to use Simons' terms, usually include religious schools and cults, authoritarian social movements, chauvinist minority groups, racist collectivities and inherently deprived communities which have reason to believe that democracy is a fraud. While none of these is inherently violent, many members consider violence a legitimate avenue to protect their interests in case of a serious threat or significant decline in their sociocultural status. Dramatic changes in the status quo in almost any democracy are largely expected to trigger violence.

The contradiction between democracy at home and military: occupation abroad

Modern political thinkers from Spencer to Lasswell have argued that a democracy cannot face a constant stress from abroad without becoming a garrison state. From 1948 to 1967, Israel may have been an exception to that maxim, but not after 1967. The expectations of many Israelis that the 1967 occupation of the West Bank, Golan Heights and Sinai, and the formation of an undemocratic military government in the occupied territories, could be implemented without corrupting Israeli democracy and culture were unrealistic. While some violent tragedies of the last 30 years were avoidable, the rise of Jewish extremism and violence seems inevitable. Democracy at home and military government in a neighbouring area across the border simply do not square. There is no humane occupation.

Democracy, violence and anticipated conflict resolution

While this article focuses on the violence introduced to Israeli politics by several of the nation's less than democratic movements, the Israeli experiment with democracy may also be used to illustrate the ways in which prudent democratic leaders reduce the potential to violence through accommodation, sensitivity to religious minorities and anticipated conflict management. Given the dearth of Jewish experience with Western liberal democracy, featured by the Russian and Polish non-democratic origins of the founding fathers of Israel, and the enormous military challenges too, the Jewish conflicts in the nation's relatively short history should be appreciated. There are, thus, serious reasons to support the proposition that Israel's public life could have been more violent in at least two areas of constant sociopolitical friction: the uneasy relationships between Orthodox and Secular Jews and the Sephardi–Ashkenazi conflict.

Having lost the 1996 election to a coalition of conservative right-wingers and Orthodox Jews, who have since imposed on the Jewish state significant clerical demands, Israeli liberals are increasingly critical of the nation's 'original sin'. They believe that if the founding fathers of Israel had the wisdom to follow the American example of separation of church and state at a time when Israeli secularism was predominant, all issues presently dividing Jews would not have existed. What many of these distinguished critics seem to miss is the counterfactual argument about what the consequences of this decision might have been. The prime minister, David Ben Gurion, agreed that all state institutions would observe religious dietary laws and that Halakhic law would prevail in personal matters such as marriage, divorce and burial. He also allowed separate state-supported religious schools and an annual exemption from military service of a select group of a lifetime yeshiva students. A later law offered Israeli women who wish to be exempt from military service on religious grounds the right to do so.[41] It appears to me that these momentous concessions, made out of generosity and not political blackmail, have reduced dramatically the potential for Israeli religious violence. They expressed great deference to Jewish tradition and a genuine interest in creating a workable consensus in the newly established state.

The government of Israel, as mentioned earlier, did not do a good job initially in absorbing Middle East and North African Sephardi Jews. The reality behind the Zionist rhetoric of the 'ingathering of the exiles', dominant in the 1950s, was gloomy. These weak populations, most of whom came penniless and devoid of Western education, were for years left behind to compete with the educated and skilled Israelis of European origins. This created in the 1960s and early 1970s an explosive situation and led to violent social protest. But despite the animosity and anger generated among Ashkenazim by the aggressive Sephardi rebellion, the Israeli political elite responded to the challenge quickly, decisively and positively. It took the government less than three years to change its socio-economic priorities and allocate large sums of money to education and construction in Sephardi areas. Affirmative action in education became the order of the day. The political system, long monopolized by the Ashkenazim, had also opened up and started recruiting young Sephardi politicians. While neither Labor nor Likud governments have been sufficiently persistent in their efforts to close the 'ethnic gap', the whole Sephardi rebellion, with its great violent potential, had been defused.

The future of Israeli political violence

While the post-1967 intensification of Israeli political violence may be looked upon as an unanticipated and unchecked consequence of the occupation of Arab territories and people, our comparative analysis of Israeli political violence suggests that in other areas of potential conflict, violent consequences were anticipated, acted upon and contained. This is an important conclusion because it shows that although democratic processes may generate political violence, violence is neither inevitable nor necessary. Violence may, in fact, be contained through learning processes which focus, among other things, on national traumas created by unintended consequences. The Rabin assassination is a case in point.

There are plenty of indications that the Rabin assassination, the most extreme expression of Israeli political violence ever, traumatized not only the Israeli left, but also Israel's religious right. While the leading authorities of the Gush Emunim camp were stunned by the disconfirmation of their messianic dreams and considered Yitzhak Rabin a traitor, they were neither eager to see him dead nor attracted by a possible Jewish civil war. Interviews with a number of Gush rabbis known for their pre-assassination extremism suggest that while none of them pleaded guilty or took responsibility for Yigal Amir's cultural upbringing, the assassination created in them a deep sense of guilt: guilt for allowing their extremist followers to take over the rhetoric of the anti-government campaign; guilt for overreacting to the acts of the Rabin government; and guilt for allowing the free yeshiva discussions of *Din Rodef* and *Din Moser*.[42] The only people who have not expressed remorse over the assassination are followers of Rabbi Kahane, but the murder totally isolated them.[43]

The main consequence of the trauma over the Rabin assassination has been a conscious rabbinical effort to downplay the rhetoric of the extreme right and to rule out political violence. The post-assassination struggle for Eretz Israel and the fulfilment of the messianic dreams has, thus, moved to the realm of hyperactive religious and political activity. This shift is supported strongly by Rapoport and Festinger's generalizations. While violence and terrorism are to be expected in situations of acute messianic crises, they are not the only alternatives. More likely is, in fact, hypernomic activity by the movement's authorities and an effort to resolve the contradictions of reality by new interpretations. The most popular among these are arguments about God's infinity and the inability of humans to fully understand His mysterious ways. This is what is presently heard in Israel, especially after Prime Minister Benjamin Netanyahu, the favourable candidate of the religious right, committed himself to the Oslo Agreements.

At the time of the writing of this article (June 1998), while Israelis remain as divided as ever, domestic violence has diminished. The only condition capable of bringing back intense messianic violence in Israel is a significant evacuation of ancient Jewish territories in the West Bank together with dramatic intensification of Palestinian violence. Muslim terrorism had played a major role in the radicalization of extremist Jews, and will probably do so in the future. What remains to be seen is whether the movements involved will remember the lessons of the Rabin assassination and continue to control their members, or whether they will repeat the grave mistakes of the past.

NOTES

1. E. Sprinzak, *Brother against Brother: Violence and Extremism in Israeli Politics from Altalena to the Rabin Assassination* (New York: The Free Press, 1999) ch.3.
2. Ibid., ch.4.
3. Ibid.
4. See reference to Menachem Begin's approach to violence in Victor T. Le Vine, this volume.
5. Shlomo Nakdimon, *Altalena* (Jerusalem: Efanim Publishers, 1978; in Hebrew).
6. Kathy Marton, *A Death in Jerusalem* (New York: Pantheon Books, 1993).
7. Isser Harel, *Security and Democracy* (Tel Aviv: Edanim Press, 1989; in Hebrew) pp.179–96.
8. Michael Bar-Zohar, *Ben Gurion* (Tel Aviv: Am Oved, 1977; in Hebrew) Vol. II, pp.922–3.
9. No one yet has documented and measured the partisan violence exercised in Israel's early elections. But as a young school boy I still remember vividly the physical confrontations in Rehovot, my home town, between members of left-wing and right-wing youth movements. For a discussion of electoral violence see David C. Rapoport and Leonard Weinberg, this volume.
10. Tom Segev, *The Seventh Million* (Jerusalem: Keter, 1991; in Hebrew) ch.5.
11. Ehud Sprinzak, 'Extreme Politics in Israel', *The Jerusalem Quarterly* 5 (1977) pp.35–7.

12. Rael Jean Issac, *Israel Divided* (Baltimore: Johns Hopkins University Press, 1976) chs.3–4; Ehud Sprinzak, *The Ascendance of Israel's Radical Right* (New York: Oxford University Press, 1991) ch.2.
13. Ehud Sprinzak, 'Gush Emunim: The Tip of the Iceberg', *The Jerusalem Quarterly* 21 (Fall 1981).
14. Ehud Sprinzak (note 12) ch.7.
15. Ibid., pp.87–93.
16. Ibid., pp.94–9.
17. Ehud Sprinzak, 'Violence and Catastrophe in the Theology of Rabbi Kahane: The Ideologization of the Mimetic Desire', *Terrorism and Political Violence* 3/3 (Autumn 1991).
18. Ibid., pp.54–9.
19. Ben Kaspit, *Ma'ariv*, 4 March 1994.
20. See Rapoport and Weinberg's discussion of the general issue (note 9).
21. Lan Greilshammer, 'The Likud', in Howard R. Penniman and Daniel J. Elazar (eds), *Israel at the Polls* (Bloomington, IN: Indiana University Press, 1986) pp.89–91.
22. Ned Temko, *To Win Or Die* (New York: William Morrow, 1987) pp.257–8.
23. Ibid, p.258.
24. Meron Benvenisti, *The West Bank Data Project* (Washington, DC: American Enterprise Institution, 1984) pp.57–60.
25. Mordechai Bar-on, *Peace Now* (Tel Aviv: Hakibbutz Hameuchad, 1985; in Hebrew) p.50.
26. Ibid., p.54.
27. Ibid., pp.58–9.
28. Quoted in Bar-On (note 25) pp.62–3.
29. Leon Festinger, 'When Prophecy Fails', in Stanley Schachter and Michael Gazzaniga (eds), *Extending Psychologicla Frontiers: Selected Works of Leon Festinger* (New York: Russell Sage Foundation, 1989).
30. David C. Rapoport, 'Messianic Sanctions for Terror', *Comparative Politics* 20/2 (1988) pp.195–211.
31. *Report of the State Investigation Committee in the Matter of the 1994 Massacre in Hebron's Cave of the Patriarchs*, p.76.
32. Meir Kahane, *Forty Years* (Miami: Institute of the Jewish Idea, 1983).
33. Note 31, pp.76–80.
34. *Report of the State Investigation Committee in the Matter of the Assassination of Prime Minister, Mr. Yitzhak Rabin* (1996) pp.88–9.
35. Rabbi Dov Lior, Rabbi Daniel Shilo and Rabbi Eliezer Melamed, 'What is the Rule about this Bad Government?', in Dana Arieli-Horowitz (ed.), *Religion and State in Israel, 1994–1995* (Jerusalem: Center for Jewish Pluralism, 1996; in Hebrew) pp.120–23.
36. This information is included in the undisclosed and confidential part of Amir's investigation. The author was allowed to see the document under the condition that no specific references are made.
37. Ibid.
38. Rapoport and Weinberg (note 9).
39. Adrian Guelke, this volume.
40. Anna Simons, this volume.
41. For a recent discussion of the religious complexity of Israel, as well as the debates, see 'Israel at 50: After Zionism', *The Economist* (a special supplement), (25 April–1 May).
42. The author conducted interviews with several Gush Emunim rabbis in December 1995 and January 1996.
43. One accusation Kahane's followers made after the Rabin assassination had to do with the 1994 outlawing of Kach (following the Hebron Massacre). The argument was that Igal Amir, who was close to Kach, acted the way he did because of the lack of legitimate avenues of political participation and protest. The party's outlawing was, according to this proposition, highly counterproductive. The issue of outlawing anti-

democratic parties is discussed in John Finn's article, this volume. There is, in my opinion, not a shred of evidence to support Kach's interpretation. Amir, who never was a Kahane follower, had all the opportunities to protest and demonstrate against the Oslo accords without Kach, and he did. The legal existence of Kach would have made, in my opinion, no difference whatsoever in the events of 1994–95, and I am not familiar with any systemic damage caused by this particular proscription.

11

Violence and Democracy in Eastern Europe

ANDRZEJ KORBONSKI

This discussion between violence and democracy in Eastern Europe excludes the regions of the former Soviet Union and Yugoslavia. In the interwar period, ethnic animosities were aggravated by the demands of treaties imposing the protection of minority rights. After World War II, however, tensions were eased by the reduction of the minority element in states throughout Eastern Europe. In addition, the horrors of World War II and the violence of the Communist seizure of power caused a massive and radical transformation of popular attitude toward both violence and democracy (at least in some East European countries), thus assuring that the majority of post-Communist transitions were conducted in a relatively peaceful manner.

Introduction

The purpose of this article is to examine the relationship between violence and democracy in Eastern Europe. To some extent, it may be seen as a pioneer study. Although by the second half of the 1990s the sheer volume of literature dealing with Eastern Europe has become quite impressive, its coverage has been rather uneven. Not surprisingly, the research on the region has often been policy-driven and closely correlated with the rapidly changing political landscape. Thus, in the past decade or so, the focus has been on the collapse of the communist rule and the ensuing process of transition to democracy, and there seems to be no end to the stream of publications dealing with this issue.[1] In fact, a new subfield of what used to be called 'communist studies' emerged in the process, that of 'transitology,' and some of the best talents in the Soviet/Russian and East European field went at each other with gusto, trying to come up with the most complete and/or realistic paradigm or model of transition to democracy.[2]

This represented a veritable sea change from the 1970s and 1980s, when scholarly interest in Eastern Europe concentrated either on the situation in the individual countries increasingly faced with the problem of liberalization versus democratization or on the emergence of organized dissent in the region.[3] There were two characteristic features of the latter: a conspicuous absence of any discussion of the possibility of the dissent ultimately becoming violent, and a rather simplistic assumption that any opposition to communism – peaceful or violent – was aimed automatically at the establishment of democracy. One of the objectives of this article is to show that the latter premise, which ultimately allowed for the possibility of a democracy being born in violence, often reflected wishful thinking on the part of many Western observers of the East European scene, and that the reality proved to be much more complex. The other purpose of the article is to investigate the relationship between elections and violence and to see whether in the East European context 'ballots so frequently produce[d] bullets'.[4]

Of the three concepts under discussion, only that of 'democracy' can be reasonably well defined, although even here some definitional problems do exist.[5] 'Eastern Europe' has been seen by many as a Cold War concept, and since the collapse of communism in the region it has been increasingly replaced by either that of East Central Europe or South Eastern Europe. In this particular case, my preference is still for the older term, covering the 14 countries located between Germany and the former Soviet Union.[6]

Earlier, I asserted that the task of examining the relationship between democracy and violence in Eastern Europe could be viewed as a pioneering effort. The main reason is a sheer lack of published research. A search at the UCLA University Research Library revealed that out of more than 2,000 titles listed in the catalogue under the heading of 'violence', only one was specifically focused on Russia and Eastern Europe.[7] There are many studies of organized terror in the Soviet Union and Eastern Europe, especially during the Stalinist period, but, valuable as they are, they are only marginally relevant to the task at hand.

The interwar period

The record shows that Eastern Europe, as it came to be known, emerged from the ruins of four empires – the Austro-Hungarian, German,

Ottoman and Russian – that disintegrated in the wake of World War I. Out of the seven countries in the region, Czechoslovakia, Poland and Yugoslavia, model creations of the Treaty of Versailles, were not even on the map in 1918 while the remaining four states, Albania, Bulgaria, Hungary and Romania, saw their boundaries significantly redrawn.

Most East European countries initially adopted democratic constitutions, modelled primarily after the American and French. This was hardly a surprise in light of the victory of Western democracies in World War I and the early belief on the part of the new, mostly Western-educated East European elites that the future of their states was closely linked to the preservation of the democratic order. The only major exception was Hungary which, following a brief democratic interlude, was taken over in 1919 by a Soviet-type republic, headed by Bela Kun, characterized by something akin to a rule of terror. Here was an opportunity for the Communist republic overthrown and for democracy to be restored by violence, yet Hungary, disillusioned with the democratic experience and scarred by the Communist terror, adopted instead a military-bureaucratic authoritarian system which persisted until the end of World War II.

Democratic systems elsewhere in the region fell by the wayside in the course of the 1920s.[8] This again was not a surprise; the new states had little if any experience with democracy. Their rulers simply could not cope with the various pressures exerted by national minority conflicts, endemic poverty augmented by population pressure, the Great Depression, excessive defence burden, religious conflicts, and persistent hostility of both Germany and the Soviet Union. Last but not least, there was total indifference and lack of support from Western democracies which, after being largely responsible for putting several East European countries on the map, were unwilling to help them in time of need, best illustrated by the example of Czechoslovakia during the Munich crisis of 1938.

The gradual emasculation and ultimate elimination of democracy in Eastern Europe was paralleled by a rapid decline in the significance and relevance of the electoral process. Although elections were held after the disappearance of democracy, they were hardly free and frequently boycotted by the opposition. In time, elections in the region became essentially symbolic and largely irrelevant. At the same time, the 20-year interval between the two wars witnessed no mass violence preceding the establishment of autocratic regimes, except for previously mentioned Hungary, and for Poland where the military *coup d'état* of May 1926 cost several hundred lives.

One of the factors which undoubtedly contributed to the gradual demise of democracy in the region was the growth of organized and individual violence. Above all, it was the governments in power which used violence against their real or imaginary enemies, ostensibly in the name of preserving the independence and integrity of their newly formed states. Prominent among the enemies were the national minorities which, in most cases, refused to recognize the legitimacy of the new and/or transformed states whose boundaries, fixed by Versailles, often cut across ethnic lines, leaving national irredentas highly dissatisfied with the status quo. In Poland in particular, the so-called 'pacification campaigns' directed against the Ukrainians were characterized by violence.[9] Next in line were the Communists who, at least until 1923, were still committed to the revolutionary ideology imposed by the Comintern and thus also strongly opposed to the post-

TABLE 1
NATIONAL MINORITIES IN EASTERN EUROPE 1930
(PERCENTAGES)

	Albania	Bulgaria	CSR	Hungary	Poland	Romania	Yugoslavia
Albanians	95.8						4.8
Bulgarians		86.8				2.0	0.4
Croats				0.3			23.8
Czechs			53.0		0.1	0.4	0.2
Germans		0.1	22.5	5.5	2.3	4.1	0.4
Gypsies		1.3	0.2	0.1		1.5	0.5
Hungarians			4.9	92.1		7.9	3.1
Jews		0.5	1.4		8.6	4.0	
Poles			0.7		68.9	0.3	
Romanians		0.3		0.2		71.9	1.1
Serbs				0.1		1.5	40.5
Slovaks			16.4	1.2			0.5
Slovenes							9.0
Turks		10.2					0.6
Ukrainians			3.9		17.4	5.4	0.3
Others	4.2	20.8		0.5	0.7	1.0	11.8

Notes: For Albania: 1945; for Bulgaria: 1934; for Poland: 1931; for Yugoslavia: 1948. The category 'Ukrainians' includes also Russians and Ruthenians. Totals do not always reach 100 per cent because of rounding.

Source: Paul S. Shoup, *The East European and Soviet Data Handbook* (New York: Columbia University Press, 1981) pp. 135–9 and 143.

Versailles territorial arrangements. Finally, especially during the Great Depression, strikes by often desperate workers and peasants were suppressed violently by the governments.

A separate chapter in the application of violence was represented by waves of periodic anti-Semitic pogroms, especially in Poland and Romania, both with large Jewish populations. The escalation of anti-Jewish violence was closely linked, first with the deteriorating economic situation, and secondly with the rise of nazism in Germany which spawned the formation of fascist-like parties in Hungary (the Arrow-Cross), Poland (the Falanga), Romania (the Iron Guard) and Slovakia (the Hlinka Guard). These extremist parties, with initial tacit approval not only of the governments but also of the Catholic and Orthodox Churches, engaged in violent excesses against the Jewish population.

It may also be argued that the rise in anti-Semitism, especially in Poland, was due to the blame placed on Jews for the Minority Protection Treaties, that Poland and other East European countries had been forced to sign in 1919 as part of the Versailles arrangement. Joseph Rothschild points out, 'Poland resented this treaty as implicitly denigrating her sovereignty', and formally denounced it in 1934.[10]

Violence bred more violence and the interwar period witnessed a series of violent reprisals performed by the persecuted minorities and other discontented groups. Two heads of state,[11] three prime ministers[12] and several cabinet ministers were assassinated. The purpose of the violence was in many respects similar to that which motivated the Russian Narodniki and other terrorist groups to assassinate Czar Alexander II and Prime Minister Stolypin: it was to force the ruling oligarchies to take repressive and violent countermeasures that would ultimately mobilize the masses against the regime and destabilize the existing political systems.[13]

This brief overview shows that on the eve of World War II, violence became commonplace in most East European countries, with the possible exception of Czechoslovakia and Hungary. In the former, despite the presence of significant national minorities, democracy managed barely to survive, but mostly in procedural terms, until the country's collapse in 1938–39. In the latter, the previously mentioned imposition of the authoritarian rule early in the post-war period kept things under control until World War II, preventing the outbreaks of violence comparable to those in the rest of the region which, particularly in the 1930s, was experiencing a sort of routinization of violence. To be sure, it was a far cry from the mass terror in the Stalinist Soviet Union or later in Nazi Germany but, nevertheless, violence was always there and what was more important, its presence was generally accepted or ignored by the majority of the population in the respective countries.

What was the reason behind the violent behaviour by various regimes, the seemingly popular tolerance of violence, and the replacement of democracies by non-democratic forms of government in nearly all East European countries? There is no single satisfactory explanation that would answer this question. Undoubtedly, a major reason was the climate of insecurity generated by the post-Versailles international system. It led to the subordination of East European societies to their rulers who proclaimed that the *raison d'état* was the preservation of national independence and sovereignty at all cost. The newly formed states felt themselves surrounded by enemies, foreign and domestic, and in order for these states to survive in the hostile environment, the domestic enemies particularly, often supported from abroad, had to be suppressed by all available means. The belief in the absolute necessity of survival acquired almost religious connotation as it was being transmitted from an already fiercely nationalistic older generation, present at the creation of the new states, to its successors who, if anything, became more chauvinistic and intolerant.

There was one other factor that came into play at that time: the traditionally low value attached to the idea of human rights, be they life or property. Whether it was the result of national liberation wars and uprisings against the various occupying powers or of the carnage of World War I, life was considered cheap in Eastern Europe. There was also a belief that no price was too high to pay for achieving and safeguarding national independence. The big difference, however, was that blood spilled had little to do with the desire for democracy. The citizens of the only functioning democracy in the area, Czechoslovakia, were known for their aversion to violence, which often cited to explain why, in contrast to Poland, Czechoslovakia did not resist the Germans in 1938 and 1939 and the Communists in 1948 and 1968.

The value of individual property in Eastern Europe also had a different meaning than in Western Europe or the US. The writings of Locke were not well known in the region, which was overwhelmingly agricultural, and hence poor, and where the bourgeoisie or the capitalist class was not only marginal but mostly of foreign origin. This clearly also intensified the ethnic conflicts which in several cases intertwined with class antagonisms.[14] The idea of private property was not well developed and internalized, not considered one of the fundamental rights, and the abolition or restriction of private ownership of land and capital was not perceived as a major violation of human rights.

World War II and the Communist takeover

The benign attitude toward violence underwent dramatic changes during and after World War II. To begin with, the sheer magnitude of human losses – whether victims of the Holocaust or non-Jewish casualties – could not help but deeply impress even the most violence-prone segments of the East European populations. While virulent anti-Semitic elements saw the Holocaust as the solution to the 'Jewish problem', and the war and the horror of the German occupation induced a fundamental change in popular perception with regard to violence, especially in countries like Poland which lost about 20 per cent of its pre-war population, it may be hypothesized that this newly found aversion to violence and unwillingness to suffer still additional losses in lives and property was one of the factors responsible for the relatively weak resistance to the Communist takeover in the aftermath of World War II.

The defeat and collapse of pre-war, largely non- or semi-democratic regimes did not result in a mass embrace of democracy. The record shows that while the various East European governments-in-exile tried to dissociate themselves from their non-democratic predecessors, if only to please their American and British patrons, and while most anti-German resistance movements at home also espoused democratic principles, the masses appeared too apathetic and too concerned with sheer physical survival to embrace the new faith. Some old habits and prejudices proved too deeply rooted to change, even when exposed to the horrors of the occupation, as witnessed in the persistence and revival of often violent anti-Semitism in the early post-war years in Hungary, Poland and Romania.

The post-war Communist seizure of power in Eastern Europe was accompanied by varying degrees of violence directed primarily, but not exclusively, against the domestic opposition to the takeover. Poland was the primary target and the period 1944–47 witnessed what some observers called a veritable civil war between the supporters and opponents of the new regime. Communist-led violence in Albania, Bulgaria, Hungary and Romania was focused mostly on the adherents of the former pro-Nazi regimes. While the takeover of Czechoslovakia was achieved incrementally in a non-violent manner, considerable bloodshed in Yugoslavia affected mostly the members of the fascist Ustasha party in Croatia or the remnants of the largely Serb pro-royalist anti-Tito Chetnik movement.

Not all the violence was entirely government-sponsored. The expulsion of the German population from Czechoslovakia and Poland sanctioned by the Potsdam Conference in the summer of 1945 was often accompanied by violence. Curiously enough, it was the Czechs, whose collaborative stance *vis-à-vis* the German occupiers was recorded by historians, who appeared to be particularly vicious in their treatment of the expellees. The revelation of the latter, the details were kept under wraps almost until the late 1980s, represented a big stumbling block to a Czech–German reconciliation in the mid-1990s.

Although the number of German refugees from Poland was much larger than that from Czechoslovakia, the Poles' behaviour, although sporadically violent, was seldom, if ever, discussed during the Polish–German negotiations aimed at normalization of relations between the two countries. It may be speculated that it was the Germans' own memories of their cruel occupation of Poland that persuaded them to adopt a more conciliatory posture.

While the Polish behaviour toward the Germans was relatively restrained, the same was not true with regard to their treatment of the Ukrainians and the Jews. In their fight against the Ukrainian Insurgent Army (UPA), the Polish Communists, emulating Stalin, decided to deport most of the Ukrainian population from its homes in south-eastern Poland to new settlements in the north-western part of the country. As part of the striking revival of traditional anti-Semitism, in July 1946 the inhabitants of the city of Kielce massacred over 40 Jews in what was the worst example of violence used against innocent, albeit racially different, Polish citizens.

To sum up, violence deployed in Eastern Europe in the early post-war period was not for the purpose of defending liberty and democracy but to destroy the budding democracy forming on the ruins of pre-war regimes. The concept of democracy is stretched clearly here as large segments of the anti-Communist opposition were less motivated by their love of democratic principles and much more by their desire to return to the status quo before the war. It should also be mentioned that the mass terror deployed by the Communists between 1948 and 1953 had nothing to do with democracy, as its principal targets were mostly top members of their own oligarchy who fell victim to factional bloodletting, as well as the remnants of the pre-war political and military elites.

This also suggests that, in sharp contrast to the interwar period, one violence-generating factor – the presence of national minorities – was either absent or considerably reduced in such countries as Poland and Czechoslovakia. As shown in Table 2, in the rest of the region the ethnic breakdown remained basically unchanged. But even in countries with sizable minorities such as Bulgaria, Romania and Yugoslavia, the traditional, often violent ethnic conflicts were kept under wraps by the local regimes almost until the end of Communist rule. The model here was the Soviet Union which strongly opposed any overt expression of nationalism, while formally paying lip service to the symbolic features

TABLE 2
NATIONAL MINORITIES IN EASTERN EUROPE 1970
(PERCENTAGES)

	Albania	Bulgaria	CSR	Hungary	Poland	Romania	Yugoslavia
Albanians	97.0						6.4
Bulgarians		87.9					0.3
Croats				0.3			22.1
Czechs			65.1				0.1
Germans			0.6	0.3	0.8	1.7	
Gypsies	1.8			0.3		1.1	0.3
Hungarians			4.0	98.5		7.9	2.3
Jews						1.1	0.2
Poles			0.5		97.9		
Romanians				0.1		88.1	0.4
Serbs				0.1		0.2	39.7
Slovaks			29.1				0.4
Slovenes							8.2
Turks		9.5				0.1	0.6
Ukrainians		0.1	0.4		1.3	0.4	0.1
Others	3.0	0.7	0.2	0.4		0.4	18.9

Notes: For Albania: 1955; for Bulgaria: 1965; for Poland: 1975; for Romania: 1977; for Yugoslavia: 1971. The category 'Ukrainians' includes also Russians and Ruthenians.

Source: Paul S. Shoup, *The East European and Soviet Data Handbook* (New York: Columbia University Press, 1981) pp.135–9 and 143.

of national identities, as institutionalized in its federal structure. The old 'ancient hatreds' were forcibly suppressed, only to resurface violently in the early 1990s.

Eastern Europe after Stalin: the next 30 years

The death of Stalin in March 1953 opened a new chapter in Eastern Europe's post-war history. It caused a mixture of shock, confusion and consternation among both the region's leaders and their respective populations; yet more was to come. The first visible sign that things would not remain the same was an unexpected popular explosion in East Berlin in June 1953 which had to be put down – without a loss of life, however – with the aid of Soviet tanks. Yet the reason behind the mass demonstration was not a sudden upsurge in demand for more democracy in the DDR but a much more mundane protest against high work norms.

Soon thereafter came the news of the arrest and execution of the Soviet secret police chief Lavrentii Beria, together with several of his henchmen, and the subsequent downgrading of the terror apparatus in the USSR. On its heels came the announcement of mass amnesty which soon became emulated by the Soviet satellites in Eastern Europe. The importance of this for the future of Communist rule cannot be overstated. The reduction in the power of the secret police, followed by a rapidly escalating criticism of its practices, inaugurated a new era especially in the satellite countries. For the first time in years people were no longer afraid to meet and talk about public affairs. The mass release of political prisoners resulted in the creation of a quasi-dissident lobby, not afraid openly to condemn and criticize governmental policies.

But this was only the beginning. Dramatic changes in the official Soviet doctrine – proclamation of 'peaceful coexistence', followed by the introduction of the concept of 'peaceful transition to socialism' – represented an official disavowal of the hallowed doctrines of 'inevitability of war', 'class struggle' and 'dictatorship of the proletariat', strongly emphasizing the non-violent character of the new dogmas. The changes took a while to sink into people's consciousness, but in practical terms they meant further relaxation of governmental controls, initiated earlier by the *ex cathedra* denunciation of Stalinist methods and practices.

Ever since the Communist takeover, the regimes in Eastern Europe felt rather insecure, knowing full well that if the Cold War were ever to be transformed into a shooting war they would soon be swept from power by what they assumed would be the victorious West – hence the official paranoia which was ultimately translated into mass terror. With 'peaceful coexistence' becoming the official Soviet doctrine, the danger of a violent East–West confrontation was removed for the foreseeable future and the East European regimes felt less threatened and could afford to become more lenient in their policies.

Khrushchev's condemnation of Stalin and Stalinist practices resulted in two well-documented cases of violence. Chronologically, the first was a major strike, accompanied by attacks on secret police and the Communist party in the Polish city of Poznan, in June 1956. The strike was bloodily suppressed by the military with a loss of life on both sides. The Poznan demonstration was notable for several reasons. It was not only violent, but also for the first time in post-war East European history it involved industrial workers heretofore considered natural and staunchest allies of the ruling Communist party. It also marked the first time that the country's military units were brought into action amid rumours of fraternization between soldiers and the striking workers, which from the Communist point of view did not augur well. Although ostensibly the main purpose of the strike was the workers' determination to express frustration with working conditions, the event itself was triggered by the government's flagrant indifference toward workers' complaints. As a result, among the signs calling for 'more bread', there were others demanding 'more freedom'.

While it would be far fetched to describe the Poznan demonstration as an opening salvo in the struggle for democracy in Eastern Europe, there is little doubt that the seeds of subsequent liberalization of Communist rule, at least in Poland, were planted at that time. The political character of the strike was recognized by the ruling party which did not punish the strike leaders and also embarked on a process of soul searching, which included the removal of some of the worst features of the Stalinist system that culminated in October 1956 in the ouster of the discredited party leadership and its replacement by a new team headed by Wladyslaw Gomulka.

This last event sparked a much more violent reaction in the form of the Hungarian Revolution which had to be forcibly suppressed by the intervention of the Red Army in November 1956. The revolt, well covered in the literature, once again raised the fundamental question: was its goal the establishment of democracy in Hungary, or was it simply an emotional outburst against the worst abuses of the hated Communist regime? One is tempted to say that the former was indeed the case, and that the valiant Hungarian freedom fighters struggled to establish democratic rule in their country, as shown by their call for a multiparty system and a pluralistic society. On the other hand, one may also be equally prone to assert that the insurgents, in their zeal to destroy the Stalinist system and take revenge on its leaders, paid little or no attention to the pursuit of democracy. To the contrary, the uprising was accompanied, among others, by an outburst of anti-Semitism, a throwback to Hungary's non-democratic past suggesting that the creation of a civil society as a first step on the road to democracy was not yet seen as a high priority.

And yet, in the enthusiasm for the brave Hungarians, willing to risk their lives fighting the Soviet oppressors, the darker sides of the revolt were quickly forgotten or ignored, especially in the West, and the Hungarian Revolution became a symbol of a perennial struggle of liberty-loving people for democracy. Thus, a myth was born suggesting that any violent outburst against communism was tantamount to a drive for democracy. It was this myth that dominated Western perception of Eastern Europe for more than 30 years, until the collapse of communism in 1989.

The period 1956–70 was relatively quiet, interrupted only by the Prague Spring of 1968 and the Baltic Coast riots in Poland in December 1970. The former, with its objective of achieving 'socialism with a human face', was characteristically non-violent, as illustrated by an essentially passive popular reaction to the Soviet military intervention, in sharp contrast to the Hungarian armed resistance against a similar intervention 12 years earlier. While much has been written about the 'Manifesto of 2,000 Words' or about the new programme of the Czechoslovak Communist party, it may be argued that the overall thrust of the Prague Spring was not so much in the direction of creating a democratic system, as in achieving a significant relaxation of the Communist rule which had shown little change since the death of Stalin, as compared, for example, to Hungary and Poland.

The bloody suppression of the workers' strikes on Poland's Baltic Coast in December 1970 represented a repetition of a similar confrontation between the workers and the military in Poznan, 14 years earlier.[15] Human lives were lost, there was considerable property damage, and the discredited Gomulka regime had to give way to a new oligarchy. Was all this another example of Polish workers willing to spill their blood in favour of more democracy? I would argue in the negative. The trigger once again was economic: it was a reaction against a sharp increase in the price level of foodstuffs and consumer goods, shortly before Christmas. There was no evidence of any mass or spontaneous demands for the liberalization of the existing system. Moreover, in contrast to the crisis of October–November 1956, when in Hungary and Poland a coalition of workers and intellectuals rose up against the post-Stalinist regimes, the Polish workers in 1970 were rebelling on their own: their erstwhile allies decided to sit this one out, remembering bitterly the events of March 1968 when the anti-party demonstrations, led by students and intellectuals, were violently put down by police with the help of the workers.

Although it may be hypothesized that democracy did not figure prominently in the minds of the rioting Gdansk workers, it may also be argued that the Baltic Coast events represented another stage in the learning process being undergone by the Polish workers. Even the most simple-minded among them must have realized that their political clout was growing: twice in 15 years they rioted and twice they were violently suppressed. Yet, each time they also succeeded in forcing the dismissal of the party leadership and its replacement by what appeared to be a more liberal regime. It was perhaps too early to expect a groundswell of demand for democracy: the workers were still more concerned with their economic well-being to pay much attention to democratization, but it could be argued that it was only a matter of time before the largely economic demands would give way to demands for more freedom and democracy. After all, Lech Walesa, the leader of the victorious Solidarity movement of 1980 admitted that it was the experience of December 1970 that taught him lessons which he successfully applied 10 years later.

Still another wave of strikes in Poland in June 1976, caused by another thoughtless governmental price increase, showed that the learning curve was rising, but this time it was rather the government more than the workers that benefited from it. The authorities, remembering what happened in December 1970, refused to deploy mass violence and instead simply cancelled the price increase, thus ensuring their survival for next four years.

Nonetheless, the 1976 strikes represented another important turning point in Poland's turbulent post-war history. The repressive measures taken by the government gave rise to the creation of a Worker Defense Committee (KOR) which marked the return of the intellectuals to collaboration with the workers. Although KOR focused primarily on providing legal aid to arrested workers, the revival of the earlier workers–intellectuals alliance implied that sooner or later the list of purely economic demands would be supplemented by political desiderata. From the beginning, the KOR leaders expressed strong aversion to violence, urging the workers to adopt a peaceful stance in articulating their demands, so as not to provoke the government to react violently to worker discontent.

A convincing test case of the policy of non-violent resistance was provided in 1979 by the visit of the new pope, John Paul II, to his homeland. The visit, which clearly worried the authorities, afraid that popular demonstrations in support of the Pope might get out of hand, ended up as an impressive demonstration of mass, albeit peaceful, loyalty to the Pope. It also suggested that the end of Communist rule in Poland was in sight and demonstrated the potential strength of a non-violent popular movement that could be mobilized for a cause.

This was exactly what happened in 1980 when the striking workers on the Baltic Coast presented the government with a list of 21 demands which clearly represented a departure from the past.[16] Although most of the demands still focused on bread and butter issues, there was at least one significant demand that was a novum: it was a demand for the recognition of Solidarity as the first truly independent and self-governing labour movement in Communist Eastern Europe. This time there was no ambiguity; the government's agreement to recognize Solidarity was seen as a major crack in the monolithic façade of the system, depriving the ruling party of the monopoly of political and economic decision-making, and thus it could be counted as a major victory for the pro-democracy forces. The government steadfastly resisted the temptation of sending troops to seize the striking factories, showing again its predilection for non-violent conflict management.

The next several months witnessed a gradual escalation of the conflict. On the one hand, the radical wing of Solidarity raised the temperature of the confrontation by sharpening the tenor of its demands, making them increasingly political. On the other, the hardline elements within the party reacted by resorting to countermeasures, which proved largely ineffective. Interestingly enough, the hoped-for demonstration effect, whereby the example of Solidarity would be emulated by workers in the neighbouring countries, did not materialize, and toward the end of 1981, for a variety of reasons, Solidarity became increasingly isolated from within and without, and an easy prey for government intervention, taking the form of martial law imposed on the country in December 1981, which effectively put an end to the democratic interlude. For once, violence could not be fully contained, but the loss of life was remarkably low. Solidarity itself, despite impressive membership figures, was easily dismantled, which testified to the skilful implementation of the military takeover.

The success of martial law produced several lessons which were apparently absorbed by both sides. For the ruling party, it represented the loss of whatever marginal legitimacy it may have still enjoyed, forcing it to turn to the military to ensure its survival. The military, still smarting from its highly criticized involvement in the suppression of the 1970 strikes, proved to be a highly reluctant participant in implementing martial law: perhaps it would refuse to be drawn in a similar crisis in the future? In the wake of its staggering defeat, Solidarity leaders realized that despite its impressive size the movement turned out to be an empty shell, that their increasingly shrill pronouncements without a follow-up action fell on deaf ears and succeeded only in alienating the population. All this meant that much time and effort would be needed to achieve victory over the Communists.

The next watershed event in Eastern Europe was the arrival on the scene in 1985 of Mikhail Gorbachev with his ideas of *perestroika*, *glasnost* and *demokratizatsiia*. This also had the effect of taking the spotlight off Poland and focusing it on Eastern Europe as a whole. The key question concerned the ability of Gorbachev to persuade his allies in the region to follow suit and implement his reform blueprint in their respective countries. It soon became apparent that only two of them, Hungary and Poland, were willing to do it. The remaining five countries, Albania, Bulgaria, Czechoslovakia, East Germany and Romania, exhibited either hostility or indifference, and Yugoslavia was facing problems that surfaced after Tito's death. It was clear that the Soviet-led monolith in Eastern Europe was falling apart.

1989 and after

In 1989 the individual East European countries were on their own for the first time in 44 years and some of them took full advantage of this opportunity. Not surprisingly, it was Poland which again took the lead. Following two waves of strikes in 1988, the Communist party agreed to initiate round table negotiations with the Solidarity-led opposition with an eye to arriving at a peaceful transfer of power. Partly free elections in June 1989 brought defeat for the Communists and a subsequent formation of the first non-Communist government in the region since the ouster of the Benes government in Czechoslovakia in February 1948.[17] Next was Hungary (July), followed by Bulgaria (October), East Germany and Czechoslovakia (November), Romania (December) and Albania (March 1990), which meant that by the spring of 1990, communism as it had been known for more than four decades was no longer there.

This brief summary does not suggest that the collapse of Communism and the transition to a new non-communist system were accomplished smoothly and non-violently. This was true, above all, in the case of Hungary and Poland. In Romania the ouster of the Communist regime necessitated the execution of its top leaders, followed by weeks of violence, involving considerable loss of life, centred on Bucharest. While transitions in Sofia, East Berlin and Prague were bloodless, they were triggered by mass demonstrations which forced the Communist governments to surrender to popular pressure.

Insofar as the DDR was concerned, it was the month of October which witnessed a massive escalation of popular discontent. After remaining under wraps for a long time, the dissatisfaction with the system spilled over into the streets and assumed a form of so-called 'People's Marches' in several key East German cities, especially in Leipzig.[18] It appears that shortly before his own ouster from leadership, Erich Honecker contemplated applying the Tienanmen strategy to quell the demonstrators, but his orders to do so were countermanded by local party and security leaders. The last straw was Gorbachev's order to the commander of Soviet forces in East Germany to keep the troops confined to the barracks and not let them intervene in the escalating crisis. There is no doubt that both these measures did go a long way in avoiding bloodshed in East Germany.

In Czechoslovakia the population, encouraged by the successes achieved by the anti-Communist opposition elsewhere in the region, also began to demonstrate in major cities, especially in Prague. During one of the rallies on 28 October, the traditional Czechoslovak independence day, rumours spread that one of the demonstrators had been killed by the police. This proved not to be true, but the anger generated by the news escalated so much that the government gave up and agreed to initiate a round table dialogue with the opposition.

The events in the rest of the region were bound to influence the developments in Yugoslavia which for decades, under the leadership of Marshal Tito, tended to march to a different drummer. Following some confusion after Tito's death, a new leader, Slobodan Milosevic, rose to power in Serbia, the largest and strongest republic within the Yugoslav federation. Seeing himself as another Tito, Milosevic proceeded to augment his power in order to expand Serbian-controlled areas, which included the autonomous regions of Voyvodina and Kosovo, the latter inhabited mostly by Albanians.

Milosevic's action was strongly resented by Croatia and Slovenia, which decided to take advantage of the creeping disintegration of the Yugoslav Federation and declared independence. Serbia's effort to stop it failed miserably in Slovenia, but it triggered a bloody confrontation with Croatia which provided a dress rehearsal for the carnage in Bosnia that followed soon after, and for a similar conflict in Kosovo which began two years later. The Dayton peace accord confirmed the breakup of the former Yugoslavia with one democratic country (Slovenia), two Communist-ruled states (Serbia and Montenegro) and three states (Bosnia, Croatia and Macedonia) whose political-constitutional order cannot be unambiguously defined.

All this meant that the disappearance of communism in Eastern Europe was not automatically followed by the establishment of stable and viable democratic systems. The transition process proved generally successful in Czechoslovakia, Hungary and Poland, much less so in Albania, Bulgaria, Romania and the former Yugoslavia. The idea of retaining a democratic, albeit socialist-oriented, East Germany entertained by some members of the anti-Communist opposition was quickly abandoned and the country merged formally with the German Federal Republic in October 1990.

Space does not allow a detailed discussion of the reasons behind the difficulties encountered by democracy in the Balkans and subsequently in Slovakia which separated peacefully from the Czech Republic in 1995. It suffices to say that in the cases of Bulgaria and Romania it took between seven and eight years for the post-Communist regimes to be finally displaced by genuinely democratic governments. It did not come easily and it took many mass demonstrations, without bloodshed, to force the governments in power finally to give up and agree to new elections which produced democratic majorities. A somewhat higher degree of violence occurred in Serbia where the anti-Communist opposition demonstrated in the streets of Belgrade for many months, before Milosevic accepted its demands to recognize the results of municipal elections that gave victory to the opposition. It was not a complete victory for democracy but definitely a setback for the Communists.

Albania presents still another example of mass violence which almost succeeded in destroying the fabric of the fledgling democracy. What started initially as a mass protest against various 'pyramid' schemes which managed to rob the Albanian population of more than one billion dollars, soon became transformed into a violent uprising against the government accused of participating in the schemes in order to finance its own election campaign. For several weeks in the spring of 1997, it appeared that the government would not be able to contain the growing anarchy and that it was only a matter of time before the country would succumb to mob rule. Considering the huge amounts of weapons in the hands of the insurgents who acquired them forcibly from both the military and police, the loss of life was relatively low. The situation was clearly getting out of hand and it was only the intervention of NATO troops, headed by Italy, that, at the last minute, prevented the total collapse of the Albanian state.

Conclusions and a look into the future

What conclusions can be drawn from this brief survey of the relationship between violence and democracy in Eastern Europe?

The record shows that insofar as the interwar period was concerned, with the possible exception of Czechoslovakia, violence had been deployed rather routinely by both the governments and the opposition. The governments, which represented a variety of authoritarian regimes, dispensed violence, for the most part indiscriminately, against rebellious national minorities and disenchanted segments of the population in the name of maintaining the independence and integrity of the state. The opposition engaged in violent, occasionally terrorist acts, in an attempt to bring down the governments or force them to grant concessions to the dissatisfied minorities. It was obvious that the application of violence had little, if anything, to do with democracy. Neither the governments nor the opposition pretended to be democratic and violence was not used to transform the existing political landscape in the direction of establishing or safeguarding democracy, but rather to preserve the status quo or to obtain some minor concessions for the opposition.

The violence appeared generally to be sanctioned by the local populations. This was because of several factors: the presence of large, unsophisticated masses of rigidly conservative peasants, generally alien to the ideas of democracy and human rights; the power in the hands of military-bureaucratic oligarchies, for whom the end – the preservation of the newly established states – sanctified whatever means were necessary, including violence; the failure of the institutions – some of which, like the churches, enjoy considerable respect – to intervene in order to modify governmental and opposition behaviour; general indifference toward violence on the part of the middle and upper classes, primarily interested in safeguarding their privileged status; and finally the absence of foreign-based institutions and organizations concerned with the issue of human rights.

The roots of this far-reaching indifference and neglect could be traced to the absence of genuine civil society and the dominance of a non-democratic political culture in the region, both strongly reminiscent of the trends prevailing in Germany and some other West European countries. Their characteristic features included the glorification of the state, dislike of compromise solutions, disrespect for other people's views, and low value put on human rights. In those circumstances, tolerance of violence and contempt for democracy were not really surprising.

The horrors of World War II and the often violent nature of Communist seizure of power in the region induced a process of change which ultimately achieved a radical transformation of the popular attitude toward both violence and democracy, at least in some East European countries. Government-sponsored violence, including loss of life, occurred on a larger scale for the last time in Poland in December 1981, in the early stages of martial law. It caused a massive popular revulsion which has persisted until today, as the members of the security forces responsible for the largest killing were recently proclaimed not guilty after a lengthy and controversial trial. It took much longer for mass violence to disappear in Bulgaria and Romania, leaving only Albania and Bosnia which still experience sporadic violence. The new *cause célèbre* is, of course, Kosovo, where the danger of mass violence appears greater than in Bosnia because of growing involvement of its neighbours such as Albania and Macedonia.

There has also been a similar change in the popular attitude toward democracy, although here the progress has been uneven, with the Balkan countries lagging behind those in East Central Europe. In the spring of 1998, none of the countries can be described as model democracies, yet each successive year has been marked by an expansion of democratic space and a gradual build-up of incipient civil society. The remarkable aspect of the democratic transformation has been that it was being accomplished essentially in a non-violent manner, testifying to a revolutionary change in popular consciousness.

What about the future? The apparent general aversion to violence, fuelled by memories of the past, seems to provide a guarantee that neither the governments nor the opposition would ever again resort to violent behaviour in order to accomplish their goals. Does it mean that, at least in the foreseeable future, the still fragile East European democracies are no longer threatened by outbreaks of violence which could destabilize the laboriously constructed political and economic systems?

Two, possibly three, potential dangers still loom on the horizon. The first one is the continued persistence of ethnic conflicts. To be sure, the intensity of ethnic animosities has significantly declined in some countries, yet elsewhere the conflict continued unabated. Poland is the best example of the former: since the collapse of communism in 1989, the Poles have greatly improved relations with their traditional enemies – the Germans, the Ukrainians and the Lithuanians – who today account for most of the national minorities. The rest of the region has shown much less progress. While this was not unexpected in the case of the Balkan countries, the recent surfacing of anti-gypsy behaviour in the Czech Republic has been surprising in view of the highly positive outside perception of the country as the most stable and advanced democracy in the region.

Do I exaggerate the threat of ethnic conflicts as a source of violence that may destroy democracy? In his recent study of the disintegration of Czechoslovakia and Yugoslavia, Andrew Janos claims that while 'ethnic fragmentation may complicate matters … there is no good psychological explanation as to why it should propel people toward violence' and he seeks explanation in the 'hoary concept of culture'.[19] Similarly, Susan Woodward, while stating that 'few states are free of the potential for animosity along ethnic, religious, racial, or communal lines' and that 'tensions along ethnic, racial, or historical fault lines can lead to civil violence', denies that this provided an explanation of the Yugoslav crisis.[20] Both authors point to the US and Czechoslovakia as examples of societies where ethnic conflicts are resolved non-violently and, as is the case of the US, the 'ethnic differences are valued for enhancing the quality of life through variety and creative tension'.[21]

My own attitude is much less sanguine. As mentioned earlier, the example of benign Czechoslovakia strikes me as misplaced and I am not convinced that racial animosity in the US improves the quality of life there. One can also point to the conflict in Northern Ireland as an example of supposedly 'civilized' people willing to shed blood in defence of their narrow sectarian interests. Of course, one could cite other examples of 'ancient hatreds' that have been resolved peacefully, to mention only France and Germany or Germany and Poland, but both these antagonisms took a long time and a bloody world war to be put to rest. Thus, to sum up, in the near future I see ethnic conflicts as a real threat to democracy, at least in some East European countries.

The second danger facing democracy in the region is a massive rise in crime and failure to generate proper respect for the rule of law. East European statistics indicate a sharp increase in violent and non-violent crime since the downfall of communism in 1989, with the rise being particularly high among the youth. Among the reasons cited has been the relative passivity of the police, weak and inefficient judiciary, easier access to weapons and alcohol, the appearance of drug culture imported from the West and, in the case of youth, the breakdown of family and social networks.

The fact is that the police and the judiciary, both understaffed and underpaid, and aware of past criticism, have been increasingly fearful of being accused again of violating human rights. Hence, in some countries they adopted a benign and tolerant attitude toward individuals and groups guilty of violent and non-violent crimes. The dramatic rise in corruption in the public and private sectors, and the rather indifferent official attitude toward it, has hardly enhanced the respect for law and order. No one has better emphasized the importance of respect for the rule of law than President Vaclav Havel of the Czech Republic, saying that 'the most important thing is that this respect take root in people's minds so deeply that it becomes a matter of honour to observe the laws, not to flaunt or circumvent them'.[22]

The rise in youth crime deserves a special comment. Not only official statistics but also journalistic accounts, point to a spectacular increase in violent behaviour of young people from late teens to mid-20s. The 'skinheads' in the Czech Republic, the former DDR and Poland have been guilty not only of killing their own but also of lynching and murdering gypsies and 'fellow human beings simply because they have a different colour of skin'.[23] While the numerical strength of right-wing violent and openly fascist groups in the region remains small, their persistence and ability to recruit new members are striking.

Perhaps the best explanation of the continuing presence of fascism in the new democracies is provided by Ralf Dahrendorf, who states that:

> Its prime characteristics is the sudden impact of the forces of the modern industrial world on a society which is unprepared because it has retained many of the characteristics of an older, status ridden, authoritarian age. The two simply do not match. As a result, important groups find themselves dislocated and disoriented. They hate capitalism as much as socialism, the newly rich as much as the newly poor ... But the extent to which outdated social structures have been preserved in the Communist countries is striking.[24]

There is no easy remedy to cure this ill, which is often linked to the previously discussed ethnic conflicts. Time, as always, is a factor, as is the success of the new democracies in alleviating social and economic problems, such as unemployment and poverty of which many of the youth are the principal victims, and in instilling respect for the rule of law.

Part of the problem lies in different perceptions of the meaning of democracy. In the zeal to propagate their views, some political groupings as well as individuals are beginning to violate norms of acceptable behaviour in the name of democracy which, they claim, legitimizes their actions in the name of free speech and/or freedom of assembly. It remains to be seen how long will it take the new democracies in Eastern Europe to find ways to restrain such behaviour without, in turn, violating fundamental rights and freedoms.

Are these the only dangers facing the new East European democracies? No – the above two were discussed at some length because of their high correlation with violence. Another threat is the failure of the new states to ensure economic well-being for all social classes and groups. Here, one has to agree with Adam Przeworski that the 'central dilemma facing the new democracies' is that they 'face the challenge of having to consolidate the nascent political institutions when material conditions continue to deteriorate'.[25] Still another one is the need to preserve national sovereignty and security. Both threats and needs deserve a separate treatment and could not be dealt with here for reasons of space.

Finally, there is still perhaps the greatest danger of all – the failure to build a viable and dynamic civil society. Contrary to many observers of the East European scene, I have argued elsewhere that civil society has never really existed in the region prior to the Communist downfall and I have attributed the wave of scholarly enthusiasm for the concept to what Leszek Kolakowski called the 'revolutionary hangover', which characterized the search for an explanation of what happened in Eastern Europe in 1989.[26] Dahrendorf is right on target in proclaiming that 'civil society is the key' and that 'people should be "civil"': that is, 'polite, tolerant and, above all, *non-violent'* (my italics).[27]

Does it mean that the idea of creating a civil society in Eastern Europe is a pipe dream? Personally, I think it is, at least in the near future. But then, Dahrendorf is also right in underscoring the key role of the time dimension and in stating that while it may take relatively little time to push through economic and constitutional reform, it is likely that two or even three generations might be needed to lay down the foundations for a viable civil society. If true, the task facing the new East European democracies is daunting, but not hopeless.

NOTES

1. Karen Davisha and Bruce Parrott (eds), *The Consolidation of Democracy in East-Central Europe* (Cambridge: Cambridge University Press, 1997); Grzegorz Ekiert, *The State Against Society* (Princeton, NJ: Princeton University Press, 1996); Jon E. Elster (ed.), *The Roundtable Talks and the Breakdown of Communism* (Chicago, IL: Chicago University Press, 1996); Adam Przeworski, *Democracy and the Market* (Cambridge: Cambridge University Press, 1991).
2. Valerie Bunce, 'Should Transitologists Be Grounded?', *Slavic Review* 54/1 (1995) pp.111–25; 'Paper Curtains and Paper Tigers', *Slavic Review* 54/4 (1995) pp.965–87; and 'The Place of Place in Transitions to Democracy', unpublished AAASS (Seattle, 1997); see also T. L. Karl and Phillippe Schmitter, 'From an Iron Curtain to a Paper Curtain', *Slavic Review* 54/4 (1995) pp.965–78; S. M. Terry, 'Thinking About Post Communist Transitions: How Unique Are They', *Slavic Review* 52 (1993) pp.333–7;

and K. Von Beyme, *Transition to Democracy in Eastern Europe* (New York: St Martin's Press, 1996).
3. Jane Curry, ed., *Dissent in Eastern Europe* (New York: Praeger, 1983); Andrzej Korbonski, 'Conformity and Dissent in Eastern Europe', in P. J. Potichnyj and J. Zacek (eds), *Politics and Participation under Communist Rule* (New York: Praeger, 1983); Zygmun Bauman, 'Social Dissent in East European Political Systems', *European Journal of Sociology* XI/I (1971) pp.41–50; H. Gordon Skilling, 'Opposition in Communist East Europe', in Robert Dahl (ed.), *Regimes and Oppositions* (New Haven: Yale University Press, 1981).
4. David C. Rapoport, and Leonard Weinberg, this volume.
5. The conceptual confusion surrounding the term 'democracy' is illustrated by David Collier and Steven Levitsky, who identified more that 550 subtypes: see 'Democracy with Adjectives: Conceptual Innovations in Research', *World Politics* 49/3 (1997) pp.430–451.
6. Albania, Bosnia, Bulgaria, Croatia, the Czech Republic, East Germany, Hungary. Macedonia, Montenegro, Poland, Romania, Serbia, Slovakia and Slovenia.
7. Felix Gross, Violence in Politics: Terror and Assassination in Eastern Europe and Russia (The Hague: Mouton, 1972).
8. Poland 1926, Yugoslavia 1929, Bulgaria 1935, Romania 1937. Albania was a feudal country and Czechoslovakia could hardly be called a model democracy.
9. The seeds of the Polish-Ukrainian antagonism, which persisted throughout the interwar period, were planted prior to World War I by Vienna in the name of the old adage, 'divide and rule'.
10. Joseph Rothschild, *East Central Europe between Two World Wars* (Seattle: University of Washington Press, 1974) p.39
11. President Narutowicz, Poland 1922 and Alexander II, Yugoslavia 1934.
12. A. Stamboliski Bulgaria 1923, and two Romanians, I. Duca and A. Calinescu 1933 and 1939.
13. Gross (note 7) pp.23–38
14. This was well illustrated by land reforms decreed by several East European countries that discriminated against ethnic minorities (Ramat, 1995, p.74.)
15. Luba Fajfer, 'The Polish Military and the Crisis of 1970', *Communist and Post-Communist Studies* 26/2 (1993) pp.202–25.
16. Mariusz Janicki and Wieslaw Wladyka, 'Manifest Sierpniowy '80', *Politykal* (Warsaw, 27 Aug. 1997).
17. Evidence exists that hardliners in the Polish Communist Party wanted to annul the elections, but were overruled by the leadership apparently stunned by events in Tienanmen Square in Beijing and who could not begin a similar action in Poland.
18. Suzanne Lohman, 'Dynamics of Informational Cascades: The Monday Demonstrations in Leipzig, East Germany, 1989–91', *World Politics* 47/1 (Oct. 1994), pp.42–101.
19. Andrew Janos, *Czechoslovakia and Yugoslavia: Ethnic Conflict and the Dissolution of Multinational States* (Berkeley, CA: International and Area Studies, 1997) p.54.
20. Susan L. Woodward, *Balkan Tragedy* (Washington, DC: The Brookings Institution, 1995) p.18.
21. Ibid.
22. Vaclav Havel, 'The State of the Republic', *New York Review of Books*, 5 March 1998.
23. Ibid.
24. Ralf Darhrendorf, *Reflections on the Revolution in Eastern Europe* (New York: NYT Books, 1990) pp.113–14.
25. Przeworski (note 1) p.109.
26. Andrzej Korbonski, 'Civil Society and Democracy in Poland: Problems and Prospects', in Adolf Bibic and Gigi Graziano (eds), *Civil Society Political Society* (Ljubljana: Slovenian Political Science Associeation, 1994); Leszek Kolakowski, 'The Post Revolutionary Hangover', *Journal of Democracy* 3/3 (1995) p.70.
27. Darhrendorf (note 24) p.100.

12

Violence and the Paradox of Democratic Renewal: A Preliminary Assessment

VICTOR T. LE VINE

Jefferson's famous dictum that the 'tree of liberty must be refreshed from time to time with the blood of patriots and tyrants' is examined using a counterfactual argument and empirical and normative analysis. If Jefferson is right and there is an inescapable connection between democracy and violence, his dictum must contain a paradox since democracy in the first instance also predicates the creation and maintenance of institutional mechanisms for non-violent resolution and management of conflict. What if Jefferson was wrong and the 'blood of patriots and tyrants' can destroy rather than fertilize the tree of liberty? Positing the counterfactual suggests (and permits analysis of) three derivative subhypotheses: (1) that democracies born in violence are more prone to periodic 'violent challenges' than those born peacefully; (2) that periodic violent challenges in democracies leave them less, rather than more, stable; and (3) that when democracies break down they usually do so when a culture of violence is created. Overall, the analysis tends to confirm the counterfactual hypothesis.

What country before ever existed a century and a half without a rebellion? And what country can preserve its liberties, if its rulers are not warned from time to time, that this people preserve the spirit of resistance? Let them take arms ... What signify a few lives lost in a century or two? The tree of liberty must be refreshed from time to time with the blood of patriots and tyrants. It is its natural manure.

Thomas Jefferson, Letter to William Stevens Smith, Nov. 13, 1787 (my emphasis)[1]

The tree of liberty only grows when watered by the blood of tyrants.

Bertrand Barère de Vieuzac,
Speech in the National Convention, 1792[2]

In 1787 Jefferson had been in Paris three years, first as Commissioner, then as successor to Benjamin Franklin, and remained until 1789 as Minister of the new American republic. When he wrote to William Stephens Smith he had already been exposed to the spirit and fiery rhetoric of those soon to launch their own revolution. Barère certainly knew Jefferson since he also approvingly quotes Jefferson as endorsing the French Revolution.[3] He may even have met Jefferson and borrowed the 'tree of liberty' phrase from him; possibly the phrase may already have been common currency among Paris' would-be revolutionaries. It has been suggested to me that it was simply hyperbole, meant to emphasize Jefferson's defense of Shays' Rebellion[4] against British propaganda which had characterized it as American anarchy, testimony to the unfitness of England's former colonies to govern themselves.[5] However, I have seen nothing to indicate that Jefferson did not mean what he said, because Shays' Rebellion had already been put down, and he had enough time to reflect on its meaning and consequences.

If Jefferson is right, there is an inescapable connection between democracy and violence; violence may be necessary not only for the birth of democracy, but for democracy's maintenance and renewal. But therein lies a paradox: if democracy is to be preferred because (*inter alia*) it provides institutionalized mechanisms for non-violent conflict resolution and management, then society must also forego the cleansing and restorative action that only violence – and the 'blood of patriots and tyrants' – can bring. The paradox is worth exploring, in part because Jefferson's thesis was expressed, with appropriate modification, by Barère five years later, but also much more recently by Sartre and Fanon[6] in *The Wretched of the Earth*, by various contemporary scholars, and in the ideological justifications offered by a whole range of 'National Liberation' and other oppositional groups including today's 'Patriots' movement and its ultra-conservative allies.[7] The latter, distant heirs of John C. Calhoun's theory of the 'compact republic', cite Jefferson to legitimize their own violent resistance to a multitude of real and imaginary injuries visited on them by what they deem despotic local and federal governments. It could be added that Machiavelli, who advocated the periodic use of (state) violence both as means of keeping populations fearful and as a reminder of the ethos of the founding period, saw innate turbulence in republics: 'There is [in republics] greater life, greater hatred, and more desire for vengeance; they do not and cannot cast aside the memory of their ancient liberty' (*The Prince*, ch.6). To be sure, this is part of his advice to whoever becomes ruler of a free city: if he does not destroy it, it will destroy him, because 'it will always find a motive for rebellion in the name of liberty and its ancient usages' (ibid.). Because of his harsh prescription, Machiavelli gave republics a backhanded, if unintentional, compliment; they are difficult to subjugate because rebellion is in their nature.

The paradox is also worth exploring because, in the first instance, both Jefferson and Barère may simply have been wrong in positing the connection, and that in fact exactly the contrary may be true – that 'the blood of patriots and tyrants' can destroy rather than fertilize the tree of liberty, in the process making democracy more difficult or less likely to achieve. Not only does the proposition appear to license violence against democracy itself, but it deprives those who espouse the proposition of any moral ground in defending democracy against violent attack. I think it likely that neither Jefferson nor Barère imagined that the very violence which gives birth to or restores liberty could also 'poison the well' of democracy by implicitly legitimizing bloody violence as an agent of change; nor could they have known that they had provided an excellent example of the paradoxical (and ironic) possibilities of the law of unintended consequences.

Demonstrating the implications of the paradox

Jefferson might have claimed to have demonstrated his proposition by asserting the salutary effect of Shay's Rebellion: the Republic (he intimated) is the better for it, in that had the rebels remained 'quiet under such misconceptions [about the facts of their grievances], it is a lethargy, a forerunner of death to the public liberty'.[8] Thus it was a good thing that the Rebellion occurred, in that it allowed the rebels to articulate their grievances, even at the cost of a few lives, since to remain silent would have been worse, presaging a general unwillingness to exercise 'the public liberty', and in that 'lethargy', its 'death.' 'Honorably conducted', the Rebellion evoked its remedy, that is, 'to set them right as to the facts, pardon and pacify them'.[9] So too,

Barère, for whom the blood of royalists, as 'water' for the French version of the tree of liberty,[10] could only have salutary effect on its growth. And so also Fanon, for whom violence was a form of individual and collective Algerian national therapy, and from Jefferson to Barère to Fanon to today's 'Patriots' and militiamen, the proposition or one of its variants is usually defended, by assertion, as self-evident and self-justifying.[11] Even those scholars, like David Apter and Lynne Iglitzin, who make the case without mentioning Jefferson tend to do so as part of a polemic against (for example) social injustice and the violence of the state. However, Iglitzin, to her credit, does recognize the paradox in her argument; I cite her statement because it is one of the clearest acknowledgements of the problem:

> The paradox implicit in this paper is that violence, the complete antithesis of the spirit and nature of the democratic ethic, is nonetheless a necessary part of the democratic process. Every act of violence ... is an affront to someone's dignity, his peace of mind, his very life. Harmful and costly in its immediate effects, in the long run it may serve as a catalyst in the operation of the necessarily imperfect democratic society. In forcing the system to a reexamination of its weaknesses and to a readjustment of its values, violence thereby performs a useful function which is therapeutic to the body politic.[12]

A more nuanced argument is advanced by Ernest van den Haag, who argues that the disenfranchised in a democracy 'may try (often with the help of some of the enfranchised) to persuade the government to enfranchise them. As a last resort, they may do so by engaging in *persuasive* [mainly non-violent] civil disobedience. Since usually ... persuasion is more likely to be effective than violence'.[13] On the other hand: 'If one believes in the legitimacy of the government, yet one is outraged by a law or a policy which, despite persuasion, despite even persuasive civil disobedience, the majority continues to support, coercive [violent] civil disobedience – and ultimately, insurrection – is justifiable.'[14] (The difference between persuasive and coercive civil disobedience, according to van den Haag, lies in the belief of the 'disenfranchised' or the aggrieved about the possibility of redress: if they believe they can still be heard, and their grievances resolved, they will resort to persuasive disobedience; if they believe that all avenues of redress have been closed, they may turn to coercive disobedience or insurrection. Thus, demonstrators – perhaps attending a proscribed gathering – may appear with placards if they think their message will get through, and possibly persuade those to whom it is directed; if they appear with weapons, that means they no longer think that possible, and have ratcheted their disobedience from persuasion to violence.)

Now whether Jefferson, or the others, *prove* the argument is another matter. Van den Haag himself admits that 'the outrages which would justify coercive civil disobedience in a democracy fortunately are rare [and thus] the effectiveness of coercive civil disobedience in attaining its ultimate, as distinguished from its temporary aim, must be doubted, in most cases'.[15] Van den Haag has little sympathy for violence, yet, in the end, cannot bring himself to condemn it outright. Moreover, all that said, the form of the defence appears almost invariably in the illogic of *post-hoc ergo propter hoc* argument, which is no proof at all. Either way, however, proven or not, the paradox remains.

The paradox as I have stated it is in the form a counterfactual hypothesis,[16] and can be tested in part by logic and in part by empirical means. The question, then, becomes not whether democracy, be it at the outset or subsequently, is periodically 'refreshed' by the blood of tyrants and patriots, but whether such violence demonstrably harms democracy, from the beginning, or later. I argue that, on balance, the evidence supports the counterfactual hypothesis. Since the truth or falsity of counterfactual hypotheses are demonstrated in the same manner as any other, a beginning to the proof of this particular hypothesis can be made by examining in turn three possible questions about violence that attends the birth of democracies, which challenge them during their lifetimes, and which may precipitate their collapse. Before turning to these subhypotheses, however, it is necessary to clarify briefly a distinction made, but not argued here: the difference between the *justification* of violence at the founding of democracies, or later, and its *consequences*.

Is blood a price worth paying for liberty? In his memoirs about his role in the founding of Israel (*The Revolt*, 1972), Menachem Begin argues that the violent Jewish resistance to the British mandatory regime was dictated by the need to seek freedom from imperialist oppression and 'serfdom', and intimates that had it not been for that resistance, grounded in a hatred for oppression, the Jewish state would never have been born. Moreover, the resistance rejuvenated Jewry, creating a new kind of Jew whose identity was forged in the struggle.

Descartes, according to Begin, had it wrong: the new Jews say, 'We fight, therefore we are.'[17] General George Grivas, who led the violent post-World War II Cypriot revolt against the British, makes much the same argument, suggesting that without his revolt (1955–59) an independent Cyprus would have been impossible. He quotes approvingly Archbishop Spiridon, Primate of all Greece: 'Freedom is never won without bloodshed.'[18] Though the Greek Cypriots and Grivas began the revolt to achieve *enosis* (union) with Greece, and had to settle for independence, the result was the same: a new Greek, proud and free. My point is that Begin and Grivas' arguments are in the line of the classic moral arguments on behalf of violent corporate resistance to tyranny (e.g. from the *Vindiciae contra tyrannos* of 1579, to the Declaration of Independence of 1776) – in effect, *justifications* for violence, be it for violence on behalf of the creation of a free government, or simply on behalf of the preservation of democracy. Moreover, as does Fanon, both Begin and Grivas argue the *transformative* effects of violence: Fanon says that it cleanses the spirit of both oppressor and oppressed, Begin and Grivas that it rejuvenates and crystallizes collective identity. So too argues van den Haag, since his analysis is part of a series of formal moral arguments about violence and civil disobedience. In any case, I make no brief here either to affirm or deny justifications for violence at the founding of democracies, or later; my concern is to consider the effects, the consequences, of such violence. I concede readily that while there is a moral argument to be made in the matter, it is not the burden of my discussion, and it would take a different form of exposition than that which I make here.

That said, I return to the main line of my argument, and to the three derivative subhypotheses of the principal counterfactual.

The subhypotheses

Subhypothesis 1: Democracies born in violence are more prone to periodic violent challenges[19] than those that are born peacefully

Prima facie, here the proof should be relatively simple: first, identify democracies 'born in violence', then tabulate the number of significant violent challenges to these democratic systems since their inception, and finally establish whether the violence at inception is in any way connected to the subsequent challenges. This first group should include not only current democracies, but also those which began as democracies but failed to maintain their democratic vocations for whatever lengths of time. The continuity of democratic rule, then, becomes important since discontinuities from the democratic norm have to be explained. Secondly, since the longevity of democratic systems may affect the frequency of such challenges, a distinction will have to be made between older and newer systems to discover if proximity to or distance from the founding affected the frequencies. Finally, examination of the content and contexts of the most important challenges will have to establish whether the challengers were influenced in their actions by the example of the 'founding violence'. And throughout, the comparison – in the first and second steps – is with democratic systems which were founded peacefully. (Whether violent post-founding challenges themselves, regardless of the contexts of founding, represent a kind of political learning is a question I will leave to my examination of the second subhypothesis.)

Without going into details, it suffices to report that a first look at the data – and a close examination of several systems' challenges – suggests that systems born without violence are only marginally less vulnerable to subsequent major violent challenges than those born in violence. Nevertheless, given the extraordinarily difficult tasks of data gathering and analysis that attends examination of the individual country challenges, I have to conclude that for now, the first subhypothesis must remain 'not yet proven'. Some of the considerations leading to this conclusion are summarized below.

According to Freedom House's 1995–96 *Comparative Survey of Freedom*, there were 117 'formal' democracies out of 191 independent countries. By Freedom House's criteria, only 76 of the 117 democracies were 'free', that is, had not only a full panoply of democratic institutions but also exercised them; the rest were 'partly free'[20] (see Annex A). Given the dynamic nature of democracy, in that a system can alternate between 'free' and 'partly free', the 117-country tranche is the more useful for our purposes. Moreover, it contains both the oldest and youngest surviving functioning democracies: the US and Eritrea. Excluding, for now, those democracies become defunct (e.g. the German Weimar Republic of 1919–33, the Russian Menshevik regime of 1915–17, the Spanish Republics of 1873 and 1931–39, the aborted Hungarian Republics of 1945–47 and November 1956, the 1945–48 Czech regime of Eduard Benes, etc.), some 73 cases, of which nine are now 'not free', appeared salient for our purposes.

If the durability of a democratic system affects positively its vulnerability to violent internal challenges such as coups, rebellions and the like, the historical record should show that once a democratic system is established, such challenges diminish in frequency the longer it survives. Consequently, it becomes necessary to distinguish between older and newer democracies. Three main historical periods of democracy-creation stand out:

(1) pre-World War I, from the late 1700s to 1914, during which the US and France became the exemplars of democratic revolution, and in Europe Belgium, The Netherlands, Switzerland, Italy and the Scandinavian countries emerged as democracies, as did Canada, Mexico and most of the Latin American republics;
(2) the 1918–39 interwar period, which saw the creation of democratic systems in a number territories held by Russia, and the German, Ottoman and Austro-Hungarian empires; and
(3) the post-World War II period to the present, when an extraordinary burst of global state-creation brought forth some 140 new political systems, a majority of them (at least initially) with democratic constitutions.

There are further complicating factors. It is virtually impossible, save through case-by-case analysis, to measure the political shadows cast by such extraordinary events as the collapse of empires and the two twentieth-century World Wars, all of which generated new states and democracies. Moreover, the two World Wars, it must be remembered, not only reconfigured continental maps, but also ended – or began the process of ending – no less than 10 empires: the German and Ottoman during the World War I, and the French, British, Portuguese, Dutch, Belgian, Spanish, Italian, German Third Reich and Japanese during or after World War II. (To all intents and purposes, and excepting a few minor territories in North and South America and the Caribbean, the American empires of France, Britain, Spain and Portugal disappeared during the eighteenth and nineteenth centuries.) And then there are the various states generated by the collapse of the Soviet Union in 1989, itself arguably an empire in its own right. The point is that democratic inceptions can be self-generated (rebellions, revolutions, civil wars, secessionist movements, 'national conferences', peaceful devolution, etc.), or they can be a consequence, proximate or distant, of some large-scale event as a war and/or an imperial collapse. It is much easier to decide if a democratic inception is violent or non-violent if it is self-generated, than if it follows in the wake of a war or other major international event. Hence my decision about initial violence or non-violence for each country was purely subjective, the result of my reading of the circumstances of democratic inception, and thus open to question. That being the case, the possible connections to subsequent violent challenges are equally problematic.

That said, preliminary analysis does permit some tentative conclusions, in addition to the initial finding that democracies born without violence appear marginally less prone to subsequent violent challenges than those having violent inceptions.

First, it turns out that with the exception of five systems in the post-World War II group, none had clear sailing from their inception. The data also reveal that for *both* those systems founded in violence and those born peacefully, the first five–ten years are the most dangerous: the longer a system survives, the fewer major challenges it faces *and* the more likely it is to be able to survive a major crisis of legitimacy. This appears to confirm the findings for Africa (at least through October 1987) reported by Bienen and Van de Walle.[21] Though they only tested for leaders, their conclusions apply as well to systems, given the interchangeability of governments and leaders and the fact that during most of the period they examined (1960–87) there were only two – at most three – durable, functioning democracies among the 51 African states examined by Bienen and Van de Walle.

Secondly, the fact that most (16) of the first category democracies (before 1914) were founded as a result of an anti-colonial revolt or a revolution against an established autocracy (e.g. the US, France, most of the Latin American systems[22]) appears to establish an analytical bias in favour of older democracies. How old does a democracy have to be to be 'durable'? Recent studies by Adam Pzreworski and his colleagues[23] suggest that democratic durability has more to do with economic well-being than (with) the presence or absence of violent challenges over time. That does not mean, of course, that violent challenges have *no* effect on durability: in general they do, but how much and what kind of effect remains an empirical question *with respect to each case.* My own guess is that both the Pzreworski *et al.* conclusions and the related conventional wisdom which relates democracy to violence[24] (the more democratic a system, the less it is prone to violence, and vice versa) hold up on condition that the dangerous initial transitional period is successfully negotiated.[25]

Finally, it is worth noting that recent work by Chistopher J. Anderson on system support in old and new democracies in Europe[26] lends indirect support to my argument. Anderson drew from surveys and other data from 30 systems in west, central and east Europe, with the majority of established, mature democracies in western Europe, and newer ones in central and eastern Europe. System satisfaction appeared most highly correlated across the board to current political and economic performance, but that was to some extent conditioned by the depth to which democratic political cultures themselves had become systemically rooted, that is, in Anderson's analysis, the years of *continous* democracy since 1900. Significant anti-democratic experience (e.g. Germany, Italy, Russia, etc.) appeared to depress current levels of satisfaction. My sense of Anderson's findings brings Aristotle's classic dictum to mind: that satisfied citizens do not revolt. This lends further credence to the body of research indentifying the causal vectors of civil violence examined under subhypothesis 3 below, and to the proposition that civil violence is less likely in mature democracies, and that newer democracies, especially those emerging from authoritarian experiences, are faced with more tenuous system support – and thus, with greater tendency to face violent internal challenges.

Given the above reservations and some reasonable deductions from the data, I repeat that the first subhypothesis cannot be considered 'fully proven', though the weight of the evidence and the analysis offered here lean to its confirmation.

Subhypothesis 2: Periodic violent challenges in democracies make them less, rather than more, stable (i.e. violence begets violence, etc.)

The proposition seems incontrovertible, save for the fact that a number of apparently stable democracies (e.g. the US, France, Italy) have managed to live through a series of violent challenges, some of them genuine crises of legitimacy, and remained both viable and effective, if not invariably 'stable'. For example, Italy, which has had almost 40 governments since the end of World War II, and survived confrontations with the Mafia, extreme leftists and rightists, terrorists and a home-grown elite conspiracy (the so-called P-2 (*'Pe Due'*) plot), nevertheless clings to its democratic vocation and may, in fact, have grown stronger for its trials. The French course has been fraught with even more perils since the 1789 democratic inception: five Republics, two empires, a monarchic Restoration, an insurrectionary Paris Commune, a military dictatorship (Boulanger), two foreign occupations, defeat in two painful colonial wars, a major military mutiny complete with a threat to send paratroops into Paris, recurrent violent strikes, local ethno-regional uprisings, and periodic left- and right-wing violence. Still, French democracy, crisis-prone though it may be, nonetheless appears as durable as ever, able to withstand even the most violent challenges. And of the course, US democracy survived a civil war of unprecedented (in its time) ferocity and violence, not to speak of foreign wars and other various violent challenges during the nineteenth and twentieth centuries. In addition, there are constitutional democracies, such as India and Sri Lanka, that have been under almost continuous violent challenge since their very inception, yet still manage to survive, seemingly forever teetering on the edge of the abyss of disintegration. Dennis Austin, who has examined this problem, believes the reason lies in the sheer scope and complexity of Indian politics; his explanation may also help unravel the survivability puzzle posed by the US, France and Italy:

> The paradox suggests that India is held together by its diversity whereby the see-saw of politics, pushed to excess, reasserts itself. If democracy needs space in which to maneuver, the multiplicity of disputes in Indian society provides room enough, for even when whole sections of the population are engaged in brutal conflict with one another, or against the state, the rest of the country is usually quiescent ... Taken together, these elements of restraint have probably helped India maintain its parliamentary structures of control against the violence which threatens them.[27]

So too, says Austin, Sri Lanka, though given the length and ferocity of the Tamil uprising, its future is more problematic. What all this means is, perhaps, that 'stability' needs to be redefined to include factors of survivability and the effect of multiple political spaces, and/or that economic well-being may not be as good a predictor of democratic durability as Przeworski *et al.* and Londregan and Poole[28] suggest.

The US, French, Italian, Indian and Sri Lankan cases notwithstanding, the *general* proposition remains persuasive on its face, and recent research on 'political learning' tends to support it.

Pzreworski *et al.*[29] make the trenchant observation that 'political learning' is a significant factor, among others, that determines if democracy endures:

> It is frequently argued – Russia is a favorite example – that the absence of democratic traditions impedes the consolidation of new democratic institutions and, conversely, that democracy is more stable in countries (like Chile) that have enjoyed it in the past. What this argument misses is that if a country *had* a democratic regime (note the past tense), it is a veteran not only of democracy but of the *successful subversion* of democracy. Political learning, in other words, cuts both ways. Democrats may find the work of consolidation easier when they can rely on past traditions, but antidemocratic forces also have an experience from which they can draw lessons; people know that overthrowing democracy is possible, and may even know how to do it. If the failed Russian hard-liners' coup of 1991 was more of *coup de théatre* than a *coup d'état*, it was perhaps because the coup plotters simply did not know what they were doing – an ignorance for which they were justly ridiculed by the more experienced Latin American soul mates. An overthrow of a democracy at any time during the past history of a country shortens the life expectancy of any democratic regime in that country. To the extent that political learning does occur, then, it seems that the lessons of antidemocratic forces from the past subversion of democracy are more effective than that [which] can be relied on by democrats.

Pzreworski *et al.* cite Londregan and Poole[30] to back up the point that coups breed coups.

Anti-democratic challenges do not, obviously, come out of the blue, though perhaps complacent governments who believe they have things under control may sometimes think so. Thus, democratic regimes in countries with a history of military coups, for example, have good reason to be on their guard, as the recent examples of Niger, Sierra Leone and Congo/Brazzaville all attest.[31] Even the Gambia, one of Africa's longest-lived (31 years) democracies, succumbed to a military coup in July 1994. Lt. Yahya Jammeh, who led the coup, is reported to have been inspired by the example of his cohorts in Mauritania, Guinea and Ghana. Clearly, coup-makers learn both from their predecessors and from each other.

It should be added that the observation of Pzreworski *et al.* that anti-democratic lessons are more effective than democratic ones needs to be qualified. I suspect they are right, but the strength and utility of such lessons probably also depends on the proximity of the last challenge (since lessons fade in the mind over time), and the extent to which the lessons of democratic experience (not just democratic norms) have become imbedded in a system.

An example of one way in which that latter learning becomes manifest occurred recently in Africa. Close reading of the annals of the wave of democratic national conferences that surged onto the (mainly French-speaking) African scene during and after 1989 surprisingly revealed not only references to proto-democratic experiences *before* independence (from 1946 to ca. 1960, multi-party elections, exuberant political campaigns, relatively free voting, etc.),[32] but also traces of French constitutional mythology, still taught (for example) in Beninois and Malien schools, and become part of those countries' elite political culture. That, of course, is the story of how in 1789 the French Third Estate (the popular assembly) launched the French Revolution by transforming itself into a National Assembly and then a Constitutional Assembly. Given that the African national conferences also declared themselves sovereign and sought to become constituent assemblies for new democratic systems, the familiar French model must have seemed strikingly apt to those Africans similarly involved.[33]

There is yet another way by which learning the political lessons of violence is encouraged in any political system born of violence, be it democratic or otherwise, and that is in the propagation of national symbols, myths and heroes glorifying the violence of national creation: there are the heroes of the revolution dying in its service; the slaughter of the British/Hessians/Tories/Monarchs/Tyrants/Aristocrats/etc.; the self-serving History which celebrates the founding carnage; the national anthem as an evocation of blood lust and a call to arms;[34] and the invocation of the Deity blessing Our Arms, Our Host, Our Victory. Thus, the Revolution remains a living political theme in France, and in the US, one of whose patriotic symbols is the Minuteman, one hand on the plough and the other grasping his musket, the violence of American beginnings is celebrated – and consecrated – in monument and song. These references are so commonplace, taken for granted, that their other meanings remain submerged; they not only teach and inspire patriotism, but also legitimize both the founding violence and subsequent violent challenges to American democracy.[35]

Subhypothesis 3: When democracies break down, they do so usually when citizens become accustomed to resorting to violence to get what they want, that is, when a 'culture of violence' is created

This is not the place to survey the ample literature on the roots of political violence;[36] my question remains to the inherent paradox of Jefferson's proposition and the possibility that its inverse may be as true, if not more true, than the original. If the proof of subhypothesis 1 above at least suggests that the founding violence of democracies may encourage later violent challenges, and if subhypothesis 2 is taken as proved (with the exceptions and conditions, as noted), then the breakdown of democracies follows as a possible consequence of the cumulative effect of violent challenges to them. Demonstrably, that breakdown comes when democratic systems can no longer cope with those challenges, when a culture of violence overwhelms the civic culture of democratic problem-solving. This is the fate which, according to Austin, forever threatens Indian and Sri Lankan democracy, and to which the Weimar Republic, one of the most notable democratic failures of modern times, succumbed.[37]

Support for this contention is found in the work of various scholars, notably that of Ted Robert Gurr, whose culture of violence hypotheses have been corroborated by Cooper, Hibbs, Adams and Duvall/ Welfling.[38] Put simply, Gurr argues that a culture of violence depends both on the strength of cumulative historical antecedents of political violence, and a kind of self-fulfilling prophecy of violence – an imperative expectation of recurrence – based on the frequency of past events of political violence.[39] The research covers both democratic and non-democratic systems, confirming that a culture of violence creates a predisposition for further political violence, save that established democratic systems seem better able to withstand such challenges. These latter are not, of course, invulnerable, and given a political culture of violence of sufficient breadth and scope will fail as readily as their less fortunate cohorts.

While case studies of particular instances or general conditions of political violence in democracies abound, there are few investigations of specific cultures of political violence in those systems.[40] However, a recent study of the Lebanese Shi'a by Elizabeth Picard[41] appears to confirm Gurr's hypotheses, speaks to my point, and offers a cautionary tale about the death of a promising democracy. Picard argues that the Lebanese Shi'a operated within and contributed to a political culture featuring (in Picard's terms) 'the institutionalization of oppression and the durability of agonistic segmentation'. Her latter reference is to the manner by which clientelistic patrimonialisms, incorporated in clans, families, and ethno-religious aggregates headed by individual *beys* and *za'im*,[42] and assisted by their strongmen and militias, have partitioned Lebanon into self-perpetuating spaces of political power. Violence has been not only the currency of internal discipline and redistribution within the enclaves, but the ordinary, even ritualized, norm in intergroup relations. 'Thus,' writes Picard, 'the social order was structured by a network of unequal exchanges which operated less on a clientilistic basis than through the exercise of physical and symbolic violence.'[43] It was hoped that the birth of a republican and parliamentary political system in 1920, and in particular its post-war rebirth in 1943 through the much-praised 'National Pact' (by which the several ethno-confessional groups were allocated top positions by formula) would change the terms of the equation and usher in civil peace and democracy.[44] Unfortunately, what changed was only the outward form of the system: the *za'im* became office-holders or officials, elections were held and parliaments met, but the old clientilistic networks, now refurbished as bureaucratic channels, continued to function as always. One thing did change, especially between 1943 and 1975: the old levels of violence, both intra- and intergroup, dropped considerably (save for a dramatic upsurge during the 1958 crisis). What is important for our purposes is that the Lebanon remained relatively peaceful, and became remarkably prosperous, under its democratic institutions and the National Pact during the 1943–75 period. While it is true that the underlying dynamics of the system remained unchanged, the 32-year democratic interlude with its booming economy and rising standard of living, was no illusion. It is also fair to say that many Lebanese hoped it would last, and that the old animosities and violence lay behind them. The outbreak of civil war in 1975 brought back the old system with a vengeance, as well as new, complicating factors: the presence of 150,000 Palestinians and their families (who had fled from Jordan in 1971), a Syrian 'peace-keeping' force (which still remains to this day), a full-scale Israeli invasion in 1982 and the creation of an Israeli 'security' zone in the south, international intervention, and last but not least, promotion of the southern/central Shi'a (with help from revolutionary Iran after 1979) to the ranks of principal – and even more violent – actors on the local scene.

What gives the Lebanese story its special poignancy is the birth and death of Lebanese democracy. It was imaginatively reconstructed (in 1945) through a special informal social contract, at the time hailed a triumph of political pragmatism, and it died because the culture of political violence which it was supposed to replace proved much more firmly rooted than all the pragmatists and optimists – both inside and outside Lebanon – thought it was.[45] In the end, democratic Lebanon was no match for it; the culture of violence had been cumulating its political violence and enracinating its social predicates long before the Lebanese turned to democracy.

Conclusion

If, in the opening paragraphs of this article, I made unfavourable reference to some latter-day purveyors of exaggerated versions of Jefferson's thesis – American militiamen, 'Patriots', and their right-wing ideological kin – I did not mean to say that his proposition had no academically respectable allies. Ernest van den Haag, who couched his argument in terms of civil disobedience, as did Howard Zinn,[46] are among that number, as was Lynne Iglitzin cited above. Recently, David Apter, while recognizing the dark and destructive aspects of political violence, defends what he calls its 'heroic side'. His argument is worth quoting at length:

> It becomes difficult to ignore the heroic side of political violence. Reallocations of wealth, moral teleologies of human betterment, doctrines of how to realize it, these are also inseparable from political violence. It would be hard to envisage the evolution of democracy or for that matter the English, French, and American revolutions without such violence and indeed fears of its potentiality. The list of reforms which were successfully pushed and prodded by confrontational violence is a long one. Nor can violence be completely separated from institutional politics. The right to organize, the actual organization of trade unions, or civil rights required a certain tandem connection between political violence and the ballot box, extra-constitutional protest movements and political parties. It takes confrontation outside the law to make the law itself. Few basic changes in the content and scope, logic and practices of liberty and equality occur peacefully, contained within the frameworks of institutional politics.[47]

Apter's defence, indeed restatement, of Jefferson's thesis is both eloquent and forceful. Apter is right, of course, that political violence has played a role in some of the most important reforms in American political history. (In a footnote he adds English Chartism as a further example of successful violence.) What is not certain is whether that role was always decisive, or was in fact *required* in each of the major reform movements he cites. Apter argues *post hoc* that it was easier to insist that violence was necessary for the success of the reform movements he cites than to test the counterfactual; after all, they all resulted in salutary changes. Moreover, he overlooks the fact that the American system was challenged in these matters when it was already mature enough to absorb the shocks of the violence involved. But what if the violence of, say, the civil rights struggle or the labour movement had spread beyond the ability of the civil rights and labour leaders and the government to contain it? And what if that violence, and the 'refreshing' violence of the other movements, had infected still others – always present – with urgent grievances and demands of their own, and thus gained further momentum to the point where a 'culture of violence' developed? Again, I pose the counterfactual to suggest the root danger of political violence in a democracy, that with respect to rebels and the perpetrators of political violence, it may not always be possible, as Jefferson put it, to 'set them right as to the facts, pardon and pacify them'. Political violence has gotten out of control before in democracies less durable and prosperous than America, and it may well happen again even in the United States.

Some summary comments and conclusions are now in order. First, I think it fair to say that with some reservations, noted above, and after a first look, the weight of evidence and scholarship appears to validate my three subhypotheses (or at least two of the three), and thereby the counterfactual hypothesis derived from Jefferson's statement.

My argument, then, restated in summary, is that even granting the possible positive effect of limited political violence in some democratic systems, democracies in general do not thrive on a diet of political violence, however heroic or well-intended. Political violence at democratic inception does not necessarily conduce to subsequent civil peace, nor is the democratic 'tree of liberty' necessarily 'refreshed' by periodic effusions of the blood of victims of political violence, be they 'tyrants' or 'patriots'. To the contrary: political violence does beget political violence, coups breed coups, and insurrections spawn further rebellions, all eventually to the point where a culture of political violence can come into being, and with it the very real possibility of democratic breakdown. Nor does all this recommend that those with grievances remain mute or refuse to exercise 'the public liberty' for fear of damaging it. Jefferson was right in arguing that to remain quiet could just as readily mean its 'death'. But grievances are articulated, and if the democracy is genuine and functioning then the institutions and/or mechanisms of peaceful resolution should preclude the necessity of violence. Successful, durable democratic systems can usually absorb the shocks of most, even nominally violent, challenges and can repair the damages those challenges inflict on them, make adjustments and reform, and all without falling apart in the process. Since democracies appear to thrive by trial and error, Karl Popper once suggested they were the most 'scientific' of all political systems. But there is a limit to that adaptability, arrived at sooner in new democracies than in the older ones, and the cumulative effects of political violence can overwhelm even the most resilient.

Let me also add here that a conclusion made earlier – that democratic systems whose transition to democracy was/is peaceful, or relatively peaceful, as through fair and open elections, fare marginally better (fewer subsequent violent challenges) than those born in violence – was not intended either as a judgement or to provide a hallmark of democratic legitimacy. Richard Sklar reminded us that resort to violence to achieve democratic transitions remains a matter of tactical/strategic choice for leaders of democratic oppositions, choices ranging from Ghandi's absolute prohibition of violence by his followers to Mandela's final, albeit reluctant, agreement to deadly, terrorist violence by the ANC when the earlier campaign of attacking economic targets had failed to move the ruling Nationalist regime.[48] How effective such choices turn out to be is a matter of dispute, since definitions of 'success' turn not only on the right choice of tactics/strategy, but on such things as timing, political will and the relative strength or weakness of opponents. In the cases of India and South Africa, the opposition 'won', in part but not necessarily entirely because it had chosen an effective strategy: while Ghandi's campaign of non-violent opposition certainly helped convince the British to free India, the transition was terribly scarred by the extraordinary violence of the Partition, itself also a consequence of the transition; and while the terrorism of the ANC may have helped persuade the Nationalists that that violence might portend even greater, more destructive disorder in

South Africa, the critical element in the transition was surely not ANC-inspired violence, but the collaboration between de Klerk and Mandela. Without the latter, as most South Africans of all races now concede, the system might very well have lapsed gradually into a bloody race war, without much hope of a democratic transition, much less a peaceful one. Nor is it at all clear – and it may be too early to judge – if the 16 democratic systems born of founding elections (all of them peaceful) which took place in Africa between 1989 and 1994 will remain democratic and peaceful.[49] Congo/Brazzaville, Niger, the Central African Republic, some half-dozen years after their respective democratic transitions, already appear to have succumbed to major violence, as did the Gambia, one of the continent's longest-lasting civilian regimes, in 1994. And at least one informed observer, Howard French, has some doubts about Mali's democratic future.[50] At all events, the point remains that while democratic systems born of a non-violent transition may experience fewer subsequent violent challenges, non-violent transitions to democracy are *by themselves* no guarantees of future civil peace.[51]

Now, when all is said and done, and in light of my argument, is there *any* violence in a democracy which *is* defensible? By addressing this question, I also want to clarify and expand on a suggestion made earlier about how political grievances are articulated. My argument, it must be re-emphasized, addressed political violence by citizens against a well-functioning democracy; a democracy become a tyranny is no longer a democracy, in which case (as Jefferson himself argued) resisting a government which indiscriminately violates its citizens' rights becomes a matter of legitimate self-defence. However, in genuine democracies, where the right to protest is guaranteed and redress possible through institutionalized channels, the distinction van den Haag makes between what he calls *persuasive* and *coercive* civil disobedience (see above) makes good sense. Persuasive civil disobedience, whether it takes the form of strikes, or mass protests, or demonstrations, or acts which get protesters arrested or worse, may sometimes disrupt or even appear to threaten the civil order, and thus verge on violence. If conducted without *premeditation*, persuasive civil disobedience seems both justifiable and defensible. Coercive civil disobedience, in which violence itself or the threat of violence is a deliberate *part of the strategy* of protest, and if adequate recourse to remedies or the means of finding remedies is available, seems to have little justification in a democracy. Nonetheless, political violence, premeditated or not, remains an unpredictable element even when introduced into campaigns of civil disobedience or other legitimate oppositional contexts.

This brings us, finally, to a word about the law of unintended consequences to which I alluded at the beginning of this article, and which could well be called Robert Burns' law, since his formulation, that 'The best laid schemes o' mice and men/ Gang aft agley' (*Man Was Made to Mourn*, 1786), is better known and more often quoted. In any case, it remains that political violence, however well intentioned, always has consequences. Among them is the danger that others will be inspired by it (and that precisely because it may have been well-intentioned), and thus may operate to defeat the very objectives it sought to achieve. The example of violence can be by itself enormously persuasive; it is hardly surprising that violent anti-democratic groups will take the name of an earlier 'martyred' rebel or of an 'heroic' earlier violent event (Black September). In the Mexican state of Chiapas, the violent challengers of the regime named themselves 'Zapatistas' in memory of Emiliano Zapata, hero of the Mexican revolution. The name is meant to be self-legitimizing, but it is invariably an empirical question whether such names help confer legitimacy on rebels, a fact that it rarely does so. That is also part of the inverse of Jefferson's proposition – political violence, like Shay's Rebellion, is not always 'honorably' conducted, nor can it always be contained or all of its consequences foreseen. The apt contemporary term for seen and unforeseen consequences is 'fallout', and it applies to the consequences of political violence. I suppose if all events of political violence were like Shay's Rebellion, and as 'honorably' conducted and handled thereafter, democracies would have little to fear from them. But that is emphatically not the case, and it would be in our best interest to remember the lesson.

ACKNOWLEDGEMENTS

I am grateful in particular to David Rapoport, Leonard Weinberg and Peter Merkl for their comments and useful suggestions, and in general for those generously offered by the other participants of the 'Conference on Violence and Democracy' held at the Stanford Alpine Chalet, Lake Tahoe, 12–14 Sept. 1997. My colleague Jack Knight also read a draft of this article, and I also acknowledge his insightful critique and helpful advice. Other personal contributions are acknowledged in the endnotes below.

NOTES

1. Julian P. Boyd (ed.), *The Papers of Thomas Jefferson* (Princeton, NJ: Princeton University Press, 1955) vol.12, pp.356–7.

2. Barère was a leading member of the Committee of Public Safety that ruled Revolutionary France during the period of the Jacobin dictatorship (1793–94). His harsh policies against those suspected of royalist tendencies made him one of the most feared revolutionaries. For details, see Leo Gershoy, *Bertrand Barère: A Reluctant Terrorist* (Princeton, NJ: Princeton University Press, 1962). David Rapoport (private communication, 5 Sept. 1997) adds that Barère 'was a major figure in the terror and that the terror aimed at purifying the community [by] making people fit for a republic'. See Michael Phillip Carter, 'The French Revolution: Jacobin Terror', in David C. Rapoport and Yonah Alexander (eds), *The Morality of Terrorism, Religious and Secular Justifications* (New York: Columbia University Press, 1989, 2nd ed.) pp.133–51. It should be added that Jefferson, for all his sympathy for the French Revolution, was nevertheless revulsed by the excesses of the Terror.

3. 'He [Jefferson] was not blind ... to the almost inevitable consequences of this great political movement. He predicted "that a lively resistance would be manifested by the tyrants and absolutists of the North; but definitely that man's condition throughout the civilized world would be considerably ameliorated by it."' Memoirs of Bertrand Barère (London: H. S. Nichols, 1896, transl. by De V. Payne-Payne) Vol. IV p.212. The above appears in Barère's biographical sketch of Jefferson, one of many of prominent political personalities of the day Barère described and discussed in his memoirs. See also William Howard Adams, *The Paris Years of Thomas Jefferson* (New Haven, CN: Yale University Press, 1997).

4. Daniel Shays and others led a rebellion of debt-stricken farmers in Western Massachusetts (1786–87, prior to that state's ratification of the Constitution) to protest excessive taxes, debt foreclosures and debtors' imprisonment by the Massachusetts government. In January 1987 Shays led a force of about 1,200 men in an attack on the federal arsenal at Springfield, which was quickly repulsed. After the rebellion had been put down by the state militia, Shays and a dozen others were tried and condemned to death. In 1788 he petitioned for a pardon, which was soon granted. In his old age, Shays was given a pension for his services during the Revolutionary War. For a full account of Shay's Rebellion, see G. R. Minot, *The History of the Insurrections in Massachusetts in 1787* (New York: De Capo Press, 1971).

5. For one, my departmental colleague Robert H. Salisbury. Dumas Malone, one of Jefferson's principal biographers, denies any suggestion that the phrase was hyperbole. While it '... has been tortured by later interpreters who have quoted it out of context, its essential truthfulness cannot be questioned by anyone familiar with course of human history': Dumas Malone, *Jefferson and his Time. Vol 3: Jefferson and the Ordeal of Liberty* (New York: Little Brown/Back Bay Books, 1962) p.49. So too Parrington, offering an expansive interpretation: 'An occasional revolution, he commented grimly apropos of the hue and cry over Shays's Rebellion, is salutary; if it does not come of itself it might well be brought about ... The longest delayed revolutions are the gravest': Vernon L. Parrington, *Main Currents in American Thought. Vol. I: The Colonial Period, 1620–1800* (New York: Harcourt Brace/Harvest Books, 1954) pp.357–8.

6. The first English translation of Fanon's book, by Constance Farrington, had it titled *The Damned* (Paris: Présence Africaine, 1963), given its original title, *Les damnés de la terre*. In the first part of the book ('Concerning Violence'), Fanon argues that violence not only unifies a colonized people, but 'At the level of individuals ... is a cleansing force' (ibid., p.73) necessary to purge the consequences of colonial tyranny's own violence.

7. Paul de Armond examines the ideological bases of the militant American right, including the militias and 'Patriots' in 'The Anti-democratic Movement – more than militias', *Public Goods Reports* (June, August 1995) at http://nwcitizen.com/

publicgood/reports/nullify.htm. For a recent appraisal of the militia movement, see Morris Dees, *Gathering Storm: America's Militia Threat* (New York: Harper-Collins, 1996).

8. Jefferson to William Stevens Smith, *loc. cit.*

9. Ibid. As a result of the Rebellion, the Massachusetts legislature passed laws easing the economic conditions of debtors, in effect in part remedying the grievances which led to the Rebellion in the first place.

10. I have been seeking the origins of the 'tree of liberty' metaphor, and thus far have only come up with its New England version, cited, for example, in an 1889 compendium of 'Fact, Fancy, and Fable':

In 1763 the 'Sons of Liberty' were organized under the 'Liberty Tree,' – a wide-spreading, beautiful elm, which stood in front of a grocery, near what is now the corner of Essex and Washington Streets, Boston, a tablet on the present building marking the spot: and here were exposed the effigies of those men who had opposed the odious Stamp Act. During the exciting period which followed, nearly all the great political meetings of the 'Sons of Liberty' called together by the hoisting of a flag on the staff extending through the branches of the tree, were held under its waving boughs and in the square about it. During the siege of Boston, about the last of August, 1775, this tree was cut down by a gang in the pay of the British soldiers and the Tories, after standing one hundred and nineteen years.

This compendium of trivia itself (Henry F. Redall, compiler, *Fact, Fancy, and Fable: A New Handbook for Ready Reference on Subjects Commonly Omitted from Cyclopaedias* ... (Chicago: A. C. McClurg & Co., 1889) pp.321–2) attributes one 'King' as the source of this description. Other encyclopaedic and historical sources confirm the factual outlines of this story, identify one Silas Downer as dedicating another Tree of Liberty in Rhode Island in 1766, and note that the most famous was one in New York. See also Thomas Paine's poem, *The Liberty Tree* (July 1977). Another suggestion in the literature is that the Tree of Liberty is a version of the Liberty Pole, which became part of the symbolism of the French Revolution, and the two are sometimes mentioned interchangeably, since both poles and trees were used for the same purpose in America. The French expression *arbre de liberté* (per Larousse) may in fact refer to the Liberty Pole rather than the tree itself; that may have been Barère's meaning as well. Roman tradition was that newly manumitted slaves celebrated their freedom by parading with a pole surmounted by a so-called 'Phyrgian' cap, which, as freemen, they were thereafter entitled to wear. The Phyrgian cap frequently appears in pictures of the French revolution. As for the redemptive, or cleansing, or purifying, or 'refreshing', power of blood, particularly sacrificial blood, Jewish and Christian tradition offer sufficient evidence (see, *inter alia*, Eph. 1:7), as does (James G.) Fraser's *Golden Bough* (New York: Macmillan, 1935, 3rd. ed.) esp. vol.1 p.85 *et seq*. Tertullian (Apologeticus 39), paraphrasing Saint Jerome, offers another use for the blood of martyrs, the generative: '*semen est sanguis christianorum*' (often rendered as 'the blood of the martyrs is the seed of the Church'). I should add that a similar, though much more expansive, generative metaphor is in Sura 96 of the Koran ('The Blood Clot', the first of the revelations to Muhammad): 'Recite: In the Name of thy Lord who created,/created Man of a blood-clot ...': A. J. Arberry, *The Koran Interpreted* (New York: Macmillan, 1955) p.344.

11. As does even Malone: see the quote in note 4.

12. Lynne B. Iglitzin, 'Violence and American Democracy', *Journal of Social Issues* 26/1 (1970) pp.184–5.

13. Ernest van de Haag, *Political Violence and Civil Disobedience* (New York: Harper and Row, 1971) p.20 (italics in original).

14. Ibid., p.29

15. Ibid., p.30.

16. In its simplest forms, it is 'What might have been', or 'had y happened instead of x, then ...' propositions in the natural and social sciences. A broad discussion is by David K. Luis, *Counterfactuals* (Cambridge, MA: Harvard University Press, 1973). For recent

explorations of counterfactual argument, see Philip E. Fetlock and Aaron Balkan (eds), *Counterfactual Thought Experiment in World Politics* (Princeton, NJ: Princeton University Press, 1996).

17. Menachem Begin, *The Revolt* (Los Angeles, CA: Nash Publishing, 1972) pp.xi–xiii. Meir Kahane, founder of the Jewish Defense League and proponent of anti-Arab violence, contributed a prefatory note to the book in which he praised Begin's generation which had 'watered the soil of their own land with blood' (ibid., p.iii).

18. Charles Foley (ed.), *The Memoirs of General Grivas* (New York: Frederick Praeger, 1964). The Spiridon quote is at p.18.

19. By 'violent challenges' I mean those activities which come to question the very legitimacy of the democratic system in which they occur. Here I would certainly include insurrections, secessionist rebellions, large-scale 'coercive' civil disobedience (see van den Haag, above), general strikes (with apologies to Georges Sorel), large-scale or pervasive oppositional terrorism, attempted coups, large-scale military mutinies and the like, plus civil violence which, for whatever reasons, grows to threaten the capacity of the state to deal with it.

20. The Survey has been published annually since the 1970s; our data are from the 1995–96 edition, on the Internet at http://www.freedomhouse.org/Political. The Survey's methodology section (at p.6 of printout) provides a functional definition of democracy, with which I concur: 'At a minimum, democracy is a political system in which the people choose their authoritative leaders freely from among competing groups and individuals who were not chosen by the government.' The same section also distinguishes democracy from freedom: 'Putting it broadly, freedom is the chance to act spontaneously in a variety of fields outside the control of government and other centers of potential domination.' Thus (suggests the Survey), a democracy can be free in form, but not in substance, or 'partly free', such as El Salvador and Guatemala, which replaced military governments but had not yet completed their transitions to liberal democracies.

21. Henry Bienen and Nicholas Van de Walle, 'Time and Power in Africa', *American Political Science Review* 83/1 (March 1989) pp.19–33. Their data spans the period from independence to October 1987. In spite of the wave of some eight 'national conferences', mainly in francophone Africa beginning in 1989, which upset several entrenched dictatorships, I suspect their conclusions generally still hold up. What reinforces their analysis is the fact that at least two dictators hung on to power after sponsoring 'national conferences' (Mobutu in Zaire and Eyadema in Togo), and two others (Matthew Kérekou in Bénin and Didier Ratsiraka in Madagascar) returned to power, albeit with refurbished democratic credentials, after democratic interludes.

22. Five central American republics – Costa Rica, El Salvador, Guatemala, Honduras, and Nicaragua – gained their formal independence with the dissolution of the Confederation of Central America in 1838. The Confederation itself, however, was created in 1824, three years after a revolt which ended Spanish rule in the five territories.

23. Adam Przeworski, Michael Alvarez, Jose Antonio Cheibub and Fernando Limongi, 'What Makes Democracies Endure?', *Journal of Democracy* 7/1 (1996) pp.39–55. Also relevant is 'Transitions to Democracy', in Adam Pzreworski, *Democracy and the Market* (New York: Cambridge University Press, 1991) ch.2 pp.51–99.

24. A view espoused, for example, in 'Coerciveness of Political Regimes and Political Violence', in James F. Kirkham *et al.*, *Assassination and Political Violence: A Staff Report to the National Commission on the Causes and Prevention of Violence* (New York: Bantam Books, 1970) pp. 182–6; and by Raymond Tanter, 'International War and Domestic Turmoil', and Ted Robert Gurr, 'A Comparative Study of Civil Strife', both in Hugh Davis Graham and Ted Robert Gurr, *The History of Violence in America: A Report to the National Commission on the Causes and Prevention of Violence ('Kerner Commission')* (New York: Bantam Books, 1969) pp.550–72 and 572–632, respectively. See also R. J. Rummel, 'Political Systems, Violence, and War', a paper presented in June 1988 at the US Institute of Peace Conference, Airlie House, Airlie, VA, on the Internet at http://shadeslanding.com/firearms/rummel.war.html.

25. Those first few years in a democratic transition are even more perilous than my analysis suggests. Edward D. Mansfield and Jack Snider argue ('Democratization and War', *Foreign Affairs* (May/June 1995) pp.79–97) that states undergoing democratization are at much greater risk of going to war with another state than those without regime change. The critical period for the democracies is during the first 10 years. Add that to the other factors of real and potential instability, including the violence of the transition itself, the dangers of disintegration faced by democracies with violent inceptions increases manyfold. I have not attempted to assess the effect of an early war as a possible stimulus to subsequent violent challenges; that must be left to individual case studies and later analyses.

26. Christopher J. Anderson, 'System Support in Old and New Democracies', (unpublished paper) presented at the American Political Science Association Annual Meeting, 28–31 August 1997, Washington, DC.

27. Dennis Austin, *Democracy and Violence in India and Sri Lanka* (New York: RIAA/Council on Foreign Relations Press, 1995) p.57.

28. Przeworski *et al.* (note 21); and Londregan and Poole (see note 27).

29. Przeworski *et al.* (note 21) pp.42–3.

30. John B. Londregan and Keith T. Poole, 'Poverty, the Coup Trap, and the Seizure of Executive Power', *World Politics* 42 (1990) pp.151–83.

31. Niger, which became independent in 1960, had civilian rule until 1974, when the regime of President Hamani Diori was overthrown by a junta led by Col. Segni Kountche. The military stayed in power for 17 years; in 1991 a national conference ushered in a democratic regime, but it was overthrown by another military coup in January 1996. Sierra Leone, independent in 1961, to date (July 1997) has six military regimes and three democratically elected governments. Congo/Brazzaville became independent in 1960, succumbed to four military coups and five military regimes; a national conference in 1991 ushered in democratic governance under Pascal Lissouba, challenged again (in mid-1997) by one of the former military presidents, Denis Sassou-Nguesso.

32. Some francophone Africans who remember the pre-1960 period have confided to me over the years that while independence ended French rule in Africa, they were never so 'free' as during the 1946–1960 period, when there were elections to local legislatures, to the French National Assembly, the Assemblies of the French Union and (later) the Community, and every francophone territory, fielded political parties and candidates by the dozen. That period is covered in Ruth Schachter Morgenthau's definitive *Political Parties in French West Africa* (New York: Oxford University Press, 1964).

33. See Pearl Robinson, 'The National Conference Phenomenon', *Society for the Comparative Study of Society and History* 36/3 (1994); *La Nation* (Benin, February 1992), special edition, 'Deux ans aprés ... Les dossiers de la Conférence'; Seydou Mamadou Diarrah Totoh, *Le Mouvement démocratique malien* (Bamako: no publisher given, 1996); Fabien Eboussi Boulanga, *Les conférences nationales en Afrique Noire* (Paris: Karthala, 1993).

34. For examples, see 'O Patriotic Hymns! You Enslave Us With Blood Lust and Self-Praise', *New York Times*, Sunday, 13 July 1997. The article cites passages from the national anthems of France, Vietnam, Mexico, Denmark, Belgium, China, Guatemala and Libya to make its point.

35. And, it should be added, it is not just violent victory that nations remember, but sometimes defeat: the national myth of Serbia is the Battle of Kosovo (at the so-called 'Field of the Blackbirds'), where, on 15 June 1389, an Ottoman army led by Sultan Murad I decisively defeated the Serbs under their Prince Lazar. During the civil war of the 1990s, many Serbs labelled their Bosnian Muslim enemies 'Turks', and fought to avenge Kosovo. (For a graphic account of this phenomenon, see John Kifner's article, 'Through the Serbians' Mind Eye', *New York Times*, 10 April 1994.)

36. My own choices among the lot are: Ted Robert Gurr's classic *Why Men Rebel* (Princeton, NJ: Princeton University Press, 1970), which remains a solid point of reference; Anatol Rapoport in his *The Origins of Violence: Approaches to the Study of*

Conflict (New York: Paragon House, 1989), who offers a synoptic view of the subject, as does Ekart Zimmerman, in his comprehensive review *Political Violence, Crises, & Revolution:Theories and Research* (Cambridge, MA: Schenkman, 1983). An older anthology still has much to recommend it: Ivo K. Feieraband, Rosalind L. Feierabend and Ted Robert Gurr (eds), *Anger, Violence, and Politics* (Engelwood Cliffs, NJ: Prentice Hall, 1973).

37. I have no wish to enter the lists of those arguing particular single, or multiple, causes of the fall of the Weimar Republic. While it is undoubtedly true that the Germans had little inkling what a National Socialist future would bring them, it remains that many, if not most, were attracted by the xenophobic, self-affirming message of the Nazis, and were apparently willing to tolerate the violence which they knew the Nazis would bring with them to power. As it tuned out, the Nazis did institutionalize a culture of violence amounting to an almost complete negation of the norms that governed Weimar in its best days. Hermann Rauschning, *Die Revolution der Nihilismus* [The Revolution of Nihilism] (Zurich: Europa Verlag, 1938) forcefully makes that argument.

38. Gurr (note 32); Mark N. Cooper, 'A re-interpretation of the causes of turmoil: the effects of culture and modernity', *Comparative Political Studies* 7/3 (Oct. 1973) pp.267–91; Douglas A. Hibbs, *Mass political violence: a cross-national analysis* (New York: Wiley, 1973); Hebron Elliot Adams, *The Origins of Insurgency*, PhD Dissertation, University of Lancaster, 1970; Raymond Duval and Mary Welfling, 'Social mobilization, political institutionalization in Black Africa, a simple dynamic model', *Journal of Conflict Resolution* 17/4 (Dec. 1973) pp.673–702.

39. Gurr (note 32) pp.160–83.

40. Surely the most comprehensive such study, in both categories is the 1969–70 *Kerner Commission Report*, including its staff studies and contract research. (For references, see note 22.)

41. Elizabeth Picard, 'The Lebanese Shi'a and Political Violence in Lebanon', in David E. Apter (ed.), *The Legitimization of Violence* (Washington Square, NY: New York University Press, 1997) pp.189–233, especially pp.208–15.

42. *Bey*: a Turkish survival, usually translated as 'lord', but also as 'chief/master'. *Zaim*: Lebanese-Arabic, usually translated as 'boss' or sometimes, 'godfather'. These leaders, often titular heads of important families, clans, militias and the like, run self-contained enclaves occasionally resembling mini-states, complete with their own militaries, welfare systems, taxation, banking and bureaucracies.

43. Ibid., p.209.

44. By its terms, *inter alia*, the President would always be a Maronite Christian, the Prime Minister a Sunni Muslim, the Speaker of the National Assembly a Shi'a Muslim, and the Cabinet divided in a ratio of 6:5, Christians to non-Christians. For details of the arrangement, see David and Audrey Smock, *The Politics of Pluralism: A Comparative Study of Lebanon and Ghana* (New York: Elsevier, 1975); Michael Hudson, *The Precarious Republic: Political Modernization in Lebanon* (New York: Random House, 1968); and Samir Khalaf, *Lebanon's Predicament* (New York: Columbia University Press, 1987).

45. I include myself among the optimists. I had visited Lebanon twice during the late 1960s and early 1970s, and thought I knew it well enough to share in the optimism expressed by many of my well-placed Lebanese friends. I was in good company: David and Audrey Smock, American social scientists who knew Lebanon much better than I did, even published a book comparing Ghana and Lebanon, in which Lebanon was extolled as a shining model of the possibilities of consociational democracy (*The Politics of Pluralism*). Unfortunately, the book was published in 1975, just as the Lebanese civil war was breaking out.

46. *Disobedience and Disorder* (New York: Vintage, 1968)

47. David E. Apter, 'Political Violence in Analytical Perspective', in David E. Apter (note 37) p.3.

48. Remarks to the panel on 'Democracy and Violence' at the International Political Science Association congress, Seoul, Korea, August 1997.

49. For details, see Michael Bratton and Nicolas van de Walle, *Democratic Experiments in Africa: Regime Transitions in Comparative Perspective* (New York: Cambridge University Press, 1997) pp.97–127 and 194–210.
50. Howard W. French, 'Mali's Slips Reflect Stumbling African Democracy', *New York Times*, 7 Sept. 1997.
51. Nor did I intend to suggest that the transition – that is, the succession – problem occurs only in democracies: it remains on one of the most vexing problems facing all political systems. (For useful comments on this problem, see Rapoport's article on elections and violence in this volume.) Democratic transitions, that is, both transitions to democracy and within democracies, however achieved, are of special interest at the end of the twentieth century for two reasons: first, because so many transitions to democracy occurred unannounced in Africa, Latin America and Europe during the 1990s; and secondly, because the institutionalized forms of leadership succession which democracies provide appear to offer, at least in part, one of most promising programmes for mitigating, even lessening, the seemingly endemic civil violence afflicting these countries during the past 50 years.

'FREE' DEMOCRACIES: CRISES OF LEGITIMACY AND VIOLENT CHALLENGES

Country: year statehood attained	Violent, non-violent dem. inception (a)	Democratic continuity: periods	FH 1995–96 ratings (b)	Legitimacy crises (CL) & violent challenges since democratic inception						
				Revolutions (c)	Civil Wars (d)	Rebellions (e)	Coups, attempted (f)	Coups, successful (f)	Terrorism, anti-government (g)	Violent civil unrest (h)
Andorra 1278	NV	1985–present	Free 1,1	0	0	0	0	0	0	0
Argentina 1816	RBL	1916–43 1983–present	Free 2,3	0	3–4	0	6	2	50+	50+
Australia 1900	NV	1900–present	Free 1,1	0	0	0	0	0	0	5
Austria 1918–38, 1955–	W	1918–38 1945–present	Free 1,1	0	1	0	1	0	5	3
Bahamas 1973	NV	1954–present	Free 1,2	0	0	0	0	0	0	2
Barbados 1966	NV	1951–present	Free 1,1	0	0	0	0	0	0	0
Belgium 1830	RBL	1830–1914 1918–1938 1945–present	Free 1,1	0	0	0	0	0	5	6
Belize 1981	NV	1964–present	Free 1,2	0	0	0	0	0	0	0
Benin 1960	NV(NC)	1960–	Free 2,2+	0	0	0	5	9	0	4
Botswana 1966	NV	1965–present	Free 2,2	0	0	0	0	0	0	0
Bulgaria 1908	VCR	1989–present	Free 2,2	0	0	0	0	0	0	0
Canada 1867	RBL, SVCR	1867–present	Free 1,1	0	0	0	0	0	5	3
Cape Verde 1975	RBL, VCR	1975–present	Free 1,2	0	0	0	0	0	0	0
Chile 1818	RBL	1989–1909 1932–1973 1989–present	Free 2,2	0	1	2	5	3	4	20+

ANNEX A (CONTINUED)
'FREE' DEMOCRACIES: CRISES OF LEGITIMACY AND VIOLENT CHALLENGES

Country: year statehood attained	Violent, non-violent dem. inception (a)	Democratic continuity: periods	FH 1995–96 ratings (b)	*Legitimacy crises (CL) & violent challenges since democratic inception*						
				Revolutions (c)	Civil Wars (d)	Rebellions (e)	Coups, attempted (f)	Coups, successful (f)	Terrorism, anti-government (g)	Violent civil unrest (h)
Costa Rica 1838	NV (RBL)	1899–present	Free 1,2	0	0	0	0	0	0	0
Cyprus (G) 1960	CW	1899–present	Free 1,1	0	1	0	1	0	15+	5
Czech Rep. 1918, 1945, 1989	W(2), RVL	1918–38 1989–present	Free 1,2	1 (NV)	0	0	0	1 (1945)	3 (1918–38)	3 (1918–38)
Denmark 14th C.	V/NV	1849–1940 1945–present	Free 1,1	0	0	0	0	0	0	0
Dominica 1978	NV	1978–present	Free 1,1	0	0	0	0	0	0	0
Ecuador 1822	RBL	9 short periods: 1822–1983 1984–present	Free 2,3	3+/–	1	6–7	(30+?)	60+	30+	50+
Estonia 1918, 1989	W, NV	1918–40 1989–present	Free 2+,2	0	0	0	0	0	0	0
Finland 1917	W	1918–present	Free 1,1	0	1	0	0	0	0	0
France 14th–15th C.	W, RVL	1792–1804 1848–1851 1870–1940 1946–present	Free 1,2	1	0	7	6	4	50+	50+
Germany 1871, 1949	W, RVL	1919–33 1949–present	Free 1,2	1	0	1	2	1	15	5 (1919–33)
Greece 1827	W/RBL	1974–present	Free 1,3	0	0	0	2	1	15	10+
Grenada 1974	NV	1974–79 1983–present	Free 1,2	0	0	1	0	1	2	2

Legitimacy crises (CL) & violent challenges since democratic inception

Country: year statehood attained	Violent, non-violent dem. inception (a)	Democratic continuity: periods	FH 1995–96 ratings (b)	Revolutions (c)	Civil Wars (d)	Rebellions (e)	Coups, attempted (f)	Coups, successful (f)	Terrorism, anti-government (g)	Violent civil unrest (h)
Guyana 1966	NV	1966–present	Free 2,2	0	0	0	0	0	0	1
Hungary 9th C.	W	1945–47 1989–present	Free 1,2	1	0	1	1	1	4	4
Iceland 930, 1874, 1918, 1944	W, NV	1944–present	Free 1,1	0	0	0	0	0	0	0
Ireland 1921	RBL	1921–present	Free 1,1	0	0	0	0	0	2	0
Israel 1948	W	1948–present	Free 1,3	0	0	1	0	0	50+	50+
Italy 1870	RVL	1870–1922 1946–present	Free 1,2	0	0	0	3(?)	0	50+	5
Jamaica 1962	NV	1962–presen	tFree 1,2	0	0	0	0	0	0	0
Japan 8th C.	W	1947–present	Free 1,2	0	0	0	0	0	6	2
Kiribati 1979	NV	1979–present	Free 1,1	0	0	0	0	0	0	0
South Korea 1948	W	1948–1961 1987–present	Free 2,2	0	0	0	1	0	4	1
Latvia 1919, 1990	W ,NV	1919–1939 1990–present	Free 2+,2	0	0	0	0	0	0	0
Liechtenstein 1918	NV	1921–present	Free 1,1	0	0	0	0	0	0	0
Luxembourg 1839	NV	1868–present	Free 1,1	0	0	0	0	0	0	0
Malawi 1964	NV	1992–present	Free 2,3	0	0	0	2	0	3	2
Mali 1960	NV	1991–present	Free 2,3+	0	0	1	2	3	0	4
Malta 1964	NV	1974–present	Free 1,1	0	0	0	0	0	0	0

'FREE' DEMOCRACIES: CRISES OF LEGITIMACY AND VIOLENT CHALLENGES

Country: year statehood attained	Violent, non-violent dem. inception (a)	Democratic continuity: periods	FH 1995–96 ratings (b)	Legitimacy crises (CL) & violent challenges since democratic inception						
				Revolutions (c)	Civil Wars (d)	Rebellions (e)	Coups, attempted (f)	Coups, successful (f)	Terrorism, anti-government (g)	Violent civil unrest (h)
Marshall Islands 1991	NV	1991–present	Free 1,1	0	0	0	0	0	0	0
Mauritius 1968	NV	1968–present	Free 1,2	0	0	0	0	0	0	0
Micronesia 1990	NV	1990–present	Free 1,1	0	0	0	0	0	0	0
Monaco 1861	NV	1945–present	Free 2,1	0	0	0	0	0	0	0
Mongolia 1946	W	1990–present	Free 2,3	0	0	0	0	0	0	0
Namibia 1990	RBL	1990–present	Free 2,3	0	0	0	0	0	0	0
Nauru 1968	NV	1968–present	Free 1,3	0	0	0	0	0	0	0
Netherlands 1814	W	1848–1940 1945–present	Free 1,1	0	0	0	0	0	0	0
New Zealand 1931	NV	1907–present	Free 1,1	0	0	0	0	0	0	0
Norway 1905	NV	1905–present	Free 1,1	0	0	0	0	0	0	0
Palau/Belau 1981	NV	1981–present	Free 1,2	0	0	0	0	0	0	2
Panama 1903	NV	1992–present	Free 2,3	0	0	0	0	0	0	0
Poland 1410 (?), 1919, 1945	W, RVL	1919–26 1989–present	Free 1+,2	0	0	0	0	0	0	0
Portugal 1140	W, RVL	1974–present	Free 1,1	0	0	0	0	0	0	1
St. Kitts–Nevis 1983	NV	1983–present	Free 1+,2	0	0	0	0	0	0	0
St Lucia 1979	NV	1979–present	Free 1,2	0	0	0	0	0	0	0
St Vincent & Grenadines 1979	NV	1979–present	Free 2,1	0	0	0	0	0	0	0

'FREE' DEMOCRACIES: CRISES OF LEGITIMACY AND VIOLENT CHALLENGES

Country: year statehood attained	Violent, non-violent dem. inception (a)	Democratic continuity: periods	FH 1995–96 ratings (b)	Legitimacy crises (CL) & violent challenges since democratic inception						
				Revolutions (c)	Civil Wars (d)	Rebellions (e)	Coups, attempted (f)	Coups, successful (f)	Terrorism, anti-government (g)	Violent civil unrest (h)
San Marino 1862	NV	1947–present	Free 1,1	0	0	0	0	0	0	0
Sao Tome & Principe 1975	NV	1991–present	Free 1,2	0	0	0	0	0	0	0
Slovakia 1993	NV	1993–present	Free 2,3	0	0	0	0	0	0	0
Slovenia 1991	VCR	1991–present	Free 1,2	0	0	0	0	0	0	2
Solomon Isl. 1978	NV	1978–present	Free 1,2	0	0	0	0	0	0	0
South Africa 1910	NV	1992–present	Free 1+,2+	0	0	0	0	0	0	5
Spain 1512 (?)	W	1975–present	Free 1,2	0	0	0	1	0	30+	3
Sweden 12th C., 1520, 1905	NV	1905–present	Free 1,1	0	0	0	0	0	2	0
Switzerland 1648	W	1874–present	Free 1,1	0	0	0	0	0	0	0
Trinidad & Tobago 1962	NV	1960–present	Free 1,2	0	0	0	1	0	0	0
Tuvalu 1978	NV	1978–present	Free 1,1	0	0	0	0	0	0	0
United Kingdom (excl. N. Ireland) 13th C.	W, RBL	1867–present	Free 1,2	0	0	0	0	0	20+	0
United States 1776	W, RBL	1787–present	Free 1,1	0	1	0	0	0	20+	10+
Uruguay 1828	W, RBL	1930–73	Free 2,2	0	1	2	5	2	5	3
Vanuatu 1980	RBL	1980–present	Free 1,3	0	0	(1)	(1)	0	0	2
Western Samoa 1962	NV	1962–present	Free 2,2	0	0	0	0	0	0	0

NOTES:

(1) 'Crises of legitimacy' are events which threaten the survival of regimes. 'Violent challenges', which are here reduced to two rubrics, anti–government terrorism and violent civil unrest, are events other than those under categories (a)–(f) which are of major importance, but do not threaten regime survival, or which have crossed the threshold to 'crises of legitimacy'.

(2) Columns:

(a) V = violent, NV = non–violent, RBL = rebellion, W = war, NC = national conference, VCR = violent civil unrest, SVCR = secessionist violent civil unrest, RVL = revolution.

(b) F–H 1995–96 ratings. Freedom House ratings system: averages of ratings on Freedom House's political rights and civil liberties category lists. 1–2.5 are considered 'free', 3–5.5 'partly free', 5–5.7 'not free'. The + sign is change upward (toward greater freedom).

(c) Revolution: complete change in the basic premises of a political system, as in a monarchy to a republic.

(d) Civil war: as distinguished from rebellion, a period of violence confronting two (or more) political factions fighting for control of the state, where the outcome is in doubt.

(e) Rebellion: armed insurrection.

(f) Attempted coups: failed attempts to change the government by force.

(f) Successful coups: attempts to change governments by force which succeed.

(g) Anti–government terrorism: major acts of terrorism, usually calling for major government response, including assassinations, bombings, massacres, etc. As for (h), these are estimates of events on a scale from 1 to 50; the + after an estimate means 'more than'.

(h) Violent civil unrest: large–scale riots, violent demonstrations, large–scale civil unrest.

Sources: Freedom House, *Table of Independent Countries, Comparative Measures of Freedom 1995–96*; misc. country studies and political histories.

13

The Italian Regions and the Prospects for Democracy

WILLIAM EUBANK and LEONARD WEINBERG

Using Putman's *Making Democracy Work* as the basis for our analysis, we investigate the performances of Italy's regional governments and conclude that successful democratic institutions depend upon the existence of a lively 'civic community' where citizens participate actively in public life in a variety of ways. 'Civic communities' do not appear overnight; they are the product of a long process of historical evolution. The implication of Making Democracy Work is that democracy is likely to fail in countries lacking such communities, where violence and authoritarian rule prevailed until recently. The findings reported in this article challenge this pessimistic view. They do so by calling attention to the fact that the areas of Italy with the most successful regional government and lively civic communities were also the areas where Fascism and Fascist violence were most prevalent in the years following World War I. In the Italian case at least, popular support for extreme anti-democratic forces and political violence did not pose an insuperable barrier to the formation of civic communities in later decades.

In a provocative article immediately preceding ours, Victor Le Vine raises important issues concerning the relationship(s) between political violence and democracy. For those hoping for the persistence of the new 'third wave' democracies that emerged over the last few decades, Le Vine's commentary goes to the heart of the matter. After investigating the arguments of Jefferson and others about the potentially beneficial effects of violence in promoting the formation of democracies and in stimulating progressive social change, Le Vine concludes: 'democracies in general do not thrive on a diet of political violence, however heroic or well-intended. Political violence at democratic inceptions does not necessarily conduce to subsequent civil peace, nor is the democratic "tree of liberty" necessarily "refreshed" by periodic effusions of the blood of victims of political violence, be they "tyrants" or "patriots." To the contrary …' Repeated expressions of political violence, Le Vine goes on, may lead to the appearance of a culture of political violence and eventually the breakdown of democratic rule itself.

This conclusion now seems virtually self-evident. But, to quote not Jefferson but Ira Gershwin, 'it ain't necessarily so'. Our analysis, which takes the form of a critique of an exceptionally important case study, seeks to measure the long-term consequences of Fascist violence in one country, and comes to conclusions rather different from Le Vine's.

Few recent books in political science have received as much critical attention or won as much praise as Robert Putnam's *Making Democracy Work*.[1] Like the book itself, the reasons for both the attention and the praise reach beyond the book's ostensible subject, the institutional performances of Italian regional governments over the last few decades.[2] Further, the author's most specific finding, that regions in the Italian South, the *Mezzogiorno*, have done poorly when compared to their counterparts in the far more prosperous central and northern sections of the country, will not seem particularly surprising or unexpected to many Italians or to foreign observers. Writers have been emphasizing the profound differences between North and South since the achievement of Italian unification in 1860. By now the literature on the subject in Italian is virtually oceanic in volume. However, it is not the particular, the idiographic, but the general aspects of *Making Democracy Work* that has excited the interest. We believe the principal reason the book has engendered such excitement has to do with the conclusions it reaches concerning what it takes to make democracy work, and not merely in Italy but, by inference, on a global basis. Let us put the case as succinctly as possible.

Although all 20 Italian regional governments from Lombardy in the north to Calabria in the south are nominally democratic in character (e.g. their leaders are selected at regular intervals on the basis of open competitive elections), they vary substantially in what Putnam and his associates refer to as 'institutional performance'. The latter is a factor on which 12 variables show significant loadings.[3] The factor, and the variables from which it is composed, reflect two considerations: responsiveness and effectiveness. By the former Putnam and his collaborators mean the willingness on the part of regional bureaucracies to respond to citizens' inquiries both written and in person. They identify effectiveness with 11 other measures including such variables as cabinet stability, budgetary promptness and legislative innovation. Putnam and his collaborators rank the regions based upon their level of institutional performance, the extent to which they are both responsive and effective, and conclude that, by and large, regional governments located north of Rome perform far better than those in the south (including the islands of Sicily and Sardinia). Why should this be true? Or, in other words, what makes democracy work better in some places than in others?

One frequently cited answer is wealth, or the level of economic development. Over the years various analysts have reported the existence of strong positive relationships between GNP, level of economic development and democratic success. In fact, Putnam and his collaborators do consider the possibility that the differences in institutional performance among the Italian regions are explicable in terms of these economic considerations.[4] What they find, however, is that while the latter do have an impact, and explain some of the variance, they do not tell the whole story. Illustratively, Campania, the region in which Naples is located, is substantially more advanced economically than Molise and Basilcata, but the government of the former is significantly less effective than that of the latter.

Rather than economic success, the most powerful explanation for the regional differences in effectiveness, Putnam reports, is the prevalence of a 'civic community'. Writing in theoretical terms (ones strongly influenced by de Tocqueville), the author stresses a number of values that promote such a community. These include 'civic engagement', where citizens active in public affairs display a public-spiritedness; and 'political equality', when in political dealings or personal interactions in general, horizontal relationships dominate over vertical or patron-client based ones. The 'civic community' is also one in which the values of solidarity, trust and tolerance are widely shared. All of these values are promoted and, reciprocally, they promote an extensive network of civil associations. These voluntary organizations have both internal and external benefits. They encourage habits of cooperation, solidarity and public-spiritedness among their members, while simultaneously achieving a variety of important social and political tasks (e.g. interest articulation, interest aggregation, economic advancement) for the community at large.

Putnam and his associates then test the theory. To do this, they operationalize the presence of 'civic community' in Italy's regions by employing four variables: membership in local associations (sports clubs in particular), newspaper readership, voter turnout at national referenda, and the frequency of individual preference voting at parliamentary elections. This variable, until recently a device used for the maintenance of patron-client networks in the *Mezzogiorno*, loads negatively on the 'civic community' factor. The 'Civic Community', Putnam and his associates report, provides the most powerful explanation for differences in the effectiveness of Italy's 20 regional governments. More than anything else it is the strength of this factor that explains what makes democracy work.

But how is a civic community formed? Where does it come from? If a civic community is indispensable in making democracy work then the answers to these questions become exceedingly important not merely in the Italian case, but in assessing the democratic prospect for all those countries that have only recently undergone transitions to democratic rule.

The answer Putnam and his collaborators furnish is not one that makes for great optimism concerning the likelihood of democratic survival in much of the world. This is the case because they see the contemporary manifestations of civic community in central and northern Italy as the outgrowth of a long-term historical process, one that originated in the 1300s or earlier and proceeds to the present time. Specifically, *Making Democracy Work* reports two discoveries. First, areas of Italy that developed traditions of local self-government and republican rule at the end of the Middle Ages tended to be the same places where a pattern of 'civic involvement' appeared in the decades between Italian unification in 1860 and 1920, the immediate aftermath of World War I. (The concept of 'civic involvement', 1860–1920, becomes a factor composed of five variables: strength of mass political parties, 1919–21; incidence of cooperatives, 1889–1915; membership in mutual aid societies, 1873–1904; electoral turnout, 1919–21; and local voluntary associations before 1860.) Secondly, regions with strong traditions of civil involvement are almost always the same as those ranking high on the contemporary measure of civil community.[5] In other words, the die was cast long before regional governments were established in 1970. The appearance of civic community, and hence the success or failure of democratic institutions, is the result of a long chain of historical practices, each one influencing the other, largely determining the contemporary outcome. If this is true, then it is difficult to hold out much hope for making democracy work in parts of the world lacking the apparatus of civic community. But is it true?

A review of the same historical record examined in *Making Democracy Work* suggests that it is not true. Contemporary differences in the democratic effectiveness of Italy's 20 regional governments may very well be explained by the presence of civic community as Putnam and his associates report. But the effort to explain the appearance of civic community as the outcome of a long and virtually unbroken chain of historical occurrences seems to be seriously flawed. We will devote the balance of this article to explaining why this is the case, and why the historical record is far more contingent than suggested in *Making Democracy Work*.

First, it is worth calling the reader's attention to the fact there was nothing inevitable about the creation of the Italian regional governments themselves. Whatever may be said about what makes them work or not work, their formation was far from historically inevitable. In the aftermath of World War II, pressures growing out of separatist sentiment in Sicily and Sardinia and the demands expressed at both domestic and international levels, of ethnic minorities in the Aosta Valley (French) and Trentino-Alto Adige (Austrian), caused the Italian government to assign these areas grants of special regional autonomy.[6] For similar reasons, but more than a decade later and after an exceptionally acrimonious parliamentary debate, the government did the same with respect to the region of Friuli-Venezia Giulia. Because of a dispute with Yugoslavia over the status of Trieste and its surroundings (which contain a minority Slovenian population), the area's internationally recognized border was settled only in 1954. And it was only in 1962 that an internally divided Christian Democratic government in Rome was able to pass the required enabling legislation to establish the regional governments.[7]

The formation of the remaining 15 regions followed a far more Byzantine path. When the Italian constitution was drafted in 1947, its framers reacted against the country's Fascist experience of highly centralized rule from Rome. At the Constituent Assembly, and for reasons reflecting their parties' historical and philosophical commitments, Christian Democratic (DC) and Republican (PRI) deputies led a successful effort to include provisions on regional decentralization in the new constitution.[8] Over the often vigorous objections of Communist (PCI) and Socialist (PSI) parties (their deputies said they feared the regions would become outposts of conservatism and reaction) Title V (Articles 114–132) called for the division of Italy into regions along with provinces and *communi* (municipalities) over which the former would play a supervisory role. Although the constitutional provision identified the regions (both those to be granted special autonomy and those with 'normal' grants of policy-making ability) and described how they were to be established, how their own basic statutes (*statuti*) would be drafted and approved, how they would be structured and what they would or could do etc., Title V was not self-enforcing: there was a need for enabling legislation. In fact, the new Constitution's 'Final and Transitional Dispositions' contained a timetable of from one to five years for the passage of this legislation and the creation of the regions.

The years went by, but what were to have been the 15 new 'normal statute' regions were not brought into being. With one exception (the Law of 10 February 1953, n. 62, which in fact weakened the regions' now hypothetical powers), none of the requisite enabling laws were enacted by the Italian Parliament.[9] What went wrong?

The answer is that the major party political contestants had changed their minds. Specifically, after the Christian Democrats became the country's ruling party, its leaders, rhetorical flourishes notwithstanding, lost interest in the regional project. The kind of decentralization involved in the formation of the new regional governments would likely have meant a certain amount of power-sharing and the potential loss of some patronage opportunities. Worse yet, the likely beneficiaries of the reform would have been the Communists and the Socialists. Given the distribution of electoral support in the country during the 1950s and early 1960s, these leftist parties (running in alliance with one another at the local level) would have dominated regional governments in the centre, or 'red belt', of Italy (Emilia-Romagna, Tuscany, Umbria, the Marches). In other words, the unintended consequence of regional decentralization would have been more power for the Communists, not exactly an item high on the Christian Democrats' agenda.[10]

For their part, the Communist and Socialist party leaders did an about-face and began to express strong commitments to the cause of regionalism. Their justification was couched in terms of support for democratic economic planning and popular participation at the grass-roots level. In other words, rather than acting as backward-looking outposts of reaction, the Left redefined the regions as likely instruments of economic progress and social justice. However, with the Christian Democrats ruling the country from Rome in coalition with strongly anti-regional rightist parties, the Liberals, Monarchists and, *sotto voce*, the neo-fascist Italian Social Movement, the likelihood that Title V would be implemented appeared bleak. It would take a major change in the composition of Italy's governing coalition before this objective could be reached.

Such a transformation occurred in the 1962–63 period when the *apertura a sinistra* (opening to the left) was achieved, and the Socialists joined the government. The Socialists insisted that the implementation of Title V be made a part of the programme of reform and renewal on the basis of which they agreed to participate in a centre-left coalition with the Christian Democrats. The latter agreed to the proposal, but insisted that the Socialists sever their local ties to the Communists (with whom they had continued to form majority coalitions to run various provinces and municipalities). The Socialists agreed and the deal was struck.[11] The regions, however, were not forthcoming. The opposition of right-wing factions within the Christian Democratic party prevented passage of the necessary legislation.

Title V was only transformed into reality in the late 1960s, a consequence of a particular political climate. Parliamentary elections were scheduled for 1968. Christian Democratic and Socialist leaders were fearful that they would be vulnerable to Communist complaints that the centre-left coalition had achieved very little, and that few, if any, of its reformist goals had been reached. To reduce their vulnerability to this charge, the Christian Democrats and Socialists overcame the longest filibuster in the history of republican Italy (one conducted by right-wing deputies) to pass a regional framework law in 1967. 'As a reform, regionalism demonstrated the will to constructive action. As decentralization, it had a democratic participatory ring. Finally, since it was limited, somewhat technical, and easily rendered vague, it was less controversial than many other issues.'[12]

Final measures concerning how the regions were to be financed and conduct their elections were enacted in 1970. The immediate impetus for action on this occasion was apparently the 'hot autumn' of 1969. Italy had been thrown into turmoil as the result of massive student and worker protests in the major cities of the north. Neo-Fascist bands launched a terrorist campaign in order to destabilize the government and jeopardize the country's democratic institutions. In this atmosphere, the ruling centre-left coalition succeeded in passing the additional regional laws as a means of avoiding the widespread and growing impression of impotence and irrelevance.[13]

It is clear, then, that the formation of Italy's 15 'normal' regions was to a significant extent the consequence of a series of *ad hoc* bargains and deals, with the key parties involved shifting their views to suit the political exigencies of the moment. With this understanding in mind let us take up the question of how the regions' subsequent performances should be understood.

In *Making Democracy Work* the chain of historical causation runs from the Middle Ages to the 1980s. To recapitulate a bit, those sections of Italy where republican communal governments had developed by circa 1300 and where civic involvement had taken hold from 1860 to 1920 are almost precisely the same locales where the virtues of civic community are most prevalent today. And it is civic community more than anything else that makes democracy work.

What happens, though, when this historical chain is examined more closely? What happens if, for example, history is stopped closer in time to the appearance of republican self-government and, per force, the development of civic traditions? Here we have in mind the years following World War I, the *dopoguerra*, and the advent of Fascist dictatorship in 1922. More specifically, what is the relationship between Fascism and the two historical predictors of contemporary civic community identified in *Making Democracy Work*?

To answer this question we assembled data which we then aggregated by region on membership in the Fascist movement (*fasci di combattimento*) between March 1921 and May 1922. We repeated this procedure for reported incidents of political violence. In this case we recorded event data on the incidence of Fascist attacks on Socialist targets over the first six months of 1921, a period of frequent Fascist assaults on various targets associated with the Socialist movement. In both cases, the data were compiled originally by the Italian interior ministry and reported in Renzo De Felice's *Mussolini il fascista: La conquista del potere, 1921–1925*.[14] To conform to the procedure used in *Making Democracy Work*, we ranked the 20 regions based upon the relative strength of the Fascist movement and the level of political violence.[15] We then compared these rankings with those based upon the republican and civic tradition displayed in the Putnam volume.[16]

The results of our analysis are quite compelling. We discover strongly positive and statistically significant relationships between both

TABLE 1
FASCIST ACTIVITIES AND TRADITIONAL COMMUNITY

	4th Century Republicanism (Fig. 5.1)	Civic Traditionalism 1860–1920 (Fig. 5.2)
Socialist Fascist Violence	.57***	.54**
Fascist Sezioni (March 1921)	.69***	.65***
Fascist Members (March 1921)	.47*	.47**
Fascist Sezioni (May 1922)	.72***	.67***
Fascist Members (May 1922)	.62***	.63***

Spearman rho: *** $p < .001$; ** $p < .01$; * $p < .05$.

the existence of republican communal governments during the Middle Ages and the civic traditions of the nineteenth and early twentieth centuries with the strength of the Fascist movement in 1921. In other words, Fascism caught hold most in those regions of North and Central Italy where republican self-government and the civic tradition had become most prevalent earlier. The same observation occurs with respect to the incidence of Fascist violence. The most violent regions are almost precisely the ones where the suspected seeds of civic virtue had already been planted.

Thus, if we were willing to draw our history to a close on, say, 29 October 1922, the date of Mussolini's March on Rome, we would be forced to conclude that republicanism and the civic tradition do not predict the virtues of civic community and hence promote democracy. These independent variables forecast the growth of the highly anti-democratic Fascist movement, a movement whose leaders held the values of parliamentary democracy in the utmost contempt, and the kind of violence that contributed so mightily to the breakdown of Italy's fragile democracy in the post-World War I era.

What happens now if we start or restart the historical record in 1920 and investigate the relationship between the Fascist movement's strength and the incidence of Fascist-Socialist violence, and the contemporary indicators of civic community and institutional performance found in *Making Democracy Work*? The results of our calculations this time are even more startling than the earlier ones (see Table 2).

They disclose the existence of strong and positive relationships between our two measures of Fascist vitality in the early 1920s – membership size and level of violence – and the strength of civic

TABLE 2
FASCIST ACTIVITIES AND CONTEMPORARY COMMUNITY

	Institutional Performance (Fig. 4.1)	Civic Commitment (Fig. 4.4)
Socialist Fascist Violence	.46**	.38*
Fascist Sezioni (March 1921)	.49**	.51**
Fascist Members (March 1921)	.24	.26
Fascist Sezioni (May 1922)	.52**	.49**
Fascist Members (May 1922)	.43*	.40*

Spearman rho: *** $p < .001$; ** $p < .01$; * $p < .05$.

community during the 1970s and 1980s. Regions where Fascism seemed to take root, Emilia-Romagna, Tuscany etc., tended to be the same ones where the virtue of 'civic community' was most prevalent in recent years. In fact, the magnitudes of these associations are actually higher than those reported in the Putnam volume between republican rule, the civic tradition and contemporary civic community! Perhaps most astonishing of all, our two indicators of Fascist vitality are also linked to Putnam and his collaborators' measure of institutional performance. In other words, the better governed the region in the 1970s and 1980s, the more likely it is that Fascists and Fascist-related violence was most common and widespread immediately before Mussolini came to power.

It seems clear by now that an effort to apply the ideas of de Tocqueville from *Democracy in America* concerning the merits of voluntary association to the Italian experience is a seriously flawed undertaking. Our findings suggest that at the regional level, a Fascist past provides a healthy soil from which both civic community and effective democratic government has grown. Why do we reach such a seemingly and monumentally paradoxical judgement? A further review of the historical record provides a plausible answer.

First, the record suggests that there is nothing incompatible between outbreaks of collective violence and the civic tradition. Certainly, the city-states that evolved in northern and central Italy during the Middle Ages were anything but tranquil communities. When not engaged in warfare with one another (Florence and Sienna for example) they were highly susceptible to intra-communal fighting. The latter usually involved disputes or vendettas among the leading families.[17] Economic differences and religious concerns, the Guelfs and the Ghibellines, were obviously major factors as well.

This linkage between the civic tradition and collective violence also applies to the era between Italian unification in 1860 and the immediate aftermath of World War I. During this period central and northern Italy abounded with manifestations of industrial worker, share-cropper and farm labourer protest. Government repression often led to violent responses on the part of those seeking to improve their social and economic circumstances.[18] Charles Tilly reports that industrial and farm worker strikes were most common in those regions Putnam and his associates identify with the growth of the civic tradition.[19] In fact we find a strong, positive association between the two variables.

Secondly, in seeking to understand the relationship between support for Fascism, Fascist violence in the early 1920s and the contemporary attributes of civic community in the successful regions, we need to pay closer attention to the conditions that prevailed in central and northern Italy in the decades following national unification. In this case, *Making Democracy Work* is certainly right in pointing out to the reader the proliferation of voluntary associations and cooperative organizations of various kinds. The problem arises, we believe, in the conclusion to be derived from these developments.

In the period after 1860, particularly after 1880, northern and central Italy began to undergo the process of industrial development. Illustratively, steel manufacturing plants were established in growing cities located in the regions of Liguria, Piedmont, Lombardy and Tuscany. Somewhat earlier agricultural cultivation, especially in the Po Valley, also experienced significant structural change associated with the growth of capitalism.[20] Among other things, as land ownership became more concentrated the number of landless labourers, *braccianti*, increased. The effect of these trends was the initiation of a process Charles Tilly, Sidney Tarrow and others identify as 'social mobilization'.[21]

To some extent building on previously existing 'friendly societies' or mutual aid organizations, new trade unions, labour exchanges and industrial and farm worker cooperatives were formed to defend the social concerns and advance the economic interests of those whose lives were being transformed by the economic changes at work in Italy. Concomitantly, with the formation and growth of these groups, new political forces were organized. Occurring overwhelmingly in the north, anarchist, syndicalist and socialist groups were created to take up the cause. Illustratively, the first congress of the anarchist Italian Federation of the International Working Men's Association was held at Rimini in 1872. A Worker's Party was established in Milan in 1882 and the Socialist Party held its first congress in Genoa in 1892.[22]

There were exceptions, to be sure (e.g. Turati's followers), but these new organizations were not supportive of parliamentary democracy at least as then constituted. Capitalist enterprise was not widely admired and the Italian state, not without cause, was identified with the interests of the former. Episodes of 'collective action', 'Red Week' 1914 for instance, were relatively common, as were the violent police and military responses undertaken by various governments to repress them.

In sum, the explicit purpose of many economic and political associations formed in central and northern Italy in the 1860–1920 period was the elimination or radical modification of the country's economic and social order and the displacement of Italy's highly flawed and only partially democratic state. The state's frequently violent and repressive reaction to the challenge posed by the numerous strikes, mass protests and other forms of collective action promoted widespread feelings of mistrust and suspicion of the poor and weak for the rich and strong and vice versa.

Enter the Fascist movement. This is not the appropriate place to enter the now extended debate over the nature of Italian Fascism (much less fascism as a generic term). For our purposes, it should suffice to say that within an astonishingly short period of time a movement fostered by Mussolini in the northern city of Milan (the formative congress was held in June 1919) was able to win hundreds of thousands of adherents, principally in the northern and central parts of the country, and bully its way into power by the end of October 1922.[23] Productionist and ardently nationalist in outlook, violent and authoritarian in temperament, Fascism promoted the mobilization of other social strata. By waging a campaign of violence against putatively revolutionary Socialist organizations in the cities and countryside of northern and central Italy, the Fascist movement managed to attract the support of many lower middle- and middle-class Italians tired of the economic and social chaos around them and fearful of the possibility of Red revolution. We could do worse than to quote Juan Linz: 'we could define fascism as a party of revolutionaries linked with the middle classes of city and/or countryside.'[24] In effect, the Fascist movement's role in this post-World War I era was to promote the mobilization of these segments of Italian society for the purpose of establishing a modern dictatorship.

How do we move from the situation that existed in central and northern Italy at the advent of Fascism to the contemporary conditions depicted in *Making Democracy Work*? Further, what lessons may students of constitutional democracy learn from the Italian experience?

So far as the answer to the first question is concerned, we should recall that the relationship between the presence of Fascist militants, Fascist violence and the contemporary 'civic community' was strong and positive. If there had been no linkage between developments in the early 1920s and current conditions, we could have concluded that the earlier occurrences had not posed an insuperable barrier to the growth of civic community. But this was not the case.

The 'civic tradition' (1860–1920), meaning to a large extent the growth of labour and farm labour organizations and left-wing political parties, was associated with support for Fascism and manifestations of Fascist violence. (And these variables, in turn, were both related to the presence of civic community in the current era.) These findings suggest, at least in the Italian case, that a high level of political mobilization and organizational activity was a precondition for the appearance of 'civic community'. Political engagement in and of itself, even on behalf of causes committed to authoritarian solutions, seems to have been the necessary condition. The sufficient condition was likely the calamitous performance of the Fascist regime along with the defeat and humiliation it brought to the Italians during World War II.

Our observations make it possible to generalize from the Italian experience about the democratic prospect in other parts of the world. The lesson we learn though is very different than the one to emerge from *Making Democracy Work*.

Instead of the appearance of 'civic community' or civil society depending on a long, unbroken chain of historical causation, we discover that support for authoritarian movements, Marxist or fascist, as well as serious episodes of political violence do not prevent the emergence of this evident prerequisite for effective and responsive government.

Further, the fact the establishment of the regions themselves was not historically inevitable, but rather was the result of short-term, self-interested calculations of powerful political parties, is also suggestive. If in the late 1960s the Christian Democrats and Socialists had not perceived the passage of the enabling legislation to be to their immediate electoral advantage there would have been no 'ordinary' regions for Putnam and his associates to study.

What these results really indicate is that the democratic prospect may be far brighter than suggested in *Making Democracy Work*. Countries in the Third World or formerly part of the Soviet Empire in Eastern Europe and Central Asia, places where domestic political life was long dominated by now discredited 'mass mobilizing' dictatorships, may still develop civic communities and effective democratic governments. If we use the Italian case as a guide, a history of serious civil strife and dictatorial rule does not pose an insuperable barrier to the emergence of both.

Making Democracy Work supports this pessimistic judgement. It does so by suggesting that successful democratic performance in Italy and elsewhere is dependent on a long uninterrupted chain of political development leading to the formation of a civic community. Our findings point in virtually the opposite direction. They suggest that serious episodes of violence between competing political movements and widespread support for anti-democratic forces do not constitute a Mark of Cain. The values of civic community may be achieved and, therefore, the supports for effective democratic government put in place, without such a long-term pattern of progressively narrower historical constraints. Further, serious episodes of political violence (e.g. the US in the 1860s, 1880s and 1960s), in and of themselves, do not appear to prevent the emergence of civic communities in Italy and, by inference, in the new democracies as well.

NOTES

1. Robert Putnam with Robert Leonardi and Raffaella Nanetti, *Making Democracy Work: Civic Traditions in Modern Italy* (Princeton, NJ: Princeton University Press, 1993).
2. The book has stimulated a fair amount of thoughtful criticism: see Filippo Sabetti, 'Path Dependency and Civic Culture: Some Lessons from Italy about Interpreting Social Experiments'; Ellis Goldberg, 'Thinking About How Democracy Works' and Margaret Levi, 'Social and Unsocial Capital: A Review Essay of Robert Putnam's *Making Democracy Work*', all in *Politics and Society* 24/1 (1996) pp.8–44; and Sidney Tarrow,'*Making Democracy Work* Across Space and Time: A Critical Reflection on Robert Putnam's *Making Democracy Work*' *American Political Science Review* 90:2 (1996) pp.389-397.
3. Putnam (note 1) pp.63–82.
4. Ibid., pp.83–6 and 121–62
5. On the formation of these 'special statute' regions see Enrico La Loggia, *Autonomia e rinascita della Sicilia* (Palermo: IRES, 1953) pp.55–7; Claude Palazzoli, *Les Regions Italiennes* (Paris: Libraire Générale de Droit et de Jurisprudence, 1966) pp.257–358; Brian Chapman, *The Problem of Regionalism in Italy* (unpublished Doctoral Thesis,

Magdalen College, Oxford, 1951); For the regional statutes themselves see Ministero Dell'Interno, *Ordinamento delle Regioni* (Rome: Istituto Poligrafico dello Stato, 1961).

6. See e.g. Vladimiro Lisiani, *Good-bye Trieste* (Milan: Mursia & Co., 1966); Norman Kogan, *Italy and the Allies* (Cambridge: Harvard University Press, 1956) pp.133–40.

7. For a discussion see Vittorio Falzone, Filippo Palermo and Francesco Cosentino, *La costituzione della repubblica italiana con i lavori preparatori* (Rome: Editore Carlo Colombo, 1954).

8. Ministero Dell'Interno (note 5) pp.75–100.

9. See e.g. Endo Santarelli, *L'ente regione* (Rome: Riuniti, 1960) pp.112–27.

10. Umberto Segre, 'La tensione ideologica del centro sinistra,' *Comunita'* (March–April, 1963) pp.3–5; and Luigi Granelli, 'L'azione delle DC per la riforma autonomista dello stato democratico', in *L'impegno della democrazia cristiana per le regioni* (Rome: Edizioni Cinque Lune, 1964) pp.66–7.

11. Peter Gourevitch, 'Reforming the Napoleonic State: The Creation of Regional Governments in France and Italy', in Sidney Tarrow, Peter Katzenstein and Luigi Graziano (eds), *Territorial Politics in Industrial Nations* (New York: Praeger Publishers, 1978) p.47.

12. Norman Kogan, *A Political History of Italy: The Postwar Years* (New York: Praeger, 1983) pp.255–6.

13. Renzo De Felice, *Mussolini il fascista: La conquista del potere, 1921–1925* (Turin: Einaudi,1966) pp.8–11, 36–9.

14. Ibid., pp.134 and 150.

15. When these data were originally constructed, the 14 regions were ranked from the most (1) to the least (15) on each of Putnam's four measures. The measures of Fascist activity were coded by their raw numerical count. Because the regions with the highest number of attacks are those with the lowest numerical indicator of rank, 1, correlating these ranked measures will produce a negative result. This can result in unnecessary confusion for the reader. Converting the raw numerical counts of Fascist or Marxist activity to ranks resolves this potential confusion. The region with the most acts of violence would be ranked first and so forth through the 14 regions. Correlating these ranked measures with Putnam's, using rho, will produce results numerically identical to the previous approach but positive in sign. We report the results based on the correlation of ranks in Tables 1 and 2. A positive correlation does not support Putnam's position; a negative correlation does. See Siegel and Sidney, *Nonparametric Statistics for the Behavioral Sciences* (New York: McGraw Hill, 1956) pp.202–13.

16. See e.g. Daniel Waley, *The Italian City-Republics* (New York and London: Longman, 1988) pp.88–156; and John Larner, *Italy in the Age of Dante and Petrarch 1216–1380* (New York and London: Longman, 1980) pp.106–27.

17. See e.g. Giampiero Carocci, *Storia D'Italia Dall'Unita Ad Oggi* (Milan: Feltrinelli, 1982) pp.65–181; Denis Mack Smith, *Italy* (Ann Arbor, MI: University of Michigan Press, 1959) pp.157–217.

18. Charles Tilly, *The Rebellious Century* (Cambridge, MA: Harvard University Press, 1975) pp.159–60.

19. See e.g. Giorgio Candelero, *Storia Dell'Italia Moderna: Lo sviluppo del capitalismo e del movimento operaio,1871–1896* (Milan: Feltrinelli, 1978) Vol. 6, pp.166–275.

20. For theoretical statements see Charles Tilly, *From Mobilization to Revolution* (Reading, MA: Addison-Wesley,1978) pp.69–97; and Sidney Tarrow, *Power in Movement* (New York: Cambridge University Press, 1994) pp.31–150.

21. See e.g. Daniel Horowitz, *The Italian Labor Movement* (Cambridge, MA: Harvard University Press, 1963) pp.17–47.

22. For a brief summary see Stanley Payne, *A History of Fascism* (Madison: University of Wisconsin Press, 1995) pp.87–106.

23. Juan Linz, 'Some Notes Toward a Comparative Study of Fascism in Sociological Historical Perspective', in Walter Laqueur (ed.), *Fascism: A Reader's Guide* (Berkeley and Los Angeles, CA: University of California Press, 1976) p.7.

14

Originary Democracy and the Critique of Pure Fairness

ERIC GANS

Thucydides' account of Pericles' funeral oration demonstrates that the first democracy was sensitive to what generative anthropology considers the central function of political systems: holding in check the resentment inevitably generated by inequality among beings whose possession of language instills in them a 'moral model' of 'symmetrical reciprocity'. Pericles' words demonstrate an awareness that the increased fairness of democratic choice only exacerbates the resentment of those not chosen.

Democracy emerged in Athens as a liberation from the traditional system of sacrificial tribute. It could not survive in antiquity because the liberation from the economic activity associated with payment of tribute depended, in Rome as in Athens, on slave labour. Modern democracy emerged in tandem with the modern market, and, in contrast to the politics-centred world of the polis, is auxiliary to civil society. In liberal democracy the political sphere functions to provide a secure basis for economic life and to permit the negotiation of the resentments that emerge within it.

This system is maximally stable and fair, but its stability cannot become absolute because its fairness can never eliminate resentment. Whereas the opposition of ethnic and other ascriptive minorities can in principle be reduced by an increase in fairness, this is not true of the opposition of 'losers' who blame their failure on betrayal by the system. Such persons are tempted by the self-justifying extremist refusal to negotiate their resentments within the political system; they consequently represent a permanent danger to liberal democracy.

Introduction: democracy, envy and the incompleteness of history

Near the beginning of Pericles' *Funeral Oration* in Thucydides, Book II, we find the two following statements, separated by a single paragraph:

> 35: ... He who is a stranger to the matter [i.e., the glorious deeds Pericles is about to commemorate] may be led by envy to suspect

exaggeration if he hears anything above his own nature. *For men can endure to hear others praised only so long as they can severally persuade themselves of their own ability to equal the actions recounted; when this point is passed, envy comes in and with it incredulity ...*

37: Our constitution does not copy the laws of neighbouring states; we are rather a pattern to others than imitators ourselves. Its administration favours the many instead of the few; this is why it is called a democracy. If we look to the laws, they afford equal justice to all in their private differences; if to social standing, advancement in public life falls to reputation for capacity, class considerations not being allowed to interfere with merit; nor again does poverty bar the way, *if a man is able to serve the state, he is not hindered by the obscurity of his condition.* The freedom which we enjoy in our government extends also to our ordinary life. *There, far from exercising a jealous surveillance [hypopsia = suspicion] over each other, we do not feel called upon to be angry with our neighbour for doing what he likes, or even to indulge in those injurious looks which cannot fail to be offensive,* although they inflict no positive penalty ...[1]

These passages from the first great statement of democratic ideology contrast with the political discourse of today in their frank references to the prevalence of 'envy' and 'suspicion' in society and to democracy's special capacity for allaying them. The speaker draws no parallel between the two categories, yet their implicit conjunction is at the heart of Athenian democracy. Because envy is aroused by actions one is unable to conceive oneself as accomplishing, equality of opportunity makes the Athenian citizenry unsuspicious of each other. If no one is prevented by external authority from serving the state and, in private life, from 'doing what he likes', each can imagine himself doing whatever anyone else can do. 'Serving the state' may be placed in parallel with 'doing what he likes' because neither in public nor in private life need the Athenian citizen answer to superiors in a permanent hierarchy.

But a more careful reading weakens this simple causal relation and reveals the vulnerability of the first democracy to what I call the 'critique of pure fairness'. Pericles does not say that everyone can serve the state, but that 'reputation for capacity' and 'merit' are favoured over 'class considerations'. In other words, Athens has a *fair* method for selecting those best suited for office, in contrast to the hierarchical societies that surround it, where birth and wealth are the sole criteria. But for that very reason, this method is bound to arouse 'envy and incredulity'. Fairness is based on a determination of suitability, and such a determination requires judgement. The fairer one wants to be, the more specific the evaluation one must make for the specific task at hand, and the more unpredictable the results. Hence, contrary to what might appear at first glance, fairness is inversely proportional to objectivity; it is the unfair criteria of birth and wealth that are objective, applicable with a minimal exercise of judgement.

Hence the fairer the society, the more an individual not chosen for a particular task is likely to disagree with society's judgement. In a democracy, I am far more likely than in a hierarchical social order to expect more honour than I receive, and to condemn as unfair the system that fails to grant it. That I can 'persuade [myself] of [my] own ability to equal the actions' that found the superior reputation of those elected makes me more, not less resentful of them, because what I fancy to be my 'ability' is not joined to the opportunity of equalling these actions. By giving everyone an equal chance, democracy arouses equal ambitions, most of which are bound to remain unsatisfied. If, on the one hand, democracy eliminates the 'external envy' that divides relatively impenetrable classes, on the other it foments the more intense 'internal envy' that arises from failed competition.

The presence of these references to envy and suspicion in the primary statement of Athenian democratic self-consciousness lends support to the view that the avoidance of such mimetic emotions and their potential for provoking violence is the crucial function of the social order. All political forms face this problem, but democracy forces its members to reflect on it. Democracy thematizes the primal danger to human society that had been held in check by the preventive terror of authoritarian systems: the danger of the resentment generated by endemically unsatisfied desire.

The ethical result of democracy's self-consciousness is the striving for fairness. But the impossibility of perfect fairness is a consequence of the paradoxical structure of desire, itself dependent on the paradoxical interaction of reality with our representation of it. Desire is grounded on the sign's originary transcendence of reality; this structure makes utopian thought inevitable but the historical realization of utopia impossible.

Generative Anthropology's Hypothesis of Human Origin

Generative anthropology attempts to explain the origin or 'generation' of the human in the most parsimonious way possible, by constructing a model, on the basis of a minimal set of assumptions, of a hypothetical event from which derive all the elements of human culture, e.g. language, morality, religion, art.

The human is defined by the use of representation, the production of intentional signs, of which those of language are the most fundamental. The genesis of the human is the genesis of language. But language, like all representation, is a form of *mimesis* or imitation. We therefore hypothesize (the 'originary hypothesis') that representation was invented/discovered at the moment in which the pre-human capacity for mimesis became a source of danger to the protohuman social order. Mimesis is in the first place the imitation of others like oneself; it is the primary form of learning, and the capacity for it is the basis of 'intelligence'. Man, *dixit* Aristotle, is the most mimetic animal; after man, the honour goes to the next most intelligent animals, his fellow primates. But the advantages of mimesis are accompanied by dangers; to imitate the gestures by which another appropriates a desired object is to risk coming into conflict with him or her over this object.

As a result of their enhanced capacity for mimesis, protohuman ancestors come to pose a greater danger to themselves than do the dangers of the outside world. At some point, the contagious force of mimesis becomes great enough to lead to a breakdown of the pecking-order hierarchy by which pre-human societies avoid intraspecific violence. The desires of the protohuman group become too strong to be constrained by their instinctive deference to the 'alpha' animal. This moment of *mimetic crisis* provides the minimal condition for the *originary event* or *scene* in which the group members, instead of appropriating the central object of their desire, emit a *sign* that originates as an 'aborted gesture of appropriation'. By means of this sign imitating or representing the common object of desire, the human community avoids self-destructive conflict: it 'defers violence through representation'. The designation of this central object situates it on an inaccessible higher plane. As the focus of collective desire, it appears to incarnate a sacred force greater than any available within the group itself – a force that is the resultant of the mimetically reinforced desires of all the participants.

In this event, all participants symmetrically emit and understand the sign that designates/sacralizes the central object: the originary scene is characterized by *linguistic reciprocity*. This reciprocity constitutes the basis for our *moral sense*: the sentiment that all human beings are equal on the scene of human culture. Rather than a set of propositions, morality is more properly understood as a model (the *moral model*) of fully reciprocal interaction.

Both politics and economics can be traced to moments of the originary event: politics, to the inaugural exchange of signs; economics, to the subsequent distribution of things that the exchange of signs makes possible. The 'equal distribution' of the central object of desire can only be carried out subsequent to each member's renunciation, mediated by the sign, of his attempt to appropriate this object in the context of pre-human appetite. This deferral of appetitive satisfaction establishes both the power of the political sphere and the productivity of the economic. The portions of the sacrificial feast possessed by each participant are, as the first objects to have an equivalent value, the first objects of virtual and, subsequently, of real exchange.

The human economy is from the first a political economy; its products, however profane, exist on the sufferance of the sacred central power. Just as the equalitarian politics of the originary scene are prior to their economics of equal distribution, so there is no historical distribution system that is not mediated by a representation system. In pre-democratic societies, neither politics nor economics are conceived as independent domains; power relations are inseparable from the ritual system of distribution as enacted in sacrificial feasts. In primitive hunter-gatherer societies, this system remains equalitarian: no individual can appropriate more for him or herself than is available to others. The pattern of ritual sacrifice equalizes the burden and the rewards of preparing and consuming the feast; the so-called 'totemic' systems of Australian tribes are means to maintaining this equality.

Hierarchy and the historical origin of democracy

With the advent of agriculture and the accumulation of surpluses of food and consequently of labour, a human hierarchy usurps the redistributive function of the sacrificial rites that had hitherto maintained symmetry within the community and makes its own decisions concerning the allocation of resources. As I attempted to show in *The End of Culture*, the 'big-man', the earliest form of chieftain described by Marshall Sahlins in *Stone-Age Economics*, takes over the central ritual function of distribution that had been shared among the various subgroups ('totems') of tribal society.[2] As Sahlins points out, the 'big-man' has no power, only added responsibility; he and his dependants must work harder than the rest to accumulate the surplus that will be consumed at the feast. But domination of the ritual distribution system is the path to political domination as well. From this beginning there emerge the first states and their extended forms, the archaic empires; the 'big-man' evolves into a god-king. The originary decision that renunciation of the central object should precede its consumption as sacrifice is now reformulated as the ideology of the ruling hierarchy, who determine the redistribution of the sacrificial surplus extracted from the population.

The reciprocity of the originary scene has but a single degree of freedom: assent to the renunciation of the central object and the production of the sign. The social order thus generated has as its prime concern preserving everyone's equality of distance from the centre. Only through human usurpation of the centre can a decision-making process concerning economic redistribution be instituted. But this usurpation in turn, by generating resentment in those excluded from the power of decision, generates pressure to restore reciprocity, this time as an active operation with more than a single degree of freedom at its disposal.

The *sine qua non* of the hierarchical decision-making process is economic: the redistribution of goods through taxes and tribute from the producers to their lords. Having arrogated to themselves the goods and services with which to conduct military operations, the members of the ruling hierarchy fight among themselves for supremacy at home and the chance of conquest abroad. But in pre-democratic Athens, with the weakening of central control by the remnants of the old Mycenaean palace hierarchy, the small producers who provided the basis of the tribute economy had increasingly less reason to tolerate it. At the same time, the need to assure control over a growing network of dependencies made the rulers increasingly dependent on their tributaries for military service.

The historical origin of democracy was in the late sixth century BC, but the key step in the creation of Athenian democracy was Solon's abolition of debt-enslavement (*seisachtheia*) at the beginning of the century. The democratic citizen is 'free' (*eleutheros*) in that he has been freed from dependency on the ritual distribution system and its vestigial aristocratic remains. This creates a historically new conception of human identity: the citizen as a free producer who can be imposed upon only by the community within which he participates equally with his fellows. The immense energy expended by the Athenians on choosing citizens not only for leadership functions (*archon*, *strategos*) but for numerous posts in the council and the courts, as well as on the apparently anomalous procedure of ostracism, measures the intensity of their desire to prevent domination of their polity by any faction or individual. This same desire explains their general preference for lot ('sortition') over election, the latter being reserved for positions requiring a special skill, particularly military.

The Athenian assembly emerges historically from the old ritual system, as reflected in the clan-based organization of the council (*boulé*); its transformation from the passive popular assembly of the Homeric epics into a power-wielding democratic body is a consequence of its members' new-found economic independence. The freedom of the Athenian citizen is a generalization of the aristocratic centrality of the 'big-man' in a local distribution system. Individual citizens are heads of family economies (*oikoi*), independent producers with an established identity in their *deme* rather than abstractly defined inhabitants of the polis, let alone human beings in general. The freedom of Athenian democracy is not understood as a 'human right' nor, conversely, is the degradation of slavery condemned. At most, political independence is detached from economic independence with the extension of citizenship rights (presumably by Solon) to propertyless citizens (*thetes*).

For the first time, the alienation of individual freedom to the centre that is a necessity of all social organization becomes a reflective, voluntary act rather than one imposed by the sacred necessity of deferring violence. The freedom to 'do what one likes' extolled in the *Funeral Oration* is that of the free producer unbound by traditional tributary obligations. Some features of this freedom anticipate and even exceed those of modern *homo economicus*. The Athenian citizen was not, like the Roman, subservient to a family he was obliged to perpetuate. As in the contemporary United

States (but not in France), Athenian parents could disinherit their children; conversely, there was no equivalent to the Roman *patria potestas* that affirmed the authority of the father over his adult sons.[3]

In the Athenian political and judicial system, the violent *agon* of physical conflict was deferred not by ritual prescription, but by its systematic transformation into the peaceful *agon* of words. Aeschylus' *Eumenides* celebrates this revolution in human self-consciousness. Athenian democracy is the first form of social organization that consciously implements our originary intuition of linguistic reciprocity.

The classical question of ancient history is why classical civilization did not survive the onslaught of the 'barbarians', and the classical explanation is that it practised slavery. Reciprocity in one area of society had to be paid for by its absence in another. But a sharper analysis is possible. The instability of Athenian democracy, and of ancient republican rule in general, may be attributed to the economic inefficiency inherent in a system that frees politics from the old ritual hierarchy but leaves the economy under the strict control of the political system. The Athenian citizens' political autonomy was not accompanied by similar autonomy in the economic sphere. Politics was bound to dominate economics because the economy itself was dependent on 'political' ie., military activity. Athens' obsession with the political process was the counterpart to the imperial nature of her economy: what concerned the Athenian democracy above all else was finding the means to extract slaves and tribute from her dependencies to replace the free citizens no longer willing to perform labour in field, mine and manufacture. Economic liberation from the tributary hierarchy had produced a citizenry for whom the only acceptable form of service was military. Because labour-for-another was precisely what democracy had abolished, the contractual freedom of wage-labour that might have permitted the Athenian economy to evolve into the ever-expanding free market of 'capitalism' could not emerge.[4]

Liberal democracy and the market model

The triumph of modern liberal democracy signalled by the breakup of the Soviet Union was declared by Francis Fukuyama in a famous article to signify the 'end of history'.[5] This rash and paradoxical Hegelian claim has aroused much controversy. But no one has been able to undermine the author's central thesis that liberal democracy is the least constrained form of social organization and that no other form can prove superior in the long run in either political freedom or economic productivity. As recently as a decade ago, many believed that socialism in one form or another could eliminate the inequities of the market system; this dream has now been laid to rest.

Liberal democracy consists of two essential components; (1) a democratic political system in which sovereignty ultimately resides in the citizenry as a whole and is regularly expressed in elections; and (2) a free market economy, subordinate to the political system but dominating it as a focus of individual action. Political theory has ignored the analogy between these two central institutions. Both the free market and democracy are minimal or 'natural' institutions, points of greatest stability or 'valleys' in institutional space, because they embody the originary human reciprocity inherent in the symmetrical interchange of language. Democracy is the political actualization of our 'moral sense' that all persons are equal with regard to the exchange of linguistic signs, just as the market realizes our originary freedom as participants in the exchange of things.

Both the market and the elective political order are decision-making mechanisms that, as in the hypothetical originary scene, but with multiple degrees of freedom, aggregate the uncontrolled inputs of many individual participants. Both market prices and election returns are the resultants, indeterminable in advance, of a multitude of individual decisions, each based on varying degrees of knowledge and judgement. Just as each citizen casts his or her vote as he or she sees fit, each participant in the market buys and sells as he or she sees fit, in both cases within the limits of what is available to buy, sell or elect. Because popular demand is the ultimate source of both political and economic power, where there is a demand for either goods or political programmes, the mechanisms of both institutions insure that, as a general rule, someone will eventually attempt to supply it.

When political thinkers construct a fictional scene of origin in a 'social contract' or John Rawls's 'original position', they pay homage to the intellectual necessity of the originary hypothesis, if not to its anthropological necessity.[6] These scenes are used either to justify a moral sense of human equality, or to explain why ethical reality cannot honour it. But our intuition of this equality precedes these artificial constructions, which are in fact designed to permit us to explore its consequences. In contrast with social-contract theories, the originary hypothesis models *in actu* the connection between linguistic competence and moral equality that is later made explicit in the democratic slogan 'one person, one vote'. It explains as well, in contrast to the a *posteriori* rationalism of contract theories, why the slogan not very long ago referred not to 'one person' but 'one man', that is, why women were excluded from the original notion of human equality and denied voting rights in democracies until very recent times. If the deferral of violence is the fundamental necessity of human systems of representation, then it is understandable that these systems have been elaborated and used primarily by the sex that is particularly prone to violence.

Once the conditions for liberal democracy have been met, it requires the least expenditure of real or potential physical violence to maintain itself. At a given moment, the best price or course of action might be one dictated by an enlightened despot. But the means required for the latter to impose his choice independently of the will of the citizenry and to suppress the expression of their resentment represent a dead loss of energy and information, whereas liberal democracy recycles both political and economic resentments into the system.

Modern liberal democracy emerges not, as in Athens, as a new political redistribution system to replace the old ritual-based system, but as the political accompaniment to the growing market that asserts, whether gradually or abruptly, its incompatibility with any such system. Hence liberal democracy is characterized by a self-conscious thinness of political activity relative to the economic activities of 'civil society' within which the general population define their lives, through both their public careers and their private consumption patterns. The political order, as the Preamble to the US Constitution makes clear, is intended to maintain the conditions necessary to permit the free exchange system of 'civil society' to flourish: 'justice', 'domestic tranquillity', 'common defense', 'general welfare' – in other terms, external and internal security, the rule of law, protection of the commons.

Domestic politics in liberal democracy is centred on the legislative process, the redistributive and regulative activity of which, beyond general considerations of the sort listed in the Preamble, is driven by the negotiation of resentments or sentiments of injustice generated within the economic sphere. The analogy between the political process and the market is most direct in quantitative policy decisions such as tax rates and spending levels, which are, like market values, unpredictable compromises arrived at through negotiation, but even in apparently non-negotiable moral issues like abortion the process tends to generate equally unpredictable compromise positions with which neither side is altogether satisfied.

The instability of democracy in Europe before the advent of modern 'consumer' society demonstrates that democratic politics can only be as it has always been in the United States – a supplement or counterweight to the marketplace, not a utopian substitute for it. The exemplary failure of the French Second Republic (1848–51) was a consequence of its political enfranchisement of the *classes laborieuses* who, although essential factors in the economy, remained, as suppliers of 'labour power', *objects* of the market system rather than its *subjects*, that is, relatively uncoerced buyers and sellers of goods and services. Democratic politics cannot serve such clients because, impatient with its limitations, they expect it to modify the market's fundamental structures – in the case at hand, by guaranteeing full employment in the *ateliers nationaux*. (In contrast, in more advanced societies the 'underclass' and other clients of social welfare do not generally pose such a threat; indifferent to the market's operation, they merely require funding from its surplus.) The working-class riots of June 1848, put down by the bourgeois *Garde Nationale*, revealed the impossibility of normal political negotiation between the components of the erstwhile Third Estate. Later in the year, the 'Prince-President' Louis-Napoleon was elected to maintain order, which he eventually assured by abolishing the vestiges of democracy in the *coup d'état* of December 1851. The lesson of these events was that the liberal bourgeoisie could maintain its economic interests against the resentments of its workers only by effectively disenfranchising itself, an ironic end to romantic illusion in the political sphere that inspired the inaugurators of cultural modernity, Flaubert and Baudelaire.

The key moment of the hypothetical scene of human origin is the 'political' exchange of signs, but its closure comes only with the 'economic' distribution of the body of the sacred victim, which incarnates the meaning of the sign in materially assimilable form. When economic goods are produced in such quantity and variety that they function more like the sign that defers mimetic violence than like the object that incites it, the average citizen need not feel obliged to contest through the political *agon* what he can obtain through the peaceful reciprocity of the marketplace. The 'deferral of violence through representation' that is the minimal function of human culture no longer requires deferral of the pleasures of consumption as well.

No aspect of market society has been so bitterly denounced by the intelligentsia as consumerism. Ever since Veblen's critique of 'conspicuous consumption',[7] consumer society has been disparaged for its encouragement of futile desires that distract its members, particularly those with revolutionary potential, from considerations of social justice. But what these critics see as the degradation of the political process is more usefully understood as its democratization. It is the circulation and negotiation, along with class, gender and ethnic differences, of the old oppositions between politics and economics, word and thing, sacred and profane, that best guarantees social stability.

The democratic process requires that the large majority of citizens have, 'a stake in the system'. But this stake is best measured not by a certain level of economic success, but by the capacity to construct an individual 'message' of identity through the consumption of 'product-signs' offered on the market.[8] The individual act of consumption is not a knee-jerk response to an advertiser's manipulation of desire; it is the outcome of a continually updated apprenticeship. The consumer must learn to use the system of 'product-signs' to express in constantly evolving ways the nuances of his or her personal identity, which is precisely that which in him *resists* or remains invariant under the operations of exchange. That consumer society continually sells the means by which some express their opposition to it ('commodify[ing] your dissent', as a recent collection calls it[9]) is anything but a sign of 'late capitalism's' imminent decline; on the contrary, the ability to express one's political disaffection from the liberal democratic system through an economic transaction within the system itself is a measure of its stability. What its diehard opponent Herbert Marcuse called 'repressive tolerance' is liberal democracy's insurance against the horrors of centralized political control.[10]

The historical success of liberal democracy is perhaps best demonstrated by the fact that its remaining enemies have been forced to abandon the traditional economic and political battlegrounds of the competition of social forms. Today's virulent anti-Western ideologies promise their adherents not only less political freedom but, unlike the Bolsheviks of old, less economic productivity as well. The present era's resentful revolutionaries, like the peasant in the Russian tale, are so enraged by the success of the market system that they are happy to lose one eye for the pleasure of seeing their neighbour lose both.

And yet we cannot for all that declare ourselves at 'the end of history'.

The critique of pure fairness: the imperfection of democracy

In order for democratic politics to function, politicians must be willing to consider market-generated resentments not as moral truths, but as negotiable interests. The distribution of economic goods resulting from market activity arouses feelings of injustice that, if unresolved within the political system, risk being turned against the market as a whole in the form of utopian revolutionary movements. Communists, Fascists and Nazis alike shared contempt for both the political and the economic structure of liberal democracy.

Historically, these movements were at their most powerful during the 1930s, which was the low point in public confidence in the market system but also, seen in retrospect, the birth of liberal democracy's mature self-consciousness, the watershed between *laissez-faire* 'capitalism' and market society as an integrated, all-inclusive politico-economic system. Right-wing anti-capitalism lost credibility with the fall of Nazism and Fascism and, a generation later, the failure of Soviet-style communism ruined the hopes of its left-wing cousin. Now that liberal democracy is without serious challengers to its global dominance, the only significant limitation to its ability to defer violence is henceforth the limitation inherent in its fairness at any given moment – a limitation that, as we have seen, was already implicit in the words of Pericles' *Funeral Oration.*

Our specific concern is to determine in what way the resentment generated by democratic fairness circulates through the exchange system. Is it confined to disaffected individuals, or does it tend to proliferate in members of ascriptive and/or voluntary groups? Most critically, can it be reabsorbed within the system before manifesting itself as violence? How do the esthetic or self-expressive features of consumer society affect the answers to these questions? But we must first distinguish the problems of democracy that reflect our 'critique of pure fairness' from those for which, on the contrary, an increase of fairness promises a solution.

Internal ethnic conflict

A frequent source of violence in modern democracy is the disaffection of economically successful minorities, such as the Basques in Spain or the Tamils of Sri Lanka and, more ambiguously, the Québecois minority in Canada. In these cases, economic success contrasts with demographic and consequently political weakness; the minority, not unreasonably, perceives discriminatory economic policies or cultural affronts such as resistance to teaching and using its language as

reflecting majority resentment of its economic strength. The division of
societies along ethnic fault-lines puts in question the model of liberal
democracy. When the circulation of desires in the marketplace fails
sufficiently to integrate the separate communities, political tension
results. The ease with which market society allows the creation and
reinforcement of images of personal identity by means of the 'product-
signs' of consumption makes any such perceived failure of
communication dangerous.

But this problem is amenable to an increase in fairness, in the sense
of a less restricted circulation of socially useful values, in either of two
ways. If the minority group is not only concentrated in a compact
geographical territory (as are all three minorities mentioned above), but
economically autonomous as well – a situation more common in
propaganda than in reality – the fair solution to the minority's sentiment
of political exploitation by the majority is secession. If this solution is
resisted by the majority, it may be concluded that the society as a whole
suffers from a deficit rather than from a surfeit of fairness.

In contrast, if the minority group forms a socioeconomic whole with
the majority, then the expansion of the market-system toward greater
inclusivity offers to its dissent what is, in principle, a self-correcting
mechanism. As the minority's sentiment of political non-inclusion
expresses itself in the marketplace, its cultural vocabulary is adopted and
transmitted by others, notably by the omnipresent youth culture that
absorbs and retransmits all signs of disaffection. This in turn reduces the
ascriptive quality of ethnic divisions and transforms them into
complexes of transmissible and ultimately 'fungible' signs. Because the
minority critique of modern democracy is directed at the incompleteness
rather than the completeness of its circulation of values, it operates as a
feedback loop rather than a vicious circle. As the critique is expressed, it
is assimilated within the system and ultimately defused, leading to the
damping over in the long term of the threat of ethnic conflict. This will
almost certainly be the outcome in the Basque and Québecois cases, and
there are signs that it will be true of the Tamils as well.

Natural inferiors? The Bell Curve problem

Resentments can only be politically negotiated so long as they permit an
implicit appeal to a moral sense of equality. My resentment and yours
may have different causes, but our sense of injustice is one; we both have
a presumptively equal claim to the ultimate re-establishment of

reciprocity. This basis for political negotiation is endangered by the 'Bell Curve' thesis that one group's resentments are founded not on potentially reversible social interactions, but on an inferiority that, whether genetic or merely environmental, is irreversible in the short term.[11]

Permanent group inferiority, understood as a group's measurably inferior ability to engage in reciprocal human dialogue, is 'unspeakable' in the liberal-democratic context because it contradicts the originary model of human moral equality and puts into question the democratic system based on it. (Whence, conversely, the implicit necessity of a claim of genetic inferiority to rationalize any intentional exclusion from this system, as witness Aristotle's concept of the 'natural slave' and the racial doctrines that justified the enslavement of Africans or the extermination of Jews.) If we are obliged to accept the Bell Curve thesis, the basis for democratic political negotiation in the originary moral model breaks down.

But what is an appropriate demonstration of 'inferiority'? We can presumably measure IQ, but there is no definitive way to measure the fundamental human capacity to use representations. However seductive the Bell Curve thesis may appear from study of current data, the anthropological foundation of liberal democracy requires that we operate on the assumption that, in the long run, the cultivation of different representational skills and techniques among racial and ethnic groups – the most significant dividing line being no doubt that which separates oral- and written-dominated subcultures – is determined culturally rather than biologically.

The criterion of intellectual parsimony must be determined not by the data alone, but by the necessity of accounting for these data within the context of a universally shared ethic. Liberal democracy is 'natural' only on the implicit assumption that all human beings can trace their origin back to the same hypothetical originary scene of language and culture. Hence it must be assumed that an increase of fairness will lead, on the one hand, to the greater cultural and genetic integration of various groups and, on the other, to the broadening of the means by which the talents cultivated by various subcultures can contribute value to the economy.

Social 'losers': extremism

The foregoing notwithstanding, at any given time there are bound to exist locally intractable phenomena of resistance to liberal democracy.

The fact that the system grows ever fairer by increasing the number of relevant criteria for merit, opening up opportunities for the less favoured and so on, will not prevent the existence of 'losers', and whatever the possibilities of a yet more inclusive fairness in the future, it cannot be assumed that all will be content to view their present failure against the horizon of these potential improvements.

To the extent that market society's politico-economic processes are stable, they appear to be founded on teachable principles: thrift, sobriety, hard work, training and so on. But in order to remain an autonomous source of information, the market processes must be irreducible to any set of rules of conduct. In contrast with the ethics of traditional societies, which prescribe socially useful actions to their members, the ethic of market society is exclusively negative: sins of commission are punished rather than sins of omission. What might be called the implicit positive ethic of this society, the imperative to produce socially useful goods, can operate only as a horizon of action, not as a decision-making procedure; all principles conducive to productivity are themselves subject to negotiation in the market.[12]

Hence when individuals who 'follow the rules' fail to achieve what they consider to be an appropriate reward for their efforts, they are tempted to denounce the social order as illegitimate for having broken its implicit promise to honour these 'rules'. Rather than participate in the political negotiation of economic resentments, which requires that all parties accept limits on their demands and on the principles that inspire them, they may prefer to make negotiation impossible by exceeding these limits, even at the risk of committing and suffering violence. This is called *extremism*. Extremist behaviour operates in a vicious circle: when the extremist's own violence provokes the social order to enact violence against him or her, he or she declares this proof of the despotic nature of this order.

There are extremists on both ends of the political spectrum, but they tend to be concentrated on the ideologically dominant side, condemning their party's leadership as treasonous for refusing to implement uncompromisingly their proclaimed 'true beliefs' – whence the bizarre *déjà vu* of radical-rightists in the 1990s expressing the same paranoia toward the FBI, ATF or CIA as did the New Leftists of the sixties. The forces once accused of racism, bigotry and fascism (i.e., of betraying the nation's liberal ideals) are now denounced as agents of godless communism and racial impurity.

There are extremists among the Basques and Tamils; there are also extremists among the American Blacks who were the target of the Bell Curve hypothesis. But even if we may be optimistic about the eventual pacification of the relations between these minorities and the majority culture that surrounds them, we cannot anticipate the elimination of voluntary groups formed by the banding together of 'losers'. Nor, however limited their present power, can we guarantee that such groups will not some day unleash a major perturbation that leads to the destruction of the liberal-democratic system. The paradoxical conclusion of the 'critique of pure fairness' is that, although Fukuyama's thesis that liberal democracy is the ultimate political system is justified, it will never be possible to proclaim the 'end of history'.

NOTES

1. Thucydides, *The Peloponnesian War* (New York: Modern Library, 1951) pp.103–104.
2. See Eric Gans, *The End of Culture: Toward a Generative Anthropology* (Berkeley: University of California Press, 1985); and Marshall Sahlins, *Stone Age Economics* (Chicago: Aldine-Atherton,1972).
3. See Raphael Sealey, *The Athenian Republic* (Harrisburg: Pennsylvania State University Press, 1987) ch.2.
4. See Ellen Wood, *Peasant-Citizen and Slave* (London: Verso, 1988).
5. Francis Fukuyama, 'The End of History', *The National Interest* 16 (1989) pp.3–18.
6. John Rawls, *A Theory of Justice* (Cambridge, MA: Harvard University Press, 1971).
9. Thomas Frank and Matt Weiland (eds), *Commodify Your Dissent: The Business of Culture in the New Gilded Age: Salvos from the Baffler* (New York: Norton, 1997).
8. Jean Baudrillard, *Le système des objets* (Paris: Gallimard 1968); *La société de consommation; ses mythes, ses structures* (Paris: SGPP, 1970).
7. Thorstein Veblen, *The Theory of the Leisure Class: An Economic Study in the Evolution of Institutions* (London: Macmillan & Co., 1899).
10. Herbert Marcuse, *One Dimensional Man: Studies in the Ideology of Advanced Industrial Society* (Boston: Beacon Press, 1964).
11. Richard J. Herrnstein and Charles Murray, *The Bell Curve: Intelligence and Class Structure in American Life* (New York: Free Press, 1994).
12. See Eric Gans, 'The Unique Source of Religion and Morality', *Anthropoetics* http://www.anthropoetics.ucla.edu/ap0101/gans.htm (June 1995), 10pp. Revised version in *Contagion* 3 (Spring 1996) pp.51–65.

15

The Political Context of Terrorism in America:
Ignoring Extremists or Pandering to Them?

CHRISTOPHER HEWITT

This article examines the political context of four waves of terrorism in the United States: by White racists in the South during the civil rights period, by Black militants in the late 1960s and early 1970s, by left-wing revolutionaries in the 1970s, and by contemporary anti-abortion extremists. Two alternative theories are considered; that citizens resort to violence because their views and interests are ignored by politicians; and that politicians by 'pandering to extremists' incite them to violence. The evidence appears to support the first theory. In the cases examined, a sizable number of people felt very strongly about some social/political issues – segregation, racial equality, the Vietnam war, abortion – and also felt that the political system ignored, or was hostile to, their concerns. Terrorism was most likely to occur under presidential administrations hostile to the goals of the terrorists, rather than under sympathetic administrations.

Why is terrorism so common in free and democratic societies? In this article, using the United States from 1954 to the present as a case study, two alternative explanations for why democratic politics lead to social violence are examined. One view is that citizens resort to violence because their views and interests are ignored by politicians. The other view is that politicians by 'pandering to extremists' incite them to violence.

Excluded opinions and extremism

Proponents of the first view argue that people who see the political system as responsive to their concerns will not resort to violence. The existence of terrorism is therefore an indicator of political alienation. This truism implies that in order to understand terrorism, are must consider whose opinions and interests are being ignored. Pluralists emphasize that a wide variety of opinions and interests are allowed to organize and compete in the political arena, but in practice certain groups are excluded from the process. Such exclusion may occur for several reasons. Sometimes political cleavages coincide with ascriptive identities and produce permanent minorities, as in Northern Ireland and other ethnically divided societies. Blacks in the United States were, until recently, disfranchised in many states, and continue to be underrepresented in terms of voting strength, political power and influence. Consequently, insofar as political issues have a racial character, Black interests and concerns will often be disregarded. Another reason why certain positions are excluded from political debate involves the logic of political competition. In most Western democracies, political opinions can be seen in terms of a left–right continuum. Electoral competition in a two-party system results in a drive for the centre. Consequently, those who are at the ideological extremes, Communists and Socialists, Birchers and neo-Nazis, find themselves ignored. Indeed, such positions are often normatively defined as being 'beyond the pale', absurd or even wicked.

Groups and individuals resort to terrorism because they are frustrated by an unresponsive political system. Schmid and de Graaf[1] consider terrorist violence as a form of communication – 'the outgrowth of minority strategies to get into the news'. Other demands may become the subject of political debate, but fail to achieve any satisfaction. Presumably, the greater the strength of 'extremist' sentiments, and the larger mobilization by 'extremist' groups, the more likely it is that terrorism will occur.[2]

Encouraging Extremism

However, others argue that terrorist violence results not from the fact that politicians ignore certain issues and opinions, but because they play up and pander to them. Mullins[3] sees the mid-1980s as providing 'an opportune political environment for the right-wing terrorist ... It did not take long for the far-right to pick up on the signals being sent by the Washington administration ... Some increases in hate-crime activity can be attributed both to the recession and the conservative political climate in the country.'

Following an attack on an abortion clinic, an editorial in *The Nation* (23 January 1995) argued that 'John Salvi was no lone gunman ... After

twenty years of denunciation of 'baby-killers' from pulpit, Oval Office
and TV studio, it was only a matter of time before someone took the
rhetoric at face value. There were a lot of fingers on Salvi's trigger.'
Jesse Jackson blamed the burning of Black churches on those 'who use
thinly coded, veiled race symbols when they say welfare and crime and
anti-affirmative action. They're sending signals, they're sending
messages more profound than their language ... they're laying the
groundwork for those who burn churches.'[4] Blanchard and Prewitt[5] in
their study of anti-abortion violence suggest two aspects of the political
context that affect the level of violence; the general orientation of the
administration, and what significant political figures, such as
presidents, say about the issue. Their argument implies that a general
pattern should be found whereby, for any particular type of extremist
violence, there will be more violence under sympathetic than under
hostile administrations. Rhetoric that provokes violence is not, of
course, confined to presidents and (as the views quoted above reveal)
those blamed for violence include conservatives, Republican politicians
in general, and religious leaders as well as presidents. This article for
the most part concentrates on presidential speeches and actions,
although the effects of Southern governors and local Black political
power are also examined.

In order to test these alternative models, four waves of terrorism are
examined: white racist terrorism in the South during the civil rights
period; Black terrorism in the late 1960s and early 1970s; left-wing
terrorism in the 1970s; and contemporary anti-abortion terrorism.

White racist terrorism in the South

The School Desegregation decision of 1954 and the civil rights
campaigns in the 1960s provoked a violent response from White racists.
A resurgent Klan bombed and shot at civil rights activists in an attempt
to intimidate Blacks from exercising their rights. Other groups such as
the National States Rights Party were also active. The violence began in
1955 and was largely over by 1971 (see Fig. 1). A total of 588 incidents
were reported in Southern states during this period, with at least 65
fatalities.[6]

The existence of a sizable group of 'extremists' among white
Southerners is undeniable, although one needs to be careful about how
the term is defined. While a majority supported segregation, only a

FIGURE 1
KLAN VIOLENCE (1954–1971)

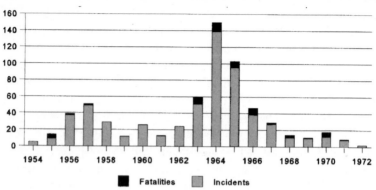

minority supported violence. According to Gallup polls, in 1965 four per cent had a highly favourable view of the Klan, compared to 59 percent with a highly unfavourable view. By 1970 opinions were even more polarized, with 6 per cent having a highly favourable and 80 per cent a highly unfavorable view of the group. Translated into raw numbers this implies that there were about 1,300,000 Klan sympathisers in 1965 and 1,660,000 in 1970.

Klan membership itself is difficult to determine for obvious reasons. However, all sources agree that membership increased dramatically in response to civil rights activity, reached a peak in the mid-1960s, and then declined precipitously. The Anti-Defamation League estimated the total at 42,000 in 1965, 55,000 in 1967, and a mere 5,000 in 1973. These trends obviously correlate, in a general sense, with the rise and fall of racist violence.

To what extent, if any, did the political context have an observable effect on terrorist violence? None of the presidential administrations during the period can be defined, in any way, as pro-segregationist. Eisenhower's civil rights bills of 1957 and 1960 were the first since Reconstruction. He ended segregation in the D.C. schools, and expressed the hope that this would become a model for other school systems. He took strong action to enforce the desegregation orders of the federal courts, and during the crisis in Little Rock 'federalized' the Arkansas National Guard and sent the 101st Airborne Division to protect Black pupils.

Kennedy was an outspoken advocate of school desegregation, although critics complained that his presidential performance did not live up to his campaign promises.[7] Kennedy twice asserted federal power, once against Governor Ross Barnett of Mississippi and once against Governor George Wallace of Alabama. Twenty thousand troops were sent to Mississippi, and both Governor Barnett and Lieutenant Governor Johnson were indicted for contempt of court when the University of Mississippi was integrated. The Kennedy administration also established a Committee on Equal Employment Opportunity, issued an executive order prohibiting racial discrimination in federally assisted housing, and used the threat of withholding federal funds to encourage school desegregation.

The Johnson administration enacted major civil rights legislation including the omnibus Civil Rights Act of 1964, the Voting Rights Act of 1965 and the Housing Act of 1968. The Johnson era legislation went far beyond that of previous administrations. For example, the 1968 Housing Act covered 80 per cent of all dwellings, compared to the 18 percent affected by Kennedy's executive order. The Voting Rights Act, in effect, enfranchised Blacks in the South for the first time since Reconstruction.

There was no major civil rights legislation under Nixon, and critics charged that in pursuit of his Southern strategy the administration was reluctant stringently to enforce desegregation policies. Civil rights leaders were openly mistrustful. At the NAACP's 1970 Convention, one speaker claimed that 'for the first time since Woodrow Wilson, we have a national administration that can be rightly characterized as anti-Negro'. The US Commission on Civil Rights claimed in October 1970 that there was a major breakdown in the enforcement of laws against racial discrimination.[8]

There appears to be no link between the policies of each presidential administration and the amount of violence that occurred. However, since the struggle over segregation was at the same time a struggle over states rights, it is likely that the state-level political situation was more significant than the national political situation. A study of the Southern reactions to desegregation by Sarratt,[9] found that the border states generally accepted the 1954 court decision, but that even in the Deep South there were variations in the intensity of the opposition, with Arkansas, Mississippi, Alabama, South Carolina, Louisiana, Georgia and Virginia being the most uncompromising. Within this group,

Mississippi, Alabama and Arkansas were marked by the intensity of their opposition to desegregation. On the other hand, Governors Collins of Florida and Sanford of North Carolina were noticeably moderate on the issue. 'Although a number of Southern governors recognized the legal force of the Brown decision, no other defended the Supreme Court as did LeRoy Collins, governor of Florida,' while Sanford's position was 'that the courts had settled the question of desegregation and that race was a closed issue in North Carolina politics'.[10]

The political rhetoric of the governors paralleled the positions taken by their administrations:

> Governor Faubus of Arkansas likened the federal courts to the Nazi judiciary under Adolf Hitler ... George C. Wallace, governor of Alabama at the decade's end was especially vitriolic in his attacks on the federal judges, whom he described at various times as 'the sorriest in the world,' 'lousy and irresponsible,' 'a bunch of atheistic pro-Communist bums,' and 'bearded beatniks and faceless, spineless, power-hungry theorists and black-robed judicial anarchists' ... Governor Ross Barnett of Mississippi pledged that he would 'rot in a federal jail before he will let one nigra cross the sacred threshold of our white schools.'[11]

The variation between the Southern states offers the possibility that we can identify the factors that were most significant in affecting the level of violence. In Table 1 the states are ranked according to the number of incidents that took place within their borders. In addition, three measures of extremist sentiments are shown for each state. These include an estimate of the number of Klansmen in early 1967 and the combined segregationist vote in the 1960, 1964 and 1968 presidential elections. In the final column, the state response to the desegregation issue is summarized as extreme, strong or moderate.[12] Not surprisingly, there is a correlation (.48) between the number of incidents and Klan strength. However, there is only a negligible (.04) correlation between the number of segregationist voters and the number of incidents.

The fact that the two most violent states were also the ones in which the governors, took extreme positions – even to the extent of defying the courts – could be taken as showing the effect of political leadership on the level of violence. However, the low level of violence in Arkansas, where Faubus engaged in a similar brinkmanship, makes this a dubious argument. A more plausible explanation for the correlation

TABLE 1
SEGREGATIONIST VIOLENCE AND STATE CHARACTERISTICS

State	Incidents	Klan	Vote	State Response
Mississippi	240	5830	888,000	Extreme
Alabama	117	1300	1,351,000	Extreme
Georgia	52	1580	1,153,000	Strong
Louisiana	38	1050	1,087,000	Strong
Tennessee	32	275	945,000	Moderate
Florida	30	770	1,530,000	Moderate
North Carolina	26	7520	1,121,000	Moderate
Texas	18	200	1,543,000	Moderate
South Carolina	17	1050	524,000	Strong
Arkansas	13	255	513,000	Extreme
Virginia	8	1250	803,000	Strong

between state policies and extremism is put forward by Sarratt, who concluded that 'almost without exception, the governors based their positions on the will of the people of their state'. In those few cases where governors took a more liberal position than their constituents, they lost to segregationist challengers. Thus Collins in Florida, Folsom in Alabama and Coleman in Mississippi 'failed in bids for re-election against candidates who were more vigorous in their support of segregation'. Newspapers had a similar relationship with their readers, and 'the public seemed to be molding newspaper opinion as much as the newspapers were molding public opinion'. Editors who deviated from the segregationist position lost readers and advertising. Some were assaulted on the street or had their offices bombed. Hodding Carter of the *Delta Democrat-Times* was hanged in effigy.[13]

Black terrorism (1965–74)

The wave of terrorist violence by Black militants in the late 1960s and early 1970s was for the most part an urban phenomenon. Two different types of Black groups carried out violent acts; separatist Black religious cults such as the Nation of Islam, and black nationalists such as the Black Panthers. The two types of groups engaged in very different forms of violence. Black nationalists carried on a virtual guerrilla war against the police, and they killed one another in factional feuds. Black separatist cults murdered randomly selected Whites, as well as dissidents and apostates. A total of 392 incidents are recorded, with over 200 fatalities resulting from the violence.

FIGURE 2
BLACK MILITANT VIOLENCE (1964–74)

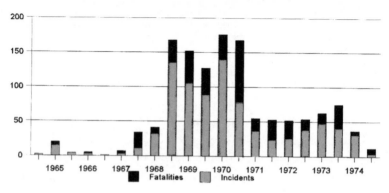

TABLE 2
FAVOURABLE ATTITUDES TOWARDS BLACK LEADERS AND GROUPS.(%)

	1963	1966	1969	1970
Stokeley Carmichael	–	7	12	26
Malcolm X	–	–	13	–
Elijah Muhammed	5	4	9	23
Black Panthers	–	–	5	25
Black Muslims	4	4	4	–
Eldridge Cleaver	–	–	–	30
Bobby Seale	–	–	–	23

Support for Black militants can be gauged from several polls. Those favouring a 'separate negro nation' increased from four per cent in 1963 to 21 per cent in 1969. Attitudes towards Black leaders and organizations also suggest an increase in nationalist and separatist sentiments in the late 1960s. Table 2 shows the proportion of Blacks who rated various groups or individuals as 'doing an excellent job'.

Other surveys produced similar results, with 25 per cent saying that 'the Black Panthers represent my own personal views', and 18 per cent giving the Panthers a 'highly favorable' rating in a 1970 Gallup poll. Data indicate that support for militant Black groups increased sharply in the late 1960s and early 1970s, and that about 20–25 per cent were sympathisers circa 1970, which would imply a total of two to three million.[14]

Since their constituencies were virtually identical, the Black Panthers, Nation of Islam, and other groups were competing with one another for support. The Nation of Islam grew dramatically in the late 1950s and throughout the 1960s, reaching a peak of perhaps 250,000 by 1970. The Black Panther Party, founded in 1966, had between 2,000 and 5,000 members in 1968.[15] Both the public opinion data and the membership statistics show that in the late 'sixties and early 'seventies, large numbers of blacks were frustrated and alienated. The growth of extremist sentiments and organizations obviously parallels the outbreak of black violence during the same period.

The political climate in the country at large was increasingly favourable to civil rights and racial equality. Throughout the period, racial issues dominated the political agenda; and Black grievances and demands were publicized by the media. According to Wolk:

> the expressed moral commitment of President Kennedy and the executive civil rights actions taken during his administration appear in sharp contrast to enforcement efforts expended under Eisenhower. Moreover, progress made during Johnson's presidency, especially in the legislative area, far surpassed the accomplishments of all who served in that office before him.'[16]

It is very noticeable that most Black terrorism occurred during the Nixon administration, when by all accounts civil rights were de-emphasized. It is possible that the *local* political situation is also a factor in explaining terrorism by Black militants. As noted earlier, most Black terrorism occurred in large cities, and in Table 3 the rate of Black terrorist incidents (per million Blacks) is shown for the 13 largest Black communities. (Since no information could be found on Black politics for two cities, Houston and Dallas, they were dropped from the sample.) Three cities have noticeably high rates: San Francisco, New Orleans and New York. To explain the variation between cities three studies of Black political participation were consulted. Patterson compared the Black voting-age population in 14 cities (circa 1970) to Black representation on the city council. Typically, Blacks were under-represented, although there was considerable variation between cities. A publication of the Joint Center for Political Studies lists all cities which had Black mayors before 1975, and Browning ranks 21 cities according to the extent to which Blacks achieved 'political incorporation' and also gives the year when this was achieved.[17]

TABLE 3
RATES OF BLACK TERRORISM AND BLACK POLITICAL SITUATION
BY CITY

City	Attacks/million	Black representation*	Politics
San Francisco	326	-3.7	Weak incorporation
New Orleans	139	-39.7	–
New York	93	-9.0	Weak incorporation
Cleveland	59	+4.3	Black mayor
Chicago	51	-0.2	–
Newark	39	-8.6	Black mayor
Atlanta	31	-21.0	Black mayor
Baltimore	31	-17.4	–
Los Angeles	30	NA	Black mayor
Detroit	24	-17.2	Black mayor
Washington DC	20	NA	Black mayor
St Louis	20	-0.2	–
Memphis	4	-13.1	–
(Average)	(47)	(-11.4)	

(* Percentage of Seats on City Council minus Black percentage of voting age population)

The evidence suggests that the extent of Black political power in each city was indeed linked to the rate of violence. Of the three cities with higher than expected levels, New York and San Francisco were singled out by Browning as having 'weak political incorporation with blacks not in the dominant coalition'. The third city, New Orleans, was the only city in Patterson's study in which Blacks had no political representation on the city council, despite constituting 39.7 per cent of the city's voting age population. Of the eight cities with below average rates of violence, five had Black mayors.

Revolutionary-left terrorism (1969–77)

Terrorism by revolutionary groups, such as the Weather Underground, began in 1967, peaked in 1971 and then declined erratically. A total of 467 incidents were recorded with bombings being the most common. Support for radical leftist groups was concentrated among students, and a 1970 Gallup survey provides two measures of its extent among this group: the proportion saying they had a highly favourable view of the Weathermen (eight per cent), and the proportion identifying themselves as 'far left' (seven per cent). Using the former measure suggests that about 604,000 students were sympathisers. The Weather Underground (as it renamed itself) was a product of the Students for a Democratic

FIGURE 3
LEFTWING VIOLENCE (1967–1984)

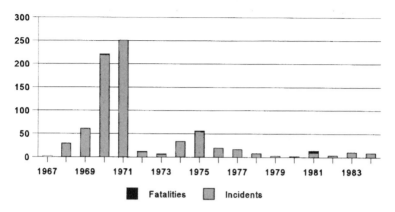

Society (SDS) split in 1969. The SDS was founded in 1962, and grew rapidly as the organizational manifestation of the radical anti-Vietnam movement. At its peak in November 1968, its membership was estimated at between 80,000 and 100,000, although it is suggested that these figures underestimate the group's true strength, since 'for every member, five others take part in SDS activities without paying dues'.[18]

The political issues that drove the student radicals were twofold: the struggle for civil rights and opposition to the Vietnam war – especially the latter. Although American involvement in Indo-China dates back to Truman and increased significantly under Kennedy, it did not become an issue in American politics until the 1964 election. As the military and political situation deteriorated, President Johnson sent large numbers of troops to Vietnam in an attempt to prevent a communist takeover. This Americanization of the war, beginning in 1965, produced the first real opposition on the campuses and in the media. As the war steadily escalated, so did the dissent. 'In its extent and intensity, the antiwar movement in the United States from 1965 through 1971 was the most significant movement of its kind in the nationn's history'.[19] Eventually, Johnson announced he would not seek a second term, and began to reduce the American involvement in Vietnam. President Nixon, elected with a 'secret plan to end the war', initially re-escalated the conflict by bombing and then invading Cambodia. However, he

continued to withdraw American forces, and the last US troops left
South Vietnam in March 1973.

Anti-abortion terrorism (1977–95)

Anti-abortion terrorism begins circa 1977 and since then, according to
the National Abortion Federation, 160 arson and bombing incidents have
been recorded against abortion clinics. In addition, there have been seven
shootings and one kidnapping. This violence resulted in five deaths and
two persons injured. Figure 4 shows the fluctuation over time.

FIGURE 4
ANTI-ABORTION VIOLENCE (1977–1995)

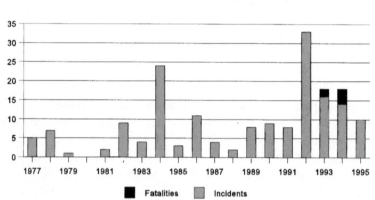

Public opinion on abortion is ambivalent, and the answers are very
obviously affected by how questions are worded.[20] The number who
feel strongly about the issue can be calculated from a 1989 poll, which
found that 32 per cent favoured overturning the *Roe* decision (compared
to 62 per cent who supported it), but that the anti-*Roe* group had more
intense opinions. Since 41 per cent of those who were anti-*Roe* had
'extremely strong' opinions on the issue, this means that 13 per cent of
the general American population were strongly anti-abortion (compared
to 10 per cent who were strongly pro-choice). As numerous studies
have shown, the primary factor predicting attitudes towards abortion is
religion. This is the case not only among the general population, but
also among activists.[21] Obviously, only a small proportion of the 13 per
cent who are strongly opposed to abortion are willing to use violence or

even to engage in any type of political action. There are no national polls that measure the degree of sympathy for extremist anti-abortion groups. However, a survey of a sample of eight conservative Protestant organizations, with a membership of approximately one million, found that 14.4 per cent felt 'very close' to Operation Rescue, suggesting a minimum of 144,000 Protestant sympathizers.[22] Since Scott and Schuman[23] found an equal number of Catholics and Fundamentalists who were strongly opposed to abortion, this implies that the national total would be about 300,000. If the number who attend the annual March for Life rallies is used as an indicator of anti-abortion mobilization, the usual turnout has been between 50,000 and 70,000, with no obvious trend since the 1970s. Operation Rescue, which advocates passive resistance against abortion clinics, claimed to have over 35,000 members in 200 cities and thousands of demonstrators have been arrested for blockading clinics.

Blanchard and Prewitt suggest two ways in which the political context affected the level of violence. First, they argue that there was more violence under Reagan than under Carter, because of the former's administration position on abortion. For example, Attorney General Meese filed a 'friend of the court' brief with the Supreme Court in July 1985, supporting the reversal of *Roe* vs. *Wade*, and in October of the same year Reagan proposed that Congress deny funding to family planning clinics that provided abortion information – the so-called 'gag rule'. 'Whatever the chief executive's actual intentions, the administration's stance on the issue was perceived by some extremists as endorsement and legitimization of private law enforcement or vigilantism.'[24]

Secondly, they argue that Reagan's speeches and writings themselves had an effect: 'The wide circulation of [an anti-abortion] essay ... was followed by a drastic increase in the rate of abortion-related violence, and the president's speeches before anti-abortion groups were interpreted by the violent radicals as tacit approval.' Indeed, his failure to speak out against clinic bombings was also a factor: 'While we cannot prove a direct cause-and-effect relationship between Reagan's silence and abortion-related violence, the correlation is evident in the decline in violence following his eventual public condemnation of it.'[25]

Although there were undoubtably significant differences between Carter and Reagan on abortion, the argument that 'Reagan's stance on

the abortion issue could only have encouraged the increase in violence'
implicitly exaggerates the differences between Reagan and Carter's
policies.[26] Carter repeatedly stated that he was opposed to federal
funding of abortion, and in one televised interview said that 'any
abortion is too much'. The National Organization of Women opposed his
candidacy in 1980, because of his lack of commitment to abortion rights.
During the Carter presidency, the House of Representatives several
times approved restrictions on federal funding of abortions, and voted in
favor of a ban on abortions being performed on military bases using
defense funds. Surely, if Blanshard and Prewitt's argument is accepted,
these actions should also have legitimated anti-abortion violence?

The Bush administration continued Reagan's policies on the
abortion issue. Bush called for *Roe* to be overturned, and twice vetoed
legislation that would have lifted the gag rule. The Justice Department
joined with Operation Rescue in an appeal to stay a preliminary
injunction banning pickets from blocking access to abortion clinics.
Like Reagan, President Bush and Vice-President Quayle spoke to the
National Right to Life Conventions. Yet despite the marked similarities
between the two administrations, abortion violence declined in
Reagan's second term but increased under Bush.

Clinton's campaign rhetoric was strongly pro-choice, and one of his
first acts was to lift abortion restrictions imposed under Reagan and
Bush. Abortion became an option in Federal Employee Health Plans,
and states were required to pay for Medicaid abortions. Under Clinton,
picketing outside abortion clinics was severely restricted by the Freedom
of Access to Clinics Entrance Law. The Justice Department launched an
aggressive probe of the anti-abortion movement in a futile attempt to
discover a national conspiracy of violence against the clinics. Clinton's
pro-choice stance was so uncompromising that he vetoed a bill calling
for the end of partial-birth abortions. If Blanshard and Prewitt's logic is
correct, this should have resulted in a decline in the number of anti-
abortion incidents. In fact, not only did the level of violence remain the
same, but the attacks became more deadly. All six murders by anti-
abortionists have taken place during Clinton's presidency.

Discussion

Based on the American experience, some generalizations can be made
about the political background for terrorism. First, sustained outbreaks
of terrorism are associated with the existence of a substantial body of

sympathizers and supporters. In all the four cases examined, a sizable number of people felt very strongly about some social/political issue – segregation, racial equality, the Vietnam war, abortion – and also felt that the political system ignored, or was hostile to, their concerns.

However, the timing of each outbreak of terrorism appears to coincide with the decline of popular mobilization, rather than with its highpoint. Thus, Klan terrorism followed the decline of the White Citizens Councils, and revolutionary left terrorism increased after the demise of the SDS. Anti-abortion violence increased along with the waning appeal of Operation Rescue. Indeed, one could argue that the failure of direct action tactics – picketing and clinic blockades – galvanized some individuals into resorting to terrorism.[27] Furthermore, there is only a weak relationship between the number of persons who have a favourable view of extremist, violence-prone organizations and the amount of violence that occurs. In Table 4, the number with a highly favourable view of the Klan, the Black Panthers and the Weathermen is compared to the number of terrorist incidents of the corresponding type, and with the number of deaths resulting. For anti-abortion terrorism, the number of persons who feel very close to Operation Rescue is shown. If these relationships are expressed as rates, it appears that revolutionary leftists are most prone to engage in violence, and that Black militants are most likely to engage in deadly violence.

As Rapoport and Weinberg point out in this volume the relationship between violence and elections has been strangely ignored, and I would like to examine further one question they discuss: the role of elections in generating violence. Since elections are the occasions when politicians are most active, one would assume that the effect of their actions will be most marked in election years. Because the electoral process involves appeals to political partisanship with consequent polarization, election years might also be marked by increases in

TABLE 4
RATES OF TERRORIST INCIDENTS AND TERRORIST KILLINGS

	Incidents	Deaths
Klan/Segregationist	354	38
Black Militant	157	79
Revolutionary	782	36
Antiabortion	560	17

Note: rate calculated per million supporters.

extremist violence. To test this hypothesis, all the presidential statements reported in *What They Said* and *Facts on File*, concerning civil rights, the Vietnam war and abortion, were counted and coded.

As expected, more presidential statements were made in election years; the average number of statements on abortion was 5.0 in election years and only 1.1 in non-election years, while for civil rights statements the ratio was 11.0 to 4.5, and for Vietnam statements 26.3 to 24.9. This does not imply that politicians are free to choose what they talk about, since some issues like Vietnam force themselves onto the political agenda. However, election issues are also determined by the candidates who raise issues that they think will help them, and try to ignore issues that hurt them. Using the number of reported statements by presidential candidates as an indicator of electoral salience, civil rights was a significant issue in 1964 and again in 1968, Vietnam in 1968 and abortion in 1984 and 1992. If these dates are compared to the figures showing the fluctuation in different types of terrorism, there is certainly a correlation. White racist violence reaches a peak in 1964, Black violence increased sharply in 1968, and anti-abortion terrorism shows two peaks, in 1984 and 1992.

In addition to the impact of elections, the effect of different administrations upon the incidence of terrorism can be examined. In order to see if there is any consistent relationship, presidential administrations were categorized according to their positions on segregation, racial equality, the Vietnam war and abortion, and then matched against fluctuations in the level of violence (see Table 5). The claim that sympathetic administrations encourage terrorism is clearly false. While terrorism is found under sympathetic administrations in three cases, it failed to occur under such administrations in two other cases. Indeed, hostile administrations are most likely to experience terrorism (five cases), and in only one case did a hostile administration *not* experience terrorism. In the three cases (all involving the Nixon administration), in which the government's position was ambiguous, terrorism declined in one case and increased dramatically in the other two.

As Davies noted in his classic study,[28] the resort to violence is most likely to take place when members of a group have their hopes and aspirations raised, but then become disillusioned with the political process. In three of the cases examined, this 'J curve' effect can be observed. Reagan raised the expectations of the religious right in

TABLE 5
PRESIDENTIAL POLICIES AND TERRORISM

		Annual average*
Segregationist terrorism and presidential policies		
Eisenhower 1953–56	anti-segregationist	13.3
Eisenhower 1957–60	anti-segregationist	25.3
Kennedy 1961–63	anti-segregationist	23.7
Johnson 1964–68	anti-segregationist	60.4
Nixon 1969–74	ambiguous	4.5
Black terrorism and presidential policies		
Johnson 1964–68	pro-racial equality	5.6
Nixon 1969–74	ambiguous	24.7
Radical terrorism and presidential policies		
Johnson 1964–68	pro-Vietnam war	0.0
Nixon 1969–73	Ambiguous	28.6
Anti-abortion terrorism and presidential policies		
Carter 1977–80	Anti-abortion	3.3
Reagan 1981–84	Anti-abortion	9.3
Reagan 1985–88	Anti-abortion	7.3
Bush 1989–92	Anti-abortion	10.0
Clinton 1993–5	Pro-choice	10.3

(* Annual number of attacks by specified type of terrorist group).

general, and anti-abortion activists in particular. Yet as columnist E. J. Dionne pointed out: 'It is striking how much loyalty Ronald Reagan won from this constituency without delivering much to them at all ... There was no school-prayer amendment, no anti-abortion amendment, no school choice program. Most of their core issues were just not dealt with.'[29] Eventually, however, frustration at the lack of results from peaceful political activity led a few individuals to turn to violence.

A similar pattern can be discerned in the anti-Vietnam war movement and the violence carried out by the Weather Underground and other radical groups. The opposition to the war took a variety of forms ranging 'from petitions and rallies and teach-ins and electoral campaigns, to public fasting, draft resistance, and even, towards the end, rudimentary forms of insurrection.'[30] One important fact should be noted about the timing of the anti-war violence: that it mostly occurred *after* 1968. Those who participated in the anti-war movement initially perceived themselves to be successful in changing both public opinion and American policy. Activists saw their efforts culminating in Johnson's March 1968 announcement that he would not run for the presidency: 'Almost immediately following the completion of his speech, students poured out of dormitories all across the nation in

spontaneous demonstrations, congratulating themselves.'[31] One
journalist concluded that the speech was a 'stunning victory' for the
anti-war movement.[32] However, this apparent victory was followed by
the election of Nixon and the continuation of the war. This led to the
'widespread belief [among activists] that the opposition to the war had
failed completely, that Johnson's defeat in 1968 had been meaningless
and empty, that Nixon was simply pursuing the war with equal
determination by other means'. The turn to violence on the part of the
Weathermen grew 'out of a sense of rage and deep frustration ... at the
continuing war in Vietnam'.[33]

The resort to violence by Black militants also fits this pattern. Civil
rights initiatives under Eisenhower, Kennedy and Johnson raised Black
aspirations, but the pace of reforms fell short of what many blacks
wanted, and their frustration led to both widespread rioting and the
emergence of violence-prone Black nationalist and separatist groups.
With the election of Nixon and 'White backlash', the gap between
Black demands and government policy became so great that it led to
widespread violence.

In the case of segregationist violence, a different explanation is
needed for the interplay between politics and violence. Segregationist
violence was essentially reactive both to challenges by the civil rights
movement and to federal intervention on behalf of Southern Blacks, and
the timing of the violence reflects this. The fact that Klan activity
declines in the late 1960s is usually attributed to vigorous law
enforcement by the FBI. Wade points out that another 'factor in the
Klan's deterioration in the late 1960s has received little attention: the
Presidential campaigns of George C. Wallace ... It's now clear that
Wallace's campaigns as the American Independent Party candidate
swallowed a lot of disaffected Klansmen. In fact Wallace offered them
the first really viable alternative to the Klan ... The Wallace campaigns
succesfully skimmed the Southern Klans of their most effective and
economically well-off supporters. There was hardly anything left of the
Southern Klan but leaderless dregs.'[34] Following the 1968 election,
Nixon's 'Southern strategy' – essentially an attempt to co-opt Wallace
voters – further weakened the Klan by providing a political alternative
to those who felt threatened by the changes in race relations.

Since politics is, in some respects, a zero-sum game in which one
group's gain is another's loss, even the most open and responsive
democracy cannot satisfy all groups consistently. For example, Black

demands for civil rights were incompatible with the maintenance of segregation. Groups that lose in the political game – particularly if they lose consistently - are likely to find the resort to violence a tempting option.

NOTES

1. A. Schmid and J. de Graaf, *Violence and Communication: Insurgent Terrorism and the Western News Media* (London and Beverley Hills: Sage, 1982).
2. Extremism can be defined in three ways: statistically, normatively and stylistically. In practice, whichever definition is used the same list of groups and ideologies is produced. See John George and Laird Wilcox, *Communists, Klansmen and Others on the Fringe* (Buffalo, NY: Prometheus, 1992).
3. Wayman Mullins, 'Hate Crimes and the Far Right.' in Kenneth Tunnell (ed.), *Political Crime in Contemporary America* (New York: Garland, 1993) p.155.
4. Michael Kelly, 'Playing with Fire', *New Yorker* 15 July 1996.
5. Dallas Blanchard and Terry Prewitt, *Religious Violence and Abortion* (Gainesville, FL: University of Florida, 1993).
6. The data on terrorist incidents used in this article are taken from a chronology compiled by the author. The chronology uses the FBI's definition of terrorism: 'the unlawful use of force or violence against persons or property to intimidate a government, the civilian population, or any segment thereof, in pursuit of political or social objectives.'
7. Although Kennedy had pledged during his 1960 election campaign to ban racial discrimination in federally-assisted housing, he delayed issuing the order until November 1962.
8. Allan Wolk, *The Presidency and Black Civil Rights* (Rutherford: Fairleigh Dickinson University Press, 1971) pp.232–4.
9. Reed Sarratt, *The Ordeal of Desegregation* (New York: Harper and Row, 1966).
10. Ibid., pp.8, 24–5.
11. Ibid., pp.6–7.
12. The statistics on the number of Klansmen in each state is taken from the House on Un-American Activities Report. The segregationist vote is defined as the vote for the National States Rights Party and 'unpledged Democrats' in 1960, the Goldwater vote in 1964, and the Wallace vote in 1968.
13. Sarratt (note 9) pp.6, 11, 248.
14. For survey data on black public opinion, see Peter Goldman, *Report from Black America* (New York: Simon and Schuster, 1970) and 'Black Mood: More Militant, More Hopeful', *Time*, 6 April, 1970.
15. Both the Panthers and the Black Muslims were drawn largely from the urban underclass. For estimates of the number and characteristics of the two groups see Stephen Bowman, *When the Eagle Screams* (Secaucus, NJ: Carol, 1994); Claude Clegg, *An Original Man: the Life and Times of Elijah Muhammad* (New York: St Martin's Press, 1997); Essien-Udom, *Black Nationalism* (Chicago, IL: University of Chicago Press, 1962); Michael Friedly, *Malcolm X: The Assassination* (New York: Caroll and Graf, 1992); and G. Louis Heath, *Off the Pigs!* (Metuchen, NJ: Scarecrow Press, 1976).
16. Wolk (note 8) p.239.
17. Ernest Patterson, *Black City Politics* (New York: Dodd Mead & Co., 1974); Joint Center for Political Studies, *Profiles of Black Mayors in America* (Washington, DC: 1977); Rufus Browning, *Racial Politics in American Cities* (New York: Longman, 1990) p.222.
18. Kirkpatrick Sale, *SDS* (New York: Random House, 1973); and Jack Newfield, *A Prophetic Minority* (New York: New American Library, 1966).

19. Melvin Small, *Johnson, Nixon and the Doves* (New Brunswick: Rutgers University Press, 1988) p.1.
20. In a 1980 poll when respondents were first asked if they supported a constitutional ban on abortions, 62 per cent were opposed while 29 per cent were in favour, but when asked if they supported a constitutional amendment 'protecting the life of the unborn child', 50 per cent were in favour and only 39 per cent opposed. Barbara Craig, *Abortion and American Politics* (Chatham, NJ: Chatham House, 1993) pp. 264–71.
21. Donald Granberg, 'The Abortion Activists', *Family Planning Perspectives* (13 July/Aug. 1981) pp.157–63; James Guth, 'Cut from the whole cloth: Antiabortion mobilization among religious activists.' in Ted Jelen and Marthe Chandler (eds), *Abortion Politics in the US and Canada* (Westport, CT: Praeger, 1994); Kristin Luker, *Abortion and the Politics of Motherhood* (Berkeley, CA: University of California Press, 1984).
22. Guth, ibid.
23. Jaquelin Scott and Howard Schuman, 'Attitude Strength and Social Action in the abortion dispute.' *American Sociological Review* 53 October 1988, 785–93.
24. Blanchard and Prewitt (note 5) p.271.
25. Ibid., p.270.
26. Reagan brought the anti-abortion movement into the Republican Party, and the 1980 abortion platform called for a constitutional amendment banning abortion. For a somewhat hysterical account of the power shift within the Republican Party, see Tanya Melich, *The Republican War Against Women* (New York: Bantam Books, 1996).
27. After the decline of Operation Rescue, some activists turned to violence. The history of one individual convicted of a series of arson attacks against abortion clinics was given in the *Washington Post* (11 Feb. 1998, p.A6): 'He was among the defendants in a civil suit filed in 1988 by several Washington state clinics seeking to enjoin protestors from blockading their facilities, and in 1990 an injunction against such blockades was issued. Officials say that Andrews then began his campaign of arson attacks.'
28. James C. Davies, *When Men Revolt and Why* (New York: Free Press, 1971).
29. Cited in William Martin, *With God on our Side: the Rise of the Religious Right in America* (New York: Broadway Books, 1996).
30. Thomas Powers, *The War at Home: Vietnam and the American People* (New York: Grossman, 1973) p.xiii.
31. Small (note 19), p.158.
32. Jonathan Schell, *The Time of Illusion* (New York: Vintage, 1976) p.18.
33. Powers (note 30) p.xix; and Nancy Zaroulis and Gerald Sullivan, *Who Spoke Up? American Protest against the War in Vietnam* (Garden City, NY: Doubleday, 1984) p.314.
34. Wyn Wade, *The Fiery Cross: The Ku Klux Klan in America* (New York: Simon and Schuster, 1987) p.364.

16

Democracy and the Black Riots: Rethinking the Meaning of Political Violence in Democracy

ABRAHAM H. MILLER and EMILY SCHAEN

The findings of two presidential commissions have dominated the understanding of the Black urban riots of the 1960s and correspondingly the general understanding of the causes of political violence. The Kerner and Eisenhower commissions each explained the causes of the riots in terms of the social science orthodoxy of the time. The riots were seen as violent responses by a community that had experienced persistent and continual frustration as a result of economic deprivation wrought by White racism. The deprivation-frustration-aggression model of violence was superimposed as a causal explanation of the riots. Social science and the popular media extolled this as the definitive understanding of the riots. Yet over the past 30 years this model has not explained empirical findings and has fallen from grace, especially among political scientists. Our research shows that even within the context of the commission reports there was evidence of other, but less politically palatable, explanations. In addition, there was the overarching issue of the occurrence of violence in democracies. Riots, like terrorism, more commonly occur within democracies than in non-democratic governmental systems. We suggest that viewed in this context, the Black urban riots are not a deviant occurrence but part of a common syndrome of violence in democracies. These riots, like others that preceded them, need to be viewed within the historical framework of the role of political violence in democracies and most specifically how democracies respond to political violence.

Introduction: an orthodoxy of explanation

Three decades after America's Black ghettos exploded in violence, the findings of two national commissions that investigated these events remain virtually unchallenged.[1] From diagnosing their causes to prescribing remedies to prevent future outbursts, the commissions' works have become, for both the popular media and the academic community, the defining statements of these events.

Each decennial anniversary of the Kerner Commission report, the best known of these reports, has been an opportunity for a public reaffirmation of the commissions findings, a rekindling of its dire predictions about the future of racial violence in America, and a lamenting of America's failure to implement the social programmes that the commission advocated as a means of solving America's racial problems. Every subsequent outburst of riot behaviour has been viewed as a confirmation of the report in all of its dimensions, from its pessimistic predictions of the future course of race relations to its original analysis of the riots as an expression of Black anger wrought from the frustration of racial discrimination and economic deprivation.

Similarly, the Eisenhower Commission, whose investigations followed that of the Kerner inquiry and reached far beyond the violence of the Black community, saw the violence of the 1960s as part of the core of American society. In an unprecedented and initially controversial fashion, what both reports did was to hold the larger society responsible for the outbursts of violence that have become an indelible part of our popular memory of that period.

The actual rioters themselves were thus depicted as no more than mere instruments of a flawed social structure. By indicting White racism as the culprit for the condition of the inner city, the burning and looting of American cities during the long hot summers of the mid-1960s was characterized as an outgrowth of racism. The Kerner Commission's most famous statement was that there was not one America but two, one that was White and prosperous and the other that was Black and neglected. Both components were separate and clearly unequal. The riots were the culmination of pent up Black rage produced by racism. The riots were a manifestation of a larger power struggle between Blacks seeking an end to the political and economic exploitation concomitant with racism and Whites seeking to preserve economic advantage.

The same theme is echoed in the subsequent Eisenhower Commission report, especially in the forward to Skolnick's *Politics of Protest*. Here, Price M. Cobbs and William H. Greier describe the Black urban riots and the student movement as attempts to bring about social reform indistinguishable from that attempted in the Boston Tea Party.[2] The riots, consequently, are covered in the mystique of one of the great undertakings of revolutionary America. Those who looted and burned their way through Los Angeles, Detroit, Newark, Chicago and lesser places become indistinguishable from those who resisted the British

Crown and from those who resisted the racial oppression of the deep South by meeting the force of the police truncheon with the dignity of non-violence.

The rioters' behaviour was interpreted as a manifestation of an observed clinical phenomenon known as Black rage, a potential for violence born of oppression and discrimination and widely dispersed throughout the Black community.[3] White racism caused the riots, in this rendition, and the end of White racism could prevent them in the future. The riots were not a law and order and social control issue, but an issue of appropriate versus inappropriate social policy. The riots were the consequence of persistent and visible racial degradation imposed by White society. The rioters were not criminals but victims in need of understanding.

With the imprimatur of both the federal government and distinguished social scientists, these ideas were not received as partisan opinions or speculations, but as conclusions emanating from careful scientific research. If ever there were a social science orthodoxy concerning any phenomenon, this was it, but not only was this the social science orthodoxy of the late 1960s; it would be an orthodoxy renewed with the passage of time and with each eruption of riot behaviour in the Black community.

An even stronger consensus was reached concerning what policies should be undertaken to prevent future riots. For while the academic community and most of the members of the commissions held tenaciously to these explanations of the riots as scientific fact, not everyone was in agreement. President Lyndon Baines Johnson found the Kerner Commission report too sweeping in its indictment of American society and refused to accept it, a response that would be pointed to later as responsible for the continuing problems of the inner city. The McCone Commission, which investigated the Los Angeles riots, argued that young, alienated newcomers to Los Angeles were responsible for the riots, and managed by invoking an appeal to the 'riff raff' notion of rioters to offend most liberals and members of the Black community.[4] Yet the McCone Commission advocated policies basically indistinguishable from those of the other commissions. President Johnson maintained a strong commitment to social programmes for the inner cities. When it came to policy advocacy, views about the causes of the riots had little to do with the policy prescriptions to prevent their future occurrence.

When it comes to interpreting the causes of post-1960s episodic outbreaks of violence in the Black community, the claim is made that the failure to implement social programmes as the Kerner Commission advocated is responsible for each such conflagration. These conclusions are as political and as flawed as the Kerner Commission's original explanation of the causes of the riots, for this conclusion assumes that there was no subsequent investment in programmes for the inner cities after President Johnson rejected the Kerner Commission report. Moreover, they further assume that these programmes worked. The latter is a most difficult assumption in the wake of overwhelming bipartisan calls at all levels of government for welfare reform, and the growing approach within some components of the civil rights community to replace government programmes with private capital. One testimony to that policy was seen on 15 January 1999, when the Reverend Jesse Jackson, flanked by President Clinton, and with the support of major American corporations, was on Wall Street appealing for private capital and investment outreach for the inner city. Our purpose here is not to enter into a debate over the viability of 'Great Society' type programmes, but to note the concomitant relationship between the persistent justification of these programmes and the interpretation of the causes of the riots.

After a Simi Valley, California, jury on 29 April 1992 acquitted police charged with the beating of Rodney King, a Black motorist who led Los Angeles police on a high speed chase in an effort to avoid a traffic citation, Los Angeles exploded in riots. Nationally syndicated and respected journalist Meg Greenfield attested to the stature of the Kerner Commission report when she told her readers of her initial reaction to the maelstrom that ripped through Los Angeles. Greenfield's immediate reaction was to reach for the Kerner Commission report to search for an explanation of the riots. As she wrote, 'Not surprisingly there were plenty of echoes that still rang true, discouraging evidence of how little things that needed changing have changed.'[5] Greenfield was not alone in hearing echoes from the past and seeing the way to prevent future riots lay in the Great Society programmes of the past. Vesta Kimble, spokesperson for the Milton Eisenhower Foundation, issued a silver anniversary update of the Kerner Commission Report imploring Congress to enact a 10-year plan that would allocate no less than $30 billion annually to job training and education to solve the problems of the inner city.[6]

Such clarion calls to bridge the racial divide appeared to ignore the good news of 25 years of racial progress that saw the emergence of a prominent and successful Black middle class, without the massive infusion, for two and a half decades, of federal spending. The racial divide was closing – and rapidly. The predictions of a persistent separation of two societies, one Black and one White, and the occurrence of riots as a common feature of the inner-city summer, proved false. Instead, the future saw the arrival of a Black middle class. Nearly half of all African-American households are now firmly in the middle class, and 40 per cent of African-American households own their own homes. In one generation the number of Black suburbanites tripled. These are not segregated suburbs, as six in 10 White Americans now report having Black neighbours. Two out of three Whites and eight in 10 Blacks count members of the opposite race as friends. Interracial marriage, once a taboo, is no longer an issue for half of the White community. From 1963 to 1993, America witnessed a 120 per cent increase in intermarriage.[7]

In terms of its predictions, the two commission reports were wrong. And as we illustrate below, prediction was not the only component of its theoretical value that must be re-examined, for if the reports failed to *predict*, did they also fail to explain? Simply because the inner cities tend to be areas of economic deprivation and the riots occurred in those areas, did those social scientists who wove a theoretical explanation of the 'causes' of the riots really do more than conclude *post hoc, ergo propter hoc?* And if the predictions and explanations are as flawed as we argue they are, why has the status of the reports not suffered accordingly?

The latter answer rests in politics. Bad news on race, as Shelby Steele has noted, serves certain vested interests with strong political agendas.[8] Moreover, bad news on race, like bad news generally, has a far greater appeal to the media.

Seeking other modes of explanation

Although social science theories are far more vulnerable to challenge than those in the natural sciences, such theories, when sustained by a predisposition of what people want or need to believe, are far more difficult to disprove. The standards of evidence are not just scientific ones, (or scientific ones locked in the sociology of knowledge, where old theories are maintained simply because of a conservative process in the evaluation of new evidence); rather, the standards of evidence confront a situation where social science functions not as the conduit for objective data, but as the means to legitimate political interests.

To understand more fully the implications of this, one should consider that from an historical perspective the Black urban riots of the 1960s are the deviant cases. The more common riot scenario in America has been one where the White community, often with the active or tacit approval of the police, have rioted against the Black community. Some of these riots were directed by elite elements of the community and designed to reassert and reaffirm the normative structure of White dominance. Others were unorganized, spontaneous undertakings of the lower elements of White society where the violence was often worse than in the 'elite' riots. And in the 1960s, non-violent civil rights demonstrators in the American South encountered yet another type of riot, the police riot, the use of civil violence under cover of law to deny the Black community its basic civil rights and the use of civil liberties to communicate its grievances.

If riot behaviour can be subsumed under some general social science theory, then it would make sense that there is not going to be one theory that explains the behaviour of Blacks and a different theory that explains the behaviour of Whites. If there is a general deprivation-frustration- aggression model that leads to violence, as the commission reports note, then this model should apply to all rioters, White or Black.

Consider then from this perspective that the commission reports provide an explanation of the Black urban riots by seeing the members of the Black community as inadvertent participants directed by social forces beyond their control. To us, the absurdity of this argument is best noted when it is applied to the riots of the White community. Would one argue that the lowest elements of the White community, the people who commonly rioted against the Black community, the typical scenario in American history, where directed by social forces beyond their control?[9] No one has attempted to make such an argument. This is, perhaps, because the fatuousness of such an explanation is far and away too obvious when applied to the White community, as absurd as it should be when applied to the Black community.

The commission reports are most compromised intellectually in their failure to consider riots as a form of political violence – like terrorism as an expression of political violence – occur most commonly in democracies. The only difference was that Blacks, traditionally the victims of political violence, became the perpetrators. Yet riots themselves are part of the political landscape in democracies.

From our perspective, the commissions also failed to note that rioting itself is also a trace finding. (The McCone Commission is the one singular exception in this regard.) Although typically one refers to the Black community as rioting, the Black community did not riot. In Los Angeles' formidable and severe Watts riot, for example, less than 2 per cent of the immediate community was involved in the riot.[10] To deduce from the larger community the characteristics and motivations of this unrepresentative behaviour is to commit an error in deductive reasoning. Similarly, to infer from the rioters' behaviour the experiences of the larger community is an equivalent error in reasoning.[11]

The commissions sought, as did many social scientists of that era, to explain the riots in the popular social science thinking of the time. This meant trying to explain the riots in terms of relative or absolute deprivation. Subsequently, empirical investigations have failed to provide confirmation for this theoretical orientation.[12]

Indeed, the relative and absolute deprivation theorists failed to deal adequately with the issue of why the most severe riots occurred in the urban North rather than the rural south where any form of deprivation, relative or absolute, was far and away higher. As obvious and repugnant as discrimination in the North was, it was tepid when compared to the deep South, especially in its most rural and backward counties with large African-American populations.

Our contention is that this very factor should have prompted both the commissions and the social scientists of the day to take a look at more macro-level factors. If one looks at American democracy, however imperfectly practised when it came to the Black population, then the disproportionate occurrence of the number of riots and their severity in the urban North becomes far and away more comprehensible. Theorists who looked at the macro-level factor of democracy itself would have easily predicted that the occurrence of riots as northern events was not an anomaly. Indeed, that is what one would have expected, had one argued that riots are more likely to occur where an aggrieved group has *greater*, not less, access to the political system.

Despite the problems northern Blacks faced in dealing with the ambiguous and inconsistent world of northern racism, Blacks were an emergent political force in the North, especially in areas where racial segregation led to safe constituencies for Black politicians. Even in those instances such as Richard J. Daley's Chicago machine where for a time White aldermen ran Black neighbourhoods, the demands of voting constituents could not be ignored totally, and ultimately the machine succumbed to the reality of having Blacks represented by people of their own race.[13] All of this stood in the sharpest contrast to the Southern experience were a repressive political oligarchy that played the race card to preserve its dominance kept Blacks from having access to the basic democratic rights and liberties. The oligarchy continued to exercise its dictatorial powers over Blacks through the unrestrained and unaccountable use of the police power at every level of government, and for a time the federal government acquiesced in this system as when federal law enforcement viewed the indiscriminate beating of Blacks on federal property as a matter for local law enforcement.

Had the purveyors of the deprivation-frustration-aggression model of the riots looked not at social and economic variables but at fundamental political variables, they would have seen that both the lower frequency and severity of riots in the South were not aberrations that had to be ignored but were a fundamental component of any theoretical explanation. Moreover, the major Black riots took place in those large northern cities where as a community Blacks were better off, indicated by the rise and triumph of Black political leaders in America's largest cities. Beyond that, riots were more likely to occur in those cities were Blacks were less likely to experience unemployment and where the income differential between Blacks and Whites was smallest.[14]

Riots and democracies

To understand riots, we argue that one must quite simply come to grips with an obvious political rather than socioeconomic fact: across time and geography democracies are more likely to have riots than are non-democratic regimes. The conditions under which Blacks lived in the North, however imperfect, were more akin to living in a democracy than not, while the conditions faced by their kinsmen in the South were more like those experienced in a repressive regime. Consequently, it is not surprising that the Black urban riots disproportionately occurred in those parts of America were Blacks had the most vital community structures, the greatest impact on the political process, and the least (relatively speaking) economic deprivation.

A similar line of reasoning can be found in the path-breaking work of Eubank and Weinberg, which focuses on the relationship between terrorism and democracy as distinct from riots and democracy. Using empirical statistical analysis, Eubank and Weinberg found that both terrorist groups and terrorist violence were more likely to be found operating in democratic as opposed to non-democratic settings.[15]

In the same theoretical vein, but far and away more in accord with the focus of this research as it relates to the relationship between riots and democracy, is the work of Tilly, Tilly and Tilly.[16] They looked at the relationship between repressive and democratic eras in the same countries, over time, and riots as a dependent variable. Examining the democratic and repressive regimes in France, Germany and Italy during the nineteenth and twentieth centuries, the researchers observed that repressive regimes were more successful in preventing acts of civil violence.

During the two regimes of Louis Napoleon (Napoleon III), first as president from 1848–51 and then as self-styled emperor (1852–71), and during the Vichy and Nazi periods from 1940 to 1944, there was a massive decline in the incidents of collective violence in France as compared to the preceding periods of democratic regimes. Similarly, the ascendance of fascism in Italy under the dictator Benito Mussolini (1925–45) brought with it a sharp decrease in collective violence. In Germany, collective violence surged during the Weimar period (1919–32) and decreased dramatically with the coming to power of the Nazi dictatorship (1933–45). Of course, parenthetically, one might note that the Nazis were responsible for a good deal of the collective violence in Weimar and once they achieved power they created and exercised a state monopoly on violence.

Although we social scientists take great pride in our arrival at conclusions that are counterintuitive, this one seems extraordinarily obvious: a riot met by a determined and disciplined police or military force that is unaccountable to any constituency other than the rulers can scatter rioters to the wind. Similarly, the expectation of harsh, determined and violent police action is itself a deterrent to civil violence.

The Canadian military historian D. J. Goodspeed makes a similar observation. Writing about *coup d'états* and not civil violence (although a carefully reading of Goodspeed in terms of the partitioning of the daily events of the February 1917 uprising in St Petersburg shows numerous acts of riots and civil violence), Goodspeed argues that the success or failure of a coup is a function of the ability of a single company of armed men to stand firm, adhere to discipline and fight.[17] Goodspeed's characterization of events seems inconsistent with conventional wisdom of great surges in dynamic political and social forces that inevitably change history. Rather, Goodspeed reminds us of something we wish not to be reminded of – the role of chance, played by those determined to raise their rifles repeatedly and fire into the mob.[18] Lenin seems to have understood this role, fleeing to Finland on the eve of the October 1917 uprising and returning only in response to extreme difficulties.

In a quantitative and comparative study of those countries with the greatest frequency of riots, Denise Di Pasquale and Edward L. Glaeser found that democracies more than any other form of government are most likely to have riots.[19] Thus, their broad-based comparative study lends confirmation to that of Tilly, Tilly and Tilly. Gurr found that regime coercive control is a fundamental component in preventing collective violence, although Gurr saw the relationship as curvilinear rather than varying directly.[20] Tilly, Tilly and Tilly sum up the importance of repression in preventing rioting: 'collective violence ... was rare under conditions of heavy repression, not because few people were aggrieved or because the state eschewed violence, but because collective action grew too costly for any group which did not already have the state's protection.'[21]

Democracies are not only more likely to incur riots; they are more likely to be less effectual in containing them. Both the Kerner and Eisenhower commissions noted the point, but were reluctant to pursue it with any emphasis. Riots that could have been contained quickly grew out of control because of a failure of police response. The amount and severity of force a democratic government can use to contain a riot is in no small measure a function of its ability to find both legitimacy and constituency support for such measures. And while riot containment is a matter for local law enforcement, increasingly in America the constituency will extend far beyond the domains of local politics smack into the glare of the television camera. This is especially true when these are acts of collective violence with a strong ethnic dimension. Such political pressure, along with the fact that in a democracy the rioters themselves will have a constituency, severely limit the actions police can take.

In a study of three riots, Eugene H. Methvin argues that some of the most violent riots of the 1960s were those where the police exercised the most restraint in response to early signs of disorder. In Los Angeles (Watts), Newark and Detroit the police immediately retreated from the sight of disorder.[22] In Newark, Director of Police Dominick Spina reported that when he arrived on the scene of the riot, he found his police officers 'crouching behind vehicles, hiding in corners and lying on the ground'.[23] In Detroit, the police removed street cordons, permitting the looters to have freer access to their booty. Such passivity gave looting a green light as reflected in the observation of one participant in the enterprise:[24] 'Those first hours, when the cops pulled out, were just like a holiday … All the kids wandered around sayin' real amazed like, "The fuzz is scard; they ain't goin' to do nothin"'.[25] Another participant told of the first brick unintentionally shattering the window of the Esquire Clothing Store. At first the small cluster of people stood aghast. Expecting the police to return, the crowd waited. A few young men then ventured into the store. Then more followed. After 20 minutes, when a police cruiser approached the store with its siren blaring, 50 looters fled in panic. The police, however, did not stop. They turned the corner and drove off. A cry went up from the dismayed crowd, 'The police ain't doin' nothin'! Let's get what we want!' With that, small groups of young men smashed windows and began looting.[26]

In Watts, the LA police found that the riot techniques in which they had trained were inappropriate to the kind of rioting they encountered. The police had been trained to disperse large crowds through close-rank marching with batons and shields. Instead, they faced small groups of rioters who carried out sporadic acts of violence fleeing from one street corner to another.[27] Instead of responding immediately and with ingenuity to this unanticipated tactic, the police responded to the ideology of the time that the police presence itself would exacerbate the violence and that the best way to contain the conflagration was for the police to withdraw. Even after that tactic proved only to give encouragement to the rioters, Chief William Parker, concerned about the criticism of his department as harbouring racism, was reluctant to take decisive action. Only after the riot spread, grew in numbers and intensified did Chief Parker give permission for a mobile processing unit to be established for the implementation of mass arrests. Once the procedure of mass arrests and on-site processing was implemented, the rioting began to abate dramatically, leading some to conclude that implementing that tactic much earlier would have had a profound impact on the course of the riots.[28]

Even so, in 1992 the Rodney King riots witnessed that the LA police had either learned nothing or were reluctant to implement what they had learned. More so than in Watts, the police abdicated their responsibility, leaving the Korean-American community, who were merchants in the riot torn area, vulnerable to the mob. Heavily armed Koreans, positioned on the roofs of their stores, as if they were a picture from a stockade under siege in the nineteenth century West, stood as testimony to the abandonment of the police responsibility to maintain public order. Some of the Korean small businessmen were wiped out in the process, and news and pictures of their plight led to anti-American riots in South Korea.

By 1992, more so than in Chief Parker's day, the Los Angeles police not only faced the fall-out from the Rodney King episode, but they also faced a variety of administrative, social and political factors that grew directly out of the democratic process and affected the manner in which the police conducted their business. The Los Angeles police by 1992 were under the control of a civilian board which reported to Mayor Tom Bradley.[29]

A consummate politician, Bradley drew support from all segments of Los Angeles' racially segmented community. Yet the Rodney King episode eroded police legitimacy in Bradley's own African-American community more than anywhere else. The civil disorder erupted in this community in the wake of the not guilty verdicts of the police who beat King, verdicts handed down by a predominately White, suburban, Simi Valley jury. It would be difficult to imagine that the riots did not have tacit support of large segments of the Black community.

Even before the riots, police had stopped some of their more aggressive policing tactics, especially the controversial 'profile stops', where those who fit the generalized description of criminals, usually young Blacks and Hispanics, were stopped and questioned without additional justification. These aggressive procedures have been upheld by the courts, but the police, in an attempt to change their public image, reduced their aggressiveness, attempting to find a middle ground between protecting the community from crime and being responsive to the concerns of the Black and Hispanic communities.[30]

The attempt to find a middle ground ultimately proved disastrous in the Rodney King riots, as the media captured the LAPD retreating from confrontations with individual rioters and looters who could easily have been arrested. Los Angeles's Webster Commission concluded that failure of the police to react was a primary reason for the violence and disorder.[31]

Both Los Angeles riots (although nearly three decades apart) illustrate not only the potential for riots to erupt in democracies, but the intrusion of political and constituency issues on their containment. Riots, like forest fires, start from preconditions. As the ability of fires to grow and spread and resist containment are a function of the abilities and resources at the disposal of firefighters, so too the ability of riots to grow, expand and persist is a function of the resources at the disposal of the police and their willingness to use them. Even the Kerner Commission report noted that a common pattern of violence usually began with rioters testing the waters to see how the police would react. When it became clear that the police would not bring enough force to deal effectively with the initial acts of violence, the violence grew in scope, duration, intensity and by the number of those subsequently emboldened to engage in such acts.[32]

Every society has an aggrieved element. The willingness and ability of the aggrieved to go into the streets and precipitate acts of civil disorder and bring them to a point where they can virtually bring an entire city to its knees and close its international airport to commerce, as the Rodney King riot did in Los Angeles, is largely a function of the intrusion of democratic politics and interest group sensitivities on the police power. Nothing explains the virulence of the 1992 Los Angeles riots as does the failure of police countermeasures.

Where the police power of the state was either prevented from acting, or where it sided with the rioters, civil disorder often turned to revolution. Contemporary experiences from Iran and the Philippines illustrate the inability or unwillingness of the police and military to put down riots, and allowing them to evolve into acts of revolution. The same case can be made for the collapse of the bourgeois government that retreated to the Winter Palace in St Petersburg in 1917.

Riots are not a single event but a series of events sliced up into temporal, psychological, geographic and political dimensions. To look at riots solely in terms of alleged underlying factors, as the deprivation-frustration-aggression school has done, is to ignore the fact that the flame of civil disorder once ignited can also be readily extinguished. Those who participate in riots often attend them for different reasons and in the course of time, through an unfolding riot, the participants' own motivations and behaviours can change. Part of that change will be a direct consequence of the efficiency and severity of the police response.

Such statements do not sit well with those who have argued in the face of disconfirming data that repression enhances the conflagration rather than ends it. Those who seek to use the riots as a means of documenting racism and exploitation, and as a means of arguing for the advancement of a political agenda based on an expansion of social programmes, find the riots both serve to sustain that agenda and give it credibility. There is little that would work so strongly against such purposes as the notion that riots are frequently episodic events that can be easily contained by a significant and efficient use of force, or that riots are a price that one pays for living in a democratic society. And in such societies, even the legitimate use of force by the civic authority is subject to interest group pressure and general political considerations.

Such analysis cannot be readily dismissed, for even the much praised Kerner Commission report noted, however hesitantly, that rioters do test the waters of police response. Perhaps it appears easy to dismiss such thinking when it comes from the observations and experiences of Los Angeles Police chief Daryl Gates or from *Reader's Digest* editor Eugene Methvin. But we do not think so – not only because such analysis can be found in the Kerner Commission report itself, but because it is also found in the observations and analysis of Morris Janowitz, one of the leading social scientists of our age.

As Janowitz notes, in speaking of the urban riots of the 1960s:

> There can be no doubt that the countermeasures employed deeply influence the course of rioting – even in prolonging the period of reestablishing law and order … Differences in police strategy are partly the result of conscious policy, since law enforcement officials have a past record to draw on, and since they are continuously alerted to the possibility of riots.[33]

Janowitz underscores this by noting the tolerant policy toward rioters and looters in Detroit, a conscious decision by Ray Girardin, the Police Commissioner, who believed erroneously that the local civilian Black leadership could itself contain the violence.

Riots, like political terrorism, are part and parcel of democratic society. They are the price societies are willing to pay whenever liberty is valued above order. But riots are also indicative of what happens when collective violence is permitted to escalate through slices of time without significant opposition. Understanding riots thus requires far and away more than an investigation of underlying social forces. Understanding requires an appreciation for the simple fact that countermeasures do influence the course riots take, either in facilitating or making more difficult the ultimate re-establishment of law and order.

Future research should revisit the major riots of the 1960s, looking at police logs, policy, the speed and efficiency in which counter-measures were implemented and their ultimate impact on the course of the riots. If riots are not single events, but events divisible by narrow segments of time and events to which participants come because of different motivations and follow different courses of action through those segments of time, then those events need to be studied in terms of the way in which countermeasures hindered or facilitated the ultimate development of a riot. For now, the best summary and anecdotal evidence available strongly suggests that countermeasures, more than any other variable, might just be the ultimate determinant of the development, scope, intensity and duration of a riot.

ACKNOWLEDGEMENTS

Some of the ideas presented here are from a presentation by Abraham H. Miller to the International Sociological Association World Congress, Montreal, 1998. The support of the Charles P. Taft Foundation, University of Cincinnati, is gratefully acknowledged.

NOTES

1. The best known and most prominent of these reports is *The Report of the National Advisory Commission on Civil Disorders* (New York: E. P. Dutton and Co., *New York Times*, p.b. edn, 1968). The commission was chaired by Illinois governor Otto Kerner, whose name has become synonymous with the report; hence, it is known as the Kerner Commission report. A now less remembered but equally important commission that ultimately defined the causes of violence in America in the 1960s was the National Commission on the Causes and Prevention of Violence, chaired by Milton Eisenhower, university president and brother of President Dwight D. Eisenhower. Its work was seen in the assembling of a series of task force reports. Most prominent among these was Jerome Skolnick's, *The Politics of Protest* (New York: Clarion, 1969). Although the work of the Eisenhower Commission extended beyond the Black urban riots, the commission paid significant attention to this phenomenon, yielding essentially the same conclusions as did the Kerner Commission.
2. Price M. Cobbs and William H. Grier in Skolnick (note 1) p.xi.
3. Ibid., pp.xiii and xiv.
4. Governor's Commission on the Los Angeles Riots, *Violence in the City – An End or Beginning?* Reprinted in Robert M. Fogelson (ed.), *The Los Angeles Riots* (Salem, NH: Ayer, 1988).
5. Meg Greenfield, 'Then and Now', *The Washington Post*, 4 May 1992, p.A23.

6. Chris Reidy, 'A Dream Deferred', *The Boston Globe*, 4 April 1993, Focus Section, pp.69–72.
7. Business Wire Inc., via Lexis-Nexis Information Systems, 'Reader's Digest Highlights Good News on Race', 23 Feb. 1998, p.2. The data are based on Stephan and Abigail Thernstrom, *America in Black and White* (New York: Simon and Shuster, 1997).
8. Shelby Steele, 'Race and Responsibilities', *The Wall Street Journal*, 18 Jan. 1999, p.A18. See also Chester E. Finn Jr. and Michael J. Petrilli, 'Education Ratings Employ Double Standards', ibid., p.A18.
9. For a discussion of the riot behaviour of Whites against Blacks see Hadley Cantril, *The Psychology of Social Movements* (New York: John Wiley and Sons, 1967) esp. chs 4–6. See also Hugh Davis Graham and Ted Robert Gurr (eds), *Violence in America: Historical and Comparative Perspectives* (New York: Signet, 1969) chs 10, 11 and 14.
10. Governor's Commission on the Los Angeles Riots (note 4) p.1.
11. Some argue, as did co-panelist Professor Peter Merkle at the 1998 World Congress of Sociology meetings, that while the rioters themselves represent a trace element that is insignificant, the significance of the riots is to be found in their support in the larger community. We find this a most speculative, unempirical and unimpressive interpretation, for if the deprivation–frustration–aggression formulation cannot be supported in empirical investigations of those who manifested riot behaviour, how can it possibly be imputed to those who did not participate but only gave verbal affirmation, in retrospect, to some pollster? This must be one of the strangest analyses of the relationship between a psychological experience and its behavioural manifestation. Those who actually manifested the behaviour are not as significant as those who did not but, perhaps, wish they had. One could only imagine Pavlov arguing that the dogs that salivated were not as important as those who did not but who barked when the others did so. Regrettably, this is the kind of thinking that pervades a politically charged issue where it is vital and necessary at every intellectual price to provide the proper political spin.
12. For a detailed analysis of this issue see Abraham H. Miller, 'Black Civil Violence and White Social Science: Sense and Nonsense', *Journal of Contingencies and Crisis Management* 7/1 (1999) pp.20–29.
13. Milton Rakove, *Don't Make No Waves ... Don't Back No Losers: An Insider's Analysis of the Daley Machine* (Bloomington: Indiana University Press, 1975) pp.271ff.
14. Stanley Lieberson and Arnold R. Silverman, 'The Precipitant and Underlying Conditions of Race Riots', in Allen D. Grimshaw (ed.), *Racial Violence in the United States* (Chicago: Aldine, 1969) pp.365–6.
15. William Lee Eubank and Leonard Weinberg, 'Does Democracy Encourage Terrorism?', *Terrorism and Political Violence* 6/4 (Winter 1994) pp.417–43. As with any empirical investigation in the social sciences, Eubank and Weinberg's work raise some interesting commentaries. See in this regard Abraham H. Miller, 'Comment on Terrorism and Democracy', ibid., pp.435–9; Christopher Hewitt, 'Some Skeptical Comments on Large Cross-National Studies', ibid., pp 439–41; and William Eubank and Leonard Weinberg, 'A Response to Miller and Hewitt', ibid., pp.442–3.
16. Charles Tilly, Louise Tilly and Richard Tilly, *The Rebellious Century* (Cambridge: Harvard University Press, 1975).
17. D.J. Goodspeed, *The Conspirators* (Toronto: Macmillian of Canada,1983)..
18. Ibid., pp.225–58.
19. Denise DiPasquale and Edward L. Glaeser, 'The Los Angeles Riot and the Economics of Urban Unrest', *Journal of Economics* 4 (1998) p.63.
20. Ted Robert Gurr, *Why Men Rebel* (Princeton: Princeton University Press, 1970) p.364.
21. Tilly *et al.* (1975) p.256.
22. Eugene H. Methvin, *The Riot Makers* (New Rochelle: Arlington House, 1970) p.478.
23. Kerner Commission report (note 1) p.3.
24. Morris Janowitz, 'The Changing Meaning of "Racial" Violence', in Grimshaw (note 14) p.505.
25. Quoted in Methvin (note 22) p.101.

26. Ibid., p.100.
27. Daryl F. Gates, *Chief* (New York: Bantam, 1992).
28. Ibid., p.101.
29. William H. Webster and Hubert Williams, *The City in Crisis: Report by the Special Advisor to the Board of Police Commissioners* (Los Angeles: n.p., 1992) – hereafter the 'Webster Report'.
30. Ibid., pp.14–21.
31. Ibid., p.24.
32. Kerner Commission (note 1) p.485.
33. Janowitz (note 24) p.505.

17

Conclusions

DAVID C. RAPOPORT and
LEONARD WEINBERG

At the beginning of the twenty-first century, communism, fascism, national socialism and lesser ideological blueprints for human betterment largely have passed from the scene, no longer capable of exciting genuine enthusiasm of any but small handfuls of individuals. It is difficult to imagine that only a few years ago these ideological blueprints, promoted by various political organizations, captivated millions and won converts among our most prominent artists, scientists and intellectuals. For reasons that have become obvious to virtually all, disillusionment followed as these ideologies became 'the god that failed'. Is a similar process of disenchantment now at work on democracy?

Recent commentaries in widely circulated periodicals suggest the answer is 'Yes', at least among some intellectuals. For instance, Robert Kaplan and Fareed Zakaria, writing in *The Atlantic Monthly* and *Foreign Affairs* respectively, argue that many new post-Cold War democracies represent transitional stages in their countries' historical experiences.[1] New democracies are often weak and corrupt weigh stations on the road to chaos and secession. Among other things, Kaplan notes that the populations of many Third World democracies are composed disproportionately of young unemployed males, a group which is both highly susceptible to violence (the new democratic South Africa is among the most violent places on earth) and likely to support extremist solutions in the arena of electoral politics. And Zakaria adds:

> Elections require that politicians compete for peoples' votes. In societies without strong traditions of multiethnic groups or assimilation, it is easiest to organize along racial, ethnic, or

religious lines. Once in power, an ethnic group tends to exclude other ethnic groups. Compromise seems impossible; one can bargain on material issues like housing, hospitals, and handouts, but how does one split the difference on a national religion? Such political competition rapidly degenerates into violence ...[2]

Thus the outcome of democratization in many cases is 'illiberal democracy'. Zakaria has in mind executive dominated governments, as in Belarus, Peru, Croatia, Serbia, Azerbaijan and Kazakstan, whose leaders ignore or selectively apply the rules of liberal constitutionalism. In effect, these 'illiberal' democratic are popularly elected dictatorships, a trajectory of democracy rule described by Plato, Aristotle, Mill, *The Federalist Papers* and others.[3]

Surprisingly, even the most stable and successful of the industrialized First World democracies seem to have elicited feelings of disenchantment during the 1990s. This time it is not foreign intellectuals, but the voters who display concern. Seymour Lipset notes:

> Across the developed world, opinion polls show that citizenries are increasingly distrustful of their political leaders and institutions. When asked about their confidence in government, large majorities in almost every country report they have 'none', 'little', or 'fair amount'. Those who report a high degree of trust generally are a small minority.[4]

Nor do we have to focus on certain Latin American or sub-Saharan African nations thought to possess 'cultures of violence' (see Victor LeVine) to find serious manifestations. In Scandinavian countries, once cited to be models of civic peace, there are now serious outbreaks of racist violence directed at immigrants, refugees and asylum-seekers.[5] Many carrying out these xenophobic attacks have lost faith in their governments' ability or willingness to keep foreigners out, a sentiment found elsewhere in the West.

Triumphalists' who think of democracy as a utopian cure-all for all the world's problems will be disillusioned. Still, in principle, disillusionment with democracy is not the same as disillusionment with communist or fascist ideologies. As numerous observers have pointed out, especially the contributors to *The God That Failed*, these ideologies were secular religions, faith that offered a kind of salvation along with guidance in the conduct of personal and social lives comparable to that provided by the world's revealed religions. Losing a faith that has dominated one's life for years is one thing; coming to a realistic understanding of democracy's limitations may be something else.

In this regard the link between violence and democracy should be considered. When acts of political violence occur with some frequency in democratic settings, one can claim that the political system in question is not really democratic, or that it is insufficiently democratic. Because 'real' democracies have rules for the peaceful resolution of social conflicts, displays of political violence simply reflect the departure of the mundane system from the democratic ideal.

Our contributors have not engaged in this word game.[6] Rather, they believe that democratic institutions do not always inhibit, and sometimes even encourage, outbreaks of political violence. In thinking about the emergence of democracies historically, both in Europe and elsewhere, Victor Le Vine along with Eubank and Weinberg have called out attention to the extent to which violent conflict was either a cause or by-product of this historical development. In a similar vein, Miller and Schaen notice that urban rioting in nineteenth-century Europe tended to erupt in the most free and open societies, and not where governments were most willing to use brute force to repress the opposition. Likewise, the Black riots in the US during the 1960s occurred largely in the northern cities, not in the still segregationist South. (It is worth noting here that the mass protests in Eastern Europe that led to the democratic revolutions of 1989 gathered momentum when it became clear the state was reluctant to use all the means at its disposal to repress the protests.) And writing from a substantially different perspective, Eric Gans, beginning with the experience of Athens, has emphasized the propensity of democratic societies to stimulate feelings of envy and suspicion which then become the basis for violent conflict – a dynamic that Alexis de Tocqueville and Robert Merton note too.

Further, it would be difficult to deny that this type of envy and suspicion is important in understanding the topics addressed in the contributions of Michael Barkun and Christopher Hewitt. In the case of racially motivated separatists, their resentments are palpable. They want out, and express a willingness to use violence to this end because of their envy and suspicion of minorities who they believe have received too much in American society. The same elements are present in Hewitt's account of White and Black terrorism during the 1960s and 1970s.

Free and open elections are at the heart of the democratic process. Yet as Adrian Guelke, David Rapoport and Leonard Weinberg observe, the electoral processes are not immune from violent activities. It is true that elections may be used to bring about a cessation of violence, at least temporarily, as the recent cases of Nicaragua and El Salvador illustrate. However, there is also an abundance of cases both contemporary (e.g. the conflict between the African Congress and the Incatha Freedom Party in South Africa) and historical (e.g. the street fighting between left and right paramilitary groups in interwar Austria, France, Italy and Germany, where election campaigns served to trigger violent confrontations).

John Finn treats the proscription of anti-constitutional parties in the democracies viable and notes: 'exclusion can work in ways that undercut the integrating and binding functions we attribute to democratic elections. Excluding opponents may contribute to their sense of alienation and isolation, making them more likely to resort to violence. It may change 'electoral losers and anti-system oppositions'. Of course this may be true, but electoral losers may have their feelings of alienation and isolation reconfirmed through their participation in competitive elections. Leaders of parties representing ethnic-religious minorities may conclude that they will be chronic losers in the game of electoral politics and seek to achieve their aims by other means.

Two major sources of political conflict at the end of the twentieth century are ethnic identity and religiously based apocalyptic visions. So far as the latter is concerned, Ehud Sprinzak's article makes clear that there is virtually nothing about contemporary Israeli democracy that has inhibited 'End of Times' thinking associated with some radical religious groups. And, in turn, these apocalyptic views have provided the basis, as in the case of the assassin Yigal Amir, for political murder and other political violence.

The articles by Martha Crenshaw, Anna Simons, Daniel Philpott and Andrzej Korbonski are concerned with what appears to be the most intractable of all post-Cold War problems, that of ethnic identity. From the perspective of foreign policy, India's failed effort to mediate the Tamil–Sinhalese conflict in Sri Lanka, the inability of the US to promote a peaceful resolution in Somalia or the failing effort of NATO to make peace in Kosovo, the evidence obviously suggests there are serious limits to the capacity of democracies to intervene and achieve peaceful outcomes. To the extent elected officials are sensitive to public opinion, their peace-making or peace-keeping goals may be thwarted when casualties mount and resources drain.

Raphael Israeli adds another foreign policy dimension to our discussion. Both he and Crenshaw stress that no matter how well-intentioned and high-minded the impulse, democracies may make matters worse when dealing with conflicts beyond their shores. He calls our attention to a second long-standing problem for Britain, France, the United States and other democratic states which extend asylum to individuals claiming to be the targets of political persecution in their homelands. Until recently British, Belgian and French courts, among others, have denied extradition requests from foreign governments on the grounds that the crimes alleged were of a political character and therefore could not be honoured. American courts have faced a similar problem in cases involving suspected IRA members who fled to the United States to avoid arrest and prosecution by the British authorities. As a result of such policies, the leaders and financiers of terrorist groups from around the world often have found sanctuary in the democracies. And not uncommonly, they have used their freedom to plan and sometimes carry out attacks on the governments of their home countries.

Outbreaks of violent conflict occur even in the most stable and successful of the democracies. Democracy is not a cure-all for all public problems. Problems existing outside the democratic context also exist within it, albeit in a special form.

NOTES

1. Robert Kaplan, 'Was Democracy Just a Moment?', *The Atlantic Monthly* 280/6 (December 1997) pp.55–80; Fareed Zakaria, 'The Rise of Illiberal Democracy', *Foreign Affairs* 76/6 (November/December 1997) pp.22–43.
2. Zakaria, ibid., p. 35.
3. Robert Dahl, *Democracy and Its Critics* (New Haven: Yale University Press, 1989) pp.52–79.
4. Seymour Lipset, 'The Western Allies 50 Years Later: Malaise and Resiliency in America', *Journal of Democracy* 6/3 (1995) p.5.
5. See e.g. Tore Bjorgo, *Racist and Right-Wing Violence in Scandinavia* (Oslo: Tano Aschehoug, 197), pp.72–112.
6. See e.g. William Connolly, *Terms of Political Discourse* (Lexington, MA: D. C. Heath, 1974) pp.10–41; W. B. Gallie, 'Essentially Contested Concepts', in Max Black (ed.), *The Importance of Language* (Ithaca, NY: Cornell University Press, 1969).

Notes on Contributors

Michael Barkun is Professor of Political Science in the Maxwell School at Syracuse University. His books include *Religion and the Racist Right: The Origins of the Christian Identity Movement Disaster and the Millennium*, and *Crucible of the Millennium*. He was a consultant to the FBI during the Montana Freemen standoff in 1996. He is currently completing a book on the spread of New World Order conspiracy theories.

Martha Crenshaw is John E. Andrus Professor of Government at Wesleyan University, in Middletown, Connecticut. Her edited book, *Terrorism in Context*, was published by the Pennsylvania State University Press in 1995. She also contributed the entry on terrorism for the 2001 edition of the International Encyclopedia of the Social Sciences.

William Eubank is an Associate Professor at the University of Nevada. His primary interests are in human motivation and constitutionalism, including political parties, elections and voting systems; political psychology and violence; constitutional law and choice theory. He is presently working on projects including the relationship between political violence and democracy and governmental structure.

John E. Finn is Professor of Government at Wesleyan University.

Eric Gans is the editor of *Anthropoetics: The Journal of Generative Anthropology* <www.anthropoetics.ucla.edu> and Professor of French at UCLA. His most recent book is *Signs of Paradox: Irony, Resentment, and Other Mimetic Structures* (Stanford, 1997). His current project, 'The Science of Origins', is a study of early modern and contemporary theories of the origin of language and human society.

Adrian Guelke is Professor of Comparative Politics in the School of Politics at Queen's University, Belfast. He is the director of the Centre for the Study of Ethnic Conflict (within the School of Politics). He was the

Jan Smuts Professor of International Relations at the University of the Witwatersrand, Johannesburg, in 1993, 1994, and 1995. He edited *The South African Journal of International Affairs* between 1995 and 1998. Publications include *South Africa in Transition: The Misunderstood Miracle* (I. B. Taurus, 1999); *The Age of Terrorism and the International Political System* (I. B. Taurus, 1995); *Northern Ireland: The International Perspective* (Gill and Macmillan, 1988); (with John Brewer, Ian Hume, Edward Moxon-Browne and Rick Wilford) *The Police, Public Order and the State* (Macmillan, 1996, 2nd edn); and (ed.), *New Perspectives on the Northern Ireland Conflict* (Avebury, 1994).

Christopher Hewitt is a Professor of Sociology at the University of Maryland Baltimore County. He has published extensively on political violence and is the author of *The Effectiveness of Anti-terrorist Policies* (1984), *Consequences of Political Violence* (1993) and *Encyclopedia of Modern Separatist Movements* (2000). he is currently writing a book on American terrorism, which examines its political and social context and the response by law enforcement agencies and the criminal justice system.

Raphael Israeli is Professor of Islamic, Middle Eastern and Chinese History at the Hebrew University, Jerusalem. He is the author of 15 books and some 80 articles on Middle Eastern, Islamic and Chinese matters. The most recent are *Green Crescent Over Nazareth* and *Divided Jerusalem (1947–67)*.

Andrzej Korbonski is Professor of Political Science (emeritus) at the University of California, Los Angeles. He has authored and co-authored over 100 books, edited volumes, book chapters and journal articles in the general field of Soviet, Russian and Eastern European politics and economics.

Victor T. Le Vine is Professor of Political Science at Washington University in St Louis. He teaches and has published in the fields of African and Middle East politics, international law, political corruption, terrorism and violence, and conflict resolution. The author of seven books and numerous articles in these fields, he is currently working on a book on politics in French-speaking Africa and a monograph on 'non-formal' politics.

Abraham H. Miller is a Professor of Political Science at the University of Cincinnati. His early work on the Black urban riots won a Pi Sigma Alpha Award for research from the Western Political Science Association. He has served as an academic fellow with the National Institute of Justice, as a Lynde and Harry Bradley Foundation Fellow with the Heritage Foundation, and three terms as chairman of the Intelligence Studies Section of the International Studies Association. His work on political violence appears in numerous academic and popular publications.

Daniel Philpott is Assistant Professor of Political Science at the University of California, Santa Barbara. He is the author of *Revolutions in Sovereignty: How Ideas Shaped Modern International Relations* (Princeton University Press, forthcoming, 2001). He has written on the role of ideas and religion and international relations, self-determination, and ethics in international relations.

David C. Rapoport is Professor of Political Science at the University of California, Los Angeles, Founding Editor of the journal *Terrorism and Political Violence*, Founding Director of the Center for Study of Religion at the UCLA, author of *Assassination and Terrorism* (1971), editor and co-editor of four other volumes, and numerous articles on political theory, political violence, and religion.

Emily Schaen is a doctoral student in the Department of Political Science at the University of Cincinnati and a commissioned officer in the United States military currently serving in Kuwait.

Anna Simons is Associate Professor of Anthropology at UCLA and Visiting Associate Professor at the Naval Postgraduate School. She has conducted fieldwork in Somalia, as well as with the US military. Recent publications include 'War: Back to the Future', *Annual Review of Anthropology* and 'Making Sense of Ethnic Cleansing', *Studies in Conflict & Terrorism.*

Ehud Sprinzak, Hebrew University Professor of Political Science, has retired recently to become the Founding Dean of the Lauder School of Government, Policy and Diplomacy at the Interdisciplinary Center in Herzliya, Israel's first private university. He is the author of five books and over 60 articles. His book *Ascendance of Israel's Radical Right* (Oxford University Press, 1991) won Israel's 1992 Michael Landau Prize for the best political science book on Israel and the Middle East. Sprinzak's most recent book, *Brother against Brother: Violence and Extremism in Israeli Politics from Altalena to the Rabin Assassination* (The Free Press, 1999) was a finalist for the Jewish National Book Award in the category of Israel.

Leonard Weinberg is Foundation Professor of Political Science at the University of Nevada. Over the course of his career he has been a Fulbright senior research fellow for Italy, a visiting professor at the University of Florence and the recipient of an H. F. Guggenheim Foundation grant for the study of political violence. For his work in promoting Christian–Jewish reconciliation, Weinberg received the 1999 Thornton Peace Prize. His books include *The Emergence of a Euro-American Radical Right* (1998, with Jeffrey Kaplan), *The Revival of Right-Wing Extremism in the Nineties* (1997, eds with Peter Merkl), *The Transformation of Italian Communism* (1995) and submissions to *The Journal of Terrorism and Political Violence*. He is the book review Editor of this journal.

Index